CHARITY LAW AND GOVERNANCE

This book presents a critical, in-depth analysis of the changes taking place in the governance of charities and charity law in Australia, New Zealand and England.

Delving into the transformative journey of charity law, the book reveals its dramatic shift from traditional private law regulation, governed by the courts and trust law, to an advanced, regulatory framework. This pivot is not just a legal transition; it reflects the core tension within charity itself – the balancing act between private initiative and public good.

Featuring contributions from both renowned and up-and-coming international charity law scholars, this book stands out for its comprehensive coverage. Each chapter delves into the nuanced, complex issues arising from the modernisation of charity law, providing a rich, insightful exploration of the concept of 'charity' as it straddles the realms of legal theory and state-regulated practice.

Charity Law and Governance

Private Purpose, Public Benefit, and the Regulatory Strategy

Edited by
Ross Grantham
and
Kim D Weinert

•HART•
OXFORD • LONDON • NEW YORK • NEW DELHI • SYDNEY

HART PUBLISHING

Bloomsbury Publishing Plc

Kemp House, Chawley Park, Cumnor Hill, Oxford, OX2 9PH, UK

1385 Broadway, New York, NY 10018, USA

Bloomsbury Publishing Ireland Limited, 29 Earlsfort Terrace, Dublin 2, D02 AY28, Ireland

HART PUBLISHING, the Hart/Stag logo, BLOOMSBURY and the Diana logo are trademarks of Bloomsbury Publishing Plc

First published in Great Britain 2025

A catalogue record for this book is available from the British Library.

A catalogue record for this book is available from the Library of Congress.

Library of Congress Control Number: 2025942487

ISBN: HB: 978-1-50997-927-1
ePDF: 978-1-50997-929-5
ePub: 978-1-50997-928-8

Typeset by Compuscript Ltd, Shannon

For product safety related questions contact productsafety@bloomsbury.com

FOREWORD

Too often charity law has been relegated to being a narrow area of law tied to history, rather than being recognised as what it is, an evolving area of the law which affects a broad section of the community, spanning from religious charities to animal rescue. This book brings the reader into the twenty-first century, offering a comprehensive exploration of the evolving landscape of charity law and governance, providing critical insights into the legal, regulatory and theoretical shifts shaping the charity sector in modern society, while demonstrating the ongoing relevance of understanding its historical evolution. The governance of charities has undergone significant transformation in recent years, moving away from the traditional reliance on private law, primarily shaped by the courts and trust law, to an intricate regulatory framework. This collection of chapters demonstrates that this transformation cannot be reduced to a simple matter of law reform, rather it reflects the broader societal shift that views charity as both a private initiative and a public good. As charity law transforms, stakeholders are confronted with fundamental questions about the purpose of regulation and the role it plays in ensuring the effective operation of charities while safeguarding public trust. This collection offers a timely and critical exploration of recent changes in the charity law landscape and provides a valuable resource not only for those involved directly in the charity sector but the broader legal community.

Born from the 2023 International Charity Law Symposium, hosted by the University of Queensland, this volume is a testament to the importance of international scholarship. The book extends upon the enriching discussions facilitated by the Symposium and highlights the importance of cultivating collaboration between academics, legal professionals and the judiciary, especially in areas such as charity law which are informed by nuanced legal complexities and bear far-reaching societal implications. The book's editors, Ross Grantham and Kim D Weinert, who share a wealth of knowledge in this area, bring together contributions from twelve distinguished authors who represent both established and emerging voices in the field of charity law. By bringing together scholars from diverse backgrounds and jurisdictions, the book encourages an exchange of ideas that has the capacity to challenge traditional thinking, shape future research, policy and practice in charity law, as well as being a valuable legal reference point.

At the heart of this work is the recognition of the evolving tensions between private autonomy and the public good in the governance of charities. The contributors bring a wealth of expertise, providing insight into the past and current landscape of charity law across several jurisdictions including Australia, New Zealand, England and China. The book's geographical scope enhances its relevance to international audiences and further provides a comparative exploration of regulatory approaches in different jurisdictions.

This collection is founded in the contribution of editors Grantham and Weinert which outlines the unique cross-section occupied by modern charity law which spans private sector autonomy, state regulation and public benefit. Their analysis is supported by an overview of the evolving relationship between charities, as autonomous private enterprises, state actors and market forces. The first chapter outlines the 'dual mandate' of charity law, which Grantham and Weinert describe as 'safeguarding the interests of those who benefit from charitable work while preserving the autonomy of those who establish and sustain charitable organisations'. Effectively balancing this 'dual mandate' has been a task long grappled with by the courts and common law. The recent attempts to balance this 'dual mandate' under regulatory frameworks has raised further questions as to the role of a modern charity.

The collection offers readers an opportunity to engage with the complexities of modern charity law from the perspective of eminently qualified authors who have provided well researched and thoughtful analysis in their chapters. Contributors tackle a broad range of topics including society's reliance on charities to deliver 'civility' and the place of charity in the twenty-first century, the contradicting duties of modern charities to achieve altruistic objectives and establish a commercial operation and even the implications of charity law on vulnerable furry and not so furry friends – homeless and abused animals. The diverse range of contributions contained within the collection provides an informed analysis of the development of charity law and the current complexities that practitioners and stakeholders are facing. Furthermore, the volume provides insight into potential opportunities that lie ahead as well as challenging traditional thinking and presenting alternative approaches and asking what 'charity' means and should mean in modern society. This thought-provoking exploration will be of great interest to anyone who wishes to understand charity in both its legal and broader social contexts.

This collection is a fitting response to the significant shifts taking place in charity governance, offering a rich and nuanced analysis that will inform legal scholars, practitioners, regulators and policymakers alike.

The Honourable Justice Susan Brown
Supreme Court of Queensland Court of Appeal

PREFACE AND ACKNOWLEDGEMENTS

Charity law, while a specialised discipline, has increasingly become a vibrant and dynamic area of scholarship. Scholars in this field offer critical analyses, thought-provoking discussions, and insightful critiques of charity law issues, including the often perplexing outcomes of judicial decisions. However, they are frequently positioned on the periphery of the charity sector itself. The divide between legal scholarship and the practical operations of charities sometimes results in scholars being overlooked as integral contributors to the broader charity ecosystem.

This collection seeks to bridge that gap. We hope the diverse perspectives and incisive analyses presented by the contributors demonstrate the valuable role that legal scholars can play in shaping the charity sector. We encourage readers to engage with the unique voices represented here and to reflect on how their observations and arguments influence charity law and practice across jurisdictions such as Australia, England, New Zealand, and China.

This volume is the result of the International Charity Law Symposium, hosted and partially funded by the TC Beirne School of Law at The University of Queensland in September 2023. The symposium brought together members of the judiciary, international scholars, and legal practitioners for a day of stimulating discussions on complex and pressing issues in charity law. It underscored the richness of this field and the many topics still ripe for exploration.

Finally, we wish to express our gratitude to our Research Assistant Rhiannon Kocho and Hart Publishing for their enthusiasm and expertise in bringing this project to fruition. Special thanks go to Kate Whetter and Verity Stuart, whose support has been invaluable.

Ross Grantham
Kim D Weinert
Australia Day 2025

TABLE OF CONTENTS

Foreword ... v
Preface and Acknowledgements ... vii
List of Contributors ... xi
Table of Cases ... xiii
Table of Legal Instruments ... xix

PART I
EROSION OF TRADITIONAL PRACTICES

1. *The Protracted Journey of Charity Law* ... 3
   Kim D Weinert and Ross Grantham

2. *Mrs Jelleby, Victorian Values, and the Legal Framework of the Law of Charity in Nineteenth-century England* ... 15
   Warren Swain

3. *The Australian Statutory Regime for* Cy-près *Schemes: Reform or Stagnation?* ... 35
   Ian Murray and Natalie Silver

4. *The Continued Place of Religious Charities within the Charity Sector: The Relationship between the Secular and the Religious Through an Economics Lens* ... 57
   Juliet Chevalier-Watts

5. *Re-imagining Charity in English Imagination: Advocating a Social Harm Critique of Charity as a Cornerstone for the 'Organization of a Civilized Social Life' in Twenty-First Century Britain* ... 77
   Sarah Wilson

6. *Understanding the Meaning of Charity: The Art of Doublethink* ... 101
   Kim D Weinert

PART II
ADAPTION AND TENSION

7. *Discrimination as Detriment* ... 123
   Jane Calderwood Norton

8. *Disability Injustices, Charities, and Repair: Towards Reparative Charity Law* 147
Linda Steele

9. *Assessing Charity Commission Regulation: An Empirical Investigation into Statutory Inquiries 2021–24* 173
Jennifer Sigafoos

10. *A Normative and Dimensional Analysis of the Chinese Legislative Framework for Charitable Organisations* 201
Shaoming Zhu

11. *Governing Animal Rescues Through Charity Law* 223
Sarah Singh and Marie Fox

Index 245

LIST OF CONTRIBUTORS

Jane Calderwood Norton is a Senior Lecturer at the University of Auckland, New Zealand.

Juliet Chevalier-Watts is an Associate Professor at Te Piringa – Faculty of Law at the University of Waikato and Co-Director of the Waikato Public Law and Policy Research Unit, New Zealand.

Marie Fox is a Professor at Liverpool University School of Law and Social Justice, England.

Ross Grantham is a Professor at the T C Beirne School of Law, University of Queensland, Australia.

Ian Murray is a Professor at the University of Western Australia Law School, Australia.

Jennifer Sigafoos is a Reader at the University of Liverpool, School of Law and Social Justice, England and Director of the Charity Law and Policy Unit, University of Liverpool.

Natalie Silver is an Associate Professor at the University of Sydney Law School, Australia.

Sarah Singh is a Lecturer at the University of Liverpool School of Law and Social Justice, England.

Linda Steele is an Associate Professor at the University of Technology Sydney Faculty of Law, Australia.

Warren Swain is a Professor at the Faculty of Law at the University of Auckland, New Zealand.

Kim D Weinert is a Lecturer at the T C Beirne School of Law at the University of Queensland, Australia and a 2025 Visiting Fellow of the State Library of New South Wales, Australia.

Sarah Wilson is a Reader at the University of York, England.

Shaoming Zhu is a Lecturer at the University College Cork School of Law, Ireland.

TABLE OF CASES

Australia

Aboriginal Hostels Ltd v Darwin City Council (1995) 33 NTR 104
Aboriginal Housing Office v Jacky [2002] NSWSC 916 .... 104, 171
Adamson v Melbourne and Metropolitan Board of Works [1929] AC 14.............229
A-G (SA) v Bray (1964) 111 CLR 402 12
Aid/Watch Incorporated v Commissioner of Taxation [2010] HCA 42 .... 111, 117
Angle Loop Ltd and Commissioner of Australian Charities and Not-for-Profit Commission [2021] AATA 3894 105
Attorney-General (NSW) v NSW Henry George Foundation Ltd [2002] NSWSC 1128 103
Cant v Kirby [2001] NSWSC 1193 104
Central Bayside General Practice Association Limited v Commissioner of State Revenue (2006) 228 CLR 168...117
Commissioner of Taxation v The Triton Foundation (2005) 226 ALR 293 110
Commissioner of Taxation v Word Investments Ltd (2007) 243 ALR 44; (2008) 236 CLR 204 ....9, 60, 102, 104
Countess of Bective v Federal Commissioner of Taxation (1932) 47 CLR 417 105
Free Serbian Orthodox Church Diocese for Australia And New Zealand Property Trust v Bishop Irinej Dobrijevic [2017] NSWCA 28 (MS 72).............44
Groote Eylandt Aboriginal Trust v Deloitte, Touche & Tohmatsu (No 2) (2017) NTR 1..104
Housing Choices Australia Ltd v Attorney-General (Vic) [2024] VSC 107 48
Kay v Southern Eastern Sydney Area Health [2003] NSWSC 292 .... 127, 143
Law Institute of Victoria v CMR of State Revenue [2015] VSC 604 103–04
Macedonian Orthodox Community Church St Petka Incorporated v His Eminence Petar (2008) 237 CLR 66...49
Marriage Guidance Council of Victoria v Commissioner of Pay-Roll Tax 90 ATC 4770..166
McGuvie Smith Institute v Campbelltown Municipal Council [1965] VR 238 229
Perpetual Trustee Company Ltd v Attorney General for the State of New South Wales (The Will of the Hon George Nesbitt) (2018) 17 ASTLR 126...................49
Perpetual Trustee Company Limited v The Federal Commissioner of Taxation (1931) 45 CLR 224 .... 103, 165
Plummer v Attorney General of New South Wales [2018] NSWSC 869 103

Salvation Army (Victoria) Property Trust v City of Richmond [1956] VLR 250 105
Salvation Army (Victoria) Property Trust v Fern Tree Gully Corporation (1952) 85 CLR 159 .... 106, 109
South Australian Employers' Chamber of Commerce & Industry Incorporated v Commissioner of State Taxation [2017] SASC 127 117
Tasmanian Perpetual Trustees Limited v Attorney-General for the State of Tasmania [2017] TASSC 32 49
Taylor v Princess Margaret Hospital for Children Foundation Inc (2012) 42 WAR 259....35
The University of Adelaide [2023] SASC 8....8
YWCA Australia v Chief Commissioner of State Revenue [2020] NSWSC 1798 102

Canada

Egan v Canada [1995] 2 SCR 513....140
Re Canada Trust Co v Ontario Human Rights Commission (1990) 69 DLR (4th) 321.... 127–28
Re Ramsden Estate (1996) 139 DLR (4th) 746....126
University of Victoria v British Columbia (AG) [2000] BCJ No 520....126
Vriend v Alberta [1998] 1 SCR 493 140

New Zealand

Attorney General v Family First New Zealand [2022] NZSC 80; [2022] 1 NZLR 175.... 10, 65, 111, 123–25, 128, 132–33, 141
Centrepoint Community Growth Trust v Commissioner of Inland Revenue [1985] 1 NZLR 673 60
Educational Fees Protection Society Inc v CIR [1992] 2 NZLR 115 63
Greenpeace of New Zealand v Charities Board [2020] NZHC 1999....64
Latimer v Commissioner of Inland Revenue [2002] 3 NZLR 195 (CA).... 62, 64
Liberty Trust v Charities Commission [2011] NZLR 68....60
Medical Council of New Zealand [1997] 2 NZLR 297....103
Molloy v Commissioner of Inland Revenue [1981] 1 NZLR 688; (1981) 5 TRNZ 1 (CA)....63
New Zealand Society of Accountants v Commissioner of Inland Revenue [1986] 1 NZLR 147; (1986) 9 TRNZ 727 (CA) 63–64
Re Greenpeace of New Zealand [2014] NZSC 105; [2015] 1 NZLR 169....59, 62–64, 70

United Kingdom

Adamson v Melbourne and Metropolitan Board Works [1929] AC 142................229
Anon (1745) 3 Atk 277; 26 ER 962................25
Armstrong v Reeves (1890) 25 LR Ir 325................229
Attorney-General v Bowles (1754) 2 Ves Sen 547; 28 ER 348................18
Attorney-General v Bucknall (1741) 2 Atk 328; 26 ER 600................25
Attorney-General v Cock (1751) 2 Ves Sen 273; 28 ER 177................20
Attorney-General v Duke of Northumberland (1877) 7 Ch D 745 (Ch)................32
Attorney-General v Griffith (1807) 13 Ves Jun 565; 33 ER 406................30
Attorney-General v Lloyd (1747) 1 Ves Sen 32; 27 ER 872................18
Attorney-General v Lord Weymouth (1743) Ambl 20; 27 ER 11................18
Attorney-General v Middleton (1751) 2 Ves Sen 327; 28 ER 210................25
Attorney-General v Oglender (1790) 1 Ves Jun 146; 30 ER 324................25
Attorney-General v Peacock (1675) 73 SS 209................20, 25
Attorney-General v Pearce (1740) 2 Atk 87; 26 ER 545................21
Attorney-Geneal v Price (1810) 17 Ves Jun 371; 34 ER 143................32
Attorney-General v Ruper (1722) 2 P Wms 125; 24 ER 667................20
Attorney-General v Tyndall (1764) Amb 614; 27 ER 399................21
Attorney-General v Whorwood (1750) 1 Ven Sen 534; 27 ER 1188................20
Baker v Sutton (1836) 1 Keen 224, 48 ER 292................23
Blandford v Thackerell (1793) 2 Ves Jun 238, 30 ER 612................21
Borough of Merton Council v Nuffield Health [2023] UKSC 18................82
Bourne v Keane [1919] AC 815 (HL)................23
Buckley v Barlow [2016] EWHC 3017 (Ch)................60
Case of Sutton's Hospital (1612) 10 Co Rep 23 a; 77 ER 960................17
Cat Protection Society of Victoria [1971] VR 801................229
Catholic Care (Diocese of Leeds) v the Charity Commission for England and Wales [2010] EWJC 520; [2010] PTSR 1074................133
Catholic Care (Diocese of Leeds) v Charity Commission for England and Wales [2012] UKUT 395 (TCC)................133
Chapman v Brown (1801) 6 Ves Jun 404; 31 ER 1115................18
Charity Commission v Wright and another [2019] EWHC 3375 (Ch)................238
Commissioners for Special Purposes of the Income Tax v Pemsel [1891] AC 531 (HL)................30–31, 61, 83, 87, 89, 102, 105–06, 113, 115, 175, 229
Corporation of Burford v Lenthall (1743) 2 Atk 551; 26 ER 731................29
Corporation of Ludlow v Greenhouse (1827) 1 Bligh NS 17; 4 ER 780................25–26
Dingle v Turner [1972] AC 601 (HL); [1972] 2 WLR 523................31, 33, 63, 102
Earl of Chesterfield v Janssen (1751) 2 Ves Sen 125; 28 ER 82................21
Ex p Skinner (1817) 2 Mer 453; 35 ER 1013................27

Gables Farms Dog and Cats Rescue v Revenue & Customs Commissioners [2008] 1 WLUK 16 243
General Nursing Council for England and Wales v St Marylebone Brough Council [1959] AC 540 104
Gill v RSPCA [2010] EWCA Civ 1430 90
Gillam v Taylor (1873) LR 16 Eq 581 32
Gilmour v Coats [1949] AC 426 (HL) 6, 20
Grimmett v Grimmett (1754) Amb 210; 27 ER 140 20
In re The Trusts of the Arthur McDougall Fund Thompson v Fitzgerald [1957] 1 WLR 81 (Ch D) 103
Independent Schools Council v Charity Commission [2011] UKUT 421 (TCC) 63, 82
Inland Revenue Commissioners v Baddeley [1955] AC 572; [1955] 1 All ER 525 64
Inland Revenue Commissioners v McMullen [1981] AC 1 (HL) 109
Jones v Williams (1767) Amb 651; 27 ER 422 21
Keren Kayemeth Le Jisroel Ltd v Inland Revenue Commissioners [1931] 2 KB 465 62–63
Lehtiäki v Cooper [2020] UKSC 33 105
LF v United Kingdom [2022] ECJR (no 1983/21) 123
London University v Yarrow (1857) 1 De G & J 72 229
London Borough of Merton Council v Nuffield Health [2023] UKSC 18 82
Mitford v Reynolds (1848) 16 Sim 105; 60 ER 812 23
Moggridge v Thackwell (1803) 7 Ves Jun 36; 32 ER 15 22
Morice v Bishop of Durham (1804) 9 Ves Jun 399; 32 ER 656 .... 21, 31
Morice v Bishop of Durham (1805) 10 Ves Jun 52; 32 ER 947 .... 21–22, 31
National Anti-Vivisection Society v Inland Revenue Commissioners [1947] UKHL 4; [1948] AC 31 .... 32, 82, 108, 131, 134, 142, 230
Neville Estates v Madden [1962] Ch 832 60
Ogden v North West English Springer Spaniel Rescue (NWESSR) [2018] (unreported) 243
Ommanney v Butcher (1823) Turn & R 260; 37 ER 1098 23
Oppenheim v Tabacco Securities Trust Co Ltd [1951] AC 297 (HL) 62–65, 82, 106
Pettingall v Pettingall (1842) 11 LJ Ch 176 23
Powell v Compton [1945] Ch 123; [1945] All ER 198 CA 104
R v Archbishop of York (1795) 6 TR 490; 101 ER 664 27
R (Cornerstone (North East) Adoption and Fostering Services Ltd) v Ofsted [2021] EWCA Civ 1390 123
R (on the application of Hodkin and another) v Registrar of Births, Deaths and Marriages [2013] UKSC 77 6
R v Registrar General, Ex p Segerdal [1970] 2 QB 697 (CA) 6

R (Weaver) v London & Quadrant Housing Trust [2009] EWCA Civ 587...........144
R (Z) v Hackney London Borough Council [2020] UKSC 40......................... 123, 126
Re Central Employment Bureau for Women and Students' Careers Association Incorporated [1942] 1 All ER 232..102
Re Compton [1945] Ch 123 .... 62, 102
Re Dean; Cooper-Dean v Stevens (1889) 41 Ch D 552................................... 12, 225
Re Dominion Student's Hall Trust [1947] Ch 183 127
Re Douglas; Obert v Barrow (1887) 35 Ch D 472.. 12, 229
Re Foveaux [1895] 2 Ch 501...230
Re Grove-Grady [1929] 1 Ch 557.. 12, 229
Re Herrick, Colohan v Att Gen (1918) 52 I.L.T. 213 231
Re Hollywood, Smyth v Att Gen (1917) 52 I.L.T. 51 231
Re Keeping Kids [2021] EWCH 175 (Ch) 233
Re Lysaght [1966] Ch 191 127
Re Macduff [1896] 2 Ch 451...132
Re Mere's Will Trust (1957) *The Times* (4 May 1957) 127
Re Moss [1949] 1 All ER 495 229
Re Oldfield (No 2) [1949] 2 DLR 175 65
Re Prison Charities (1873) LR 16 Eq 129..55
Re Scarisbrick's Will Trusts [1951] Ch 622; [1951] 1 All ER 822 102
Re The Trusts of the Arthur McDougall Fund. Thompson v Fitzgerald [1957] 1 WR 81 (Ch D)...103
Re Wedgwood [1915] 1 Ch 113 229–30
Richardson v Mellish (1824) 2 Bing 229; 130 ER 294 32
Scottish Burial Reform and Cremation Society Ltd v Glasgow Corp [1968] AC 138 (HL) 30, 64, 105
Southwood v Attorney General [2000] WTLR 98
Swife v A-G (Ireland) (No 2) [1912] IR 133 12
Tatham v Drummond (1864) 4 De GJ & Sm 484..12
The Baptist Union of Ireland (Northern) Corporation Limited v The Commissioners of Inland Revenue [1945] NI 99................................ 113–14
The Charitable Corp v Sir Robert Sutton (1742) 9Mod 350; 88 ER 500 17
The Official Receiver v Atkinson & Ors [2021] EWHC 175 (Ch)..........................191
Three Counties Dog Rescue v HMRC [2011] UKFTT 817 (TC)............................243
Thornton v Howe (1862) 31 Beav 14, 54 ER 1042.. 31, 60
Independent Schools Council v Charity Commission [2011] UKUT 421 (TCC); [2012] Ch 214..105, 133, 135, 145
Thornton v Howe (1862) 31 Beav 14, 54 ER 1042.. 31, 60
Trustees of British Museum v White (1826) 2 Sim & St 594; 57 ER 473........... 19, 23
Turner v Ogden (1787) 1 Cox 316; 29 ER 1183..20
Varsani v Jesani [1999] Ch 219 (MS 92) 47
Wellbeloved v Jones (1822) 1 Sim & St 40; 57 ER 16..25
Westminster City Council v Duke of Westminster [1991] 4 All ER 136 (Ch)..........37

Williams v Kershaw (1835) 5 Cl & Fin 11; 7 ER 346 23
Williams' Trustees v Inland Revenue Commissioners [1947] AC 447 65
Zedra v HM Attorney General [2023] EWCA Civ 1332 .... 36, 47

United States of America

Bob Jones University v United States (1983) 461 US 574 126
Citizens United v Federal Electoral Commission (2010) 558 US 310 141
Dulles v Johnson (1959) 273 F 2d 362 103
Jackson v Philps (1867) 96 Mass 539 14 Allen 539 (Mass SC) 64
Regan v Taxation Without Representation (1983) 461 US 540 141
Rosenberger v University of Virginia (1995) 515 US 819 142

TABLE OF LEGAL INSTRUMENTS

Australia

Australian Charities and Not-for-Profits Commission Act 2012 (Cth)........ 57, 159
Australian Charities and Not-for-Profits Commission Regulations 2022 .... 148, 168
Charitable Trust Act 1962 (WA)........ 44, 51–52
Charitable Trusts Act 1993 No 10 (NSW)........ 44–45, 49
Charitable Trusts Act 2022 (WA)........ 44–45, 51–52
Charities Act 1978 (Vic)........ 43, 45
Charities Act 2013 (Cth) (WS52)........ 19, 57, 105, 148, 164, 170
Companies Act 1961 (Vic)........ 112, 114
Disability Discrimination Act 1992 (Cth)........ 166
National Disability Insurance Scheme Act 2013 (Cth)........ 11, 153
Trustee Act 1936 (SA)........ 43, 45
Trusts Act 1973 (Qld)........ 43, 45
Trusts Act 2025 (Qld)........ 53
Variation of Trusts Act 1994 (Tas)........ 45

China

2016 Charity Law of the People's Republic of China........ 203, 219
2023 Charity Law of the People's Republic of China........ 203, 219
2021 Civil Code of the People's Republic of China........ 201–02, 206, 220
2018 Enterprise Income Tax Law of the People's Republic of China........ 201–02, 216
2019 Interim Measures for the Management of Investment Activities of Charitable Organisations for Value Preservation and Enhancement........ 202, 213
2013 Interim Provisions on the Management of Foreign Chambers of Commerce........ 201
1998 Interim Regulations on the Registration and Administration of Private Non-Enterprise Units........ 201
Legislation Law of the People's Republic of China........ 211
2011 Management of Social Organisation Evaluation Measures........ 201

2016 Measures for the Administration of Public Solicitation by Charitable Organisations 201
2018 Measures for Information Disclosure by Charitable Organisations 201
2018 Measures for the Management of Credit Information of Social Organisations 201
2016 Measures for the Recognition of Charitable Organisations 201, 204
1999 Public Welfare Donation Law of the People's Republic of China 201
2017 Red Cross Society Law of the People's Republic of China 201
2016 Regulations on the Registration and Administration of Social Organisations 201

New Zealand

Charities Act 2005 (NZ) 19, 58, 61, 105, 125
Charitable Funds Appropriation Act 1871 (NZ) 58
Charitable Trusts Act 1957 (NZ) 42, 44, 58
Religious Charitable and Educational Trusts Act 1856 (19 and 20 Vict 1856 No 21) (NZ) 58
Religious Charitable and Educational Trusts Act Amendment Act 1865 (NZ) 58

Republic of Ireland

Charities Act 2009 105

United Kingdom

Animal Welfare Act 2006 229–30
Bubble Act 1720 (6 Geo 1 c 18) 17
Chancery Procedure Act 1852 (15 & 16 Vict c 86) 27
Charitable Donations Registration Act 1812 (52 Geo 3 c 102)
Charitable Trusts Act 1853 (16 & 17 Vict c 137) 27, 29, 31, 83
Charitable Trusts Act 1860 (23 & 24 Vict c 136) 29
Charitable Uses Act 1601 (43 Eliz 1 c 4) 3, 19, 61, 106
Charitable Uses Act 1736 (9 Geo II c 36) 18, 89
Charities and Trustee Investments (Scotland) Act 2005 .... 105, 224
Charities Act (Northern Ireland) 2008 105
Charities Act 1960 .... 30, 37–39, 42–44, 47, 57

Charities Act 1992 190
Charities Act 1993 .... 37, 39–40
Charities Act 2006 .... 39–41, 45–47, 53, 57, 64, 81–85, 90, 92, 99, 229, 234, 240
Charities Act 2011 .... 19, 32, 39–41, 45–50, 61, 63–64, 77, 80–83, 105, 174, 176–77, 179–80, 183–84, 188, 197–98, 229, 234, 242
Charities Act 2022 .... 30, 41, 50, 77, 81, 92
Charities Inquiry Act 1818 (58 Geo 3 c 91) 28
Charities Inquiry Act 1819 (59 Geo 3 c 81) 29
Charities Procedure Act 1812 (52 Geo 3 c 101) 26
Consumer Rights Act 2015 243
Dangerous Dogs Act 1991 226
Duties on Income Act 1799 (39 Geo 3 c 13) 19
Environmental Protection Act 1990 225
Equality Act 2010 126
Hunting Act 2004 231
Income Tax Act 1842 (5 & 6 Vict c 35) 19
Legislative and Regulatory Reform Act 2006 .... 179–80, 198
Mortmain and Charitable Uses Act 1891 (54 & 55 Vict c 73) 31
Roman Catholic Charities Act 1860 (23 & 24 Vict c 134) 20
Roman Catholic Relief Act 1829 (10 Geo 4 c 7) 20
Statute of Charitable Uses 1601 (42 Eliz 1 c4) 3, 5, 9, 12, 57, 82–83, 170
Taxation Act 1798 (38 Geo 3 c 16) 19
The Animal Welfare (Licensing of Activities Involving Animals) (Scotland) Regulations 2021 .... 223, 226
The Charities (Protection and Social Investment) Act 2016 .... 178, 188
Toleration Act 1688 (1 Will & Mary c 18) 20

PART I

Erosion of Traditional Practices

1

The Protracted Journey of Charity Law

KIM D WEINERT AND ROSS GRANTHAM

I. Charity Law at the Crossroads

Charity law occupies a distinctive and complex space at the intersection of private initiative and public responsibility. It operates within a legal framework that both facilitates and constrains private action for public benefit. Since the enactment of the Statute of Charitable Uses 1601 (also known as the Statute of Elizabeth),[1] charity law has evolved in response to shifting social, economic, and political landscapes. The role of the state in relation to charity has oscillated, at times embracing regulatory oversight and, at others, retreating to allow private philanthropy greater autonomy. In contemporary society, the convergence of charity law with tax policy, governance structures, and regulatory frameworks has introduced additional layers of complexity. This necessitates a critical examination of how charity law fulfils its dual mandate: safeguarding the interests of those who benefit from charitable work while preserving the autonomy of those who establish and sustain charitable organisations.

Historically, the role of charities has been inextricably linked to the shifting priorities of the state and market forces. In times of economic downturn, charities have stepped in to provide essential services, acting as a safety net where state provisions have been inadequate. Conversely, during periods of state expansion, the role of charities has sometimes been marginalised or integrated into broader public service provision. This duality has created a persistent tension between the legal recognition of charities as private entities and the broader expectation that they serve a public good. This tension has only deepened in recent decades, as charities have become central actors in the delivery of health, education, and social welfare services.

Simultaneously, public confidence in charities has been tested by high-profile governance failures, financial mismanagement, and shifting societal attitudes toward philanthropic institutions. The increasing professionalisation of the charitable sector – marked by a focus on strategic management, transparency, and

[1] 43 Eliz 1 c 4.

impact assessment – has further transformed the legal and regulatory landscape. This collection engages with these ongoing debates, offering a critical analysis of charity law's foundational principles and its evolving role in society.

Charities, as non-governmental actors, also play a vital role in shaping public discourse. They frequently advocate for policy changes, provide services that bridge gaps left by government, and act as intermediaries between the state and individuals. However, the extent to which charities should engage in political advocacy has been the subject of considerable debate, particularly in light of their tax-exempt status.[2] Some argue that such involvement blurs the line between charitable activity and lobbying, while others contend that charities are uniquely positioned to represent marginalised groups and advocate for meaningful policy reforms. These questions form a central thread in the discussions that follow in this collection, underscoring the evolving and contested nature of charity law in modern society.

II. Private Purpose, Public Benefit, and Regulatory Strategy

The chapters in this collection explore the evolving challenges and tensions within charity law, shedding light on the interplay between private initiative and public responsibility, the contested nature of public benefit, and the ongoing transformation of charity governance. These three overarching and interrelated themes highlight the legal, ethical, and regulatory considerations that shape contemporary charity law and influence how legal frameworks and regulators navigate the complexities of the sector.

A. Private Initiative and Public Responsibility in Charity Law

At its core, charity law governs an area where private action intersects with public benefit. A charitable trust or organisation originates from an individual's or group's voluntary initiative, often driven by altruistic motives, religious or social values, or a response to unmet community needs. However, despite its private origins, a charity's activities are inherently public-facing, designed to benefit broader society rather than serving the personal interests of the founder or trustees. This duality raises fundamental questions about the appropriate level of state intervention in the governance and operations of charitable organisations.

Historically, the state's role in charity law has been largely facilitative, recognising and regulating charities without imposing undue control. The legal framework

[2] See: J Calderwood Norton and M Harding, 'Charities and Politics: where did we go wrong?' (2024) 44 LS 649.

enables charitable activity by granting tax-exempt status, legal recognition, and operational privileges, while also ensuring charities meet accountability and transparency standards. However, as charities have increasingly assumed responsibilities traditionally held by the state – particularly in education, healthcare, welfare, and social services – governments have become more invested in their oversight. This shift has led to greater regulatory intervention, often driven by concerns about financial integrity, governance standards, and the effective use of charitable resources.

Since the mid-twentieth century, the privatisation of public services has intensified the blurring of boundaries between charities, nonprofit service providers, and government agencies. In many jurisdictions, governments have outsourced essential social services to the charitable sector, reducing direct state provision and relying on charities to fill the gap. This contract-based relationship between charities and governments has created new tensions: while charities benefit from public funding and tax exemptions, they also face increased scrutiny, compliance requirements, and bureaucratic oversight. Questions arise about whether charities remain independent actors serving voluntary purposes or whether they have become quasi-public entities, bound by the same expectations as government service providers.

This evolving relationship challenges traditional conceptions of charitable autonomy, raising concerns about mission drift, where charities shift their focus and behaviour from pursuing the public good to securing government contracts. Additionally, reliance on state funding or tax incentives introduces the risk of political influence, with governments using funding mechanisms to shape the charitable sector in ways that align with broader policy objectives. As legal and regulatory frameworks continue to adapt, the question remains: to what extent should the state regulate charities that operate in public service domains, and where should the boundaries of charitable independence be drawn?

B. The Contested Concept of Public Benefit

Public benefit has long been the defining characteristic of charities, distinguishing them from private entities or businesses. Since the Statute of Charitable Uses 1601, the requirement that charities serve a recognised public good has been a cornerstone of charity law. However, the meaning of public benefit has evolved over time, shaped by changing social values, economic realities, and legal developments.[3] Today, the concept is under increased scrutiny due to three interrelated pressures: fiscal considerations, the commercialisation of charities, and shifting societal expectations.

[3] cf D Halliday and M Harding (eds), *Charity Law – Exploring the Concept of Public Benefit* (Oxford, Routledge, 2022).

First, the financial privileges associated with charitable status – including tax exemptions, gift aid schemes, and donor incentives – have heightened state interest in regulating charities. Tax benefits, while intended to support public-serving organisations, have at times been exploited by entities seeking financial advantages rather than pursuing genuine charitable purpose. Cases involving wealthy private schools, exclusive membership organisations, and for-profit subsidiaries of charities have raised questions about whether these institutions truly serve the public interest or primarily benefit privileged groups.

Second, as charities have expanded their roles in public service delivery, they have become more commercialised, adopting business-like models to maintain financial sustainability. Many large charities now generate significant revenue through fee-based services, partnerships with corporations, and investment activities, raising concerns about whether their commercial pursuits align with their charitable purpose. The rise of social enterprises and hybrid nonprofitbusiness models has further complicated distinctions between charitable, commercial, and governmental functions, making it increasingly difficult to define what constitutes a 'public benefit'.

Third, shifting societal norms and ethical considerations have challenged traditional definitions of public benefit. Historically, courts relied on moral and religious justifications to determine charitable purposes. However, modern expectations of inclusivity, equity, and social justice have led to legal debates over whether certain charities – such as religious organisations that restrict membership or educational institutions that exclude disadvantaged groups – should qualify for charitable status. Notably, cases involving cloistered religious orders,[4] controversial advocacy groups,[5] and private institutions have tested the boundaries of what constitutes societal benefit in contemporary contexts.

The tension between historical legal definitions and modern social realities suggests that charity law must continue to evolve. Legal frameworks must strike a balance between respecting traditional charitable purposes and ensuring that public benefit remains relevant, inclusive, and aligned with contemporary societal values.

C. The Evolution of Charity Governance

The third major theme in contemporary charity law is the transformation of governance structures within the charitable sector. Historically, charities were small, volunteer-driven organisations, often guided by founders' values and

[4] *Gilmour v Coates* [1949] AC 426.

[5] The nature of the Church of Scientology as a religious order has been a matter of considerable debate. Lord Denning was scathing in his criticism of it in *R v Registrar General, Ex p Segerdal* [1970] 2 QB 697 (CA), but more recently the Supreme Court overturned that decision in *R (on the application of Hodkin and another) v Registrar General of Births, Deaths and Marriages* [2013] UKSC 77.

informal governance practices. However, as the sector has grown into a major economic and social force, governance has shifted toward professionalisation, regulation, and corporate oversight.

Today, many charities operate as large-scale enterprises with significant assets, international reach, and professional management teams. As a result, legal and regulatory bodies have increasingly sought to impose corporate-style governance frameworks, ensuring charities operate transparently, accountably, and efficiently. This has led to the introduction of governance structure and practices that are more consistent with corporate compliance models than purpose-led organisations.[6]

However, this transition has introduced new challenges. Unlike commercial entities, charities do not exist to generate shareholder profit but rather to fulfil a social mission. The application of corporate governance principles – such as board independence, performance metrics, and risk management – can clash with the unique ethical and operational concerns of charities. For example, an over-emphasis on financial performance may pressure charities to prioritise revenue generation over direct community impact, leading to mission drift.

Regulators such as the Australian Charities and Not-for-profits Commission (ACNC),[7] the Charity Commission for England and Wales, and other international regulatory bodies continue to grapple with these governance tensions. They must balance the need for strong oversight with the recognition that charities operate on fundamentally different principles than commercial corporations. Questions arise about how much regulatory burden should be placed on charities and whether a one-size-fits-all governance model is appropriate for a diverse sector that includes both grassroots organisations and multinational NGOs.

As charity law continues to evolve, regulators must navigate a delicate equilibrium: ensuring good governance, financial accountability, and public trust, while preserving the flexibility and ethical commitment that define the charitable sector. The challenge remains to develop regulatory strategies that uphold the core values of charity while supporting innovation and sustainability in an increasingly complex social and economic landscape.

III. Thematic Overview

The collection begins with Warren Swain's historical review of the law of charity mediated through the lens of Charles Dickens's amusingly satirised Victorian attitudes towards charity in the form of Mrs Jelleby, who devotes her time to Africa

[6] cf I Murray, 'Characterising and Changing Charitable Purpose: theories of organizational purpose' (2024) 87 (4) *MLR* 1111.

[7] The name given to the regulator itself reflects some of this tension. The elision of 'charity' and 'not-for-profit' reflects a misunderstanding of the profound differences between (a) the legal structures involved and (b) the purposes of these two types.

whilst her own home falls into ruin.[8] Older treatments of the subject had emphasised a move from individualism to collectivism as represented by the welfare state. In contrast, more recent accounts of the history of charity have stressed the very pluralistic nature of philanthropy. Charity during this period involved a combination of public and private welfare and was shaped and motivated by community practice and community values. Often, however, these values conflicted. Some evangelical Christians were advocates of individual assistance and the idea of self-help. But even within that group there were those who favoured greater state paternalism. It was just as possible in this period to view charity through a utilitarian lens as a means of increasing overall welfare. In short, the situation was complex and there is no single narrative.

Given the complex and pluralistic social setting of charity in the nineteenth century it is more than a little odd that the basic legal definition of charity should still be based on a statute of 1601. More broadly, Owen Davies Tudor the leading commentator on the law relating to charities of the time, observed that the law presents 'many anomalies'. Despite the huge historiography on charity and philanthropy in the nineteenth century the subject barely receives a mention in the relevant *Oxford History of the Laws of England*[9] and the leading legal historical treatment of the subject by Gareth Jones ends in 1827.[10] Swain's chapter examines how the law of the period tried to solve these anomalies and at the same time was shaped by broader social and legal developments of the era.

The dual nature of charity as private initiative and public concern is reflected in the doctrine of *cy-près*.[11] Natalie Silver and Ian Murray explore the doctrine as recipients of large charitable gifts.[12] Many of these gifts take the legal form of perpetual charitable trusts, creating significant endowment portfolios.[13] However, charitable trusts often contain conditions or restrictions (that are sometimes rather eccentric) that the donor has placed on the use of the funds, presenting challenges for charities in utilising these assets, particularly when the trust conditions have become impracticable or impossible to perform because they no longer reflect contemporary society or institutional practices.[14] This chapter

[8] C Dickens, *Bleak House* (first published 1853, London, Penguin, 1979) 479.

[9] William Cornish et al (eds), *The Oxford History of the Laws of England, Volume XI: 1820–1914 English Legal System* (Oxford, OUP, 2010).

[10] G Jones, *History of the Law of Charity 1532–1827* (Cambridge, CUP, 1969).

[11] GE Dal Pont, *Law of Charity* 3rd edn (Australia, LexisNexis, 2021) chs 15 and 16.

[12] For example, the charitable bequest that was the subject of *The University of Adelaide* [2023] SASC 8 had grown to almost $500,000.

[13] In a 2017 study, the National Association of College and University Business Officers found that the assets under management of all 809 US college and university endowments surveyed added up to $566.8 billion as of June 2017 (NACUBO, '2017 NACUBO-Commonfund Study of Endowments Report', National Association of College and University Business Officers, 2017).

[14] I Murray and N Silver, 'Use of Cy-près and Administrative Schemes by Australian Higher Education Providers to End Dead Hand Control of Charitable Assets' (2024) 45(2) *Adelaide Law Review* 363.

undertakes a survey of Australian *cy-près* and administrative scheme cases involving examining judicial approaches towards scheme applications, including the extent to which the promotion of both testamentary intent and the public interest in the effective use of charitable assets is considered. The chapter also examines the process involved in making *cy-près* and administrative scheme applications. It considers whether, in Australia's current regulatory environment that seeks to balance public trust and confidence in the charitable sector; with supporting an effective charitable sector, the ancient scheme provides a viable means of enabling charities to access funds controlled by donors from the grave.

The pursuit of religious belief has been intimately connected with the law of charity throughout the centuries since charity was first recognised.[15] Despite this long and close relationship there are, as Juliet Chevalier-Watts explains, criticisms of the continued place of religious charities within the 'third sector'[16] in what is becoming a more secularised world.[17] As these voices grow ever louder the social legitimacy of religious charities falters. In light of the pressures facing religious charities to maintain their stronghold within the sector, this chapter considers some of those pressures and how religious charities may continue to be justified not through the legal lens, but through the lens of economics. In doing so, the chapter demonstrates the continued value of religious charities not only to religious communities but also to society, generally through religious charities' capacity to contribute to social and economic life.

Sarah Wilson's chapter continues the questioning of the role of traditional charity values and, in particular, the articulation of those values in law. Wilson borrows from EL Woodward's classic *Oxford History of England – The Age of Reform*[18] to frame the chapter's interest in the place and role of charity in society in the United Kingdom in the twenty-first century, and the argument that too little critical attention is given to the place occupied by it. The chapter explores the desirability, and even necessity, of charity in today's society, and the concomitant importance attached to law as a mechanism to support charity as much as possible. The critique offered in this chapter focuses primarily on contributions made by charity to 'civilised social life' in the twenty-first century in the United Kingdom which illuminates the extensive partnering which can be found between the State and charitable organisations (as part of the third sector). From this, and

[15] The 'advancement of religion' was one of the four heads mentioned in the Statute of Charitable Uses 1601 (42 Eliz 1 c 4).

[16] The third sector is usually defined as part of an economy or a society that includes non-governmental and non-profit-making organisations or associations such as charities and voluntary groups. M Lyons, *Third Sector: the contribution of non-profit and cooperative enterprise in Australia* (Australia, Taylor & Francis, 2001) 5–7.

[17] *Commissioner of Taxation of the Commonwealth of Australia v Word Investments Limited* (2008) 236 CLR 204, [155], per Kirby J. For an interesting discussion of the trend to a secular morality, see J Hendry, *Between Enterprise and Ethics: Business and Management in a Bimoral Society* (Oxford, OUP, 2004).

[18] EL Woodward, *The Age of Reform 1815–1870 (The Oxford History of England)*, vol 13 (first published 1938, Oxford, Clarendon Press, 1963).

using examples drawn from health and social care spheres, this chapter argues it is timely to reflect on whether the very considerable reliance which is placed on charity for delivering 'civility' can cause more harm than good.

The values that underpin charity law, and which inform the concept of public benefit, is also the subject of Kim Weinert's chapter. In this contribution, Weinert argues that despite steadfast efforts to locate a determinate methodology to set the contours of charity law doctrines, the task remains elusive, mainly owing to a 'halo' projected onto charities.[19] The halo effect projected onto charities tends to frame a benevolent expectation of the law for an entity to achieve an altruistic purpose for those in need. It is this ideal, Weinert argues, which is the myth. In Weinert's view, discussion of how modern charities balance an altruistic mission with commercial operation is framed by the Orwellian concept of 'doublethink' – holding contradictory beliefs simultaneously. Charities are increasingly expected to function like businesses while maintaining their traditional moral identity, leading to contradictions in governance and regulation. Fundamentally, Weinert questions whether charity law can reconcile its historical moral foundations with contemporary economic realities suggesting that its meaning will remain contested as legal, social, and political forces shape its future.

Jane Calderwood Norton's chapter, 'Discrimination as Detriment', comes at the idea of public benefit from a novel and hitherto under-analysed perspective. Courts and regulators commonly focus on the benefits of charitable purposes. They have historically been reluctant to explicitly assess detriments or harm, including those caused by discriminatory practices. The goal of the chapter is to examine whether charities with discriminatory purposes can still provide public benefit and whether permissible discrimination (eg affirmative action) undermines public welfare. Calderwood Norton's approaches this task through a careful analysis of the New Zealand Supreme Court's distinctly opaque reasoning in *Attorney General v Family First New Zealand*[20] that a charity's purposes were discriminatory but nevertheless conferred a public benefit. The chapter argues that public benefit should be assessed through a transparent evaluation of benefits and detriments, rather than through vague public policy exclusions. The chapter concludes that public benefit analysis should explicitly weigh the harm caused by discrimination, rather than relying on judicial avoidance techniques. It contends that while charity law should not become an extension of discrimination law, ensuring that charitable status is not granted to organisations that cause societal harm, is essential to maintaining public trust and upholding the core values of charity law.

In recent decades, charities have emerged as major providers of services for those in the community with disabilities. As the state has withdrawn from the direct provision of social services, including services that support and empower those with disabilities, charities have moved to fill the void. This is particularly

[19] The terms 'halo' or 'halo effect' were coined by Edward Thorndike, 'A Constant Error in Psychological Ratings' (1920) 4 *Journal of Applied Psychology* 25.

[20] [2022] NZSC 80.

evident in Australia with the introduction of the National Disability Insurance Scheme.[21] Under this scheme, the Federal government has effectively out-sourced disability services to a range of organisations, many of whom are charities. Linda Steele's chapter explores the darker side of disability support services and the contemporary role of charities in the perpetuation of disability injustices. Perhaps unintentionally, charities nevertheless contributed to the disability injustices committed during twentieth century. The more recent shift to the so-called 'choice and control' model of the National Disability Insurance Scheme has resulted in charities rebranding themselves and erasing their pasts. Steele concludes that there is a need for a radical re-evaluation of charity law's role in disabled people's lives and their access to support. The recognition that charity law has played a role in harming disabled people is an important step if the socio-legal relations of disability support are to be reconceived.

One of the most profound and far-reaching changes to have occurred in the charities sector is the ways that and means by which charities are regulated. While historically, the civil courts, with some oversight by the Attorney General as *parens patriae*, were the primary mechanism of oversight and accountability for charities, more recently in many jurisdictions, including the United Kingdom and Australia, regulatory agencies have been created to exercise active monitoring and control of charities and those who administer them. In doing so, these agencies have in many respects displaced the courts as the primary regulator of charitable purposes. An important question posed by these new regulatory bodies is: are they effective regulators? Jennifer Sigafoos's chapter explores this question with the first comprehensive empirical investigation of the most significant regulatory interventions by the Charity Commission for England and Wales. The analysis reveals that the Charity Commission responds to issues raised by the media, police, and individuals making complaints rather than being a proactive monitor of charities' activities. Not surprisingly, the study finds that it is the larger charities, with substantial revenue, that are the most likely to face statutory inquiries. The chapter emphasises the careful balance between regulatory enforcement and sectoral support that is needed and questions whether the current framework has achieved that balance. The findings highlight the ongoing challenges in maintaining effective, proportionate, and transparent charity regulation.

Shaoming Zhu's chapter also considers the governance of charities and offers a rare insight into China's legislative framework for charitable organisations. Zhu identifies as a central issue facing the development of charities in China the inconsistencies in the legislative and administrative governance regime. There are multiple regulatory instruments and the Charity Law 2016 must coexist with tax laws, civil codes, and ministerial regulations, leading to confusion over legal status, tax exemptions, and compliance requirements. Ultimately, the chapter argues that effective governance in China's charitable sector requires a unified legal

[21] National Disability Insurance Scheme Act 2013 (Cth).

framework, better incentives, and clearer roles for trustees and regulatory bodies to ensure sustainable growth and public trust in charities.

The final chapter in this collection addresses a subject that may, at first glance, seem to have little to do with the law of charity: the plight of homeless and abused animals. Yet, this should not come as a surprise. The dedication of significant sums of money, whether by will or through trusts, to the welfare of animals (or specific animals)[22] has a long history, and animal welfare is a long established charitable purpose.[23] Maria Fox and Sarah Sing's chapter examines the role of charity law as a governance mechanism for regulating animal rescue organisations in England and Wales. It highlights how charitable status impacts governance, financial accountability, and public trust while exposing governance failures that may compromise animal welfare. The authors argue that charity law serves as a regulatory mechanism in the absence of a dedicated statutory framework for animal rescues. The Charity Commission plays a crucial role in governance by investigating financial mismanagement, conflicts of interest, and inadequate trustee oversight in rescue organisations. However, inquiries often reveal that trustees misunderstand or fail to comply with their legal duties, leading to financial instability and operational failures. The chapter also highlights that governance failures often correlate with animal welfare breaches, as inadequate financial oversight can lead to animal neglect or mistreatment. While charity law helps identify governance risks, the authors argue that its light-touch regulation is insufficient to ensure high animal welfare standards. They conclude that a sector-specific statutory framework is necessary to enhance governance and protect both animals and public trust, while charity law remains an essential but limited tool in regulating animal rescues.

IV. Charity Law in Flux

The legal framework governing charitable organisations stands at a pivotal moment in the early twenty-first century. Charity law, with its deep historical roots tracing back to the Statute of Charitable Uses 1601, occupies an increasingly intricate position at the juncture of private initiative and public responsibility. As charitable organisations have evolved from their origins as vehicles for private philanthropy into sophisticated institutions that frequently serve as critical providers of public services, the regulatory landscape has become correspondingly complex. The contemporary charitable sector faces unprecedented challenges that test the limits

[22] A trust established for the benefit of a specific animal will not be charitable, but may still take effect as a private trust so long as it does not breach the rule against perpetuities: *Re Dean; Cooper-Dean v Stevens* (1889) 41 Ch D 552.

[23] *Re Grove-Grady* [1929] 1 Ch 557, 582; *Tatham v Drummond* (1864) 4 De GJ & Sm 484; *Re Douglas; Obert v Barrow* (1887) 35 Ch D 472; *Swife v A-G (Ireland) (No 2)* [1912] IR 133; *A-G (SA) v Bray* (1964) 111 CLR 402.

of traditional legal frameworks while simultaneously presenting opportunities for innovation and reform.

The historical development of charity law reflects an enduring dialogue between private philanthropic impulses and public regulatory oversight. From its ecclesiastical origins through its codification in the Statute of Elizabeth and subsequent evolution in common law jurisdictions, charity law has exhibited a remarkable capacity for adaptation while maintaining certain foundational principles. This adaptability has been central to its continued relevance; yet, it has also generated tensions between competing interests and objectives that remain unresolved in contemporary legal practice.

Modern charity law inherits this complex legacy while confronting new and distinct challenges. The dramatic expansion in the scale and sophistication of charitable organisations, their increasing role in the provision of essential services, and the emergence of novel forms of philanthropy all test the boundaries of traditional legal paradigms. These developments raise fundamental questions about the nature of charity, the appropriate balance between private initiative and public oversight, and the evolving role of charitable organisations in contemporary society.

One of the most profound transformations in recent decades has been the shift of charities from supplementary service providers to indispensable components of social service delivery systems. This change has unfolded against a backdrop of shifting government policies, economic pressures, and evolving societal expectations. The withdrawal of the state from direct service provision in various sectors has created a space that charitable organisations have increasingly been called upon to fill.

This transformation carries significant implications for charity law. Traditional legal frameworks, originally designed to ensure the proper stewardship of charitable endowments and prevent fraud, must now accommodate organisations that function as quasi-public institutions. These developments have prompted calls for reforms that better align charity law with contemporary realities while preserving the distinctive attributes that make charitable organisations valuable social institutions.

The chapters in this collection engage with these fundamental challenges, offering diverse perspectives on how charity law might evolve to meet contemporary needs while safeguarding its essential function as a framework for promoting public benefit through private initiative. They represent crucial contributions to ongoing debates about the future of charity law and its role in modern society.

Through rigorous analysis of these themes and challenges, this collection aspires to contribute to the development of more effective legal frameworks for charitable activities in the twenty-first century. The diversity of viewpoints presented in these chapters underscores the complexity of the issues at hand and highlights the necessity of considering multiple perspectives in shaping appropriate legal responses to the evolving landscape of charity law.

2

Mrs Jelleby, Victorian Values, and the Legal Framework of the Law of Charity in Nineteenth-century England

WARREN SWAIN

> One other singularity was, that nobody with a mission – except Mr Quale, whose mission … was to be in ecstasies with everybody's mission – cared at all for anybody's mission. Mrs Pardiggle being as clear that the only one infallible course was her course of pouncing upon the poor, and applying benevolence to them like a strait-waistcoat; as Miss Wisk was that the only practical thing for the world was the emancipation of Woman from the thraldom of her Tyrant, Man. Mrs Jellyby, all the while, sat smiling at the limited vision that could see anything but Borrioboola-Gha.[1]

Charity is more than a good subject for satire. It also raises complex issues for lawyers, even if it has attracted relatively little attention from legal historians. The leading account remains Gareth Jones, *History of the Law of Charity 1532–1827*.[2] In recent decades, social historians[3] have stressed the complexity of charitable activity, including its public and private aspects.[4] By 1700, public Poor Law relief, provided by parishes, already supported five per cent of the population.[5] A century later, the New Poor Laws brought about radical changes to this system.[6] The character of private as well as public charity altered fundamentally as well. This was a more gradual process that occurred from the

[1] C Dickens, *Bleak House* (first published 1853, London, Penguin, 1979) 479.
[2] G Jones, *History of the Law of Charity 1532–1827* (Cambridge, CUP, 1969).
[3] C Jones, 'Some Recent Trends in the History of Charity' in MJ Daunton (ed), *Charity, Self-Interest and Welfare in the English Past* (London, UCL Press, 1996).
[4] J Innes, 'The "Mixed Economy of Welfare" in Early Modern England: Assessments of the Options from Hale to Malthus (c1683–1803)' in Daunton (n 3).
[5] P Slack, *Poverty and Policy in Tudor and Stuart England* (London, Longman, 1988) 172. For a summary of poor relief until the 1830s, see MJ Daunton, *Progress and Poverty: An Economic and Social History of Britain 1700–1850* (Oxford, OUP, 1995) 448–59.
[6] The same individuals might be involved in both a public and private sphere: N McCord, 'The Poor Law and Philanthropy' in D Fraser (ed), *The New Poor Law in the Nineteenth Century* (London, Macmillan Press, 1976).

mid-seventeenth century to the mid-nineteenth century. By 1850, some charities had become large, wealthy, and complex organisations. The existing legal and regulatory framework proved unequal to the task of ensuring that they were properly managed. Victorian England was also an era that saw large-scale law reform. Some of these wider changes – for example, relating to the operation of the Court of Chancery – were highly relevant to the way that charities were regulated. Other shifts were more conceptual in the way in which the substantive law was structured. These events occurred against the backdrop of debates about the proper reach of the nineteenth-century state.

I. Individual Giving and Charitable Associations

Charity takes many forms. At its simplest, charity might consist of modest donations to friends and acquaintances.[7] In the 1660s, Samuel Pepys described several types of charitable activity in his diaries. His personal poor box[8] was a variation on the tradition of poor boxes in churches or alms-houses.[9] Poor boxes are a good illustration of the small, localised, and communal character of most charities from Medieval times into the early modern period.[10] By the seventeenth century, this model was changing, as some charities started to become large and complex organisations. Pepys was involved with two of them: Christ's Hospital, a school set up as a charitable foundation, and the Greenwich Hospital.[11] These types of charity had certain common features:

> These bodies no longer relied on [state or church] authority either for the setting of policy goals or for funding. They were thus more flexible organizations: they were not tied to the need to seek recruits from any pre-existing geographical area, or occupational status or even religious grouping. … [T]hey were subscriber organizations, dependent on an individually committed set of members for their continued existence, requir[ing] them to be both publicity-conscious and inclusive in organization. Subscribers needed to be given a sense of participation in management and managers needed to project a sense of awareness of their accountability to subscribers.[12]

[7] Examples can be found in Elizabeth Freke's seventeenth-century commonplace book: Elizabeth Freke, 'Remembrances, 1671–1714' (2001) 18 *Royal Historical Society Camden Fifth Series* 37, 117 (3 and 4 January 1709).

[8] R Latham (ed), *Pepys's Diary* (London, Folio Society, 1996) vol 1, 5 March 1662.

[9] ibid 27 February 1660. On the history of the poor box, see Nicholas Dean Brodie, '"An ancient box": *The Queen v. Robert Wortley and John Allen* (1846); or, A History of the English Parochial Poor Box *c.* 1547' in AM Scott (ed), *Experiences of Charity, 1250–1650* (Farnham, Ashgate, 2015).

[10] M Rubin, *Charity and Community in Medieval Cambridge* (Cambridge, CUP, 1987).

[11] R Ollard, *Pepys: A Biography* (London, Hodder and Stoughton, 1974) 323; C Tomalin, *Samuel Pepys: The Unequalled Self* (London, Penguin, 2002) 303, 362–65.

[12] MJD Roberts, 'Head versus Heart? Voluntary Associations and Charity Organization in England, c. 1700–1850' in H Cunningham and J Innes (eds), *Charity, Philanthropy and Reform: from the 1690s to 1850* (London, Macmillan Press, 1998) 67.

The large sums of money that a charity like Thomas Coram's Foundling Hospital attracted through subscriptions created an impetus to finally address the legal personality of charities.[13] The hospital itself was a corporation under Royal Charter.[14] In *The Case of Sutton's Hospital*,[15] Coke CJ explained that a corporation of this kind operated through the idea of a *persona ficta* or an artificial legal person.[16] When the Charitable Corporation for the Relief of Industrious Poor collapsed amid allegations of embezzlement and fraud,[17] Lord Hardwicke observed that 'this is in the nature of a private trust for other persons; and in this view the committee-men are responsible to the corporation for breaches of trust, either by commissions or omissions, for acts of malfeasance or nonfeasance'.[18] Lord Hardwicke conceded that it was possible to impose joint liability on the directors in a case of fraud but stressed the dangers of making it 'too perilous for honest men to accept offices of trust, by making them liable to losses in the execution of them'.[19] Deed of settlement or joint stock companies, which emerged after the Bubble Act 1720,[20] operated as unincorporated partnerships governed by the law of contract and trusts.[21] Charitable, as well as business organisations, began to follow the same model.

Rather than the trouble and expense of resorting to the law, it was believed that the best check on corruption was to employ a large number of governors.[22] Governors could expect some social cachet and there were more tangible benefits for subscribers.[23] Coram's Hospital was largely run on commercial lines.[24] Some charities might be dominated by one individual like Thomas Firmin.[25] Others had moral or religious purposes, such as the Methodist Strangers' Friend Societies or the more aristocratic Ladies' Charitable Society.[26] The moral panics of the late eighteenth century created a fertile environment for the creation of many new

[13] RK McClure, *Coram's Children: The London Foundling Hospital in the Eighteenth Century* (Hartford, Yale University Press, 1981).

[14] ibid 32.

[15] (1612) 10 Co Rep 23 a; 77 ER 960.

[16] For the influence of this idea more broadly, see S Watson, *The Making of the Modern Company* (Oxford, Hart Publishing, 2022) 35–36.

[17] There was clearly a profit motive because shareholders were paid a dividend. P Brealey, 'The Charitable Corporation for the Relief of Industrious Poor: Philanthropy, Profit and Sleaze in London, 1707–1733' (2013) 98 *History* 708.

[18] *The Charitable Corp v Sir Robert Sutton* (1742) 9 Mod 350, 355; 88 ER 500, 503.

[19] ibid 356; 504.

[20] 6 Geo 1 c 18.

[21] A Televantos, *Capitalism Before Corporations: The Morality of Business Associations and the Roots of Commercial Equity and Law* (Oxford, OUP, 2020) 35–52.

[22] For eg: Coram's Hospital had 375 governors in the original charter: McClure (n 13) 167.

[23] P Langford, *Public Life and the Propertied Englishman 1689–1798* (Oxford, OUP, 1991) 498. For example, in having access to hospital beds.

[24] McClure (n 13) 179–89.

[25] P Dixon, 'Firmin, Thomas (1632–1697)' Oxford Dictionary of National Biography (online edn, 6 January 2011).

[26] Roberts (n 12) 67–73.

charities.[27] Evangelicals like William Wilberforce promoted charities that included the Society for the Suppression of Vice[28] and others.[29] The Society for Effecting the Abolition of the Slave Trade was founded in the 1780s by a small group of prominent Quakers and Anglicans.[30] The rise of a subscription model of charities allowed the growing middle class to become involved in philanthropic activity and marked a shift from the typical older model in which wealthy individuals left legacies to charity.[31] This small list of examples illustrates the way that charitable activity had become very varied by 1750 and went beyond the relief of poverty, education or hospitals

A testamentary gift to charity involves four interested parties: the testator, the executor, the charitable beneficiary under the will, and the testator's heirs who might wish to challenge the validity of any bequest that diminished the estate.[32] The Charitable Uses Act 1736 imposed restrictions on bequests of real property to charity – the so-called mortmain restriction.[33] In the absence of a deed in the presence of two witnesses, at least a year prior to death, the bequest was void.[34] The legislation was designed to prevent deathbed legacies from diminishing family estates.[35] It generated a significant amount of litigation.[36] Lord Hardwicke recognised the dangers associated with deathbed bequests,[37] but he remained reluctant to apply the legislation too strictly. In 1801, Sir William Grant made the point that later judges were more willing to interpret a bequest as falling within mortmain.[38]

[27] ME Fissell, 'Charity Universal? Institutions and Moral Reform in Eighteenth-Century Bristol' in L Davison et al (eds), *Stilling the Grumbling Hive: The Response to Social and Economic Problems in England, 1689–1750* (New York, Alan Sutton, 1992).

[28] This society was more concerned with fears around social order than questions of sensual vice. In the aftermath of the French Revolution, this was perhaps not that surprising: MJD Roberts, 'The Society for the Suppression of Vice and its Early Critics, 1802–1812' (1983) 26 *Historical Journal* 159.

[29] B Hilton, *A Mad, Bad, and Dangerous People? England 1783–1846* (Oxford, OUP, 2006) 178; J Innes, 'Politics and Morals: the reformation of manners movement in later eighteenth-century England' in E Hellmuth (ed), *The Transformation of Political Culture: England and Germany in the late Eighteenth Century* (Oxford, OUP, 1990).

[30] JR Oldfield, *Popular Politics and British Anti-slavery: The Mobilisation of Public Opinion Against the Slave Trade, 1787–1807* (Manchester, Manchester University Press, 1995) 41–69.

[31] Langford (n 23) 491. For the emergence of a middle class around this time. See: P Earle, *The Making of the English Middle Class: Business, Society and Family Life in London, 1660–1730* (London, Methuen, 1989).

[32] This was even more complicated when there were different versions of the will: *Attorney-General v Lloyd* (1747) 1 Ves Sen 32; 27 ER 872.

[33] 9 Geo 2 c 36, s 1.

[34] ibid s 1. There were some exceptions (in s 4) including gifts to Oxford and Cambridge colleges.

[35] The preservation of landed estates was a wider concern that was reflected in other legal doctrines, including decisions about dealing with expectancies: W Swain, 'Reshaping Contractual Unfairness in England 1670–1900' (2014) 35 *JLH* 120, 133–34. Medieval concerns about mortmain were motivated by concerns over the loss of feudal incidents by alienation of land to religious bodies, or in modern terms, a form of tax avoidance: P Brand, *The Making of the Common Law* (London, Hambledon Press, 1992) 233–44.

[36] Jones (n 2) 113–19.

[37] *Attorney-General v Lord Weymouth* (1743) Ambl 20, 23; 27 ER 11, 12–13.

[38] *Chapman v Brown* (1801) 6 Ves Jun 404; 31 ER 1115 referring to Lord Hardwicke in *Attorney-General v Bowles* (1754) 2 Ves Sen 547; 28 ER 348. For Lord Hardwicke's approach more generally, see: Jones (n 2) 114–15.

Certainly, some early nineteenth-century cases on mortmain adopted an extensive definition of charity.[39] One enduring consequence of the 1736 Act was to ensure that the legal definition of what amounts to a charity (and within the Act) became, for the first time, a much more central concern for lawyers.

II. The Legal Definition of Charity

Mortmain was not the only reason that it became necessary to determine if an organisation was a charity.[40] Income tax was introduced at the end of the eighteenth century.[41] The Assessed Taxes Act 1798[42] excluded 'Royal or public hospitals',[43] whereas the Duties on Income Act 1799[44] contained a more general exemption for 'charitable purposes', which were still left undefined.[45] When income tax was permanently reintroduced in 1842,[46] the legislation stated that income 'vested in trustees for charitable purposes' and 'applied to charitable purposes' might be refunded.[47] The charities tax exemption was only seriously challenged in the 1860s by Chancellor of the Exchequer, William Gladstone.[48] His proposals were dropped in the face of lobbying from charities,[49] but by the late nineteenth century, tax had become the main setting for discussions about the legal definition of charity.[50]

From the nineteenth century, the starting point for a legal definition of charity has been the Preamble to the Charitable Uses Act 1601.[51] Traces of this approach can still be found in modern legislation.[52] It was not the original purpose of the

[39] *Trustees of the British Museum v White* (1826) 2 Sim & St 594; 57 ER 473.

[40] In addition the rule against perpetuities did not apply to charities. O Davies Tudor, *The Law of Charitable Trusts* 2nd edn (London, Butterworths, 1862) 251.

[41] For the early history, see M Emory, 'The Early English Income Tax: A Heritage for the Contemporary' (1965) 9 *Am J Legal Hist* 286; M Gousmett, 'A Short History of the Charitable Purposes Exemption from Income Tax of 1799' in J Tiley (ed), *Studies in the History of Tax Law*, vol 5 (Oxford, Hart Publishing, 2011).

[42] 38 Geo 3 c 16.

[43] ibid s 29. This exemption mirrored earlier legislation: Gousmett (n 41) 134–35.

[44] 39 Geo 3 c 13.

[45] ibid ss 5, 87, 88. See: Gousmett (n 41) 143.

[46] Income Tax Act 1842 (5 & 6 Vict c 35).

[47] ibid sch A, vi.

[48] Roy Jenkins, *Gladstone: A Biography* (London, Random House, 1997) 241–43. This affair is covered in detail in an unpublished PhD: MJ Gousmett, 'The Charitable Purposes Exemption from Income Tax: Pitt to Pemsel 1798–1891' (PhD thesis, University of Canterbury 2009) 292–339.

[49] An account of a meeting between charities and Gladstone was carried in the press: *The Times* (London, 4 May 1863) 5. See Gousmett (n 48) 293–95.

[50] FA Martin, 'The History of the Taxation of Charities: How the Common Law Development of a Legal Definition of "Charity" Has Affected the Taxation of Charities' in J Tiley (ed), *Studies in the History of Tax Law*, vol 4 (Oxford, Hart Publishing, 2010).

[51] 43 Eliz 1 c 4.

[52] Charities Act 2011 (UK), s 3; Charities Act 2013 (Cth) s 12. The UK and Australia have elaborated on the traditional four-fold classification. The old approach is most strongly retained in New Zealand: Charities Act 2005 (NZ) s 5.

Preamble to provide a definition of charity. Rather it was intended to list those activities that fell within the remit of commissioners whose role it was to ensure that charitable donations were carried out in accordance with the intentions of the donor. A contemporary reading by Francis Moore in Middle Temple in 1607 argued that charity should be widely construed because it encapsulated a wider principle of which relief of poverty was just the main manifestation.[53] The Act of 1601 dates from the same period as the Elizabethan Poor Laws.[54] It also coincided with growing public anxiety about the weakening of community and the values of neighbourliness.[55] In this context, a desire to ensure some regulation of charities was understandable.

The extent to which the Preamble was regarded as a definition of charity before the nineteenth century should not be overstated.[56] There are certainly examples of courts using the Preamble in the eighteenth century.[57] Lord Hardwicke said that, 'The establishment of learning is a charity; and so considered on the statute of Elizabeth',[58] but it was also stressed that whilst the statute was 'a great enumeration of charitable uses' it 'does not affect to mention all'.[59] Yet as his remarks show, the Preamble was not seen as an exhaustive definition[60] and a purpose might be charitable and fall outside of it.[61] Value judgements going beyond mere definitional questions were involved and reflected in Lord Hardwicke's statement that, 'This is a different sort of charity from those pretended ones in times of popery and monkery.'[62] Religion provided one obvious context for changing social values. More than 60 years after the Toleration Act,[63] a non-conformist charity would receive the same treatment as a charity under the established Church of England.[64] Catholic emancipation took longer,[65] and Catholic charities only received equal treatment in 1860.[66]

[53] G Jones, 'Francis Moore's Reading on the Statute of Charitable Uses' (1967) 25 *CLJ* 224.
[54] Slack (n 5) 122–31.
[55] A Wood, *Faith, Hope and Charity: English Neighbourhoods, 1500–1640* (Cambridge, CUP, 2020).
[56] For a contrary view, see *Gilmour v Coats* [1949] AC 426 (HL), 442–43 (Lord Simonds).
[57] *Attorney-General v Ruper* (1722) 2 P Wms 125, 126; 24 ER 667, 667.
[58] *Attorney-General v Whorwood* (1750) 1 Ves Sen 534, 537; 27 ER 1188, 1190.
[59] *Turner v Ogden* (1787) 1 Cox 316, 317; 29 ER 1183, 1183.
[60] ibid.
[61] *Attorney-General v Peacock* (1675) 73 SS 209, which suggests that the King ultimately 'ought to be the great protector of all charities' even if they fell outside the statute.
[62] *Grimmett v Grimmett* (1754) Amb 210, 213; 27 ER 140, 142.
[63] Toleration Act 1688 (1 Will & Mary c 18) established religious freedoms for non-conformists.
[64] *Attorney-General v Cock* (1751) 2 Ves Sen 273; 28 ER 177.
[65] Roman Catholic Relief Act 1829 (10 Geo 4 c 7); GIT Machin, *The Catholic Question in English Politics, 1820 to 1830* (Oxford, OUP, 1964).
[66] Roman Catholic Charities Act 1860 (23 & 24 Vict c 134). Catholic charities became quite important in relief for the poor. JA Sheetz-Nguyen, '"Father of the orphan, his helper and his judge": Roman Catholic Response to the English Poor Law System' in MD Button and JA Sheetz-Nguyen (eds), *Victorians and the Case for Charity: Essays on Responses to English Poverty by the State, the Church and the Literati* (Jefferson, McFarland, 2014).

The idea that a charity involved a *public* benefit, arguably highlighted by Moore in the early seventeenth century,[67] began to feature more prominently in the case law[68] but was not yet a legal requirement for a body to be classed as a charity. There were good reasons why a prescriptive definition of charity was still some way off. Aside from inconsistencies in the application of the 1736 Act,[69] an insistence on a rigid definition of charity would have been contrary to Chancery practice of the period. The equitable jurisdiction was becoming more structured from the late seventeenth century, but any attempt to define legal concepts tended to favour very broad definitions rather than narrow ones.[70] This approach made sense as a way of avoiding deliberate evasion of equitable protection. Like fraud, had charity become rigidly defined, one consequence would have been to make it easier to avoid falling within mortmain restrictions and would therefore run counter to judicial rhetoric about the need to prevent evasion.[71]

Something closer to a legal definition of charity did finally emerge in 1805. From this point, the words of the Preamble were more than just a factor to consider but were used to determine whether the purpose was charitable. The leading authority, *Morice v Bishop of Durham*,[72] was not a mortmain dispute. It involved an attempt by the next of kin to challenge the validity of a bequest relating to the residue of the estate for 'such objects of benevolence and liberality as the Bishop of Durham in his own discretion shall most approve of'.[73] One of the leading lawyers of the day, Sir Samuel Romilly,[74] argued that the trust was too vague to be enforced. Romilly conceded that objection could be overcome if the trust was treated as charitable; he focused on the term 'liberality', which he argued was not charitable: 'not even importing anything of a public nature; from which the public is to derive any benefit'.[75] Sir William Grant MR agreed that the bequest was not charitable. He was influenced by the fact that the testator failed to use the word 'charity'.[76] But he suggested that 'liberality and benevolence' could potentially include any activity that fell within the Preamble but also activity that fell outside of it. The Preamble

[67] Jones (n 2) 127. For a more sceptical view on Moore's use of public benefit, see M Mills, 'The Development of the Public Benefit Requirement for Charitable Trusts in the Nineteenth Century' (2016) 37 *JLH* 269, 280.

[68] *Attorney-General v Pearce* (1740) 2 Atk 87, 88; 26 ER 454, 454; *Jones v Williams* (1767) Amb 651, 652; 27 ER 422, 422. For some other examples, see Jones (n 2) 122.

[69] Jones (n 2) 109–19.

[70] The definition of fraud is a good example: *Earl of Chesterfield v Janssen* (1751) 2 Ves Sen 125; 28 ER 82.

[71] *Attorney-General v Tyndall* (1764) Amb 614, 27 ER 399; *Blandford v Thackerell* (1793) 2 Ves Jun 238; 30 ER 612.

[72] *Morice v Bishop of Durham* (1804) 9 Ves Jun 399; 32 ER 656 [*Morice* (Ch)]; *Morice v Bishop of Durham* (1805) 10 Ves Jun 522; 32 ER 947 [*Morice* (Ch App)].

[73] *Morice* (Ch) (n 72) 399; 656.

[74] Romilly was an important figure in law reform as well as a lawyer and politician. P Medd, *Romilly: A Life of Sir Samuel Romilly* (London, Collins, 1968).

[75] *Morice* (Ch) (n 72) 400; 657.

[76] ibid 406; 659.

was henceforth critical in defining the scope of charity in law: 'Those purposes are considered charitable, which that Statute enumerates, or which by analogies are deemed within its spirit and intendment; and to some such purpose every bequest to charity generally shall be applied.'[77] On an appeal from the Bishop, Lord Eldon conceded that 'there is no magic in words; and if the real meaning of these words is charity or charitable purposes, according to the technical sense, in which those words are used in this Court, all the consequences follow'.[78] This legal definition of charity was one 'which the determinations have affixed to that word in this Court: viz either such charitable purposes as are expressed in the Statute, or to purposes having analogy to those'.[79] Lord Eldon recognised that there was a wider sense of charity: 'the great and extensive sense of the word "charity," in the Christian religion'.[80] In a legal sense, however, charity was a narrower concept than 'liberality'.[81]

The reasons why Lord Eldon and Sir William Grant MR were so determined to define charity using the words of the Preamble in *Morice v Bishop of Durham* were not made explicit. The decision nevertheless fits within the wider movement to begin structuring equitable doctrine.[82] In a slightly different charitable context, some words of Lord Eldon are on point: 'but, notwithstanding that, it seems to me, the cases have gone a length, upon principles wise or otherwise is not for me to determine, which has formed a precedent, that binds me in this Court'.[83] A definition provided certainty. Other evidence shows that the Preamble was becoming prominent in the legal discourse of the period. A year before *Morice v Bishop of Durham*, Richard Bridgeman reprinted Moore's reading on the statute, along with George Duke's *The Law of Charitable Uses* of 1676.[84] By the late eighteenth century, charitable status was becoming more significant for tax purposes as well as for mortmain, and this may have made it more desirable to create a fixed legal definition of charity.

None of this speculation explains why the Preamble was chosen as the legal definition of charity. The fact that it was so well established was one advantage. Another strength was that the Preamble covered the core of standard typical charitable activity, especially when extended by analogy. One unintended consequence was that it allowed potential charities to argue that the gift was for a public purpose rather than charitable and therefore fell outside the restrictions put in place by the mortmain legislation. Even if judges were sometimes prepared to stretch the

[77] ibid 405; 659.

[78] *Morice* (Ch App) (n 72) 542; 955.

[79] ibid 541; 954 (citation omitted).

[80] ibid 543; 955.

[81] ibid 530–31; 950.

[82] For the same process in relation to contract doctrine. See: Swain (n 35).

[83] *Moggridge v Thackwell* (1803) 7 Ves Jun 36, 68; 32 ER 15, 25.

[84] R Bridgman, *The Law of Charitable Uses* (London, W Clarke, 1805). On Duke, see Jones (n 2) 232–33.

legislation to ensure that mortmain restrictions applied,[85] it might not be a coincidence that a decision like *Morice v Bishop of Durham* in which a bequest was held not to be charitable was also outside mortmain.[86]

The Preamble was a means of excluding gifts for a public purpose that were difficult for a court to oversee. As a result, enforceable public purpose trusts were confined to a short list of exceptional categories.[87] Sir Thomas Plummer MR in *Ommanney v Butcher* made the point,

> In all cases the general principle is, that the trust must be of such a tangible nature as that the Court can deal with it; when it is mixed up with general moral duty it is not the subject of the jurisdiction of a Court of Justice.[88]

Whilst some judges were reluctant to enforce vague bequests of the kind in *Morice v Bishop of Durham*, the authorities from this period were not altogether consistent. It is not immediately obvious why a gift 'for such religious and charitable institutions and purposes as the trustees should think fit' is valid[89] and one 'for such benevolent, charitable and religious purposes, as [the trustees] in their discretion shall think most advantageous and beneficial' is void.[90] Beyond the legal definition of charity, the ongoing oversight of charity was an increasingly important activity both for the Court of Chancery and as a result of wider regulation.

III. Charity in Early Victorian England

By the eighteenth century, philanthropy 'had become more various and more self-consciously purposeful'.[91] A century later, charity was one element in the broader discourse of voluntarism, in which some advocated ideas like self-help and the absence of state intervention.[92] Centuries-old forms of community relief, which included a custom in which the gentry supplied food and fuel to the poor around Christmas, were still going strong in the 1840s.[93] The overall picture was a very diverse one, albeit there were some broad trends. Martin Gorsky's study of nineteenth-century Bristol shows a further decline in endowment charities

[85] *Trustees of the British Museum v White* (n 39).

[86] On this important point, see Jones (n 2) 131.

[87] This includes care for a particular animal (*Pettingall v Pettingall* (1842) 11 LJ Ch 176); the maintenance of a monument (*Mitford v Reynolds* (1848) 16 Sim 105; 60 ER 812); saying of a private mass (*Bourne v Keane* [1919] AC 815 (HL)).

[88] *Ommanney v Butcher* (1823) Turn & R 260, 273; 37 ER 1098, 1102–03.

[89] *Baker v Sutton* (1836) 1 Keen 224, 233; 48 ER 292, 295.

[90] *Williams v Kershaw* (1835) 5 Cl & Fin 111; 7 ER 346.

[91] P Slack, *From Reformation to Improvement: Public Welfare in Early Modern England* (Oxford, OUP, 1998) 163.

[92] A Tyrrell, 'Voluntarism and Self-Help' in M Hewitt (ed), *The Victorian World* (London, Routledge, 2012).

[93] D Roberts, *Paternalism in Early Victorian England* (London, Croom Helm, 1979) 114–16.

from the 1830s and a growth in subscription charities.[94] The rhetoric of mutuality, which was still preserved in the Friendly Societies, began to be replaced by a model of hierarchical patronage in organisations like hospitals.[95] Other charities remained closely identified with religious groups.[96] This period also saw the emergence of national charities as diverse as the Royal National Lifeboat Institution and the Royal Society for the Prevention of Cruelty to Animals.[97]

The first treatises devoted to the law of charities appeared in the 1830s. William Boyle, in his *A Practical Treatise on the Law of Charities*, saw his role as 'elucidating the principles' out of a mass of authority.[98] Leonard Shelford gave a more detailed justification for his book:

> The numerous Charities existing in this country … the number of decisions already made and likely hereafter to arise in courts of equity upon difficult and intricate questions concerning charities – and the want of a modern and more systematic arrangement of the law upon that subject … are sufficient reasons for offering to the Profession and the Public a new work upon it.[99]

Claims about a 'systematic arrangement' were standard for nineteenth-century legal writers irrespective of the subject matter.[100] In the case of charities, it was no easy task. Shelford's book ran to over a thousand pages. The complexity of mortmain was one reason. It was just as difficult to describe the various regimes for regulating charities.

The remit of the Elizabethan charity commissioners was to ensure that funds were used in accordance with the intention of the donor.[101] The old system was moribund by the mid-eighteenth century.[102] Shelford argued that commissions had 'long fallen into disuse, partly by their abuse and partly because they were found insufficient in prosecuting the claims'.[103] With the decline of the charity commissions, the Court of Chancery was once again the main forum for redress. Unfortunately, the court had also become a byword for expense and delay, famously portrayed by Charles Dickens in *Bleak House* in the 1850s.[104] The reasons for these problems were complex. Some were structural, but judges, litigants, and lawyers

[94] M Gorsky, *Patterns of Philanthropy: Charity and Society in Nineteenth-Century Bristol* (Martlesham, Boydell Press, 1999).

[95] ibid 128–34.

[96] ibid 160.

[97] D Owen, *English Philanthropy 1660–1960* (Cambridge, Harvard University Press, 1964) 176–80.

[98] W Boyle, *A Practical Treatise on the Law of Charities* (London, Saunders and Benning, 1837) vii.

[99] L Shelford, *A Practical Treatise of The Law of Mortmain, and Charitable Uses and Trusts* (London, S Sweet, 1836) preface.

[100] S Waddams, 'Nineteenth-Century Treatises on English Contract Law' in A Fernandez and MD Dubber (eds), *Law Books in Action: Essays on the Anglo-American Legal Treatise* (Oxford, Hart Publishing, 2012).

[101] For the operation of the commissioners, see Jones (n 2) 29–56.

[102] Owen (n 97) 85.

[103] Shelford (n 99) 278.

[104] Dickens (n 1).

all share some of the blame.[105] Much of the earliest Chancery litigation relating to charity involved claims by parties to a trust or legacy.[106] A charity might more often have a wide class of beneficiaries. In these cases, the Attorney General was usually required to be a party on behalf of the Crown by way of an information[107] based on a complaint from a relator.[108] An information differed from a standard bill,[109] and a relator could be 'most remote' from the charity and still have standing.[110] In the late seventeenth century, Lord Nottingham explained the origins of this process: 'the King as *Pater patriae* may and ought to be the great protector of all charities which were not within the regulation of the statute of 43 Eliz., for he was so at Common Law before that statute'.[111] The relator, rather than the Crown, was potentially liable for costs. In *Attorney-General v Middleton*, Lord Hardwicke awarded costs against a relator who brought a claim 'from a private motive of revenge'.[112] Shelford observed that cost orders against relators were 'frequent'.[113] When combined with the other deficiencies of Chancery, it can hardly have inspired much confidence. Evidence collected in 1818 showed that between 1785 and that year, 569 suits had been filed by the Attorney-General. This works out to less than 20 actions a year, many of which might not have reached a courtroom.[114] It hardly suggests a rigorous system of equitable oversight of charitable activity.

Speaking in Parliament in 1818, Sir Samuel Romilly said that 'it was impossible, through the court of Chancery, to obtain redress for the abuses of charitable institutions'.[115] He highlighted long delays and the risk of payments in costs. He had already made a similar point in a debate about charity registration in 1811, where he suggested that, 'The best remedy would be to enable the Chancellor to interfere in a summary way on petition. Most of the abuses would soon be reformed by this simple regulation.'[116] Romilly's proposal was taken up as part of legislation requiring charitable donations to be registered[117] and more general legislation designed

[105] For a good summary of these problems, see Michael Lobban, 'Preparing for Fusion: Reforming the Nineteenth-Century Court of Chancery, Part I' (2004) 22 *LHR* 389, 391–97.

[106] For examples of early Bills, see, Jones (n 2) 171–201.

[107] *Wellbeloved v Jones* (1822) 1 Sim & St 40; 57 ER 16. A private charity that operated as a voluntary society was held not to need the involvement of the Attorney-General: *Anon* (1745) 3 Atk 277; 26 ER 962.

[108] On the requirement of a relator, see *Attorney-General v Oglender* (1790) 1 Ves Jun 246; 30 ER 324. For details, see R Hinde, *The Modern Practice of the High Court of Chancery* (London, E Brooke, 1785) 73–75; J Harrison and J Newland, *The Practice of the High Court of Chancery* (London, J Butterworth, 1808) vol 1, 95–96; Shelford (n 99) 398–408.

[109] C Barton, *An Historical Treatise of a Suit in Equity* (London, W Clarke, 1796) 25.

[110] *Attorney-General v Bucknall* (1741) 2 Atk 328; 26 ER 600.

[111] *Attorney-General v Peacock* (n 61) 209. See also: *Corp of Ludlow v Greenhouse* (1827) 1 Bligh NS 17, 48; 4 ER 780, 791.

[112] *Attorney-General v Middleton* (1751) 2 Ves Sen 327, 330; 28 ER 210, 213.

[113] Shelford (n 99) 476.

[114] *Account of Petitions to Lord Chancellor and Master of Rolls, and Bills in Court of Chancery on Abuses in Charities or Charitable Donations* (1818) [372] PP vol xv 305.

[115] (1818) 38 PD (2nd Series) 1230–31 (3 June 1818).

[116] (1811) 19 PD (1st Series) 516 (26 March 1811).

[117] Charitable Donations Registration Act 1812 (52 Geo 3 c 102).

to bring a remedy for abuses of charitable trusts.[118] The idea was that this reform would replace the cumbersome information process with a faster, cheaper and more efficient summary procedure. It was not untypical of the sort of piecemeal reform of Chancery from this period.[119]

The apparent benefits of an informal process failed to materialise. John Mitford argued in 1826 that the experience showed that summary procedure was not the answer to the problems of Chancery.[120] In his work on Chancery procedure the following year, he wrote that the new process caused 'great inconvenience'.[121] He argued that the absence of a record in summary process made it difficult to determine against whom judgment should be given, especially those whose interests might be affected. He also referred to a recent judgment of the House of Lords in *Corp of Ludlow v Greenhouse*,[122] in which the author, as Lord Redesdale, gave one of the speeches in which he was openly critical of the new legislation. His deeper concern expressed there was that:

> Many things have lately passed with respect to charities, which have had a very unfortunate effect. I know that a great many persons now refuse to be trustees for charities: they say, we are exposed in such a manner to proceedings against us, that we must beg leave to decline being trustees for a charity; and the effect will be to prevent respectable persons being trustees for charities, if they are to be exposed to the sort of proceeding which unfortunately this Act of Parliament has more than once given rise to.[123]

Lord Redesdale pointed out that in the information procedure, the Attorney-General had control over whether litigation proceeded,[124] which he thought should be retained by the new summary process.[125] The legislation was also confined to breach of trust rather than one where the dispute concerned the way that funds were distributed.[126]

Lord Redesdale would defend Lord Eldon against those who argued that he was responsible for the delays in Chancery litigation.[127] The two men also shared a desire to limit the application of Romilly's legislation.[128] Lord Eldon stressed that a signature of the Attorney-General was required and that no case should proceed,

[118] Charities Procedure Act 1812 (52 Geo 3 c 101).

[119] This approach is best illustrated by the report of the Chancery Commission in the 1820s. P Polden, 'The Court of Chancery, 1820–1875' in William Cornish et al (eds), *The Oxford History of the Laws of England, Volume XI: 1820–1914 English Legal System* (Oxford, OUP, 2010) 652–55.

[120] J Mitford, *Considerations Suggested by the Report Made to His Majesty Under a Commission Authorising the Commissioners to Make Certain Inquiries Respecting the Court of Chancery* (London, John Hatchard, 1826) 98.

[121] J Mitford, *A Treatise on the Pleadings in Suits in the Court of Chancery* (London, J and WT Clarke, 1827) 19.

[122] *Corp of Ludlow v Greenhouse* (n 111).

[123] ibid 50; 792.

[124] ibid.

[125] ibid 51–52; 792.

[126] ibid 66–67; 798.

[127] DS Greer, 'Mitford, John Freeman-, first Baron Redesdale (1748–1830)' *Oxford Dictionary of Natural Biography* (online edn, 3 January 2008).

[128] For more detail see: Jones (n 2) 165–66.

which would not be approved under the older information process.[129] He also limited the summary process to actions between beneficiaries and trustees where there was a 'plain' breach of trust by a trustee.[130] Hostility to these reforms may, in part, have been motivated by a dislike of summary process and fears that it would be extended more widely.[131] By the 1850s, approval by the Charity Commission was required for a summary claim,[132] but the attempt to stop the rise of summary procedure had failed.[133] This did not mean that all the problems of the Court of Chancery had been solved. More significant reforms would be necessary in the 1870s and even these only went someway to speeding up the legal process.[134] Fortunately, there were some other options for regulating charities.

IV. The Re-Emergence of the Charity Commission

By the second decade of the nineteenth century, it was obvious that bringing about even the smallest reforms to the Court of Chancery would be difficult. At the same time, widespread abuse of charitable funds highlighted by the scandal around educational charities was plain to see. In the 1790s, Lord Kenyon had commented on the poor state of many charitable schools: 'In some instances that have lately come within my own knowledge, there was not a single scholar in the schools though there were very large endowments to them.'[135] Henry Brougham, a future Lord Chancellor who had a special interest in education, took up the issue in Parliament.[136] Brougham went on to chair a parliamentary inquiry which produced several reports showing the misappropriation of funds and a failure to educate the poorest children in London.[137] He argued that throughout the country, funds had 'been grossly misapplied, often no doubt from ignorance of the best method of employing them',[138] going on to allege that some educational charities taught very few or even no children and pressed for the creation of a charity commission. Two typical examples that Brougham gave include a school founded

[129] *Ex p Skinner* (1817) 2 Mer 453, 456; 35 ER 1013, 1014–15.

[130] ibid 457; 1015.

[131] Owen Tudor made this point in the 1860s: Tudor (n 40) 178.

[132] Charitable Trusts Act 1853 (16 & 17 Vict c 137) s 17. The Attorney-General retained the power to instigate proceedings in s 18 without approval of the Charity Commission.

[133] Polden (n 119) 665. For example: Chancery Procedure Act 1852 (15 & 16 Vict c 86) s 45.

[134] P Polden, 'The Judicature Acts' in William Cornish et al (eds), *The Oxford History of the Laws of England, Volume XI: 1820–1914 English Legal System* (Oxford, OUP, 2010) 757–73.

[135] *R v Archbishop of York* (1795) 6 TR 490, 493; 101 ER 664, 666.

[136] R Stewart, *Henry Brougham, 1778–1868: His Public Career* (London, Bodley Head, 1985) 120–27. Brougham was an important figure in law reform of the period as well. M Lobban, 'Henry Brougham and Law Reform' (2000) 115 *English Historical Review* 1184.

[137] *Report from Select Committee on the Education of the Lower Orders in the Metropolis* (1816) [498] PP vol iv 1. For examples of evidence, see *First report. Minutes of Evidence Taken Before the Select Committee Appointed to Inquire into the Education of the Lower Orders of the Metropolis* (1816) [427] PP vol iv 5.

[138] (1818) 37 PD (2nd Series) 817 (5 March 1818).

in Norfolk in 1680 for 40 poor pupils that has an income of £300 a year and no pupils, and another school in Yorkshire with an income of £1,300 a year and just six pupils.[139] One objection to reform was that a charity commission was inconsistent with the rights afforded to private property. But, as Brougham pointed out, a commission was hardly novel.[140] Chancery may not have provided a realistic remedy for many people, but it nevertheless showed that charities were not a form of private property that could escape scrutiny.[141]

The proper role of regulation of charities was just one element in contemporary debates about the proper reach of law and state.[142] Both main political parties were divided on these sorts of issues. Free-market Liberals took a different view from their allies amongst the more interventionist Whigs.[143] But these positions were not rigidly held. Brougham, who is usually seen as a member of the free-market faction, favoured what were, for the period, relatively invasive regulation of charities. A Tory-dominated House of Lords was largely hostile to reform. The Bill was so extensively amended that Brougham complained that 'he could scarcely recognise his own offspring'.[144] Whilst Brougham reluctantly accepted the amendments,[145] he continued to criticise the Act outside of Parliament. He went on to publish a polemic arguing for more significant reform, which attracted a lot of attention.[146] Brougham was particularly critical of the way that schools that used visitors as part of their governance were excluded from the legislation, but he also stressed the limits of his proposals, noting that the commissioners 'were only empowered to inquire and to report; to discover abuses, and to lay them before Parliament and the country'; they had no wider legal powers.[147] Brougham tried to strengthen his cause by threatening a new committee.[148]

In 1819, during the third reading of the Charitable Foundations Bill, Robert Peel furiously attacked Brougham's committee for exceeding its remit.[149] Brougham responded with sarcasm, saying of Peel: 'And the speech was wholly made up of invective, save and except the portion devoted to those denials of any design to inveigh.'[150] Superficially, the main ground of disagreement was about whether charities with visitors should be included in the legislation. As with other forms

[139] (1818) 38 PD (2nd Series) 599–600 (8 May 1818).

[140] ibid 603.

[141] (1818) 38 PD (2nd Series) 603–04 (8 May 1818).

[142] These ideas are often represented by the idea of laissez-faire, but there was a great deal of variation in the application of these principles, which were often contested: AJ Taylor, *Laissez-faire and State Intervention in Nineteenth-century Britain* (London, Macmillan, 1972).

[143] For a short summary see Hilton (n 29) 520–21; P Mandler, *Aristocratic Government in the Age of Reform: Whigs and Liberals 1830–1852* (Oxford, OUP, 1990).

[144] (1818) 38 PD (2nd Series) 1246 (3 June 1818).

[145] Charities Inquiry Act 1818 (58 Geo 3 c 91).

[146] H Brougham, *A Letter to Sir Samuel Romilly, MP, Upon the Abuse of Charities* (London, Longman, 1818). It was a somewhat surprising bestseller: Stewart (n 136) 125.

[147] Brougham (n 146) 20.

[148] (1819) 39 PD (2nd Series) 552 (22 Feb 1819).

[149] (1819) 40 PD (2nd Series) 1300–08 (23 June 1819).

[150] ibid 1319.

of Victorian regulation, there was an element of class interest in play.[151] It was possible to support regulating charities aimed at the poor whilst at the same time deploring the way that Oxford and Cambridge and the major public schools might be brought within the regulations. Brougham lost the battle on the issue of visitors, but the legislation significantly increased the powers of the charity commissioners. More commissioners were appointed, many of whom were salaried, and they were given oversight of all charities, not just educational ones.[152]

The Charity Commission was not a permanent body during this period, which left its future uncertain.[153] The final renewal expired in 1837.[154] The increase in the activities of the Commission in the 1830s[155] had created powerful enemies in the church, universities, and charitable corporations.[156] After several failed attempts, a permanent Board of Commissioners was created in 1853.[157] The new body had powers to investigate charities and require the submission of accounts, but it was not able to instigate an inquiry on its own initiative.[158] A court order was required before a charity could be reorganised. In 1860, the Commission was finally given some quasi-judicial powers, but initially these could only be applied to smaller charities.[159]

V. The Limits of Regulation and the Law of Charity

A dual system of charity regulation using the courts and commissioners described by Lord Hardwicke in the 1740s[160] was never very secure before the 1860s. In modern times, we are used to private law operating within a framework of public law regulation. In some instances, it might even be argued that regulation has become the dominant partner.[161] The nineteenth-century landscape was quite different and may explain some of the resistance to the existence of a Charity Commission.[162] The Commission survived, and the new structure remained

[151] KT Hoppen, *The Mid-Victorian Generation 1846–1886* (Oxford, OUP, 1998) 100–01. For the issue of class interest in charities into the twentieth century: J Hackney, 'The Politics of the Chancery' (1981) 34 *CLP* 113.

[152] Charities Inquiry Act 1819 (59 Geo 3 c 81).

[153] For a useful overview of the charity commission in the nineteenth century, see: JJ Fishman, 'Charitable Accountability and Reform in Nineteenth-Century England: The Case of the Chancery Commission' (2005) 80 *Chi Kent L Rev* 723.

[154] R Thompson, *The Charity Commission and the Age of Reform* (London, Routledge & Kegan Paul, 1979) 117.

[155] ibid 168–72.

[156] ibid 202–03.

[157] Charitable Trusts Act 1853 (16 & 17 Vict c 137).

[158] Through the Attorney-General: ibid s 20.

[159] Charitable Trusts Act 1860 (23 & 24 Vict c 136). Charities with an annual income of more than £50 were beyond these powers.

[160] *Corp of Burford v Lenthall* (1743) 2 Atk 551, 553; 26 ER 731; 732.

[161] H Collins, *Regulating Contracts* (Oxford, OUP, 2002).

[162] Charities are, however, not unique for the time in sitting within a regulatory framework. Loan transactions and compensation for injured workers are other examples: PWJ Bartrip and SB Burman, *The Wounded Soldiers of Industry: Industrial Compensation Policy 1833–1897* (Oxford, OUP, 1983).

largely unchanged for a further century.[163] Courts were still left with a lot to do. The infelicities of Chancery procedure were a significant problem. It was not an area of the law in which radical change from judges was ever very likely. There was more to this than mere kneejerk conservatism of some Chancery judges. By the nineteenth century, a body of law and practice had grown up over hundreds of years. Lord Eldon articulated this attitude when he said that although 'Charity Estates all over the kingdom are dealt with in a manner grossly improvident; amounting to the most direct breach of trust' for a great length of time, it was a 'dangerous mode of dealing' for a court to unravel longstanding arrangements.[164]

Some of the major charities were venerable institutions by this point. The leading schools and universities may not have welcomed scrutiny and had powerful supporters. The fact that they used visitors was a justification for giving them slightly different treatment. These arrangements long predated modern ideas about charitable governance.[165] Nineteenth-century governments first became involved in charities out of necessity in the context of education. Even then, there was some political resistance. The legislation was a compromise and any extension to the regulatory framework was only achieved in piecemeal fashion.

The courts faced several challenges. Nineteenth-century judges were put in the position of applying old law during a period when charitable activity was changing. This did not always lead to a satisfactory outcome, or at least a very neat one, as illustrated by the history of the *cy-prés* doctrine as a means of redirecting charitable funds when a charitable purpose has failed.[166] Once charities are legally defined, there is an obvious tension between ensuring that meritorious organisations are not excluded from the benefits accruing to charitable status whilst resisting a free-for-all.

The foundations of the modern law of charity were laid down in a speech of Lord Macnaghten in *Pemsel* in the 1890s when he listed four heads of charity: poverty, education, religion, and 'other purposes beneficial to the community'.[167] When 80 years later, Lord Wilberforce warned that these words 'must not be given the force of a statute',[168] he was not motivated by a desire to limit the definition of charity but the opposite. From the modern perspective, especially following

[163] Charities Act 1960 (UK).

[164] *Attorney-General v Griffith* (1807) 13 Ves Jun 565, 580; 33 ER 406; 411.

[165] For examples, see GH Martin and JRL Highfield, *A History of Merton College* (Oxford, OUP, 1997) 14; GL Harriss, 'William Waynflete and the Foundation of the College, 1448–1486' in LWB Brockliss (ed), *Magdalen College Oxford: A History* (Oxford, Magdalen College, 2008) 1, 30. A more unusual arrangement can be found on the foundation of Hertford College where the Visitor and the Principal possessed absolute authority: R Newton, *Rules and Statutes for the Government of Hertford College* (London, John Osborn, 1747).

[166] The scope of the original *cy-prés* doctrine was relatively narrow but was stretched by judicial interpretation. For details, see Jones (n 2) 138–53; LA Sheridan, *The Modern Law of Charities* 4th edn (Chichester, Barry Rose, 1992) 212–44. These rules are now overlain by statutory powers to amend charitable trusts: Charities Act 1960 (UK); Charities Act 2022 (UK).

[167] *Comrs for Special Purposes of the Income Tax v Pemsel* [1891] AC 531 (HL) 583.

[168] *Scottish Burial Reform and Cremation Society Ltd v Glasgow Corp* [1968] AC 138 (HL) 154.

rather broad statutory definitions of charitable purpose, it may seem that there was a degree of inevitability about this approach.[169] A more pertinent but rarely asked question is less about whether the definition of charity is broad enough but whether, given the benefits that charitable status entails, it is far too broad.[170] Depending on one's preferences, it is easy enough to identify more than a few non-meritorious organisations that have secured charitable status.[171]

From the perspective of the 1890s, the direction of travel was less certain. By the time *Pemsel* was decided, mortmain restrictions were largely a dead letter.[172] Assuming the policy of the protection of landed estates is a valid one, there was an obvious justification for treating an organisation as a charity and therefore within the scope of mortmain. By the late nineteenth century, the landed gentry was declining as a powerful political block and the great estates were a less important source of wealth and political power than in earlier centuries.[173] Mortmain creates a pressure to treat a body as a charity. The tax exemption of charities may point in the opposite direction, even if this is a truth that most judges have proved remarkably resistant to articulating.[174]

Pemsel is usually remembered for Lord Macnaghten's definition of charity. It built on the judgments in *Morice v Bishop of Durham*[175] in that it relied on the Preamble.[176] But more narrowly, it was based on a classification used by Sir Samuel Romilly during argument before Lord Eldon.[177] *Pemsel* was nevertheless a majority decision. Lord Halsbury LC and Lord Bramwell dissented. Both favoured confining charity to the relief of poverty.[178] Lord Bramwell made the point:

> I think a charitable purpose is where assistance is given to the bringing up, feeding, clothing, lodging, and education of those who from poverty, or comparative poverty, stand in need of such assistance ... That a temporal benefit is meant, being money, or having a money value. This definition is probably insufficient. It very likely would not

[169] As listed in (n 52).

[170] The only seriously contested matter of charitable status are private schools: C Bennett, 'Relieving Britain's private schools of their state handout shame is surely an act of charity' *The Guardian* (3 December 2022) www.theguardian.com/commentisfree/2022/dec/03/relieving-britains-public-schools-state-handout-shame-acto-of-charity. A good case can be made for arguing that several other types of charity should not escape scrutiny. Tax exemption is not a zero-sum game. Tax revenue avoided by charities must be collected elsewhere.

[171] *Thornton v Howe* (1862) 31 Beav 14, 54 ER 1042 (a charity promoting the works of Joanna Southcote, who claimed to be the mother of the second messiah). For a thoughtful account that supports Sir John Romilly MR's assertion of legal neutrality and points out that the outcome meant that the bequest fell within mortmain, see P Ridge, 'Legal Neutrality, Public Benefit and Religious Charitable Purposes: Making Sense of *Thornton v Howe*' (2010) 31 *JLH* 177.

[172] Mortmain and Charitable Uses Act 1891 (54 & 55 Vict c 73).

[173] For this story, see D Cannadine, *The Decline and Fall of the British Aristocracy* (Hartford, Yale University Press, 1990).

[174] For a rare example: *Dingle v Turner* [1972] AC 601 (HL) 624–25.

[175] *Morice* (Ch) (n 72); *Morice* (Ch App) (n 72).

[176] This position relying on the Preamble as the definition of a legal charity was enshrined in legislation: Charitable Trusts Act 1853 (16 & 17 Vict c 137) s 66.

[177] *Morice* (Ch App) (n 72) 532; 951.

[178] *Pemsel* (n 167) 552 (Lord Halsbury LC).

> include some charitable purposes, though I cannot think what, and include some not charitable, though also I cannot think what; but I think it substantially correct, and that no well-founded amendment of it would include the purposes to which this fund is dedicated.[179]

Public benefit emerged in the nineteenth century as a condition of the existence of a charity. It has been suggested that the new requirement reflected a growing plurality of charitable activity and provided a useful means of setting the boundary of charity alongside a list of defined charitable activities.[180] Lord Bramwell's speech shows that a policy choice is involved in what is included within the definition of charity. Equally, behind the innocuous and objective sounding requirement of 'public', there is more than a hint that public policy is at work. There is no need to labour the point because some charities that are far from public in the usual sense of the term have been treated as charities. Setting aside those charities like Eton College, which are only public in the same way that the Dorchester and Savoy Grill are public, the so-called 'poor relation' cases are the most obvious example of this phenomenon.[181] Equally, there is a policy choice in the rule that a benefit is prima facie assumed where the charity involves the relief of poverty, religion, or provides education.[182]

The emergence of a requirement of public benefit may not be coincidental. By the 1850s, judges were increasingly wary about entering the choppy waters of public policy.[183] This is not to say that public policy disappeared entirely. The fourth edition of Tudor's leading work on charity as late as 1906 gave examples of courts using public policy as a ground for rejecting charitable status.[184] It is nevertheless fair to say that as an explicit principle, public policy became more muted. These sorts of questions came to be addressed more obliquely, either under the guise of public benefit or behind the question of whether the activity fell within the definition of charity.[185]

[179] ibid 564–65.

[180] Mills (n 67).

[181] *Attorney-General v Price* (1810) 17 Ves Jun 371; 34 ER 143 (poor kinsmen and offspring within Brecon); *Gillam v Taylor* (1873) LR 16 Eq 581 (lineal descendants of Richard Wilson); *Attorney-General v Duke of Northumberland* (1877) 7 Ch D 745 (Ch) (poorest of my kindred). On the rather confused eighteenth-century authorities, see Jones (n 2) 260–62.

[182] *National Anti-Vivisection Society v IRC* [1948] AC 31 (HL) 41–42 (Lord Wright). Any presumption of benefit is now abolished in England: Charities Act 2011 (UK) s 4. This and earlier legislation are poorly drafted. The requirements of public and benefit are separate. There was never a presumption that any class of charity was public: J Hackney, 'Charities and Public Benefit' (2008) 124 *LQR* 347.

[183] Public policy was famously described as an 'unruly horse': *Richardson v Mellish* (1824) 2 Bing 229, 252; 130 ER 294, 303. But the authorities did not all speak with one voice and certainly public policy continued to play a role, even in an area like contract law which might otherwise be thought to be rather rule based: W Swain, 'Contracts "Not for the Public Good" and the Classical Law of Contract' (2022) 43 *JLH* 1.

[184] L Bristowe, Cecil Hunt and Halford Burdett, *The Law of Charities and Mortmain* 4th edn (London, Sweet and Maxwell, 1906) 44–45.

[185] It would be preferrable to have a proper debate about the philosophical merits of the existing definition of charity. For an example of this approach, see M Harding, *Charity Law and the Liberal State* (Cambridge, CUP, 2014).

The modern law of charity remains a curious mix of the old and new. The definitions of charity in recent statutes strongly reflect modern bien pensant concerns.[186] But the hand of history also sits heavily.[187] There remains a good deal of truth in a statement made nearly two hundred years ago by Joseph Story when he observed that:

> But, however strange some of the doctrines already may stated seem to us … yet they cannot now be shaken, without doing that … in effect, which no Judge will avowedly take upon himself to do, to reverse decisions, that have been acted upon for centuries.[188]

[186] For a summary, see L Driscoll, 'England and Wales: *Pemsel* plus' in M McGregor-Lowndes and Kerry O'Halloran (eds), *Modernising Charity Law* (Cheltenham, Edward Elgar, 2010).

[187] *Dingle v Turner* (n 174) 616–17 (Lord Cross).

[188] J Story, *Commentaries on Equity Jurisprudence: as administered in England and America* 2nd edn (Boston, Little and Brown, 1839) vol 2, 419.

3

The Australian Statutory Regime for *Cy-près* Schemes: Reform or Stagnation?

IAN MURRAY AND NATALIE SILVER

I. Introduction

The *cy-près* doctrine has evolved from a general equitable doctrine based on judge-made law to a contemporary statutory doctrine, providing mechanisms for *cy-près* schemes to approve changes to the charitable purpose for which property is held:[1]

> It was a process developed by the English equitable judiciary to remedy frustrating events that a perpetual charity may encounter such as impracticability of charitable purpose, inadequacy or surplus of funds. The judiciary attempted to apply the frustrated funds to a purpose as near as possible to the original purpose and intention of the donor.[2]

Furthermore, as observed by Edelman J, the 'courts have struggled with the operation and limits of this doctrine for at least 350 years'.[3] In Australia, this struggle continues as the state-based statutory regime, largely copied from the English legislation, no longer reflects the contemporary English statutory *cy-près* doctrine. This is because the English statute has been progressively reformed in the twenty-first century to permit change more flexibly and to provide greater discretion to the Charity Commission of England and Wales. In contrast, Australia's statutory *cy-près* doctrine has not evolved beyond the English statute as enacted in 1960 and relies on judicial decision-makers and state Attorneys-General.

This divergence from England both in terms of statutory language and legal processes relating to *cy-près* calls into question the continuing precedential value of contemporary English case law, such as the recent United Kingdom's

[1] See generally: GE Dal Pont, *Law of Charity* 3rd edn (Australia, LexisNexis, 2021) chs 15 and 16.
[2] M McGregor-Lowndes, *Inquiries, Empirical Research and Regulatory Failure* (Queensland University of Technology, Working Paper, 1993) 9.
[3] *Taylor v Princess Margaret Hospital for Children Foundation Inc* (2012) 42 WAR 259, [48].

Court of Appeal case *Zedra Fiduciary Services (UK) Ltd v Attorney General*.[4] It also raises an issue of whether the current Australian statutory *cy-près* doctrine promotes the most effective use of charitable assets that reflect contemporary society.

Section II of this chapter explores the history of the *cy-près* doctrine and its statutory evolution in England; Section III examines the development of Australia's statutory *cy-près* doctrine and the judicial approach to *cy-près* schemes; Section IV considers the implications of the statutory divergence that has occurred between England and Australia; and Section V provides concluding thoughts in light of recent reforms to Australia's statutory *cy-près* doctrine.

II. Historical and Current Approaches to *Cy-Près* Schemes in England

The precise origins of the English *cy-près* doctrine are open to some dispute. What can be said with certainty is that it was a judicial development, with the English Court of Chancery regularly employing modern *cy-près* principles from the seventeenth century, culminating in *Moggridge v Thackwell*[5] as the leading modern authority on judicial *cy-près*.[6] In doing so, the Court of Chancery drew on the practice of the ecclesiastical courts, which in turn drew on analogous principles from Roman Law.[7]

The doctrine required that (a) a gift on trust 'be directed toward a charitable object'; (b) that 'charitable object has become impossible or impracticable to carry out' – the grounds or occasions stage; and (c) that a substituted scheme for application of the relevant property be devised that 'is "as near as possible" to the donor's intention' – the alternative scheme or similarity stage.[8] The criteria of 'impossibility' or 'impracticability' in (b) have been described as 'a reasonably high threshold',[9] that 'severely restricted the application of the doctrine of cy-près';[10] while (c) means that 'the purposes of the charitable trust are modified to purposes

[4] [2023] EWCA Civ 1332 (*Zedra*).

[5] (1802) 7 Ves 36.

[6] RP Mulheron, *The Modern Cy-près Doctrine: Applications and Implications* (Abingdon, Routledge-Cavendish, 2013) 8–9; CR Sherman, *The Uses of the Dead: The Early Modern Development of Cy-près Doctrine* (Washington DC, Catholic University of America Press, 2018) 1–23.

[7] Mulheron (n 6) 6–7; H Picarda, *The Law and Practice Relating to Charities* 4th edn (London, Bloomsbury, 2014) 439–40. Although, for discussion about the extent to which the Court of Chancery created its own principles, rather than drawing on them fully formed, see, eg, Sherman (n 6).

[8] Mulheron (n 6) 53 (in the event of initial failure of a charitable object, it was also necessary to demonstrate a general charitable intention). See also W Henderson, J Fowles and G Hogan, *Tudor on Charities* 11th edn (London, Thomson Reuters, 2022) [10-050]–[10-053], [11-014].

[9] Mulheron (n 6) 58.

[10] Henderson, Fowles and Hogan (n 8) [10-050].

which are similar in theme to the original purposes but allow for modern conditions'.[11] Typically this required 'a close analogy between the donor's intention and the [proposed] cy-près scheme …'.[12]

Lord Nathan chaired a review of the law and practice relating to charitable trusts, resulting in an influential 1952 report that specifically considered the general law *cy-près* principles and recommended statutory provisions that would widen the availability of schemes, on the basis that the grounds of impossibility and impracticability were too narrow.[13] The background to the Nathan Report was an earlier report of 1948 by Lord Beveridge into Voluntary Action in the United Kingdom. That report called for an inquiry into the *cy-près* rule in light of numerous instances of charitable trusts dating back to the fourteenth to nineteenth centuries that were no longer of benefit to the public due to changed circumstances.[14] This had resulted in the political desire of 'putting to the best possible use the country's voluntary agencies, including charitable trusts', and more specifically of achieving 'considerable additional finance from private, as opposed to public, funds by the re-allocation of the endowments of charitable trusts which were thought to be "moribund" or "dormant"'.[15] However, both reports were clear that voluntary action (as differentiated from state action) was valuable; hence the Nathan Report also emphasised 'preserving … the "spirit of the intention of the founders"' while 'keep[ing] abreast of current needs'.[16]

The Nathan Committee's recommendation was incorporated in section 13 of the Charities Act 1960 (UK), then rewritten in materially identical wording in section 13 of the Charities Act 1993 (UK), and in later iterations of the Charities Act in 2006 and 2011. Section 13 of the Charities Act 1960 provided eight separate grounds or occasions for the availability of a *cy-près* scheme, some of which (as to the fulfilment of the original purposes,[17] original purposes cannot be carried out,[18] and amalgamation[19]) reflected categories already recognised

[11] *Westminster CC v Duke of Westminster* [1991] 4 All ER 136 (Ch), 142 (Harman J), cited by Mulheron (n 6) 86.

[12] Mulheron (n 6) 87.

[13] Report of the Committee on the Law and Practice relating to Charitable Trusts, HMSO, London, 1952 (the 'Nathan Report') [365].

[14] WH Beveridge, *Voluntary Action: A Report on Methods of Social Science* (Abingdon, Routledge, 2015 edition, first published 1948) 187–200, 210–13, 309–11 (the 'Beveridge Report').

[15] Nathan Report (n 13) [15].

[16] ibid [60].

[17] Section 13(1)(a)(i): 'where the original purposes, in whole or in part – have been as far as may be fulfilled'.

[18] Section 13(1)(a)(ii) 'where the original purposes, in whole or in part – cannot be carried out, or not according to the directions given and to the spirit of the gift'.

[19] Section 13(1)(c): 'where the property available by virtue of the gift and other property applicable for similar purposes can be more effectively used in conjunction, and to that end can suitably, regard being had to the spirit of the gift, be made applicable to common purposes'.

by the general law.[20] Other grounds (as to surplus property,[21] unsuitability of class or area,[22] original purposes taken over by other providers[23]) represented a slight widening.[24] Two grounds went a little further, one applying where the original purposes have ceased to be charitable[25] (while the drafting of the provision has caused controversy, it does not appear to have been much used);[26] the other applied where the original purposes had ceased to be effective ('cessation ground'), being that:

> where the original purposes, in whole or in part, have, since they were laid down – ceased in any other way to provide a suitable and effective method of using the property available by virtue of the gift, regard being had to the spirit of the gift.[27]

This final ground reflected the main statutory extension and has been described as 'very much wider than … the old law',[28] and as 'represent[ing] a considerable liberality upon the common law doctrine'.[29] The provision squarely raises both the desirability of protecting donors' freedom of alienation of property, and also the advancement of the public good from the more effective use of property.[30] This is in part due to the need to establish that the purposes have ceased to be suitable and effective (not just that another purpose is more effective),[31] and the requirement to have regard to the 'spirit of the gift'.

The Nathan Report had drawn upon Scottish law in proposing that the formulation of any *cy-près* scheme should have 'special regard to the *spirit of the intention of the founders*'.[32] However, ultimately, the Report and the resulting legislation used the phrase, 'the spirit of the gift', not at the second stage of formulating an alternative scheme, but at the first grounds or occasions stage.[33] As to the alternative

[20] Mulheron (n 6) 100–04; Picarda (n 7) 454–56. The amalgamation category reflected authorities relating to administrative schemes.

[21] Section 13(1)(b): 'where the original purposes provide a use for part only of the property available by virtue of the gift'.

[22] Section 13(1)(d): 'where the original purposes were laid down by reference to an area which then was but has since ceased to be a unit for some other purpose, or by reference to a class of persons or to an area which has for any reason since ceased to be suitable, regard being had to the spirit of the gift, or to be practical in administering the gift'.

[23] Section 13(1)(e)(i): 'where the original purposes, in whole or in part, have, since they were laid down – been adequately provided for by other means'.

[24] Mulheron (n 6) 103–06. See also: Picarda (n 7) 456–58.

[25] Section 13(1)(e)(ii): 'where the original purposes, in whole or in part, have, since they were laid down – ceased, as being useless or harmful to the community or for other reasons, to be in law charitable'.

[26] Mulheron (n 6) 107–09.

[27] Section 13(1)(e)(iii).

[28] HL Nathan, *The Charities Act 1960* (London, Butterworths & Co, 1962) 77.

[29] Mulheron (n 6) 109. See also: Henderson, Fowles and Hogan (n 8) [10-070].

[30] See example: Nathan Report (n 13) 16–17, 23–28, 75; Mulheron (n 6) 110–12. For a discussion of such counterbalanced concerns more broadly in relation to the *cy-près* doctrine, see Sherman (n 6) 17; Law Commission (UK), *Technical Issues in Charity Law*, Report No 375 (September 2017) 60.

[31] See example: Henderson, Fowles and Hogan (n 8) [10-070].

[32] ibid 700. Emphasis added.

[33] As noted by Mulheron (n 6) 112.

scheme stage, the Charities Act 1960 (UK) reflected the general law, simply requiring that the property be 'applied cy-près', that is, as near as possible to the original purposes.[34]

In addition to widening the grounds of availability, the Charities Act 1960 (UK) also notably provided the Charity Commissioners for England and Wales (now the Charity Commission for England and Wales)[35] with concurrent jurisdiction to settle *cy-près* schemes in most cases.[36] Since 1960, the vast majority of *cy-près* schemes have been settled by the Charity Commission and not the courts.[37]

The Charities Act 2006 (UK) subsequently amended the cessation ground of the 1960 and 1993 legislation to add a reference to 'the social and economic circumstances prevailing at the time of the proposed alteration of the original purposes' as a factor to be given regard alongside the spirit of the gift.[38] This was achieved by amending the cessation provision to replace the words 'spirit of the gift' with 'appropriate considerations' and then defining this term to refer to both the spirit of the gift and the social and economic circumstances. The provision is repeated in materially the same form in section 62 of the Charities Act 2011 (UK). The aim appears to have been to make it easier to establish a ground or occasion where changed circumstances resulted in the use of the trust property being less effective than it might otherwise be:

> This is an amendment to what is known as the 'cy-près' rule. Currently, as many noble Lords will know, the law is rather inflexible in this area: purposes must be as close as practicable to the original purposes. Complying with the current legal position can frustrate trustees and the outcome is not always necessarily the best for the charity's beneficiaries. By also allowing the social and economic circumstances within which the charity operates to be taken into account when changing charitable purposes, the Bill will help more effective use to be made of charitable resources.[39]

At the same time, the alternative scheme stage similarity requirement was watered down by the Charities Act 2006 (UK) (and this continues in the Charities Act 2011 (UK)) to require the court (or the Charity Commission) to simply have regard to certain factors. These included two factors linked to donor intent ('the spirit of the original gift' and 'the desirability of securing that the property is applied for charitable purposes which are close to the original purposes'),[40] as well as one linked to more

[34] Section 13(1). See also: Mulheron (n 6) 129–30.

[35] The Charity Commissioners were replaced by the Charity Commission by the Charities Act 2006 (UK), s 6. The change brought a clear articulation of the Charity Commission as a statutory corporation and a greater range of functions and powers, as well as more explicit regulatory goals: Henderson, Fowles and Hogan (n 8) [15-006].

[36] Charities Act 1960 (UK) s 18(1). The current provision is Charities Act 2011 (UK) s 69.

[37] See example: Mulheron (n 6) 92; Picarda (n 7) 523; J Picton, '*Zedra Fiduciary Services (UK) Ltd v Attorney General*: the Contemporary Scope of the Statutory Cy-près Doctrine' (2024) *MLR* 1, 8.

[38] Charities Act 2006 (UK) s 15.

[39] House of Lords Debates, Vol 668, 20 Jan 2005 (Minister of State, Baroness Scotland of Asthal). See also: Picarda (n 7) 472; Henderson, Fowles and Hogan (n 8) [10-060].

[40] Charities Act 2006 (UK) s 18, inserting ss 14B(3)(a) and (b) in the Charities Act 1993 (UK). Now see Charities Act 2011 (UK) ss 67(3)(a) and (b).

effective use of property ('the need for the relevant charity to have purposes which are suitable and effective in the light of current social and economic circumstances').[41] This is a significant change, providing the courts and the Charity Commission with some discretion in settling a scheme, with the ultimate scheme being one the relevant body considers 'appropriate' having regard to (but not necessarily following) the three criteria.[42] However, as predicted by Mulheron and evidenced in the discussion of *Zedra* below, English courts have a history of conservatively interpreting broadened *cy-près* provisions, which may restrict the application of discretion by the court,[43] but is unlikely to affect that of the Charity Commission.[44]

Alongside these wider reforms, since at least 1985, the trustees of small (and sometimes old) charitable trusts have been given the power to amend the trust's charitable purposes by resolution of the trustees, subject to the trustees being satisfied of certain matters and to acceptance of the resolution by the Charity Commission.[45] These powers have generally been applied to a larger range of 'small' charities over time, and the matters about which the trustees need to be satisfied have been reduced. As at the enactment of the Charities Act 2006 (UK), charitable trusts with gross income of less than £10,000 and not holding land that had been designated to be used for the purposes of the charity, a resolution of a two-thirds majority of trustees is required for the charitable purposes to be replaced by other charitable purposes in circumstances where the trustees are satisfied that:

> it is expedient in the interests of the charity for the purposes in question to be replaced;

and

> that, so far as is reasonably practicable, the new purposes consist of or include purposes that are similar in character to those that are to be replaced.[46]

The Charity Commission could veto a resolution on the basis that the trustees had not complied with this procedure, or 'on the merits of the proposals contained in the resolution'.[47] These provisions were repeated in materially identical form in the Charities Act 2011 (UK).[48] The effect is to materially widen the grounds or occasion stage, while still retaining the similarity requirements of the alternative scheme stage. However, the provisions applied only to the trustees of small charitable trusts.

[41] Charities Act 2006 (UK) s 18, inserting s 14B(3)(c) in the Charities Act 1993 (UK). Now see Charities Act 2011 (UK) s 67(3)(c).

[42] See example: Henderson, Fowles and Hogan (n 8) [11-003]–[11-010].

[43] Mulheron (n 6) 133–34.

[44] See: Picton (n 37) 10.

[45] Picarda (n 7) 551–56. See also: Charities Act 1985 c 20 (UK) ss 2 (old trusts that are local charities for the relief of poverty – power to amend objects), 4 (small charities – power to spend capital); Charities Act 1993 (UK) s 74; Charities Act 2006 s 41 (which added s 74C to the Charities Act 1993 (UK)).

[46] Charities Act 2006 (UK) s 41, which inserted s 74C(4) in the Charities Act 1993 (UK).

[47] Charities Act 2006 (UK) ss 40 and 41, which inserted ss 74A(2) and 74C(9) in the Charities Act 1993 (UK).

[48] Charities Act 2011 (UK) ss 275, 278.

In a 2017 report, the Law Commission (UK) recommended expanding this approach to all charitable trusts.[49] This was largely to align the approach to the amendment of charitable purposes for both trusts and incorporated charities.[50] The aim was to deal with concerns that the *cy-près* grounds or occasions were too narrow, while still retaining some similarity requirements at the alternative scheme stage to provide a level of protection for donor intent.[51] This recommendation was incorporated in the Charities Act 2022 (UK), which from March 2024 enables a 75 per cent majority of trustees[52] to pass a resolution to amend the trust purposes to new charitable purposes if the trustees 'are satisfied that it is expedient in the interests of the charity'.[53] There is no longer any requirement for the trustees to be satisfied that the new purposes are similar, although a degree of similarity will still practically be required because the Charity Commission's consent to the change requires it to have regard to three factors similar to those introduced for the general cessation ground by the Charities Act 2006 (UK). Two factors are related to donor intent ('the purposes of the charity when it was established'[54] and 'the desirability of securing that the purposes of the charity are, so far as reasonably practicable, similar to the purposes being altered'); with one related to the more effective use of property ('the need for the charity to have purposes which are suitable and effective in the light of current social and economic circumstances').[55] Nevertheless, these three factors are not binding on the Charity Commission; there is no obligation to ensure that the new purposes must bear similarity – these factors are just guides.[56] Further, the potential for the factors to be in conflict (especially between the third factor relating to the effective use of property and the first two factors) is likely to increase the discretion afforded to the court or the Charity Commission.[57]

As a result of these developments, the trustees of a charitable trust in England or Wales now have a statutory power permitting them to amend the charitable purposes whenever they think it is expedient, provided that the new purposes bear some degree of similarity with the old purposes, with the extent of similarity affected by the impact of changed social and economic circumstances. Even before

[49] Law Commission (UK) (n 30) 41–62, 355–57 (recommendations 3 and 4).

[50] ibid 40, 60–61.

[51] ibid 38, 41–42.

[52] If the charitable trust has members, then the requirement is for a resolution passed by a majority of the trustees and 75 per cent of the members who are eligible and who vote: Charities Act 2022 (UK) s 3, which introduces s 280A(5) in the Charities Act 2011 (UK).

[53] Charities Act 2022 (UK) s 3, which introduces s 280A(2) in the Charities Act 2011 (UK).

[54] Oddly, not the spirit of the gift. For a discussion of this oddity, see Henderson, Fowles and Hogan (n 8) [10-033].

[55] Charities Act 2022 (UK) s 3, which introduces s 280A(10) in the Charities Act 2011 (UK).

[56] J Picton, 'The Charities Act 2022 and its Dissuasive Effects on Donors' (2023) 86(4) *MLR* 1011, 1019; I Murray and J Picton, 'The Reform of Charitable Constitutional Purposes: Should Australia Follow England's Path in Aligning Charitable Trusts and Corporations' (2024) 35 *King's Law Journal* 46, 49–50.

[57] Murray and Picton (n 56) 49.

these recent reforms, commentators had suggested that it had become 'relatively easy for trustees to achieve modification'.[58] Now, it is even easier.[59]

III. Historical and Current Approaches to *Cy-Près* Schemes in Australia

Leeming JA has observed that 'the law of charity, at least for the last four centuries, has been deeply informed by the construction of statutes'.[60] Nowhere is this more evident in Australia than the *cy-près* doctrine where statutes have been enacted in all of the states to expand the operation of the *cy-près* doctrine at general law. The primacy of statute in this area of law was acknowledged by Edelman J, who determined that in Western Australia 'there is no longer a general equitable doctrine of cy-près. … The doctrine has been replaced by a statutory regime.'[61]

All of the state statutes in Australia broaden the grounds by which the original purposes of a charitable trust or gift can be varied beyond 'impossibility' or 'impracticability' under the general law, although in general, Australian courts have 'adopted a flexible interpretation' of the terms impossibility and impracticability.[62] So why was statutory intervention needed? The answer is found in the influential Nathan Report discussed above.[63] Although, interestingly, well before the Nathan Report, New Zealand had engaged in statutory reform of the *cy-près* doctrine through section 15 of the Religious, Charitable, and Educational Trusts Act 1908 (NZ), reproduced in section 32(1) of the Charitable Trusts Act 1957 (NZ), which states:

> [I]n any case where any property or income is given or held upon trust, or is to be applied, for any charitable purpose, and it is *impossible or impracticable or inexpedient to carry out the purpose* … then (whether or not there is any general charitable intention) the property and income or any part or residue thereof or the proceeds shall be disposed of for some other charitable purpose, or a combination of such purposes, in the manner and subject to the provisions hereafter contained in this Part of this Act.[64]

As we have discussed in Section II, England implemented the recommendations of the Nathan Report in the Charities Act 1960 (UK) section 13 which provided

[58] B Crumley and J Picton, '"Still Standing?": Charitable Service-users and Cy-près in the First-tier Tribunal (Charity)' (2018) 82 *Conveyancer and Property Lawyer* 262, 262.

[59] See for example: Picton (n 56) 1017.

[60] M Leeming, *Statutory Eucalypts in the Law of Charity* (John Emerson Oration and CLAANZ Annual Lecture, University of Sydney, 29 November 2023), 15.

[61] *Taylor v Princess Margaret Hospital for Children Foundation Inc* [2012] WASC 83 [47].

[62] Dal Pont (n 1) [16.1].

[63] Nathan Report (n 13).

[64] Emphasis added.

the separate grounds or occasions for the availability of a *cy-près* scheme, including the cessation ground,

> where the original purposes, in whole or in part have since they were laid down, … *ceased in any other way to provide a suitable and effective method of using the property available by virtue of the gift, regard being had to the spirit of the gift.*[65]

The Charities Act 1960 (UK) prompted a review of charitable trust law in Australia in 1962 by the Victorian Chief Justice's Law Reform Committee.[66] In 1965, the Committee's Report on Charitable Trusts was published. It considered the meaning and effect of section 13 of the Charities Act 1960 (UK) and noted that 'possibility or practicability is no longer the test [for invoking the cy-près jurisdiction], but that it is sufficient that the original purpose is no longer suitable and effective'.[67] In 1971, the Queensland Law Reform Commission also considered the Nathan Committee Report and found that '[t]here is in Queensland no provision analogous to s. 13 of the Charities Act 1960, and we recommend the adoption of that section'.[68] The resulting provision in section 105(1) of the Trusts Act 1973 (Qld) states:

> [T]he circumstances in which the original purposes of a charitable gift can be altered to allow the property given or part of it to be applied cy près shall be as follows – (a) where the original purposes, in whole or in part – … (iii) *can not be carried out according to the directions given and to the spirit of the trust*; … (e) … (iii) *ceased in any other way to provide a suitable and effective method of using the property available by virtue of the gift, regard being had to the spirit of the trust.*[69]

Victoria followed in 1978 with the Charities Act 1978 (Vic) section 2(1) with language identical to Queensland's section 105(1), other than using 'spirit of the gift' instead of 'spirit of the trust'. Two years later, South Australia adopted similar provisions through the Trustee Act Amendment Act 1980 (SA), which added section 69B(1) to the Trustee Act 1936 (SA):

> The purposes for which property is required or permitted to be applied in pursuance of a charitable trust may be altered by a trust variation scheme in any of the following circumstances: (a) where the original purposes, in whole or in part – … (ii) *cannot be carried out, or not according to the directions given and to the spirit of the gift*; or … where the original purposes, in whole or in part – … (e) … (iii) have *ceased to provide a suitable and effective method of using the trust property.*[70]

[65] Charities Act 1960 (UK) s 13 (1)(e)(iii). Emphasis added.

[66] McGregor Lowndes (n 2) 28, citing page 1 of the report 'in our report we have to consider whether we should adopt the provision of that [Charities Act 1960 (UK)] or some of them'.

[67] Chief Justice's Law Reform Committee, *Report on Charitable Trusts*, Melbourne, 1965, 22.

[68] Queensland Law Reform Commission, *Report on the Law Relating to Trusts, Trustees, Settled Land and Charities*, No 8, 1971, 72.

[69] Emphasis added.

[70] Emphasis added. This provision was added through the Trustee Act Amendment Act 1980 (SA).

New South Wales legislation came later, with the Charitable Trusts Act 1993 (NSW) section 9(1):

> The circumstances in which the original purposes of a charitable trust can be altered to allow the trust property or any part of it to be applied cy-près include circumstances in which the original purposes, wholly or in part, have since they were laid down *ceased to provide a suitable and effective method of using the trust property, having regard to the spirit of the trust.*

The Explanatory Note to the Charitable Trusts Bill 1993 (NSW) noted that 'a similar extension has been made in other States'.[71] In *Free Serbian Orthodox Church Diocese for Australia and New Zealand Property Trust v Bishop Dobrijevic*[72] the New South Wales Court of Appeal acknowledged section 9's derivation from the English statute, stating '[b]etween 1962 and 1993 each Australian state enacted legislation in similar terms to section 13 of the Charities Act 1960 (UK), including relevantly section 9 of the Charitable Trusts Act'.[73]

However, while the statutes in Queensland, Victoria, South Australia and New South Wales enlarged the *cy-près* doctrine to broaden the grounds on which the original purposes can be varied to include circumstances where the original purposes have ceased to provide a suitable and effective method of using the trust property, having regard to the spirit of the trust or gift, Western Australia did not follow these cessation grounds. Instead, Western Australia adopted the inexpedience grounds from the New Zealand statute, which the second reading speech made clear:

> The purpose of this measure is to put it into some statutory form … [The Nathan Report] recommended a new cy-près doctrine to be super-imposed upon the orthodox doctrine … Whilst we agree with the Nathan Committee in its comments in the need for reform we are not able to agree to a solution that would result in two cy-près doctrines in place of one. In our opinion this would add unnecessarily to the complexity of the law of this subject. Instead we recommend the adoption of the relevant sections of the New Zealand Charitable Trusts Act 1957.[74]

The Charitable Trust Act 1962 (WA) section 7 (now Charitable Trusts Act 2022 (WA) section 10(1)) relevantly states:

> [W]here any property or income is given or held upon trust, or is to be applied, for any charitable purpose, and – (a) it is *impossible, impracticable or inexpedient to carry out that purpose*; … then (whether or not there is any general charitable intention) the property and income, or any part or residue thereof, or the proceeds of sale thereof, shall be disposed of for some other charitable purpose, or a combination of such purposes, in accordance with a scheme approved under this Part.[75]

[71] Charitable Trusts Bill 1993 (NSW), Act 1993 No 10.

[72] [2017] NSWCA 28.

[73] ibid [207].

[74] Hansard, Legislative Assembly, 1 November 1962, 2306. See also Edelman J in *Taylor* [57] referring to enactment of the Western Australian provisions 'against the background of the New Zealand legislation and the Nathan Report'.

[75] Emphasis added.

Tasmania's Law Reform Commission in 1984 included recommendations that Tasmania's statutory expansion of the *cy-près* doctrine include both the cessation grounds and the inexpedience grounds,[76] and in doing so, reviewed the history of *cy-près* reforms in the United Kingdom, New Zealand and other Australian states.[77] Ten years later these recommendations were largely followed in sections 5(2) and 5(3) of the Variation of Trusts Act 1994 (Tas):

> (2) If it has become *impossible, impracticable or inexpedient to carry out the original purposes* of a trust for charitable purposes in whole or in part, an application may be made for a variation of those purposes by a scheme approved under this Part.
>
> (3) Without limiting the generality of subsection (2), an application for a variation of trust may be made in the following circumstances: (a) if the original purposes, in whole or in part – … (ii) cannot be carried out, either at all or according to the directions given or to the *spirit of the gift*; … (e) if the original purposes, in whole or in part – … (iii) have *ceased to provide a suitable and effective method of using the trust property.*

As in England, in all Australian states, once the grounds upon which to request a *cy-près* scheme have been established (the grounds or occasions stage), the court must then determine whether to approve the scheme through the application of a similarity test to the original purposes or means (the alternative scheme or similarity stage). For this similarity stage, the statutory provisions refer to schemes where property is to be applied '*cy-près*' (as near as possible),[78] or 'to some other charitable purpose … that is as close as possible to the original purpose';[79] or to a scheme that 'accords as far as reasonably practicable' 'with the spirit of the [trust/original gift]'.[80] However, none of these statutes adopted the broader language in the Charities Act 2006 (UK) (now section 67 of the Charities Act 2011 (UK)) of simply 'having regard to' factors including 'the desirability of securing that the property is applied for charitable purposes which are close to the original purposes'. As a result, the Australian statutes also differ from the contemporary English statute in the alternative scheme stage.

Understanding that the impetus for, and language of, statutory *cy-près* reforms in Australia was copied from a now outmoded version of the English statute in five out of six states leaves Australia in a peculiar situation where laws that were created to reflect the English statutory regime for *cy-près* schemes now markedly diverge. As aptly summarised by Leeming JA, 'the Australian State Legislatures

[76] Law Reform Commission of Tasmania, *Report on Variations of Charitable Trusts*, No 35, 1984, 8. While the language of the recommendations adopted both grounds, in another part of the report (p 16) the Law Reform Commission recommended 'that the English/Queensland/South Australian legislation be followed'.

[77] ibid 12–16.

[78] Charitable Trusts Act 1993 (NSW) ss 9 (1), 12(1)(a); Trusts Act 1973 (Qld) s 105(1); Charities Act 1978 (Vic) ss 2(1), 4(3).

[79] Charitable Trusts Act 2022 (WA) s 10(2).

[80] Trustee Act 1936 (SA) s 69B(6); Variation of Trusts Act 1994 (Tas) ss 6(3), 7(5).

have enacted British legislation, which has long since been further refined in that country, but not updated here'.[81]

IV. Statutory Divergence and its Implications

It is well established that 'much judge-made law is best seen as a response to or a consequence of statute' and 'statute is commonly a reaction to judge made law, and is itself the occasion for future development of the law' such that 'the two are *entangled*'.[82] Matthew Harding has discussed this entanglement in charity law observing that:

> While the charity statutes that have been enacted in recent years are designed to reflect and build on case law, like all statutes they also each change the law in their jurisdiction in some way. Thus, even if the interpretation of charity statutes is likely to be informed in key ways by equity jurisprudence, it is unlikely to be exhausted by recourse to such jurisprudence. After all, to the extent that a charity statute changes the law, the content and meaning of that statute cannot be given by the very law that is changed by it.[83]

As discussed above, statutes have been enacted in Australia to expand the operation of the *cy-près* doctrine at general law, while also serving as the basis for the development of new judge-made law. This section considers the 2023 case of *Zedra* and its implications for Australia in light of the current judicial approach undertaken by the Australian courts in relation to *cy-près* schemes.

The Charities Act 2006 (UK) replaced references to the 'spirit of the gift' in section 13(1)(c), (d) and (e) – later included in section 62 of the Charities Act 2011 (UK) – with the expression 'appropriate considerations'. The recent English litigation of *Zedra*, involving a £600 million charitable trust established with a gift of £500,000 to encourage altruism by attracting further voluntary contributions to discharge the national debt, which had grown to almost £2.3 billion – involved some consideration of this language. At first instance, Zacaroli J found that *cy-près* grounds existed, not only because the original purpose could not be carried out (based on expert evidence that the chances of the fund accumulating to a sufficient size to discharge the national debt were 'vanishingly small'),[84] but also because the cessation ground was engaged. This was on the basis that:

> current economic circumstances [including a shift in economic theory and government policy from attempting to pay down the national debt to leaving it in place][85] mean that

[81] Leeming (n 60) 5.

[82] M Leeming, *The Statutory Foundations of Negligence* (Alexandria, NSW, The Federation Press, 2019) 3–4, expanding on the concept of entanglement of common law, equity and statute in *Common Law, Equity and Statute: A Complex Entangled System* (Alexandria, NSW, The Federation Press, 2023).

[83] M Harding, 'Equity and Statute in Charity Law' (2015) *Jo E* 167, 170.

[84] *Zedra* [2020] EWHC 2988 (Ch) [136] (Zacaroli J).

[85] ibid [37]–[38] (Zacaroli J).

> adherence to the original main purpose would leave the National Fund in limbo indefinitely, with no benefit accruing to charity at all.[86]

An appeal was made as to the alternative scheme stage. Lewison LJ discussed the change in language from section 13(1)(e)(iii) of the Charities Act 1960 (UK) to section 15 of the Charities Act 2006 (UK). His Lordship noted that the latter:

> substituted the phrase 'the appropriate considerations' for 'the spirit of the gift'. The spirit of the gift was one of the two appropriate considerations. The other was: '… the social and economic circumstances prevailing at the time of the proposed alteration of the original purposes.'[87]

On appeal, *Zedra* was concerned with the factors introduced in section 67(3) of the Charities Act 2011 (UK), which the Court or Charity Commission must have regard to in the alternative scheme stage. Lewison LJ stated that '[f]or the first time … Parliament specified the considerations which had to be taken into account in devising a cy-près scheme'.[88] His Lordship noted that this determination involved a 'value judgment' for the decision-maker.[89]

Lewison LJ then considered the concept of the 'spirit of the gift', which he described as a 'nebulous phrase'.[90] This is curious given he then cites Morritt LJ in *Varsani v Jesani*[91] who stated that 'the concept is *clear enough*, namely, the basic intention underlying the gift or the substance of the gift rather than the form of the words used to express it or conditions imposed to effect it'.[92] He cites Chadwick LJ in the same case, who also finds the concept quite clear, requiring 'the court to look beyond the original purposes as defined by the objects specified in the declaration of trust and to seek to identify the spirit in which the donors gave property upon trust for those purposes'.[93] Yet on this point, Lewison LJ concludes:

> What we are concerned to identify is the spirit of 'the gift'; that is to say the particular gift: not some alternative gift that the donor, actuated by the same or similar motives, could have made but did not in fact make.[94]

By limiting the phrase 'spirit of the gift' to the 'particular gift', Lewison LJ seems to be narrowing this concept to the original donor intent. This becomes clear when he concludes, 'there is no reason to travel outside the spirit of the gift'[95] and 'it is not for us to question the wisdom of the gift'.[96]

[86] ibid [137] (Zacaroli J).
[87] *Zedra* (n 4) [55]. Lewison LJ provided the sole judgment, Sir Launcelot Henderson and Asplin LJ concurred.
[88] ibid [56].
[89] ibid [57].
[90] ibid [59].
[91] [1999] Ch 219.
[92] *Zedra* (n 4) [59]. Emphasis added.
[93] ibid [60].
[94] ibid [81].
[95] ibid [82].
[96] ibid [105].

When discussing purposes which are 'suitable and effective', Lewison LJ again construes this narrowly, finding 'what is "suitable" means what is suitable for this charity in relation to these funds held on these charitable trusts. These questions cannot be divorced from the spirit of the gift or its original purposes'.[97] At the same time, he finds, '[t]he question of "effectiveness" is more elusive'.[98] Acknowledging that 'a reduction in the National Debt which will have only a minuscule or … a negligible effect cannot be described as effective', as it would make no practical difference, while 'if the trustee's scheme were to be adopted the funds could be used to produce real good',[99] he ultimately concludes '[t]o the extent that the National Fund reduces the National Debt … it is *effective* to provide charitable benefits'.[100]

English *cy-près* cases such as *Zedra* may no longer have precedential force in Australia, given the Charities Act 2011 (UK) has been extensively revised, resulting in an expanded statutory *cy-près* doctrine that goes well beyond the statutory 'reforms' enacted in Australia. So, what does this statutory divergence mean for the continuing precedential value of contemporary English case law, such as *Zedra*?

Starting with the grounds for a *cy-près* scheme, the phrase 'spirit of the trust (or gift)' has been broadly interpreted by the courts to encompass:

> a more abstract conception than the original specific purposes of the trust, being 'the basic intention' or substance underlying the creation of the trust or the making of a gift. It includes regard to the trust's history and the social context of the time at which it was established.[101]

Australian judges often take into account changed social and economic conditions to 'show that a particular purpose is inexpedient, or that it no longer provides a suitable and effective method for using trust property'.[102] A survey of higher education purpose charitable trusts suggests that judges often do so in ways that strain or simply fail to explain consistency with the statutory requirements.[103] Thus, a similar result to the first instance decision in *Zedra* and other English cases relying on the statutory reference to these factors may be achieved on some occasions in Australia. Indeed, to the extent the English statute still refers to the 'spirit of the original gift' and the need for the relevant charity to have purposes which are 'suitable and effective' there may be some precedential value at the grounds

[97] ibid [95].
[98] ibid [95].
[99] ibid [97]–[98].
[100] ibid [103].
[101] I Murray and N Silver, 'Use of Cy-près and Administrative Schemes by Australian Higher Education Providers to End Dead Hand Control of Charitable Assets' (2024) 45(2) *Adelaide Law Review* 363, 367.
[102] See eg: Dal Pont, above n 1 [16.12]. See also *Housing Choices Australia Ltd v Attorney-General (Vic)* [2024] VSC 107 [37] (Daly AsJ).
[103] Murray and Silver (n 101) 369–82.

stage. As the High Court of Australia in *Macedonian Orthodox Community Church St Petka Incorporated v His Eminence Petar*[104] observed:

> [W]here, as here, the legislation reflected and even copied laws enacted, or made, for identical or analogous circumstances in England, it was permissible and helpful to construe the New South Wales legislation with the benefit of the experience expressed in judicial observations on the English analogues.[105]

However, some Australian cases do suggest that a point of difference exists and have exhibited reluctance in referring to decisions based on the revised English provisions. For instance, Leeming JA determined in *Perpetual Trustee Company Ltd v Attorney General for the State of New South Wales (The Will of the Hon George Nesbitt)*,[106] that in construing and applying section 9 of the Charitable Trusts Act 1993 (NSW), section 62 of the Charities Act 2011 (UK) 'may be passed over because it is differently worded'.[107] That was due to the express inclusion in section 62 of reference to the social and economic circumstances in addition to the spirit of the gift. In *Nesbitt*, Leeming JA noted that it would not be possible to obtain a *cy-près* scheme solely on the grounds of a discriminatory condition.[108] That position has been reiterated in *Tasmanian Perpetual Trustees*,[109] in which the Attorney-General (Tas) requested a *cy-près* scheme under the Tasmanian expediency ground,[110] on the basis of changed social and economic conditions, to vary a provision requiring gender discrimination in the awarding of educational scholarships.[111] Wood J accepted that gender equality was a societal norm, but rejected that a ground had been made out for a *cy-près* scheme, largely due to the importance of respecting the settlor's intentions.[112]

However, with the latest English reforms, trustees of charitable trusts can apply for a scheme on the mere ground that it is expedient. Australian cases are unanimous in reiterating that the cessation and expediency grounds do not permit a *cy-près* scheme merely because it is expedient, inexpediency is required.[113]

For the alternative scheme stage, the English provisions no longer require the proposed scheme to be similar to the original purpose, though they require 'regard to' similarity and to the spirit of the gift, alongside the need for purposes which are suitable and effective in the light of current social and economic

[104] (2008) CLR 66.
[105] ibid [53].
[106] (2018) 17 ASTLR 126 ('*Nesbit*').
[107] ibid [49].
[108] ibid [42]–[44].
[109] *Tasmanian Perpetual Trustees Limited v Attorney-General for the State of Tasmania* [2017] TASSC 32.
[110] Which courts have approached in a similar fashion to the Australian cessation ground: Dal Pont (n 1) [16.7].
[111] *Tasmanian Perpetual Trustees Limited v Attorney-General for the State of Tasmania* [2017] TASSC 32 [54].
[112] ibid [63]–[68].
[113] See example: Dal Pont (n 1) [16.7].

circumstances. The Australian statutory provisions all require similarity, it is not simply a factor to which the court must have regard. *Zedra* provides a cautious interpretation of the expansive English provisions. This approach is in keeping with Australian judges, who remain mindful of donors' wishes at the alternative scheme stage, with reference to applying the gift as closely as possible to the donor's original intentions.[114] However, it is questionable whether English courts will move to a more liberal interpretation. For a start, the approach taken by Lewison LJ in *Zedra* has been criticised in that its 'conservative interpretation of the s 67(3) factors jars with the contemporary approach of the Charity Commission'.[115] As John Picton explains:

> Lewison LJ's reasoning is subject to some difficulty. His narrow interpretation of 'the spirit of the gift', and the word 'effective', strays from a natural, and fuller, reading. It can be seen that although the modern statutory *cy-près* doctrine is no longer a rule of proximation, Lewison LJ nevertheless proceeded conservatively, in his judgment, on the basis that the scheme of arrangement should exhibit a strong fidelity to the original trust instrument.[116]

The implication of Picton's comments is that the approach of reasoning by analogy to previously decided cases, by which the *cy-près* principles first arose (and which inform the need to apply property to a purpose as near as possible to the original purpose) is a different mode of reasoning to the task of statutory construction, with its focus on text, context and statutory purpose. Over time, it is to be expected that the statutory changes will drive changes in the approach of the courts to the alternative scheme stage as judges pay more attention to construing the statutory provisions.

Picton also notes the irony that at the same time *Zedra* was being decided, a further procedural reform of English *cy-près* law was taking place, providing the trustees of charitable trusts with a new power of constitutional amendment without having to show that a triggering ground for constitutional alteration has arisen.[117] Accordingly, the use of the new provisions by charity trustees is likely to mean that the decision in *Zedra* will have little impact on the Commission's 'continued and liberal administrative discretion'.[118]

As noted in Section II of our chapter, given the role of the Charity Commission in determining *cy-près* schemes, cases in the English court system are rare,[119] and likely to become even rarer with the expansion of the mechanism for charity trustees to seek a *cy-près* scheme. Myles McGregor-Lowndes has pointed out that the 'bypassing of the judiciary' in England resulting from the abandonment of the judicial process of regulating charity to administrative arms of the state has

[114] Murray and Silver (n 101) 373.
[115] Picton (n 37) 12.
[116] ibid 11.
[117] Charities Act 2022 (UK) s 3; inserting Charities Act 2011 (UK) s 280A. See: discussion in Section II above.
[118] Picton (n 37) 10.
[119] ibid 12; Crumley and Picton (n 58) 265–66.

implications for a legal system that operates on the basis of precedent, providing 'little opportunity for judges to advance the law in tune with societal expectations'.[120] Consequently, even if the statutory divergences, in respect of the grounds and alternative scheme stages are overcome, there may be little English precedent for Australian courts to draw upon.

V. Australian Reform?

We have arrived at a point of significant statutory divergence between Australia and England and Wales in relation to *cy-près* variation of charitable trusts. Over time, this will reduce the body of case law to which Australian judges can refer when considering the Australian provisions. That is because English cases will increasingly relate to materially different provisions, and because there will not be many English cases as an administrator, the Charity Commission for England and Wales will be tasked with the majority of *cy-près* approvals. In contrast, Australian jurisdictions still compel trustees to seek court approval for *cy-près* schemes, other than in the cases where Attorneys-General are permitted to approve schemes for small charitable trusts. A reduced body of English case law is likely to impact the quality of new Australian decisions and the efficiency with which new decisions can be produced.

There is also a policy question as to why Australian jurisdictions might wish to apply public institutions to support the private property rights of donors (who, in the context of perpetual charitable trusts, will no longer be living) to such a degree instead of the public benefit from the more effective and efficient use of charitable trust property (as determined by the living trustees). As set out in Section II, these policy questions were clearly considered in the context of the Nathan Report and the English and Australian legislation that flowed from it. What is surprising is not just that the Australian provisions remain relatively frozen in time, but also that in the isolated instances of modernisation that have occurred, there has been no re-engagement with this policy debate and consideration of whether changed circumstances require a new boundary to be set.

For instance, in Western Australia, the Charitable Trusts Act 1962 (WA) was repealed and replaced by the Charitable Trusts Act 2022 (WA). The main driver for change was the Attorney-General's experience of investigating and responding to alleged breaches of trust by trustees of a charitable trust intended to benefit a First Nations' community.[121] However, in addition to expanding the Attorney-General's powers of investigation and enforcement,[122] the legislation amends the *cy-près* provisions to update the processes for advertising proposed schemes and to adopt

[120] McGregor-Lowndes (n 2) 17.
[121] Explanatory Memorandum, Charitable Trusts Bill 2022 (WA) 9.
[122] See example: I Murray, 'The Charitable Trusts Bill 2022 (WA)' (2022) 33(3) *Public Law Review* 195.

a plain-English drafting style.[123] There are no material additions to the *cy-près* grounds.[124] In fact, a ground permitting small charitable trusts to be terminated where the income was low in relation to the charitable purpose[125] was removed on the basis that the circumstances were already covered under the general *cy-près* grounds.[126] The provisions permitting the Attorney-General to approve schemes for small charitable trusts (in place of the court) were also amended to require the valuation of property held by the trustee to take place on the basis of disregarding the reduction in value caused by any limits on use imposed by the trust's charitable purposes.[127] The effect makes it harder for such charitable trusts to access the small charitable trust provisions. Counterbalancing these constrictive changes, a provision excluding schemes where the lapse rule applied was removed, albeit several authorities had already interpreted this provision very narrowly.[128]

For the alternative scheme stage, the new Act replaced a provision that did not expressly impose a similarity requirement ('the property and income [to which a *cy-près* ground relates] … shall be disposed of for some other charitable purpose, or a combination of such purposes, in accordance with a scheme approved under this Part'),[129] with one that does ('The property … must, in accordance with an approved scheme, be applied to some other charitable purpose (an alternative charitable purpose) that is as close as possible to the original purpose').[130] While a line of case authority had interpreted the previous provision in a restrictive way, that approach was criticised and a new Act provided an opportunity for change.[131]

The Explanatory Memorandum and the Parliamentary Debates make no reference to the developments in England and Wales, referring only to the establishment of the Charity Commission for England and Wales in relation to another part of the Charitable Trusts Act 2022 (WA).[132] Nor do the Explanatory Memorandum or

[123] Charitable Trusts Act 2022 (WA) Pt 3.

[124] There were some very minor changes of language for clarity and a ground was shifted from a separate section (Charitable Trusts Act 1962 (WA) s 7(2)) into a combined section (Charitable Trusts Act 2022 (WA) s 10(1)(e)).

[125] Charitable Trusts Act 1962 (WA) s 7A(1): where 'the value of the property [falling below a specified low threshold] is too small, in relation to the charitable purposes, for any useful purpose to be achieved by the expenditure of only the income derived from that property'.

[126] Explanatory Memorandum, Charitable Trusts Bill 2022 (WA) 3.

[127] Charitable Trusts Act 2022 (WA) s 16(2).

[128] See for example: Dal Pont (n 1) [16.9]; Explanatory Memorandum, Charitable Trusts Bill 2022 (WA) 3.

[129] Charitable Trusts Act 1962 (WA) s 7(1).

[130] Charitable Trusts Act 2022 (WA) s 10(2).

[131] As to discussion of the line of authority and criticism of the approach in the cases, see Dal Pont (n 1) [16.8].

[132] Explanatory Memorandum, Charitable Trusts Bill 2022 (WA); Western Australia, Parliamentary Debates, Legislative Assembly, 7 April 2022, 1785–1788 (David Templeman, on behalf of the Attorney-General); Western Australia, Parliamentary Debates, Legislative Assembly, 14 June 2022, 2745–69; Western Australia, Parliamentary Debates, Legislative Assembly, 15 June 2022, 2835–40; Western Australia, Parliamentary Debates, Legislative Assembly, 16 June 2022, 2951–52; Western Australia, Parliamentary Debates, Legislative Council, 16 June 2022, 2907–09; Western Australia, Parliamentary Debates, Legislative Council, 13 October 2022, 4501–03; Western Australia, Parliamentary Debates, Legislative Council, 20 October 2022, 4787–801; Western Australia, Parliamentary Debates,

Parliamentary debates discuss any policy reason for why the grounds or alternative scheme stages were constricted rather than broadened, other than a general reference by the Attorney-General in relation to constricting the alternative scheme provision as being the desirability of keeping the new purpose in a similar category or 'stream' as the original purpose:

> Any charitable purpose approved under the scheme means that it has to be as close as possible to the original designated charitable purpose. We want to keep the thing onstream. The bill will legislate that it be closely reflective of what the courts have ruled in common law; that is, if there is going to be a new scheme, it has to be as close as possible to the charitable purpose contained in the trust.[133]

In Queensland, the Trusts Act 2025 (Qld) has recently been enacted. While it does not go as far as the most recent English reforms, it does seek to adopt the modest expansion of grounds effected by the Charities Act 2006 (UK). That is, it seeks to expand the cessation ground by requiring regard not only to 'the spirit of the trust', but also to 'the social and economic conditions prevailing at the time of the proposed change to the purposes of the trust'.[134] Oddly, this change was not recommended in the Queensland Reform Commission 's report that led to the Act.[135] The rationale provided in Parliamentary Debates, to 'enable a more modern consideration in line with societal expectations',[136] while a little inscrutable, suggests some intention to effect a slight broadening of grounds for the benefit of the public.

The Trusts Act does not adopt the Charities Act 2006 (UK) liberalisation of the alternative scheme stage, as it leaves a similarity test as a requirement. However, it also effects an administrative change by introducing an ability for trustees of small charitable trusts (where the value of trust property is $750,000 or less) to apply to the Attorney-General for approval of a scheme.[137] This is consistent with the Queensland Law Reform Commission's recommendations, made based on the disproportionate value of trust assets and the costs involved in applying to court for a scheme.[138]

Despite the slight broadening in the Act, the Queensland Law Reform Commission Discussion Paper, Interim Report and Final Report and the Explanatory Note do not discuss the *cy-près* reforms in England and Wales.

Legislative Council, 26 October 2022, 5032–40; Western Australia, Parliamentary Debates, Legislative Council, 27 October 2022, 5128–32.

[133] Western Australia, Parliamentary Debates, Legislative Assembly, 14 June 2022, 2760 (John Quigley, Attorney-General).

[134] Trusts Act 2025 (Qld) ss 199(1)(e)(iii), 199(2).

[135] Explanatory Note, Trusts Bill 2024 (Qld) 22; Explanatory Note, Trusts Bill 2025 (Qld) 22.

[136] Queensland, Parliamentary Debates, Legislative Assembly, 21 May 2024, 1628 (Yvette D'Ath, Attorney-General).

[137] Trusts Act 2025 (Qld) s 202. Though trustees are not permitted to do so if the court has previously approved a cy-près scheme amending the purposes of the charitable trust.

[138] Queensland Law Reform Commission, *A Review of the Trusts Act 1973* (Final Report No 71, December 2013) [9.44]–[9.47].

However, the materials refer to other English developments, such as amendments relating to total return investment.[139] Nor do the Final Report, Interim Report or Discussion Paper generally discuss policy rationales for reform of the grounds for *cy-près* schemes, albeit there is discussion of the breadth of the proposed approval process for the Attorney-General with reference to submissions that make implicit reference to the importance of supporting donor intent.[140]

The picture from the two most recent reform processes in Australia is thus a modest constriction of grounds and alternative scheme stages (in Western Australia) and a modest broadening of the grounds stage (in Queensland). While Queensland is attempting to make it easier to obtain scheme approval from a non-court decision-maker, Western Australia appears to have made it slightly more difficult to do so. In neither jurisdiction was there any policy discussion about the approaches adopted.

This chapter is a plea to engage in that policy discussion. To start the process, several factors raised elsewhere ought to be considered.[141] First, while the statutory grounds for *cy-près* strictly do not permit a scheme merely on the basis that better use can be made of charitable assets, in practice that is often – though not always – the outcome for trustees who incur the expense and take the time away from other activities to apply to court. For instance, as discussed in Section IV above, a survey of scheme applications for reform of higher educational purpose charitable trusts found that the vast majority were successful, even though the judicial reasoning was strained or virtually non-existent in many.[142] Further, some empirical evidence on Western Australian charities indicates that many trustees do not bother to seek formal approval for a change of purpose, preferring to instead rely on agreement with the donor or their family. All of this suggests that practice is more liberal than the formal law, raising rule of law concerns.[143] Reform could address these concerns, alongside the potential for greater public benefit from the more effective and efficient use of charitable assets.

Second, while a more liberal *cy-près* process might permit the more effective and efficient use of charitable assets, there is the countervailing concern that this might reduce the quantum of assets being donated on charitable trust. That is because the charitable trust has traditionally been seen as a vehicle to achieve perpetual strong protection for donor intent, so if that protection is watered down, the range of choice for donors is reduced, and some donors may not like

[139] Queensland Law Reform Commission, *A Review of the Trusts Act 1973 (Qld)* (Discussion Paper WP70, December 2012) [6.54]–[6.61].

[140] Queensland Law Reform Commission, *A Review of the Trusts Act 1973 (Qld)* (Interim Report WP71, June 2013) [13.46]–[13.55], [13.61]; Queensland, Parliamentary Debates, Legislative Assembly, 18 February 2025, 65 (Deborah Frecklington, Attorney-General).

[141] Murray and Silver (n 101); Murray and Picton (n 56) 61–66.

[142] See: Murray and Silver (n 101) 369–82.

[143] See example: I Murray et al, 'Restricted Philanthropic Gifts: Paradigm Clash between Law and Practice or Simply a Muddle?' (2024) 47 *UNSW L J* 139–76.

any of the remaining options.[144] As discussed in Section II, for England and Wales, greater liberalisation of *cy-près* for charitable trusts brings the charitable trust option into much closer alignment with an incorporated charitable vehicle. Empirical evidence is needed to determine the size of this risk, although general experience points to the ingenuity of donors in finding alternative pathways to achieve their purposes.[145] It is worth emphasising that it is possible to liberalise the grounds stage of *cy-près*, without liberalising the alternative scheme stage to the same extent. That is, it would be possible to adopt the English position for charitable trusts that the trustees can seek a *cy-près* scheme whenever they consider it expedient, but to still require that the scheme proposed by the trustees must bear a sufficient degree of similarity to the original purposes. As discussed in Section IV above, that is a rough approximation of the position adopted in the higher education cases we surveyed. This might go some way to reassuring donors that their gift, for example, for the relief of poverty, will not be diverted to the advancement of education.[146]

Third, shifting decision-making about *cy-près* schemes from the judiciary to a component of the executive, raises the potential not only for a simpler and cheaper process, but also better decisions in that the decision-maker better understands the charity sector and government policy relating to the sector.[147] After all, as shown by the higher education purpose survey identified above, Australian courts are taking a permissive approach at the grounds stage, even if the courts are slightly more demanding that the precise contours of a scheme be in broad accordance with donor intent.[148]

However, it is debatable whether Attorneys-General hold this expertise as opposed to a dedicated charity regulator, such as the Australian Charities and Not-for-profits Commission.[149] In an Australian federal context, this raises constitutional power issues, in that without a state referral of powers the federal government is unlikely to have the power to legislate for the Australian Charities and Not-for-profits Commission to take on such a role.[150]

If the statutory *cy-près* doctrine and processes are to be truly reformed in Australia to reflect contemporary society and promote the most effective use of charitable assets, grappling with the difficult policy questions and the significant developments in England and Wales that have taken place over the past six decades, will be essential.

[144] Murray and Picton (n 56) 61–62.
[145] See example: D Brakman Reiser and SA Dean, *For-Profit Philanthropy* (Oxford, OUP, 2023).
[146] See example: *Re Prison Charities* (1873) LR 16 Eq 129.
[147] Murray and Picton (n 56) 62; Murray and Silver (n 101) 388–89.
[148] Murray and Silver (n 101) 382.
[149] ibid 388–89.
[150] See example: Murray and Picton (n 56) 65.

4

The Continued Place of Religious Charities within the Charity Sector: The Relationship between the Secular and the Religious Through an Economics Lens

JULIET CHEVALIER-WATTS

I. Introduction

This chapter considers the place of religious charities within the charity law narrative. This consideration takes place against the background of the increasing pressure now being placed upon religious charities to justify their place within the charity sector. The place of such charities is viewed through two lenses: secular and economic. Perhaps surprisingly, this chapter concludes that religious charities are facing pressures that may be unjust and, indeed, damaging, and that religious charities continue to play a vital role in contemporary society, particularly from an economic perspective. It should be noted that discussions on the economic value of religious charities find its foundations in novel and recent research and data. This research, while limited, is nevertheless revealing. There is much scope for further research to be undertaken on this matter and such research should be welcomed by both the state and the charity sector. This is because it is argued that the findings of the research are important because they will add positively to the current charity narrative by providing objective evidence as to the economic contribution of religious charities to society, which, up until now, has not been effectively captured.

New Zealand, along with many of its common law counterparts, including the United Kingdom[1] and Australia,[2] has long since confirmed the validity of religious

[1] See eg: the Statute of Charitable Uses 1601 (42 Eliz 1 c 4); the Charities Act 1960 (UK); Charities Act 2006 (UK) and 2001 (UK).

[2] See eg: the Australian Charities and Not-for-profits Commission Act 2012 (Cth) and Charities Act 2013 (Cth).

charities[3] under the legally recognised charitable purpose of 'the advancement of religion'. In New Zealand, the key statute tasked with the governance of charities is the Charities Act 2005, which the Charities Amendment Bill has subsequently amended and came into force in July 2023.[4] Despite statutory oversight on the validity of religious charities, they also face increasing contemporary secular criticism and pressure. Hammond has observed that the world is shifting to a more secular stance.[5] Indeed, it has been said that '[i]n modernity science is the primary lens through which humans understand their worlds',[6] as opposed to finding meaning through a religious lens. Certainly, it has been argued that the traditional role of religion is diminishing in the contemporary world and with that decline comes a downward trend in religious beliefs and behaviours.[7] However, it is acknowledged that this is a complex matter, and it is not always so clear-cut as to the real trends of secularisation.[8] It is beyond the scope of this chapter to consider in detail the issues of secularisation.

Nevertheless, what is clear is that there are widespread criticisms being levelled at religion, and unsurprisingly these emanate from a secular standpoint. Accordingly, such criticisms about religion frequently manifest as either a demand to demonstrate the validity of religion in today's society or, as is the focus of this chapter, for governments to heed demands to remove religions from the legal charity register. Incidentally, and of note, as may be common knowledge, entities with registered charitable status are afforded several pecuniary and non-pecuniary benefits that are not available to non-charitable entities.

These two principal criticisms are generally highly visible, especially in the media. For example, New Zealand's leading national newspaper, *The Herald*, criticised the Government's apparent reluctance to constrain a New Zealand commercial food giant's tax benefits because of its position as a religious charity. In criticising this lack of restraint by the Government, *The Herald* asserted that New Zealand's charity law was beholden to 'archaic British law'[9] because New Zealand finds its charitable history in its British roots. The criticism, which

[3] See eg: the Religious, Charitable and Educational Trusts Acts 1856 and 1865 (19 and 20 Victoria 1856 No 21); Charitable Funds Appropriation Act 1871 (NZ); the Charitable Trusts Act 1957 (NZ); and the Charities Act 2005 (NZ).

[4] Department of Internal Affairs, Charities Services, 'Charities Act change hub' (5 October 2023) www.charities.govt.nz/charities-act-hub/charities-act-change-hub/.

[5] PE Hammond 'Introduction' in PE Hammond (ed), *The Sacred in a Secular Age: Toward Revision in the Scientific Study of Religion* (Berkeley, University of California Press, 1985) 1.

[6] S Dein, 'Covid-19 and the Apocalypse: Religious and Secular Perspectives' (2021) 60(1) *J Relig Health* 5, 11.

[7] TW Smith and B Schapiro, 'Secularization around the World' (NORC at the University of Chicago April, Report to the Templeton Religion Trust, April 2021) 2.

[8] ibid 7.

[9] D Farrar, 'Advancement of Religion Should Not Be a Charitable Purpose' (*Kiwiblog*, 23 February 2015, citing *The New Zealand Herald*) https://kiwiblog.co.nz/2015/02/advancement_of_religion_should_not_be_a_charitable_purpose.html. See also J Chevalier-Watts, 'The Social Licence of Religions' [2023] *NZLJ* 284, 285; M Soper, 'Charities', *Laws of New Zealand* (online ed, LexisNexis, 2023), Preface.

focused on this history, enabled a religious food giant to be granted significant financial benefits in terms of tax waivers because of its registered charitable status under the charitable purpose of the advancement of religion. Thus, the point which *The Herald* is undoubtedly making, although perhaps it is not that well-articulated, is that religious charities should not be privileged to be granted such benefits when religious entities promote a belief that cannot be proven.[10] In other words, the legal recognition granted to religious charities demonstrates that those religions are 'worthy enough to receive the support of the state',[11] which appears to bestow upon religions an approval by society.[12] This is despite a religious belief that can never be proven to exist, and indeed may be controversial in nature, as illustrated by the New Zealand Pentecostal Christian organisation, Destiny Church. This organisation has captured the New Zealand headlines on a number of occasions due to some of the outspoken opinions of its Apostle Bishop, Brian Tamaki. In one such example, the Bishop laid the blame for the 2023 devastating Aotearoa/New Zealand Cyclone Gabrielle firmly at the feet of 'porn, abortion and gay rights'.[13] However, this is not the first time that the Bishop has blamed a number of terrible national natural events on, in his view, the actions of 'sinners', which again includes homosexuals. These natural events included the Christchurch earthquakes of 2010 and 2011, which killed hundreds of people, as well as the Kaikoura earthquake in 2016.[14] Such views were met with alarm and ridicule by politicians and the public alike. The Bishop's outbursts added to the burden being placed on religious charities per se as to their viability within the charity sector.

Consequently, it could be argued that religious charitable purposes might be viewed in contrast to other non-religious charitable purposes, whose purposes are not a matter of belief, and whose purposes can generally be seen as offering more tangible benefits to society, and which, in truth, tend not to elicit such public outrage. Indeed, the tangibility of these benefits has been of key concern for the courts in determining the charitability of an entity's purposes.[15] Nevertheless, religion does not, by its very spiritual nature, provide tangible benefits in the same

[10] Farrar (n 9).

[11] J Calderwood, 'Controversial Charities and Public Benefit' [2018] *NZLJ* 64, 67.

[12] ibid 67, referring to P Ridge, 'Religious Charitable Status and Public Benefit in Australia' (2011) 35 *Melb U L Rev* 1071, 1073.

[13] NZ Herald, 'Cyclone Gabrielle: Destiny Church Leader Brian Tamaki Blames Porn, Abortion, Gay Rights for Tragedy' *The New Zealand Herald* (Auckland, 1 March 2023) https://nzherald.co.nz/nz/cyclone-gabrielle-destiny-church-leader-brian-tamaki-blames-porn-abortion-gay-rights-for-tragedy/VCUXZFEBDRH5HNISRXLP5D5O54/; T Manhire, 'Brian Tamaki blames porn use in Gisborne and Hastings for Cyclone Gabrielle disaster' *The Spinoff* (New Zealand, 1 March 2023) https://thespinoff.co.nz/politics/01-03-2023/brian-tamaki-blames-porn-use-in-gisborne-and-hastings-for-cyclone-gabrielle-disaster; RJ Sewell, 'Queering the Courts The Untold Stories of Takatapui/LGBTQ+/Queer New Zealanders in the District Court' (Masters Thesis, Victoria University of Wellington 2023) 23.

[14] NZ Herald 'Comments by Brian Tamaki Blaming Gays, Murderers and Sinners for Earthquakes Called "Ridiculous"' *The New Zealand Herald* (Auckland, 16 November 2016) https:nzherald.co.nz/nz/comments-by-brian-tamaki-blaming-gays-murderers-and-sinners-for-earthquakes-called-ridiculous/5BBK77ZXCW7FE2VZSZAUYM22JE/.

[15] *Re Greenpeace of New Zealand Inc* [2015] 1 NZLR 169, [120], [125].

way as, for example, a food bank or New Zealand's national ambulance service, St John's. Yet religions, regardless of their ethereal quality, may still be charitable. However, secular pressures have emanated not only from the media but, perhaps less expectedly, from some of the judiciary. This was evidenced in the Australian High Court case of *Commissioner of Taxation of the Commonwealth of Australia v Word Investments Limited*, where Kirby J expressed his disapproval of religious charities, thusly stating:

> courts must recognise that this is deeply offensive to many non-believers, to people of different faiths and even to some people of different religious denominations who generally share the same faith.[16]

Mallon J, in the High Court of New Zealand the case of *Liberty Trust v Charities Commission*,[17] also recognised the difficulties associated with recognising religions as charitable. In this case, her Honour remarked that 'whether there is social utility in the advancement of religion is "a very much more doubtful proposition"'.[18] It is interesting to note that these judicial concerns arose even though it has been stated in an earlier case that '[a]s between different religions the law stands neutral, but it assumes that any religion is at least likely to be better than none'.[19]

This latter point intimates that there should be judicial neutrality on such matters and, as a consequence, that there is an expectation that the judiciary will refrain from criticising religions within the charity law narrative, regardless of any secular views. However, as evidenced, religious charities and the benefits bestowed upon them by virtue of their charitable status can give rise to such concerns. Consequently, the fact that the judiciary feels so strongly about religions being granted charitable status that they should express public concern about such charities serves to emphasises the secular pressures facing religious charities. Such judicial criticism is even more disquieting when one realises that case law has confirmed that there should not be any further questions as to the lawfulness of religious charities unless a religious doctrine or ideology is so 'adverse to the very foundations of all religion … that they are subversive of all morality'.[20] Unquestionably, neither of the charities in *Word Investment* or *Liberty Trust* had doctrines or ideologies that would have lent themselves to being viewed as being 'subversive of all morality'. Yet, despite this, these cases gave rise to judicial criticism, demonstrating the deep-seated secular sentiments regarding religion's continued place with the charity law framework.

[16] *Commissioner of Taxation of the Commonwealth of Australia v Word Investments Limited* (2008) 236 CLR 204, [155]. See also Chevalier-Watts (n 9) 285; J Chevalier-Watts, 'Faith, Hope and Charity – a Critical Review of Charity Law's Socio-Legal Reconciliation of the Advancement of Religion as a Recognised Head of Charity' (Thesis, University of Waikato 2019) 10.

[17] *Liberty Trust v Charities Commission* [2011] 3 NZLR 68 (HC).

[18] ibid [54], citing *Centrepoint Community Growth Trust v Commissioner of Inland Revenue* [1985] 1 NZLR 673 (HL) and referring to AW Lockhart, 'Centrepoint Community Growth Trust v Commissioner of Inland Revenue' (1984–87) 5 *AULR* 244.

[19] *Neville Estates v Madden* [1962] Ch 832, 853. See also Chevalier-Watts (n 9) 285.

[20] Chevalier-Watts (n 9); *Thornton v Howe* (1862) 31 Beav 14, 20. See also *Buckley v Barlow* [2016] EWHC 3017 (Ch) (1 December 2016), [37]. See also Chevalier-Watts (n 16).

Consequently, in light of the secular pressures facing religious charities to maintain their stronghold within the charity sector, this chapter considers some of those pressures and the issues that they may have caused and how religious charities can continue to be justified not only in their legal validity but also through a contemporary economics lens. Before addressing those matters, it is important to set out the charity law framework in which religious charities are embedded so as to contextualise the following discussions.

II. Charity Law Framework

A. Overview of Charity Law

As noted earlier, New Zealand charity law finds its origins in English law. The foundational charity law statute is that of the Charitable Uses Act 1601,[21] otherwise more commonly known as the Statute of Elizabeth 1601. The statute's Preamble provided a non-exhaustive list of purposes held to be legally recognised as charitable at the time. The statute itself has been repealed, but the Preamble's statement of charitable purposes lives on in many common law jurisdictions, including the United Kingdom and, of course, New Zealand.[22] Importantly, it was Lord Mcnaghten in the renowned case of *Commissioner for Special Purposes of the Income Tax v Pemsel*[23] who summarised the purposes in the Preamble, creating four categories of charitable purposes, which are: the relief of poverty, the advancement of education, the advancement of religion, and any other purposes beneficial to the community.[24] This categorisation is still recognised today, albeit with a number of recent legislative additions in some jurisdictions (such as the United Kingdom).[25] However, New Zealand retains the four original heads of charity under section 5(1) of its Charities Act 2005. The 'advancement of religion' is the focus of this chapter.

For a purpose to be recognised legally as being charitable, a purpose must fall within one or more of the *Pemsel* heads of charity or any of the expanded heads of charity as determined in some jurisdictions; be enforceable by a court, specifically the Attorney-General, and they must fall within the spirit and intendment of the Preamble of the Statute of Elizabeth 1601 (in other words, they must be analogous to purposes already recognised as charitable).[26] Thus, whether or not a purpose is charitable is generally determined by 'the common law with an element of statutory

[21] Soper (n 9) [12].
[22] See Charities Act 2005 (NZ), s 5(1).
[23] *Commissioner for Special Purposes of the Income Tax v Pemsel* [1891] AC 531.
[24] ibid 583.
[25] See for example, Charities Act 2011, s 3(1)(a)–(m).
[26] Soper (n 9).

overlay'.[27] As an aside, and to ensure a full understanding of the advancement of religion, a religion can only fall within the head of 'advancement of religion' if it advances that religion, which is interpreted broadly. Generally speaking, to advance a religion means 'the promotion of spiritual teaching in a wide sense, the maintenance of the doctrines on which it rests and the observances that serve to promote and manifest it'.[28]

An important aspect of the questions around the continued relevance of religion in the charity sector is the fact that the common law of charities has evolved with society and the changing values of society. Thus, as noted above, it is apparent that religious charities face significant public pressure to retain their foothold in the charity law framework that is likely to be closely aligned with these changing social norms. Evidence of the evolution of the common law and charities is reflected in the New Zealand Supreme Court case of *Re Greenpeace of New Zealand Inc*,[29] where the majority acknowledged that charity can be 'found in purposes which support the machinery or harmony of civil society',[30] which was illustrated in the earlier New Zealand Court of Appeal decision in *Latimer v Commissioner of Inland Revenue*.[31] Of note is that the Court in *Latimer* held that assisting Māori[32] to prepare, present, and negotiate claims in the Waitangi Tribunal[33] was charitable. This reflected a significant legal shift away from the English authorities of *Re Compton*[34] and *Oppenheim v Tobacco Securities Trust Co Ltd*,[35] concerning the charitable requirement of public benefit. Thus, *Latimer* reflects the common law's ability to evolve to 'support the machinery or harmony of civil society',[36] that being the public benefit of assisting Māori in bringing claims in the Waitangi Tribunal with the effect of bringing closure and justice to Māori in the resolution long-held grievances against the Crown. Before *Latimer*, assisting Māori was determined as not being charitable because of the blood tie relationship found between Māori,[37]

[27] AS Butler and T Clarke, *Equity and Trusts in New Zealand* 2nd edn (Wellington, ThomsonReuters, 2009) 273.

[28] L Breach, *Nevill's Law of Trusts, Wills and Administration* 13th edn (Online edition, LexisNexis, 2018) para 6.2 referring to *Keren Kayemeth Le Jisroel Ltd v Inland Revenue Commissioners* [1931] 2 KB 465, 477.

[29] *Re Greenpeace of New Zealand Inc* (n 15).

[30] ibid [70].

[31] *Latimer v Commissioner of Inland Revenue* [2002] 3 NZLR 195 (CA).

[32] 'Māori' refers to being an 'indigenous New Zealander, an indigenous person of Aotearoa/New Zealand'. *Te Aka Māori Dictionary* http://maoridictionary.co.nz/search?keywords=maori.

[33] The Waitangi Tribunal was 'set up by the Treaty of Waitangi Act 1975 (New Zealand), the Waitangi Tribunal is a permanent commission of inquiry that makes recommendations on claims brought by Māori relating to Crown actions which breach the promises made in the Treaty of Waitangi'. Waitangi Tribunal, Te Ropu Whakamana i te Tirito o Waitangi, Ministry of Justice New Zealand, Waitangi Tribunal www.waitangitribunal.govt.nz/.

[34] *Re Compton* [1945] Ch 123.

[35] *Oppenheim v Tobacco Securities Trust Co Ltd* [1951] AC 297 (HL).

[36] *Re Greenpeace of New Zealand Inc* (n 15) [70].

[37] The blood tie relationship between Māori is based on whakapapa a 'genealogy, genealogical table, lineage, descent – reciting whakapapa was, and is, an important skill and reflected the importance of genealogies in Māori society in terms of leadership, land and fishing rights, kinship and status. It is

thus falling within the exception to public benefit found in the cases of *Re Compton* and *Oppenheim*. This chapter turns now to the legal construct of 'public benefit' to provide additional context to the issue of religious charities remaining in the charity legal framework.

B. Public Benefit

In addition to the aforementioned charitable requirements, for a purpose to be deemed charitable, that purpose must meet the public benefit test. In other words, a purpose will only be charitable if it confers a public benefit:[38] a purpose that confers private benefits, or mainly private benefits, will not be charitable. The public benefit test is said to have two closely related limbs.[39] The first limb is whether the purpose confers a benefit on the public or a sufficient section of that public. The second limb is whether 'the class of persons eligible to benefit constitutes the public or a section of it'.[40] In New Zealand, public benefit is said to be presumed for the first three heads of charity, but for the fourth head of charity, the benefit must be expressly determined.[41] Consequently, it can be seen that the public benefit under the advancement of religion is presumed, hence why the ethereal qualities of religion may be charitable even though the tangible benefit may not be readily available. Of note is that the construct of public benefit 'does evolve and can be developed by the courts'.[42] However, it has been asserted that the public benefit test can be challenging to apply.[43] By way of illustration, it cannot be argued that world peace would not be of public benefit. However, 'whether peace should be pursued through disarmament or strength is contentious',[44] thus reflecting some of the challenges in recognising the public benefit of a purpose.

Concerning *Re Compton* and *Oppenheim*, these cases illustrate some of the limitations of the public benefit and where a purpose may fail for having private benefit. Accordingly, in *Re Compton* and *Oppenheim*, the Courts confirmed that

central to all Māori institutions.' Te Aka Māori Dictionary (n 31) http://maoridictionary.co.nz/search?&keywords=whakapapa.

[38] *Oppenheim* (n 34) 305. See also *The Independent Schools Council v The Charity Commission* [2011] UKUT 421 (TCC) 18–19.

[39] *New Zealand Society of Accountants v Commissioner of Inland Revenue* [1986] 1 NZLR 147, 152, referring to SG Maurice and DB Parker *Tudor on Charities* 7th edn (London, Sweet & Maxwell, 1984) 4. See also *Dingle v Turner* [1972] AC 601, 624.

[40] *New Zealand Society of Accountants* (n 38) referring to Maurice and Parker (n 38) 4; AS Butler, 'Charitable Trusts' in *Equity and Trusts in New Zealand* (Wellington, ThomsonReuters, 2009) 288–89.

[41] Soper (n 9) [13] referring to, inter alia, *Oppenheim* (n 34) applied in *Molloy v Commissioner of Inland Revenue* [1981] 1 NZLR 688 (CA); Breach (n 27) para 6.2.2 referring to *Keren Kayemeth Le Jisroel Ltd v Inland Revenue Commissioners* [1931] 2 KB 465, 477. The presumption of public benefit has been removed from all heads of charity in the United Kingdom. See Charities Act 2011, s 4(2).

[42] *Re Greenpeace of New Zealand Inc* (n 15) 175.

[43] Butler (n 39) 289 referring to, inter alia, *Dingle* (n 38) and *Educational Fees Protection Society Inc v CIR* [1992] 2 NZLR 115, 126–27.

[44] *Re Greenpeace of New Zealand Inc* (n 15) 175.

the public benefit test would fail if there were, inter alia, a blood tie or personal relationship between the beneficiaries of the purpose and the settlor. However, in the New Zealand context of Māori, there is clearly a blood tie relationship between Māori, and this issue came to the fore in *Latimer*. In response to the issue of the blood tie relationship found within Māori, the Court of Appeal in *Latimer* confirmed that applying the English law of *Re Compton* and *Oppenheim* would be 'insufficiently responsive to values emanating from outside the mainstream of the English common law'.[45] This would be particularly important regarding the 'Māori view of the importance of whakapapa and whanau to identity, social organisation and spirituality'.[46] Consequently, and as reflected later in the New Zealand Supreme Court case of *Greenpeace*, charity law echoes social cues and the Court of Appeal in *Latimer* confirmed that in the particular circumstances, 'Māori beneficiaries of this trust, both together and in their separate iwi or hapu groupings'[47] satisfied the public benefit test.[48] Whilst it is evident that charity law can reflect changes in society, just as advocating for the abolition of slavery, promoting human rights and protecting the environment have been found to be charitable.[49] As a result, it may be that religious charities, in time, may no longer be found to be charitable as they would no longer be found to reflect the social norms of the time. Indeed, this latter point regarding religious charities is of particular relevance to this chapter. This is because the public perception of the public benefit concerning religious charities sits at the heart of secular criticisms and the question of whether religions should remain within the charity framework. Thus, public benefit runs as a theme throughout this chapter. In addition, it is acknowledged that charity law 'has developed empirically and by analogy upon analogy'.[50] This is an essential point of note because the secular influence of society appears to be shaping some policy and legal changes regarding religious charities, as will be demonstrated.

However, as this chapter demonstrates, it *is* possible to find the public benefit in religious charities, particularly in the economic benefit to society. This is because the public benefit test is:

> intangible and nebulous; its effects can only be represented as variable and unpredictable. Imprecision has resulted in illogical and capricious decisions, sometimes impossible to reconcile.[51]

[45] *Latimer* (n 30) [38].
[46] ibid [38].
[47] ibid.
[48] ibid.
[49] *Re Greenpeace of New Zealand Inc* (n 15) [70] referring to *Jackson v Philips* (1867) 96 Mass 539 14 Allen 539 (Mass SC); Charities Act 2006 (UK), s 2(2)(h) (now Charities Act 2011 (UK), s 3(1)(h)). See also *Greenpeace of New Zealand v Charities Board* [2020] NZHC 1999, [37], [84]–[101].
[50] Soper (n 9) [12] referring to, inter alia, *New Zealand Society of Accountants* (n 38) applying *Inland Revenue Commissioners v Baddeley* [1955] AC 572 and *Scottish Burial Reform and Cremation Society Ltd v Glasgow Corporation* [1968] AC 138.
[51] GHL Fridman, 'Charities and Public Benefit' (1953) 31 *Can Bar Rev* 537, 539 as cited in J Warburton, 'Charities and Public Benefit – From Confusion to Light?' (2008) 10(3) *CLPR* 1, 2.

Its very intangible and nebulous nature means that the economic contribution of religious charities to society can fall within its construct. This is not least because benefits arising from charitable purposes may be direct or indirect.[52] As a result, it is submitted that economic outputs due to religious purposes may offer an indirect public benefit. These indirect public benefits arise from, for example, government funds that would have been provided for state housing or welfare payments that can be diverted to other communities because religious charities have already provided those resources through their activities or fundraising. Consequently, it is argued that the 'production of indirect [economic] benefits'[53] is charitable. Indeed, the value in the economic analysis of legal doctrine has long been recognised as 'fruitful'.[54] This is because many legal doctrines, such as public benefit, 'are best understood and explained as efforts to promote the efficient allocation of resources'.[55] Thus, when the public benefit is demonstrated, and an entity obtains charitable status, it can allocate its resources appropriately to communities in need. Furthermore, it is not the first time that economic arguments have been presented in relation to public benefit. Thus, by way of example, in the New Zealand High Court case of *Family First*,[56] Simon France J observed that where charitable status could be 'achieved at a cost to other family models, it could affirmatively be said not to be in the public interest'.[57] Whilst his Honour is likely referring to any non-fiscal detriment to society, using the word 'cost' can also mean the fiscal detriment to society. If, therefore, there is a fiscal detriment to society, as intimated by Simon France J, then this would negate the public benefit. Consequently, if financial disbenefit to society can negate the public benefit, in the opposite, it is argued respectfully that economic outputs that benefit society should then fulfil the public benefit test.[58] In addition, it has been stated that similarities exist due to the appropriate exercise of charitable policies whereby poverty in communities is decreased, which has resulted in increased community wellbeing.[59] The appropriate exercise of such policies would have involved fiscal considerations. Hence, economics can be at the heart of charity and, thus, public benefit.

[52] Fridman (n 50) referring to *Williams' Trustees v IRC* [1947] AC 447, 458; *Oppenheim* (n 34) and *Re Oldfield (No 2)* [1949] 2 DLR 175, 182.

[53] Fridman (n 50) 540. See also: J Chevalier-Watts and F Scrimgeour, 'The Economic Value of Religious Charities in Aotearoa-New Zealand' (as yet unpublished article although under peer review) 7.

[54] RA Posner, *Economic Analysis of Law* 9th edn (New York, Wolters Kluwer, 2014) 30.

[55] ibid 31.

[56] See: *Attorney-General v Family First New Zealand* [2022] NZSC 80. See also Chevalier-Watts and Scrimgeour (n 52) referring to *Family First*, [65]. Family First appealed this decision to New Zealand's Supreme Court, where it was held that Family First was not charitable.

[57] *Family First* (n 55) [65].

[58] Chevalier-Watts and Scrimgeour (n 52) 9 referring to *Family First* [2018] NZHC 2273, [65].

[59] K O'Halloran, *The Profits of Charity* (Oxford, OUP, 2012) 441. See also Chevalier-Watts and Scrimgeour (n 52).

C. International Policies: The Impact of Public Opinion

It may be argued that the public appeal of religious charities is waning as a result of secular influences, but this does not automatically mean that religious charities will be struck off a charity register. Furthermore, it is arguable that public or judicial opinion will not negatively impact policy decisions concerning religions more generally. This is not least because religious charities have already demonstrated that they meet charity law requirements, hence being confirmed as charitable and thus signifying their legal validity. However, evidence has come to light of international policies being adversely impacted by public opposition to religion, reflecting the increasing secular stance of many contemporary societies. Such evidence is to be found in Norway and Belgium and in national policies in New Zealand. We begin by considering the issues in Norway.

i. Norway and Religious Entities

Before considering the facts relating to the Norwegian matters, it should be made clear that Norwegian religious issues do not concern religious charities per se or the advancement of religion. However, it is submitted that analogies might be drawn between Norwegian religious legal issues and those of religious charities, such that Norway is merely reflecting the growing unease about religion generally. Further, it serves as an illustration of the secular influences on state religious policies.

The Lutheran Church is the official religion in Norway and nearly three-quarters of the Norwegian population is registered as a member of that faith. Although of note, in a survey conducted in 2016, more than half the population of Norway stated that they did not believe in God.[60] Such a finding demonstrates the increasing secularisation of such countries, which likely has been the driving force behind the pressures facing some religions in Norway, as we shall consider. Nevertheless, Norway has a system of religious registration under the Act on Religious and Belief Communities (Religious Communities Act), which was amended in 2020, and this register has over 700 different religions on it. Under this Act, religions may be awarded grants and subsidies, which are provided for, among other things, under the Norwegian Constitution and 'respect the principle of equality between religious communities, whatever their size, since the Church of Norway (Lutheran) is supported by taxpayers' money'.[61]

[60] S Osborne, 'Norway's Biggest Church Loses More Than 25,000 Members After New Online System Makes it Easier to Leave' *The Independent* (London, 2 September 2016) https://independent.co.uk/news/world/europe/norway-state-church-online-registration-system-deregister-members-leave-quit-a7221331.html.

[61] W Fautre, 'Norway: A Trial About the State's Intrusion into Religious Beliefs' *Diplomat Magazine* (8 January 2024) https://diplomatmagazine.eu/2024/01/08/norway-a-trial-about-the-states-intrusion-into-religious-beliefs/.

Until 2022, no religion had been deregistered due to its practices or beliefs.[62] However, in 2022, Jehovah's Witnesses became the first religion to be deregistered and certainly the first to have its registration revoked as a result of social pressure. This resulted in Jehovah's Witnesses losing approximately US$1.5 million in a year, which was generally utilised for international relief work and furtherance of national religious practices. The Governor of Oslo and Viken made this decision as she had received complaints about the religion's practice of 'disfellowshipping',[63] which can lead to instances of 'shunning'. Disfellowshipping is a controversial practice where a person has their religious membership revoked, which may lead to that person being shunned by their former religious brethren.[64] This practice led the Governor to assert that it caused 'negative social control'[65] and violated children's rights,[66] hence the revocation of their registered status. Nevertheless, it has been argued that this practice of disfellowshipping only happens when serious violations of the religion's moral code have occurred, and the types of acts that may trigger disfellowshipping include manslaughter, adultery or illegal drug use. Further, spokespeople for the faith strongly argued that the religion does not make its members shun former members when they have been disfellowshipped or, indeed, if they have left voluntarily.[67] That is because there is no explicit monitoring or policing over the exercise of a person's faith.[68] However, if a person has been disfellowshipped and refuses congregational help to restore the person's relationship with God, then members of that faith may feel bound to follow the Bible's instructions in its entirety by choosing to shun the sinner who has been disfellowshipped, as instructed under 1 Corinthians 5:11.[69]

Following the Governor's decision, the Ministry for Children and Families upheld the decision in September 2022, and in response, the Jehovah's Witnesses filed two lawsuits in December 2022. One suit pertains to the loss of registration and the other to the loss of grants due to losing their registration. Initially, the Oslo District Court granted an interim injunction to suspend the loss of registration. However, this injunction was later removed by the District Court in 2023,[70] a decision that was also appealed. In June 2023, the Borgarting Court of Appeal dismissed that appeal.[71] The ramifications of Norway's decision have led to serious

[62] M Introvigne, 'Norway: Oslo District Court Suspends De-Registration of Jehovah's Witnesses' *Bitter Winter* (1 April 2023) https://bitterwinter.org/norway-court-suspends-de-registration-of-jehovahs-witnesses/.

[63] K Post, 'Jehovah's Witnesses Go to Trial Against Norway after State Registration is Revoked' *Religion News* (16 January 2024) https://religionnews.com/2024/01/16/jehovahs-witnesses-go-to-trial-against-norway-after-state-registration-is-revoked/.

[64] WA Grendele, M Flax and S Bapir-Tardy, 'Shunning from the Jehovah's Witness Community: Is It Legal?' (2023) 38 *JL & Relig* 290–313.

[65] Post (n 62).

[66] ibid.

[67] ibid.

[68] ibid.

[69] ibid.

[70] ibid.

[71] Fautre (n 60).

consequences for the Jehovah's Witnesses in Norway, not just in terms of financial consequences, but to other serious consequences, including members of the faith being subject to assaults, vandalism, and harassment,[72] which reflects the social feeling towards this religion as a result of losing their registration. In other words, without the state's legal validity as a registered religion, the religion appears no longer to be validated by the state and, as a result, has become a target of some public derision and hatred. At the time of writing, the Jehovah's Witnesses of Norway were suing the state of Norway; the trial started in January 2024. The trial will decide 'whether some practices of the Jehovah's Witnesses violate Norway's Religious Communities Act or whether withdrawing the Jehovah's Witnesses' registration violates their right to freedom of religion and freedom of association, as guaranteed in the European Convention on Human Rights'.[73] The outcome of the trial has not yet been determined.

ii. Belgium

Belgium also saw the Jehovah's Witnesses having to defend their practices, particularly disfellowshipping, in the Belgium Court of Cassation, the highest court in Belgium. This set of circumstances again reflects the continued secular social pressures facing religions. In brief, a former Jehovah's Witness brought a claim in the public prosecutor's office in 2015, asserting that the religion had entirely excluded and isolated that person. As a result, Jehovah's Witnesses were charged with violating Article 22 of the Anti-Discrimination Act and the trial Judge found against the religion. The Ghent Court of Appeal subsequently reversed this decision in June 2022 with the Court finding that the Jehovah's Witnesses were not discriminatory and nor that they incited harm. Further, the Court affirmed that the practice of disfellowshipping and shunning was legal. This decision was appealed. Then in December 2023, the Belgian Court of Cassation confirmed definitively that disfellowshipping is lawful and connected to freedom of association, as well as freedom of religion.[74]

Belgium has now resolved this issue in favour of Jehovah's Witnesses. However, the complaints and appeals speak to the continued pressure encountered by many religions, as a consequence of the increasing criticisms of religions' place and role within contemporary society. Such pressures may have been resolved, for the time being, at least in Belgium, but what of the similar context found within New Zealand?

[72] Post (n 62).

[73] K Post, 'Jehovah's Witnesses Sue Norway After Registration Revoked' *Baptist Standard* (18 January 2024) www.baptiststandard.com/news/world/jehovahs-witnesses-sue-norway-after-registration-revoked/.

[74] 'BELGIUM: The Cassation Court Rules in Favour of Jehovah's Witnesses' *Human Rights without Frontiers* (30 December 2023) https://hrwf.eu/belgium-the-court-of-cassation-upholds-the-right-of-jehovahs-witnesses-to-exclude-members/.

iii. New Zealand

New Zealand is not exempt from such pressures either. Interestingly, New Zealand has already felt the shockwaves emanating from Norway. Although New Zealand and Norway are about as different as can be[75] the Norway cases against Jehovah's Witnesses have created nevertheless negative media attention in New Zealand.[76] Thus, despite the distance and the differences between the two jurisdictions, the national attention that Norway has received speaks clearly as to the global secular pressures that continue to mount against religions generally. Further, New Zealand specifically changed this issue from a matter of freedom of religion to an explicit charity law issue. The news from Norway ignited calls from the media for the charity sector to investigate alleged harms caused by religions to the public and followers of religion, and indeed, there were calls for Jehovah's Witnesses themselves to face comparable state punishments to which they were subject in Norway.[77]

There is no evidence that such calls will be answered by the Department of Internal Affairs – Charities Services in New Zealand at this time. As a result, one might be of the view that New Zealand would be exempt from such occurrences as witnessed in Norway and Belgium. However, it would be true to say that, on the contrary, New Zealand has witnessed such state policies responding to social pressures and this was evidenced in the charity sector by the Charities Commission Registration Decision: Exodus Ministries Trust Board 18 August 2010 (now the Department of Internal Affairs – Charities Commission).[78] Whilst this decision did not concern Jehovah's Witnesses, it is arguable that the decision reflected the public norms about religion generally, particularly concerning the issue of public benefit of religions from a charity law perspective. The point in issue for the Charities Commission (as it was) (the Commission) was that Exodus Ministries, a Christian religion, promoted what is generally known as 'conversion therapy' for those individuals who identified as homosexual. It is also noted that at the time of the Decision, conversion therapy was still legal in New Zealand. However, under the Conversion Practices Prohibition Legislation Act 2022 (NZ), its practice is now generally illegal.

Exodus Ministries claimed that, according to Christian principles, homosexuality was a sin and thus was not accepted within that faith. Hence it promoted conversion therapy for those individuals who identified as homosexual. In response to this practice, the Commission declared that conversion therapy did

[75] Chevalier-Watts (n 9) 286–87.

[76] A Bradley, 'Something Evil' *RNZ* (10 August 2023) www.rnz.co.nz/programmes/in-depth-special-projects/story/2018901718/something-evil; M Luc, 'Request to Consider Charity Status of Abusive organisations' *FYI.org.nz* (19 April 2022) https://fyi.org.nz/request/19160-requst-to-consider-charity-status-of-abusive-organisations.

[77] Chevalier-Watts (n 9) 286 referring to A Bradley, 'Something Evil' *RNZ* (10 August 2023) https://rnz.co.nz/programmes/in-depth-special-projects/story/2018901718/something-evil.

[78] Registration Decision: Exodus Ministries Trust Board Decision No: 2010–15–18 August 2010.

not advance religion. Furthermore, it failed the public benefit test because it was contrary to public policy,[79] this was although it was perfectly legal at the time. In other words:

> promoting conversion therapy, whilst still legal … was not popular publicly, and thus the promotion of conversion therapy defeated the public benefit … Indeed, the Commission affirmed that the public benefit must be viewed in the context of contemporary society.[80]

Here, then, is clear evidence of the strength of public pressure in successfully challenging legal norms in favour of social norms. Such challenges have likely arisen as a result of New Zealand's move from a historic majority Christian country to an apparent secular country.[81] With such religious change comes change to conventional ways of thinking, and with that, the increasing number of criticisms being levelled at conventional religious practices as society questions traditionally held religious practices, as evidenced in Exodus Ministries. The result for Exodus Ministries was that it failed to obtain charitable status.

Of course, it would be irresponsible to state that conversion therapy should still be welcomed in religious practices. This is because there is much evidence as to the harm such therapy causes to those subject to the practice[82] and the author's view is that the Commission's decision was correct in the circumstances. However, it cannot be ignored that charities are not always popular and sometimes they are controversial, but this is no reason to find an entity fails the public benefit standard. Indeed, this has been expressed by the New Zealand Supreme Court in no uncertain terms, as set out by Elias CJ for the majority of in *Re Greenpeace of New Zealand Inc.*[83] That being that if the popularity of causes or lack of controversiality of a cause were considered part of the decision-making process in determining the charitability of an entity then:

> Such thinking would effectively exclude much promotion of change while favouring charitable status on the majoritarian assessment and the status quo. Just as unpopularity of causes otherwise charitable should not affect their charitable status, we do not think that lack of controversy could be determinative.[84]

[79] Charities Services, Registration Decision: Exodus Ministries Trust Board 18 August 2010, [49].

[80] Chevalier-Watts (n 9) 286.

[81] J Chevalier-Watts, *The Law of Religion in New Zealand* (Wellington, ThomsonReuters, 2021) 44–45; DH Griffiths, 'Defining the Secular in the New Zealand Bill of Rights Era: Some Cases and Controversies' [2011] *OtaLawRw* 4, 4, referring to New Zealand Human Rights Commission 'Freedom of Religion and Belief: draft for discussion' (March 2010).

[82] See generally: A Przworski, E Peterson and Al Piedra, 'A Systematic Review of the Efficacy, Harmful Effects, and Ethical Issues Related to Sexual Orientation Change Efforts' [2020] *Clinical Psychology Science and Practice* 1–23; S Boulos and C Gonzalez Canton, 'No Such Thing as Acceptable Sexual Orientation Change Efforts: An International Human Rights Analysis' (2002) 32 *Women & Criminal Justice* 185–204.

[83] *Re Greenpeace of New Zealand Inc* (n 15) [75].

[84] ibid.

This is because this would have the effect of limiting the ability of charities to respond to the needs of society generally. As noted earlier, ending slavery and promoting human rights, inter alia, have been found to be charitable. Indeed, for the former, this carried with it much controversy and, at the time, was publicly unpopular. The promotion of human rights has also carried some controversiality. Nevertheless, such purposes have been found charitable, thus reflecting the ability of the charity to support society as it evolves. Therefore, whilst the author believes that the Commission made the correct decision overall pertaining to Exodus Ministries, we still need some clarification regarding the decision-making process. Nevertheless, what was evident from the Exodus Ministries decision was that regardless of whether the religious practice in question was legal at the time, social norms changed and rendered the practice of conversion therapy as lacking in public benefit.

The Belgium Jehovah's Witnesses' final appeal demonstrated that religious freedoms should be protected, even if controversial, which is perhaps analogous to Elias CJ's view that charities should be able to operate even if controversial. That is because society has legally recognised the place of religion, whether from a charitable perspective or from a human rights perspective. Indeed, in New Zealand, freedom of religion has been entrenched through section 21(1)(c) and sections 13 and 15 of the Human Rights Act 1993 and the Bill of Rights Act 1990, respectively.[85]

Perhaps, therefore, and respectfully, the Commission in Exodus Ministries could have given further weight to the constitutional importance of religion in New Zealand. However, it is likely, and perhaps correctly so, that the Commission still would have found against Exodus Ministries. Regardless, however, it is acknowledged that this decision is difficult and as society changes it is inevitable that the law will embrace such changes. Indeed, there is much evidence that the law is influenced by society and, mainly because of the relationship between law, society and religion:

> The relationship between religion and society cannot be understood without reference to law, and the relationship between religion and law cannot be understood without reference to sociology. A sociology of law and religion is concerned with how social forces shape the legal regulation of religion and how law is used to affect religion and its social expression. It seeks to shed further light upon the complex relationship between religion, law and society.[86]

Consequently, the decisions emanating from Belgium, Norway, and indeed New Zealand, likely reflect those complex relationships, where secularism, religion, and societal norms vie for space and are subject to a variety of pressures in the ever changing societal constructs. Western societies, such as New Zealand,

[85] Chevalier-Watts (n 9) 287.

[86] Chevalier-Watts (n 16) 55 citing R Sandberg and R Catto, 'Law and Sociology: Toward a Greater Understanding of Religion' in N Doe and R Sandberg (eds), *Law and Religion: New Horizons* (Leuven, Peeters, 2010) 287.

are embracing new cultures and leaving behind some of the traditional views entrenched in historical religious norms. As a result, these new ways of life, which undoubtedly embrace a more secular stance for many individuals, mean that tensions inevitably arise between the traditional religious norms that may be perceived as causing harm and the contemporary less restrictive methods of non-religious life. Nevertheless, one must remain vigilant to ensure that popular opinion does not replace the rule of law. Certainly, the rule of law should not be dismissed merely because of secular pressures that come to bear on religious purposes and activities. Indeed, 'it would be wise to urge caution to ensure that social pressure does not become mob rule and overtake the correct legal decision-making processes'.[87]

III. The Economics of Religious Charities

Such cautionary counsel is particularly relevant when contemporary research into the economic value of religion demonstrates the tangible benefit to society of religions. Of note and relevant to society, their outworkings benefit religious and secular communities alike. Examples of religious outworkings include child and elderly care, foodbanks, and natural disaster outreach, to name but a few.[88] Whilst these activities might not appear religious in nature per se, more often than not, they are generally driven by and indeed are a requirement of a particular faith. It is relevant that these outworkings have a dollar figure that can be assigned to them, but this value has invariably been hidden from public view. This is not for any nefarious reason; rather, it is because, whilst religion is acknowledged as a vital part of many cultures, there has been little attention given to the economics of religion.[89] Consequently, there has been limited research on this aspect of religious charities and, therefore, there needs to be more literature on what this can mean for the health of society. As a result, it is submitted that this economic value provides an alternative argument to those who seek to undermine the place of religions within society, particularly within the charity narrative. This alternative argument is now gaining a foothold as some research is being undertaken nationally and internationally, and the findings as to the economic value of religion generally, as well as religious charities, are surprising, albeit welcome, at least from a religious charity perspective.

[87] Chevalier-Watts (n 9) 287.

[88] These examples have been obtained from the University of Waikato University Ethics Committee approved questionnaire conducted by Dr J Chevalier-Watts (Principal Investigator) as part of the research project, 'The Economics of Religious Charities'. Dr Chevalier-Watts acknowledges the funding granted by The Wilberforce Foundation to assist with this project). See generally: Chevalier-Watts and Scrimgeour (n 52).

[89] RJ Barro and RM McCleary, 'Religion and Economic Growth' (May 2003) National Bureau of Economic Research, United States of America Working Paper 9682, 2.

Before considering the initial findings as to the economic value of religious charities in New Zealand, it is initially worthwhile to set out some international conclusions to contextualise the value of religious charities globally. Some of the first research into the economic value of religious charities emanated from the United States of America in 2016. That research demonstrated, as a conservative estimate, that religion, including not-for-profit and charitable entities, was annually worth US$1.2 trillion to the economy in that year, which at the time was more significant than a number of tech giant companies, including Apple, Amazon, and Google.[90] More recent research emanating from Australia also provides interesting data regarding the economic footprint of religion, although this research focused on religion more generally as opposed to religious charities. However, what can be said is that many religions are registered as charities, so the data will still catch the fiscal benefits of their outworkings in this research. In brief, what was determined was that religion contributed A$20 billion generally to 'enhancing the economic and social life of all Australians and serving the common good'.[91]

Canadian research in 2020 also provides fascinating data concerning the economic footprint of religion. It was the first of its kind in Canada, utilising similar metrics to the abovementioned research conducted in the United States.[92] This research provided three estimates of the value of religion to Canadian society. The first estimate was the most conservative, only considering the revenue of religious organisations, with the estimate being that those organisations provide Can$30 billion to the economy. The second estimate was the mid-range estimate, whereby the research considered goods and services provided by religious bodies and charities and stated that this was worth more than Can$67 billion to society. That would make religion, including religious charities, Canada's ninth largest enterprise. The final and third estimate acknowledged that religious persons are influenced and directed by their faith to impact how they carry out their business, which meant that religion was worth nearly Can$690 billion to society annually.[93] It is interesting to note that when religious charities are included in the data, the

[90] Chevalier-Watts (n 16) 168 referring to B Grim and M Grim, 'The Socio-Economic Contribution of Religion to American Society: An Empirical Analysis' (2016) 12(3) *Interdisciplinary Journal of Research on Religion* 2; Religious Freedom and Business Foundation, '$1.2 Trillion Religious Economy in U.S.' https://religiousfreedomandbusiness.org/1-2-trillion-religious-economy-in-us; BJ Grim, 'Religion may be bigger business than we thought. Here's why.' (5 January 2017) *World Economic Forum* https://weforum.org/agenda/2017/01/religion-bigger-business-than-we-thought/; J Carter, 'How Much Economic Value Does Religion Provide America?' (*Action Institute Blog*, 15 September 2016) https://blog.acton.org/archives/89009-how-much-economic-value-does-religion-provide-america.html. U Osili, 'What influences American giving?' (*The Conversation*, 25 July 2018) https://theconversation.com/what-influences-american-giving-78800. Numbers are expressed in the billions of inflation-adjusted USD.

[91] 'Measuring the Economic Impact of Religious Persons Associated with Volunteering and Donation Behaviour' (August 2021) Research Report AGAPE Economics for SEIROS Working Paper, 42.

[92] B Grim and M Grim, 'The Hidden Economy – How Faith Helps Fuel Canada's GDP' (*CARDUS*, 21 September 2020) 'www.cardus.ca/research/spirited-citizenship/reports/the-hidden-economy-how-faith-helps-fuel-canadas-gdp/.

[93] ibid.

economic footprint increases significantly, reflecting the intrinsic fiscal value of such charities to society.

Turning now to the economics of New Zealand religious charities, it is worth mentioning that until very recently, there has yet to be any such research conducted in New Zealand similar to that undertaken in the United States, Canada, and Australia. As such, this chapter can only refer to the initial findings, but those of its international counterparts have also revealed the very real and valuable financial impact of religious charities on society. Of note is that the New Zealand research focuses specifically on the economic value of religious charities and not on the economic value of religions per se. Thus, the data provides a more accurate picture of the worth of religious charities. Of further note and evidence of the significant place of 28,000 registered charities in New Zealand, 10 per cent are religious charities. Their collective income ranks third after the income received by Education and Health charities.[94] These are not insubstantial numbers.

Further, the Department of Internal Affairs – Charities Services data shows that volunteer hours in 2018 were comparable to 66 per cent of paid hours.[95] In other words, 'for every 3 hours of paid staff time, 2 hours of volunteer time were also contributed'.[96] Additionally, the volunteering for religious charities was estimated to be valued at NZ$15.2 million. Overall, therefore, 'the total value contributed by religious charities in 2018 was NZ$6.1B or the equivalent of about 3% of annual Government expenditure'.[97] Taking into consideration the small population size of New Zealand, which was estimated to be 5,269,200 as at 30 September 2023,[98] this is a substantial figure and thus represents a significant economic contribution to society.[99] This is especially true when the current New Zealand population is compared with that of the United States for the year when the population was 335,445,435.[100] In Canada, its population was estimated at 40,528,396 in 2023,[101] and in Australia, its population was 26,638,544 people also in 2023.[102] It is acknowledged that the data for New Zealand refers to 2018 and not 2023, so the population figures will not be strictly comparable. However, the information generally reflects the significant difference in size between

[94] Ngā Ratonga Kaupapa Atawhai, Charities Services, 'Ngā Ratonga Kaupapa Atawhai Arotake, Ā-Tau Charities Services Annual Review 2021/2022'.

[95] Chevalier-Watts and Scrimgeour (n 52) 12.

[96] ibid.

[97] ibid.

[98] Stats NZ, 'National population estimates: At 30 September 2023' (16 November 2023) https://stats.govt.nz/information-releases/national-population-estimates-at-30-september-2023/#:~:text=At%2030%20September%202023%3A,resident%20population%20was%20provisionally%205%2C269%2C200.

[99] Chevalier-Watts and Scrimgeour (n 52) 9.

[100] US and World Population Clock, United States Census Bureau www.census.gov/popclock/.

[101] Statistics Canada, 'Canada's population estimates, third quarter 2023' (19 December 2023) www.150.statcan.gc.ca/n1/daily-quotidien/231219/dq231219c-eng.htm.

[102] Australian Bureau of Statistics, 'National, State and Territory Population' (24 March 2024) www.abs.gov.au/statistics/people/population#:~:text=Australia's%20population%20was%2026%2C638%2C544%20people,net%20overseas%20migration%20was%20518%2C100.

New Zealand and her jurisdictional counterparts mentioned here, thus demonstrating the significance of religious charities generally within the New Zealand context from an economic perspective.

Therefore, this means that religious charities make a significant financial contribution to society generally because of, for example, the volunteers, the outreach, and the tithing. If religions were to be removed from the charity sector, they would no longer receive the financial and non-financial benefits that arise from being a registered charity. As a result, it is doubtful that they would be able to operate to the extent they do, meaning their outreach would be limited, as would so many other parts of their invisible but economically impactful work. Consequently, it is asserted that the secular criticisms that are levelled at religious charities should be considered in the context of the real economic value of religious charities. Of course, the economic research being conducted in New Zealand is in its early stages and, as such, will have limited bearing on the negative views associated with religious charities. Nevertheless, regardless of its novelty, the findings still provide illuminating and objective data that may provide some support for the continued place of religions within the legal charity framework.

IV. Concluding Comments

This chapter began by noting that New Zealand, alongside some of its common law counterparts, has long confirmed the legal legitimacy of religion from a charity law standpoint. Nevertheless, religious charities face increasing criticisms from many secular perspectives, which include the judiciary, the media, and public figures.[103] It is against this backdrop of criticism that religious charities likely have to justify their continued place within the charity sector. However, it can be challenging to see where the immediate value to the public of religious charities and public pressure has led to some states making policy decisions that undermine the very legitimacy of religion, at least from a public perspective. This has led, on occasion, to harmful outcomes for those who follow those religions and, on other occasions, to lose charitable status.

Nevertheless, this chapter has revealed that religious charities have value beyond their spiritual outputs and this value has rarely been considered either from a legal or state perspective until recently. This research has found an objective value in the economic worth of religious charities to society. Whilst the research undertaken in the United States, Canada, and Australia focused on religion more

[103] See eg, Known formally as Twitter, Ricky Gervais (@rickygervais) and S Osborne, 'Stephen Fry were asked what he would say to God if they met. His answer is being investigated by police.' *The Independent* (London, 7 May 2017) https://independent.co.uk/news/world/europe/stephen-fry-blasphemy-god-ireland-confronted-by-met-a7722191.html.

generally and not specifically on religious charities, it should be noted that religious charities were still a core component of that research.

That is because religions very often have parts of their organisation registered as a charity, so it is likely that even in those three countries, the data incorporated a significant amount of data derived from religious charities. However, the research emanating from New Zealand focused more specifically on religious charities alone. This research is presented as an alternative argument for those wishing to see religious charities excluded from the charity law narrative. The research demonstrates just how economically valuable religious charities are to society. Because of their charitable status, religious charities can provide substantial community and welfare support, thus providing a significant economic benefit to the state. Consequently, if religious charities no longer existed, it would be unlikely that any government could afford to make up for the financial losses that communities would suffer due to religious charities losing their charitable status. This is especially true in post-COVID times when many states face economic uncertainty and must make serious financial decisions that can negatively impact many populations.

Therefore, it may be prudent for states to consider adopting a restrained approach when considering the place of religion within charity, and the reason is twofold. First, as has been demonstrated overseas, policy decisions about the legal legitimacy of religions can harm the religion and its followers. Second, whilst the research into the actual economic benefit of religious charities to states is currently in its infancy, the early results demonstrate that religious charities can and do significantly contribute to state economies. Without those charities, communities would likely suffer adverse consequences. Of course, it may be that the rulings made nationally and internationally are simply an indication that society is evolving and, thus, should not be viewed with any great consternation.

On the other hand, it may be wise to view those rulings with some unease because public pressure and public opinion are not equivalent to the appropriate application of law and policy, and states must be cognisant of such matters. As a result, the author respectfully asserts that states would be wise to adopt a more restrained stance when considering the legal legitimacy of religious charities to ensure that these public pressures do not replace the appropriate determination of legal or policy decisions.[104] This is because religious charities can and do substantially contribute to society. Without them, our societies, secular and non-secular alike, will be much poorer, at least certainly from an economic perspective.

[104] Chevalier-Watts (n 9) 287.

5

Re-imagining Charity in English Imagination: Advocating a Social Harm Critique of Charity as a Cornerstone for the 'Organization of a Civilized Social Life' in Twenty-First Century Britain

SARAH WILSON

I. Introduction

The analysis of the legal and social importance of charity in this chapter focuses on English charity law within the wider British legal tradition present in the United Kingdom.[1] For charity lawyers, the rationale for this legal framework lies in demarking purposes, which are considered charitable from a wider sphere of 'worthy causes' subsisting in the sphere of social life. My analysis explores the 'place' of charity in wider societal consciousness, proposing that this is complex and multifaceted, and that it can be found couched in narratives of presumed societal importance and benefit. Interrogating these ideas occurs through explaining that English law has a very longstanding tradition of conferring upon certain 'worthy causes' the special legal status of 'being charitable', which has had the effect of generating wider understandings of charity and embedding them, in particular ways. Through exploring the *journey* of English charity law, close attention is paid to the Charities Act 2011, where the legal definition of charity can be found, and to a continuing direction of travel, which is evident in the Charities Act 2022 (UK). Here, both current law, and ideas of a journey are consciously oriented towards

[1] Which requires understanding that the British (or UK) legal tradition actually comprises three separate legal systems; those of England and Wales, Northern Ireland, and Scotland. Both the former are common law traditions, while Scotland is a mixed common law and civil law-based system.

how charity appears to occupy a crucial place in the social and economic life of an advanced and sophisticated society. This vista of the present is then combined with references to the Medieval origins of charity and charity law to suggest that it is timely to ask fundamental questions about the role of charity in a complex modern society. It is suggested that looking beyond conventional narratives of charity as well as closely at them helps to create an impetus for this, and from this that contributions from cultural theology, and especially social harm analysis, might assist this.

The title of this chapter has borrowed ideas of societal complexity and 'civility' from EL Woodward's classic *Oxford History of England*.[2] This seminal whig history reflection on social, economic, and political transformations of nineteenth-century Britain's *Age of Reform 1815–1870* is considered significant in many different ways, with this channelled through how these transformations could be understood through Woodward's conceptualisation of 'The Organization of a Civilized Social Life'.[3] For Woodward, industrialisation had generated the capability for life in Britain to be much improved in comparison with previous generations, enabling the population to live easier, safer, healthier, and more kindly, lives.[4] But for this overall improvement to continue, the growing intricacy of life produced by industrialisation and its aftermath required greater organisation of lives being lived; with this considered as necessary for a complex industrial society 'as the provision of new methods of transport'.[5] Characteristic of 'whig histories', this is an overly positive account of the seismic societal shifts brought about in the making of modern Britain, and overlooks much of the immense suffering produced, but it is Woodward's identification of this core aspiration of the 'age of reform' that interests this analysis. For Woodward, the pursuit of 'civilized social life' would give life to emerging ideas of 'common affairs' and of an 'administrative superstructure' for taking charge of matters of common concern; matters which should be taken out of the realm of individual choice, and away from traditionally local organisation, and replaced with 'standardisation'.[6] For a reader in the twenty-first century, ideas of organisation, an 'administrative superstructure', and 'common affairs' presented in Woodward's 1930s retrospective are ones readily associated with 'the State' and 'public policy'.

This analysis of charity and its embeddedness in society shows many dimensions of interest in ideas of 'organization of civilised social life'. The idea of charity occupying a significant place in the social and economic affairs of a wealthy, and advanced and sophisticated society is premised on how present-day UK life might be recognised as such a setting. This is channelled through tropes of achieved and

[2] EL Woodward, *The Age of Reform 1815–1870 (The Oxford History of England) (Volume 13)* (Oxford, Clarendon Press, first published 1938).

[3] ibid the chapter title (I) beneath the commencement of Book Four within the overall work, commencing 426.

[4] ibid 426.

[5] ibid.

[6] ibid.

aspirational 'civility' for citizens,[7] and citizens' expectations in their lived experiences, together with asking how such a society might look to respond to challenges it faces. In presenting an account of how a longstanding tradition of recognising 'charity' has embedded particular ideas of what charity is, and perceptions of the importance of legal support for this, attention is paid to strong continuities which charity law shows with its origins and past iterations, and also how new directions are revealed in how it has looked to adapt to change. Many references are made to relationships subsisting between 'charity' and the State, foregrounding how this manifests in the present. This reflects how this particular take on 'journey' looks to track charity's legal meaning and social significance in the present, and also across time.

In making fleeting reference to different models of the State that can be found in UK history as part of this, conceptualisations of the twenty-first century State as the 'welfare State' are very familiar, and also useful for engaging with ideas of 'social civility'. These ideas are also helpful for scrutinising the partnerships subsisting between the State and charitable organisations, and which are identified widely across policy discourse and academic analysis. In this vein, with a different emphasis, references to evident, aspirational, and especially *expected* 'civility' could be directed towards a commonly found and related assertion that the significance of the charitable sector today can be understood through reference to a retreat in State provision in the lives of citizens.[8] But this analysis directs core ideas of 'civility' and its different presentations – achieved, aspirational, and expected – towards explaining the embeddedness of charity and its legal framing and more 'popular' facings in social psyche. And from this, it asserts that emphasis on its purported benefits has obscured how charity might harm a complex and advanced society and present barriers to the goals of a 'civilised social life' contrary to dominant ideas that it assists in delivering these.

II. The Legal Definition of Charity and Signposting Ideas of Wider Social Significance and of Charity Law's *Journey*

Explaining how charity manifests in society today involves identifying charity's presumed positives and acknowledging a widely referenced 'special place in public sentiment',[9] and seeks to understand how this might have arisen. In turn, these

[7] Certainly, on metrics such as membership of the G7 informal grouping of seven of the world's advanced economies, and performance in eg OECD Better Life Index – see www.oecdbetterlifeindex.org/countries/united-kingdom/.

[8] See: *The Journey of Charity Law: The impact of past problems today and into the future*, Symposium hosted by the University of Queensland, 29 September 2023, https://law.uq.edu.au/event/journey-of-charity-law.

[9] C Mitchell and SR Moody (eds), *Foundations of Charity* (Oxford, Hart Publishing, 2000) vii.

same reference points are directed towards suggesting that charity might actually be a source of harm for society, and present barriers to civility, and in that vein, to how they might also assist in questioning of charity's presumed benefits and in scrutinising the State-focused structural support it currently commands. From this, the analysis looks to justify a search for new understandings of charity's legal importance and social significance. From engaging with how legal analysis has sought to understand charity and critique it, the analysis looks to illuminate the value of 'social harm' analysis. Applying social harm analysis to charity is novel. Social harm analysis lies beyond legal analysis, and is most readily associated with critique of conventional evaluations of crime in society pursued within the discipline of criminology. Social harm analysis argues that the nature of criminology's dominant interest in understanding how societies are impacted by crime is typically too narrow, and too focused on individual acts of harm.[10] For pioneers like Hillyard, a social harm approach looks to widen understandings of how harms to society can also manifest beyond crime, and subsist as detriment to the welfare of individuals and a society collectively, with this in various ways originating in allocations of power within society, and channelled through (especially) the conduct of governments and corporations.[11]

Arguments for configuring charity as social harm will be made through reference to the strong structural support which is given to 'charity' by law, and from how its embedded 'special place' in societal consciousness has discouraged fundamental critique, and even 'drowned out' this. This argument is built through engaging with how English law is written, and how it is reflected on in policy and academic spheres – and through highlighting what appears to be absent in these reflections. The perceived benefits of social harm analysis for this exercise flow from how charity and English charity law *are* presented in academic analysis and, indeed, the many strengths of this literature. But it is also argued that whilst the place of 'charity' in the English context has generated a recognisable and respected, and sizable body of 'critical' analysis, even the most engaged and critical elements calling for 'fundamental reappraisal of the assumptions which inform English legal notions of "charity"' characteristically stop short of questioning its very existence.[12] Instead, this analytical tradition actually adopts many of the tropes characterising dominant analysis; namely those clustering around the presumed social benefits of charity, and recognising what is widely considered manifestly important work undertaken by charity in society.

A feature in common for the critical charity literature is its interest in legal understandings of 'charity', and this analysis is premised on how English charity law requires that for an organisation to be charitable, its purposes must be 'charitable' and must benefit 'the public', as defined by 'charity law'.[13] There is a substantial body of English charity law, much of which has been developed

[10] See P Hillyard and S Tombs, 'From "Crime" to Social Harm?' (2007) 48 *Crime, Law, and Social Change* 9, 13.

[11] ibid 12.

[12] Mitchell and Moody, *Foundations of Charity* (n 9) vii.

[13] Charities Act 2011 (UK), ss 1 and 2.

through the common law, but where the significance of this is now determined by a statutory framework. The Charities Act 2006 (UK) commenced this project of a new era for charity law, coming into force 1 April 2008, and being replaced by the Charities Act 2011 (UK), which, as consolidating legislation, did not alter the new law's substance. As a more intensified focus on a journey of charity law follows, it becomes clear that English charity law now also includes the Charities Act 2022 (UK). For this initial focus on how charity law defines and recognises charity, Charities Act 2011 (UK) provisions are central. Central for explaining what the law is, and where it can be found, and also for highlighting that 'purposes' which can be identifiable with 'doing good' and as 'worthy causes' can fall outside charity law's parameters even where they look and appear to be very similar to those which fall squarely within these.

Whilst discussion of the 'journey' *to* the Charities Act 2011 (UK) is held over for now, even introducing its very basic significance for how charity is defined through law requires understanding it as part of a reform movement. This commenced formally in 2002, and was motivated by mutually reinforcing ideas of bolstering public confidence in charity, and improving the regulation of charitable activity; and framed by ideas of continuity and change. Ideas of continuity and change reflected a prevailing consensus that aspects of traditional approaches which had functioned well should be retained, and should work alongside new directions considered necessary to achieve these twin goals in the twenty-first century. In this setting of continuity and change, many of charity law's traditional features and core principles were retained, and the significance of past law was enshrined through how the legislation references this as 'old law'.[14] From this, the effect of sections 1–4 of the Charities Act 2011 (UK) is that purposes are to be considered 'charitable' for the purposes of English charity law if they amount to worthy causes with recognised charitable character and are determined to be for 'public benefit'. For charitable character to be present (and the corollary that not all purposes will be considered to have this character) a charity's purposes must be exclusively charitable, and fall within a statutory list of accepted categories of purpose.

Both the idea of a statutory 'list' of purposes considered to manifest charitable character and a requirement of being 'exclusively charitable' have long traditions in English charity law, and the new law also demonstrates many continuities with the letter of the 'old law'.[15] The 'public benefit' requirement also has a long tradition in charity law,[16] but in theory at least, demonstrating public benefit now embodies a conscious new direction. The new approach did continue the tradition of framing public benefit through questions of whether (i) (on balance) a purpose

[14] Example: s 3 'Descriptions of purposes', by virtue of s 3(4) 'In subsection (1)(m)(i), "the old law" means the law relating to charities in England and Wales as in force immediately before 1 April 2008'.

[15] At the time S Wilson, *Todd and Wilson's Textbook on Trusts* (Oxford, OUP, 2015), had extensive discussion of what were then proposals heading towards enactment of the Charities Act 2006 (2005) and (2007) (UK) as the Charities Act was imminently coming into force in 2008.

[16] Classic authority for the public benefit requirement is *Morice v Bishop of Durham* (1804) 9 Ves 399; (1805) 10 Ves 522.

is beneficial rather than detrimental to the public,[17] and (ii) benefits the public in general, or a sufficient section of it,[18] but prior to the Charities Act 2006 (UK) many recognised charitable organisations – some existing over decades or even centuries – had never had to establish the 'first question of public benefit', as they were presumed to be beneficial rather than detrimental.[19] New approaches require *all* purposes (including established charities) to address this 'first' question thereby removing the historical presumption, with a further conscious new direction being that this question would move from a 'once-and-for-all' finding to that of ongoing demonstration.[20] As much commentary has noted, the theory and practice of 'new' public benefit requirements haven't entirely aligned, especially in the light of the decision in *Independent Schools Council v Charity Commission*.[21] For this analysis, however, the significance of the 'new law' in the journey of charity law lies firstly in how the intendment behind the Charities Act 2006 (UK) can speak to the lengths to which law can be shown to support the institution of charity. And from that thereafter, for reflecting on how relatively little by way of fundamental critique law's considerable interest in charity has generated.

Proposing the absence of critique *is* premised on there being a great deal of academic reflection on 'charity law'. It also requires acknowledging that the *journey* of charity law to the 'new law' as well as beyond it is well-documented in the academic literature. This pattern of reflection is also evident in the policy sphere, and within the space of little more than a year, the Charities Act 2006 (UK) reforms had generated both Lord Hodgson's Review of the Charities Act 2006 (UK) in 2012,[22] and the post-legislative scrutiny conducted by the Public Administration Select Committee within the auspices of the UK Parliament (PASC Report) in 2013.[23] Both policy reports also outline charity law's journey, with both going further back in time than many accounts of charity law's history in referencing the establishment of the first ever charity in 597. Both then turn to more familiar territory; namely, the Statute of Elizabeth 1601 (the Statute of Charitable

[17] *National Anti-Vivisection Society v Inland Revenue Commissioners* [1948] AC 31, as now embodied in Guidance produced by the Charity Commission in furtherance of its obligations under the Charities Act 2011 (UK), s 17.

[18] *Oppenheim v Tobacco Securities* [1951] AC 297, as now embodied in Guidance produced by the Charity Commission in furtherance of its obligations under the Charities Act 2011 (UK), s 17.

[19] As explained in debate on the Charities Bill 2004 in the House of Commons, 9 November 2005, col 25; https://publications.parliament.uk/pa/cm200506/cmbills/083/en/06083x--.htm.

[20] Much of the attention attracted by this legal shift became anchored to wider concerns about how public schools would fare in a new regime of public benefit; see P Luxton, 'Public Benefit And Charities: The Impact of The Charities Act 2006 On Independent Schools And Private Hospitals' in M Dixon and G Griffiths (eds), *Contemporary Perspectives On Property, Equity And Trusts Law* (Oxford, OUP, 2007) 181.

[21] *Independent Schools Council v Charity Commission* [2011] UKUT 421 (TCC). This decision was upheld by the Supreme Court in *London Borough of Merton Council v Nuffield Health* [2023] UKSC 18.

[22] Lord Hodgson, *Trusted and Independent: Giving charity back to charities – Review of the Charities Act 2006* (London, The Stationary Office, 2012).

[23] Public Administration Select Committee (2013–2014 Session), *The role of the Charity Commission and "public benefit": Post-legislative scrutiny of the Charities Act 2006* (London, The Stationary Office, 2013).

Uses), which is taken to be the first legal definition of charity, through its famous Preamble setting out the purposes for which a charity could be established, and then Lord Macnaghten's seminal formulation of the four heads for classifying 'charitable purposes' in *Pemsel* in 1891.[24]

The PASC Report outline of charity law's history also notes that 1960 marked the creation of the register of charities, and that in 1853 the Charitable Trusts Act established the Charity Commission.[25] Indeed, it is very significant for understanding charity law's journey that the Charitable Trusts Act 1853 (UK) established the office of charity commissioner; an office held in personal capacity by individuals until the Charities Act 2006 (UK) created the Charity Commission as a 'body corporate' to take on the functions of the Charity Commissioners in furtherance of objectives reflecting its functions and duties under the Act.[26] The PASC Report history 'overview' doesn't explain this, or how this innovation might speak to the considerable infrastructure which is seemingly necessary for supporting charity law. Neither it nor Lord Hodgson's overview explain why the Charitable Trusts Act 1853 or the Statute of Charitable Uses 1601 might have been so-called, or indeed how it ever was that charity became publicly enforceable, and that a hallmark of the institution of charity is how it 'falls to be subject to the control of the High Court in the exercise of its jurisdiction with respect to charities'.[27] What is much more apparent in general histories of charity law, and what is missing in the PASC Report outline are Medieval contributions to charity law, and to wider ideas of charity. For this, Lord Hodgson provides a lead through noting that 'those who wished to give help to those less fortunate could leave their property to monasteries and other religious or public institutions for this purpose' with the 'all-powerful Church' at the heart of this 'informal system for poverty relief'.[28]

III. Imagining Charity and its Place at 'The Heart of UK Society' – And Signposting the Continuing Significance of Medieval Contributions to Charity (and Charity Law)

In the general history of English law, Medieval times are widely credited as a time of development for English common law marking the birth of 'equity'.[29] Equity's origins as a parallel and discretionary jurisdiction of conscience, seeking to complement law as well as mitigate harsh outcomes of remedies at law where the

[24] *Commissioners for Special Purposes of the Income Tax v Pemsel* [1891] AC 531 (HL).
[25] PASC Report (n 23) 8.
[26] By virtue of s 6 of the 2006 Act; see now s 13(1) of the 2011 Act.
[27] Charities Act 2011 (UK), s 1(1)(b).
[28] Lord Hodgson (n 22) 1.3, 8.
[29] See: JH Baker, *An Introduction to English Legal History* (London, Butterworths: LexisNexis, 2002).

circumstances called for this are well-known, together with the Court of Chancery morphing from the Ecclesiastical elements within the King's Court. Alongside this, equity's *in personam* interventions would come to harden into development of property rights for those without them 'at law'. The earliest trusts appeared in this setting, and to serve this purpose. This development also marked the beginnings of the lasting association of 'charity' with 'the trust', which has continued long after most charitable purposes have ceased to subsist as 'trusts'. In the English context, charities are much more commonly unincorporated associations, or companies limited by guarantee, or (following the Charities Act 2006 (UK)) a 'charitable incorporated organisation' (CIO). How equity became involved with charitable giving at all is part of the journey of charity law, and is also part of the tale of how charity acquires a wider societal significance. This is when charity starts to become configured in particular ways by acquiring a 'public' profile – whilst trusts are paradigmatically associated with (private) beneficiary enforcement.[30] And, it is argued, it is in this early phase of development that charity starts to lose connection with its origins, and starts to become fashioned in different – and more recognisable – ways.

At all these times in the history of England, and as 'the State' looked and behaved in particular ways, charity was and is considered socially important and receives significant legal support in different ways. In the twenty-first century charity and its relationship with the State show some notable characteristics which can, and, it is argued, *should*, lead us back to the Medieval origins of charity and (then nascent) charity law. By the close of the twentieth century, charity had acquired a strong international face, reflecting domestic concern with overseas issues,[31] with a further trend 'at home' also becoming increasingly visible. This is how the State has formed close partnerships with, and commissions specialist services from, charitable organisations to support what it can achieve for its citizens, and in the pursuit of a 'civilised social life', for example, in the sphere of children's care (eg Barnardo's) and health care and medical research (eg Cancer Research UK). Elsewhere, this trend is a key dimension for analyses proposing that these partnerships might have evolved into State retreat in providing for citizens, and that it is increasingly ceding this to the voluntary sector (including charitable organisations themselves). But this analysis continues to focus on how for charity law's journey, these earliest years of the twenty-first century have seen charity law codified and reworked in some key ways, with this beginning formally with the publication of *Private Action, Public Benefit*.[32] This 2002 documentation, and what followed in the presentation and parliamentary scrutiny of the Charities Bill 2004 (UK),

[30] Certainly, for express trusts; *Morice v Bishop of Durham* (n 16). See also n 39 (below), noting that charity law also owes its origins to the simultaneous protectively oriented jurisdiction (and thereby one with a more 'collective' character) known as *parens patriae*, exercised on behalf of the King, and also within the remit of the Lord Chancellor.

[31] For example: OXFAM was established in 1942, www.oxfam.org.uk/about-us/history-oxfam/.

[32] Prime Minister's Strategy Unit, the Cabinet Office, *Private Action, Public Benefit: A Review of Charities and the Wider Non-profit Sector* (London, The Stationary Office, 2002).

shows how the primary purpose of legal change was bolstering public confidence in charity.[33]

In this reform discourse, this perceived importance of elevating charity's public appeal through improving regulation and promoting greater access to charity law for purposes with social benefit was itself closely aligned with an insistence that vital work is undertaken by charitable organisations in society today – and that more endeavour still is needed. Subsequent reflections on this movement from the PASC Report reminded that the Act's aims lay in providing a 'legal and regulatory environment to enable all charities to realise their potential as a force for good in society'.[34] PASC also reminded that reform sought to 'encourage a vibrant and diverse sector, independent of Government; and to sustain high levels of public confidence in charities through effective regulation'.[35] The PASC Report also proposed that the charitable sector is 'at the heart of UK society',[36] echoing views expressed a year earlier in 2012 in Lord Hodgson's Review of the Charities Act 2006 that 'the fundamental principles of charity and philanthropy are deeply ingrained in this country's culture'.[37] This significance of charity for today can also be read into statistics published annually by the Charity Commission, relating to England and Wales. According to the Annual Report and Accounts 2023 to 2024, published in July 2024, there were (at the recording of data on 31 March 2024) 170,056 charities on the Register of Charities, and moreover during the financial year 2023–24, £96 billion of charity income and £94 billion of charity spend were regulated.[38] Whilst these statistics exclude a small number of organisations which are either excepted or exempt from registration, they do speak persuasively to ideas of charity being 'at the heart of … society'.

Following this thread of the numerical size and financial value of the charitable sector, commentaries proposing a heightened importance for charity on account of an apparent State retreat from providing for citizens can speak a basic truth, even if these reflections don't necessarily capture the fuller and more multifarious picture of present-day State provision. This basic truth is how legal support for charity can always be seen operating alongside a strong fiscal interest in supporting those minded to assist others in need. For the Elizabethan nation State and the nineteenth-century nascent modern State, we can observe times of significant population growth and changing patterns of living, framed by perceived opportunity and also uncertainty, and similar tropes are arguably at play today in the UK. Charity is also associated with ideas that are long-standing, namely in providing beneficence and support for those who are vulnerable and unable to care for themselves, and, centrally, the young and the elderly, as well as the sick and infirm. The

[33] ibid noted in the Introduction 1.4, 11, which also references the formal announcement of the project on 3 July 2001.
[34] PASC Report (n 23) 3.
[35] ibid.
[36] ibid.
[37] Lord Hodgson (n 22) 1.2, 8.
[38] With this representing an overall increase in both metrics from the previous accounting period.

very earliest 'charity law' evident in Medieval times manifested as emergent ecclesiastical, and then early Chancery, interest in those showing willingness to 'give' to worthy causes.[39] This reflected an idea that giving to others less fortunate was a 'good' that one should be 'held to' if one expressed an intention to do so.

This application of equity's jurisdiction of conscience in this setting is consistent with a more pervasive placing of 'good conscience' within Medieval life. Conscience was an integral part of a mindset borne from Catholic religiosity, and subsisted as a dominant if not pervasive rationality, and one reflecting a strong emphasis of life on earth as preparation for the afterlife.[40] This makes the attraction of giving to others less fortunate persuasively part of a calculus of behaving with 'good conscience', and helping to 'save one's soul'.[41] The strong associations between religion and charitable provision persisted into the nineteenth century, and were also evident in Elizabethan times, but where the earlier dissolution of monasteries by Henry VIII[42] had helped to refocus religiosity in a more 'worldly' way.[43] These associations between charity and religion continue to be present,[44] through readily identifiable voluntary activities of faith organisations. Different framings of these associations, but associations nonetheless, can also be found in posited puzzlement surrounding charity's enduring appeal; given how its derivation from 'a Western Christian tradition' would make it seem 'ill-suited to the pluralist, multicultural, secular society which characterises Britain in the twenty-first century'.[45] But equity's interest in holding people to their 'giving' intentions was also greater than religiosity alone can explain. As EL Woodward's classic commentary on the nineteenth-century emergence of the modern State explains, the traditional unit of governance in place was the parish, with services provided locally, and supported by revenue generated locally, principally through 'rates'.[46] Under this system, the benefits of benevolence provided *by* others will have been keenly felt by the entire community, which would otherwise be financially responsible for its vulnerable members.

These fiscally oriented and collective reasons to encourage 'giving' to worthy causes gained early formal recognition during Medieval times, through the

[39] Alongside Chancery jurisdiction over trusts, nascent charity law was also a product of *parens patriae*, the prerogative jurisdiction exercised by the Lord Chancellor on behalf of the King; see M Harding, 'Charity and Law: Past, Present and Future' [2020] *Singapore Journal of Legal Studies* 564, 576.

[40] With profound influences on shaping ideas of law and justice. See: T Haskett, 'Conscience, Justice and Authority in the Late-Medieval English Court of Chancery' in A Musson (ed), *Expectations of the Law in the Middle Ages* (London, The Boydell Press, 2001) 159.

[41] M McMurdo, 'Faith Hope and Charity: The Resilience of the Charitable Trust from the Middle Ages to the 21st Century' (2013) 13 *QUT Law Review* 1, 5.

[42] ibid.

[43] Alongside fracturing Church provision for those unable to provide for themselves, in times of significant population growth, with the latter enabled significantly by recovery from the Black Death.

[44] See: D Stevens, 'Rescuing Charity' in Mitchell and Moody, *Foundations of Charity* (n 9) 29.

[45] Mitchell and Moody, *Foundations of Charity* (n 9) vii.

[46] Woodward, *Oxford History* (n 2) 426–27; and with some application of this to early poor law reforms at 430–40.

emerging, but pre-existing framework of the trust, with this also explaining the longstanding regard for charity law as 'trusts law' – albeit a special and distinctive type of trusts law. The special and distinctive body of 'charity law' has always thus, arguably manifested intentions to 'enable all charities to realise their potential as a force for good in society',[47] albeit in an apparently strongly fiscally oriented way. What is strikingly clear by the time Lord Macnaghten set out the *Pemsel* heads of charitable purpose is that not all worthy endeavours of assistance for others are considered to have 'charitable character' and to confer public benefit.[48] Modern charity law looks to gatekeep the status of 'being charitable' within a much wider sweep of voluntary and not-for-profit activity, commonly referenced in the present as the 'third sector'.[49] Here, it is significant that charity specifically rather than a wider notion of 'helping' others is considered 'at the heart of … society' today. Asking what is special about charity leads quickly to ideas that 'being charitable' means being subject to public scrutiny and State regulation – and even connoting attaining State 'approval'.[50] It leads as quickly to a number of perceived advantages for organisations themselves, and also for those who support them through donations, some of which are better known than others beyond specialist charity communities. Ones which are generally less well-known flow from how charity law is configured as a type of trusts law.[51] The best known, and arguably most significant, advantage flowing from charitable status relates to taxation.

Today, charitable purposes (through the organisations which pursue them) receive very generous taxation treatment in respect of a number of key UK taxes, with those giving to charity (as natural and legal person donors) enjoying generous deductions across a range of common taxes. The tax advantages received by charitable organisations and those who support them are very prominent in the perceived importance of confining the 'advantages' of charitable status to what is considered to be properly at 'the heart of … society', with the operation of this also working to *exclude* from these privileges. What is emphasised far less is just how much administration is required to 'gatekeep' charitable status in this way. Still less is said about how the tax advantages received by charitable organisations reflect an actually quite dark compact with the State; embodying that beyond these 'head start' financial advantages, organisations are left to thrive or perish, without (or with limited) active positive financial support. More is said on the latter shortly, but in following initially the thread about the modern infrastructure which is necessary to support charity, and to ensure the advantages of charitable status are

[47] PASC Report (n 23) 3.

[48] And indeed, earlier in *Morice v Bishop of Durham* (1804) (n 16).

[49] As explained by the UK National Audit Office, www.nao.org.uk/successful-commissioning/introduction/what-are-civil-society-organisations-and-their-benefits-for-commissioners/.

[50] See: Lord Hodgson's account (n 22) of the reform movement leading to the Charities Act; chapter 2; 12–19.

[51] Centrally, charitable purposes are not subject to the beneficiary principle, nor perpetuity rules, both of which can invalidate private trusts. The *cy-près* doctrine uniquely operates to protect for charitable use any property applied to a purpose which is uncertain or no longer capable of execution.

suitably contained in a structural way (beyond the substantive law defining and limiting charity), this started to solidify during the nineteenth century with the creation of the office of Charity Commissioner in 1853.

IV. The 'Modern' Origins of Charity Law Today – And the Significance of Medieval State Responses to Charity

English law in the twenty-first century generally shows in many ways a lasting legacy of nineteenth-century legal innovation and change.[52] This was when much of the legal institutional framework and architecture which supports law today, and which is familiar to students and scholars of English Law, was put in place.[53] Perhaps law's interest in charity specifically should not be surprising in a setting where legal innovation itself was considered by contemporaries to be part of a wider pattern of human boldness, endeavour, and achievement across science, innovation, and trade, and the country's material wealth.[54] At this time, charity became recognisably a 'sword and shield' for social change – a source of support for many left to the ravages of change, and breakdowns in traditional ways of living brought about by industrialisation, and also a mechanism for social reform agitation.[55] A maturing State, which sought to acquire ever-greater understandings of the demands of a modern industrial society through collecting and processing information,[56] was positioned well to understand how charity was manifesting and operating, and thus how to support this, and put limits on this. And certainly better placed than in the earliest days of conception for the 'administrative superstructure' idea[57] to perceive contributions which charity could make to the project of continuing improvement and higher overall civility, and to make connections between this and the costs of elevated civility, whilst being mindful of historical dislike for taxation amongst 'freeborn Englishmen'.[58]

[52] See: S Wilson, 'Value and Values in Higher Education: Some Reflections From the UK on the Subversive Dimensions of Historical Approaches in the Study of Law' in M Duffy et al (eds), *Critical Legal Education as a Subversive Activity* (Abingdon, Routledge, 2022) 149, 155.

[53] ibid.

[54] Council of Legal Education (Great Britain), *A Century of Law Reform: Twelve Lectures on the Changes in the Law of England During the Nineteenth Century* (London, Macmillan Publishing, 1901) 1.

[55] A Dunn, 'Demanding Service or Servicing Demand? Charities, Regulation and the Policy Process' (2008) 7 *MLR* 247, 248.

[56] D Eastwood, 'Amplifying the Province of the Legislature: the Flow of Information and the English State in the Early Nineteenth Century' (1989) 62 *Historical Research* 276.

[57] See: how ideas of a State with understanding and options in the sphere of governance and regulation, and relationships with its citizens as conceptualised in A Ogus, 'Better Regulation – Better Enforcement' in S Weatherill (ed), *Better Regulation* (Oxford, Hart Publishing, 2007) can interplay with the account of the nascent nineteenth-century State in Eastwood (n 56).

[58] See: S Dowell, *A History of Taxation and Taxes in England From the Earliest Times to the Present Day* (London, Legare Street Press, first published 1965), especially (at 260–61) discussion of Sydney Smith's 1820 missives on the 'freeborn Englishman'.

Thus, charity and its modern infrastructure are very plausibly products of an increasingly informed and resourced nascent modern State, and one mindful of the social and economic externalities of change – and also the costs of mitigating and managing them. This was a good time to look favourably on those committed to providing charity, and for supporting charity, and for developing a framework which would facilitate this. But in this narrative of understanding, resourcefulness, and incentivisation in promoting 'charity', the Medieval application of the trust to enforce charitable giving also merits attention. The trust wasn't an obvious vehicle for this, but Medieval contributions to the earliest 'charity law' nevertheless manifested innovation as well as showing determination to support charity in a structural way. That the trust was not an obvious mechanism for this, is evident from the proposition of a 'historical accident'[59] at play, and the asserted concerted effort on the part of the early Court of Chancery to hijack the charitable gift and 'squeeze[d] it (with some difficulty) into the pre-existing framework of the trust'.[60] The endeavours to formalise charitable giving, as evident in the Medieval Court of Chancery, show a very long timeframe of determination to encourage charitable giving. This narrative of charity's origins generates in turn much wonder for how ideas of charity as a source of social harm could even arise, making little suggestion even that charity has been considered unfavourably at all in its long history.

Fleeting mention has been made to the fragility in public confidence in charity, with further discussion of this still to come, following some reflection on how strong support for charitable giving creates tensions between charity and others who might otherwise receive property given to it. As *Pemsel* itself shows, charitable giving presents tensions *for* the State; the very same State which actually encourages charitable activity and giving through tax advantages and concessions. Today, it is easy to understand that where tax concessions are enjoyed by one sector of society, this is certain to affect distributions of the tax burden on other sectors in society, or reduce the scope of provision of public services, or encourage government borrowing. These implications will also have been clear in earlier pursuits of a 'civilised social life' as the nineteenth-century State became more interventionist and increasingly able to continue a trajectory of overall improvement. That is, once the emerging 'administrative superstructure' could generate improvement positively – for example, through public health initiatives and a public education movement – taking different directions from the early part of the century when stemming the risks to civility presented by spiralling poor relief spending and tackling crime had dominated. Elsewhere, as the Charitable Uses Act 1736[61] and its effects for widening the recognition of bequests as 'charitable' show, alongside the State, rightful heirs were also likely to be unimpressed with their relatives'

[59] P Matthews, 'The New Trust: Obligations without Rights' in AJ Oakley (ed), *Trends in Contemporary Trust Law* (Oxford, Clarendon Press, 1996) 1, 2.

[60] ibid.

[61] 9 Geo 2 c 36.

charitable intentions.[62] Today, the 'tax angle' continues to create controversies around decisions on what should 'be charitable' given a spectrum of viewpoints on what is socially beneficial, whilst *Gill v RSPCA* shows how donors' favour for charity continues to be a source of resentment amongst families.[63]

V. Law, Public Confidence, and Charity – A Problematic Trinity

On a broader plane, the fragility of public confidence in charity, which dominated the lead into the Charities Act 2006 (UK), continues to frame concern about the ability of charity to flourish in society. Research commissioned by the Charity Commission published in 2016 suggested that confidence in charity had been adversely affected by aggressive tactics on the part of charities to secure donations and also media reports on how charities spend donations.[64] In subsequent research published in 2023, the Charity Commission reported that public trust in charity had recovered, and indeed that trust in charity had 'increased at a time when trust in other institutions has flatlined or fallen'.[65] The nuances behind this headline included contextual reference to the cost of living crisis, and how crisis response 'has not fundamentally changed people's overall trust and confidence in charities or how relevant they believe them in general to be', and perhaps had even made charities' endeavours more visible in positive ways; and findings of overall greater trust in smaller locally focused charities over larger, international, and professionalised ones.[66] But laments of there being 'few, if any', signs of trust returning to pre-2015 levels were aligned directly with the above 2016 research findings.[67] This research is part of a much larger narrative suggesting that public confidence in charity is currently considered to be crucial but unstable. In looking now to advance why strong if not universal views of charity as a force for good might be challenged, and an alternative view of charity as a source of harm proposed, then perhaps positing this rests on the key question of why public

[62] G Jones, *History of the Law of Charity 1532–1827* (Cambridge, CUP, 1969); Chapter VII 'The Mortmain Act 1736' 109–19; and Chapter IX 'The Influence of the Mortmain Act, 1736, on the Definition of Charity' 128–33.

[63] *Gill v RSPCA* [2010] EWCA Civ 1430.

[64] *Public trust and confidence in charities: Research conducted by Populus on behalf of the Charity Commission* 2016 https://assets.publishing.service.gov.uk/media/5a800410e5274a2e8ab4dae5/Public_trust_and_confidence_in_charities_2016.pdf.

[65] *Public trust in charities: Research conducted on behalf of the Charity Commission by Yonder* 2023 www.gov.uk/government/publications/research-into-public-trust-in-charities-and-trustees-experience-of-their-role-2023/public-trust-in-charities-2023#:~:text=Trust%20levels%20still%20sit%20lower%20than%20historical%20highs&text=This%20marks%20the%20third%20year,that%20remains%20below%20historic%20highs.

[66] ibid.

[67] ibid.

confidence is so important, and why charity is capable of commanding confidence at all given the 'shocks' it frequently experiences.

These shocks include pervasive ones, and ones which are long-standing relating to concerns about how charitable organisations spend donations, and about associated administrative costs (and perceived wastes thereof). More recently, as the above 2016 research found, these established concerns had continued, but there were also newer ones relating to aggression in donor-securement tactics, including street 'chugging' and telephone 'hounding'.[68] Given the 2016 findings and a number of highly profiled scandals which have followed since, it is perhaps surprising that public confidence had recovered at all in 2023. The 2016 Report did include the AgeUK energy package 'mis-selling' and Kids Company financial mismanagement scandals,[69] but its publication timing meant that it couldn't include in its reporting on targeting donors with aggressive and manipulative tactics the subsequent suicide of a 92-year-old 'poppy seller' who was said to have received over 3,000 requests for support from charities in the lead up to her death.[70] What is perhaps the most highly profiled recent 'charity scandal' can also speak to how important charity is in English consciousness, and just how unassailable the very strongly positive associations it attracts seem to be. This concerns 'lockdown hero' Captain Sir Tom Moore, who became a national treasure on account his fundraising for the NHS during the COVID-19 pandemic, and whose endeavours have become 'part of Covid-19 pandemic history'.[71]

'Captain Tom' was knighted for this by the late Queen Elizabeth II, and his subsequent passing at the age of 100 was national and international news. So too became the charity, the Captain Tom Foundation which was set up in his honour by his family, but for all the wrong reasons. Indeed, following a scandal concerning the use of funds, and the name of the charity which was every inch as visible in the national press as Captain Tom's legendary lockdown fundraising,[72] a Charity Commission statutory enquiry was commenced in June 2022 to 'investigate serious concerns about the charity's governance and financial controls'.[73] The Charity Commission has recently confirmed that Captain Tom's daughter

[68] *Public trust and confidence in charities* (n 64) 5.

[69] ibid.

[70] S Morris, 'Poppy seller who killed herself got 3,000 charity requests for donations a year: Questions raised about charities' tactics after regulator's report says Olive Cooke, 92, was overwhelmed by approaches before her suicide', *The Guardian*, 16 June 2016, www.theguardian.com/society/2016/jan/20/poppy-seller-who-killed-herself-got-up-to-3000-charity-mailings-a-year.

[71] H Burchell, 'Captain Tom's daughter defends decision to keep book profits', *BBC News*, 12 October 2023, www.bbc.com/news/uk-england-beds-bucks-herts-67086802.

[72] P Butler, 'Captain Tom charity faces scrutiny after report of payments to daughter Hannah Ingram-Moore reportedly paid via family firm for appearances linked to charity that bears father's name', *The Guardian*, 16 August 2023, www.theguardian.com/society/2023/aug/16/captain-tom-charity-faces-scrutiny-after-report-of-payments-to-daughter.

[73] Charity Commission, Press Release 'Regulator announces statutory inquiry into The Captain Tom Foundation', 30 June 2022, www.gov.uk/government/news/regulator-announces-statutory-inquiry-into-the-captain-tom-foundation.

(Hannah Ingram-Moore) and her husband have been disqualified from being charity trustees and from holding an office or employment with senior management functions in charities.[74] Whilst the 'Captain Tom' scandal has clearly shocked the nation, the history of charity and charity law suggest that it will become part of a story which considers charity overwhelmingly – if not unassailably – an institution of good, and which contends that whilst there are organisations which occasionally give charity a 'bad name', that stricter regulatory approaches will reliably restabilise confidence.

This is the latest scandal[75] which is thus likely to produce strong vocalisation of support for charity, and 'doubling down' on insistence that it is a force for good. Indeed, some years earlier, Lord Hodgson dedicated his 2012 review of the Charites Act 2006 (UK) to the 'heroes' who work for charities and who financially support them, with the Review 'intended to help them flourish',[76] and there is little to suggest that much has changed, even with a plethora of post-2012 scandals. Lord Hodgson's Review was actually titled *Trusted and Independent: Giving charity back to charities*, and in it he also expressed his hope that charity's heroes would feel that he had 'kept the faith' (*in* charity).[77] The fate of the Captain Tom Foundation is certain to become a further opportunity to purvey that charity is at the 'heart of … society'. This is also seemingly likely from how the journey of charity *law* itself continues through the Charities Act 2022 (UK), with this legislation designed to strike a 'careful balance' between the all too familiar characterisations of cutting regulation to liberate charity resources and maintaining appropriate regulatory oversight and safeguards.[78] The Captain Tom Foundation scandal will almost certainly not be seen as an opportunity to question the very idea of charity, and why charity is supported at all in society, let alone to ask why it has such a 'special place in public sentiment', and commands very extensive support in law. It will certainly not generate thoughts on how charity could be construed as a source of social harm.

[74] Charity Commission, Press Release, 'Charity Commission confirms it has disqualified two individuals in The Captain Tom Foundation inquiry', 3 July 2024, www.gov.uk/government/news/charity-commission-confirms-it-has-disqualified-two-individuals-in-captain-tom-foundation-inquiry.

[75] NB: the findings from a Charity Commission statutory inquiry in 2021 into the affairs of 'Fashion for Relief' published 26 September 2024 resulted in British supermodel Naomi Campbell being disqualified from acting as a charity trustee (see Practice Note published by Penningtons Manches Cooper, www.penningtonslaw.com/news-publications/latest-news/2024/naomi-campbell-disqualified-from-being-charity-trustee-over-serious-mismanagement). This *is* more recent than the 'Captain Tom' events, and Naomi Campbell is a very highly profiled celebrity, but it seems unlikely that Captain Tom will be eclipsed in current British memory and imagination anytime soon.

[76] Lord Hodgson's Review (n 22) 7.

[77] ibid.

[78] Law Commission, Press Release 'Charities Act 2022 receives Royal Assent', 11 March 2002 https://lawcom.gov.uk/charities-act-2022-receives-royal-assent/.

VI. The Case for New Critical Directions and for Applying 'Social Harm' Analysis to Charity

Social harm analysis may not seem an obvious intellectual avenue for critiques of charity. This reflects its origins in and continuing associations with understandings of 'crime' – albeit through a State, rather than individual focus, and looking at crime as well as beyond it to ideas of 'social detriment' through foregrounding ideas of power and inequality.[79] But its ability to produce analyses of how citizens can be harmed by the State, or institutions supported by the State, is evident in the recognition of an already extensive range of physical and non-physical harms, with the field still actively developing. Indeed, it has been applied persuasively to everyday-life resonances found as widely as in obesity, poverty, long working hours, unemployment and social isolation for purposes of working towards understanding the features of societies which look to reduce harms, or instead to generate them.[80] Configuring charity as social harm works by recognising how the State has supported its embeddedness, and perpetuates pro-social narratives for charity, and even generates these. It also works from how the State currently pays little attention to the damaging effects on society of encouraging this support, and indeed how the State encourages a heavy reliance on charity for delivering 'civility' for its citizens. This analysis perceives these damaging effects as ones associated with undermining social cohesion and also perpetuating an unrealistic vista of what charity is able to deliver in a society which expects, and very much demands, high levels of civility.

The attraction of social harm analysis for interrogating charity's 'special place' in society and wider psyche also emanates from suggesting that even the most intellectually stimulating and critical analysis of charity within the legal canon is more premised on the tropes of charity's presumed good and deep cultural appeal than looking to challenge them. There is, of course, much critical reflection on how charity currently operates, but that does not in and of itself amount to critique of a fundamental character. A strong focus on how charities aspire to 'put themselves out of business'[81] through resolving the social causes they look to champion inevitably buys into the overarching idea of the enormous importance of charity for society. Similarly, highly profiled critiques of how charity law is being brought into disrepute in different ways, and even being made a 'nonsense of', subsist on a plane of reasoning that the law *can* be brought 'back into repute'[82] – and (with strong

[79] Example: Hillyard and Tombs, 'From "Crime" to Social Harm?' (n 10).

[80] S Pemberton, *Harmful Societies: Understanding Social Harm* (London, Policy Press, 2015).

[81] As classically associated with Chesterman's use of the slogan of housing and homelessness charity Shelter; M Chesterman, *Charities, Trusts, and Social Welfare* (London, Weidenfeld and Nicholson, 1979) 354.

[82] As is seen in the very prominent reference to Lord Campbell-Savours' remarks in the House of Lords (9 February 2005, col GCGC69) in M Synge, *The 'New' Public Benefit Requirement: Making Sense of Charity Law?* (London, Bloomsbury Press, 2015) xiii.

subtext that it) *should* be. In different ways, these narratives look to generate conversations on how to liberate charity to elicit greater contributions from it (often as part of an argument for greater empowerment of the voluntary sector), even when clothed as calls for 'fundamental reappraisal of the assumptions which inform English legal notions of "charity"', and reconsiderations of the 'foundations of charity'.[83] Whilst there *are* perspectives which do ask directly 'whether law should continue to maintain legal charity or whether it should now allow legal charity to wither and die in favour of other modes of action',[84] they can also be found to welcome the contributions of charity to 'modes of action' found in the sphere of 'social action', highlighting even its capabilities for resisting 'moral diminishment' risks presented by the 'marketization' of social spaces.[85] This analysis suggests instead that we should call out charity – and its support in law and social consciousness – as amounting to social harm.

On occasions critical charity literature *does* ask whether 'law should continue to support "charity" at all',[86] and in doing so suggests that in the twenty-first century charity might more readily be identified with unpalatable and outdated connotations of '"do-gooding" and moral superiority', and that it is based on patronising relationships between donor and recipient, which promote inequality and power imbalances within society, and discourage reciprocity and inclusiveness.[87] But even such perspectives concede that 'the idea of giving a privileged place to voluntary organisations is, if anything, becoming more widespread',[88] and align themselves with aspirations for protecting charity to allow it to flourish.[89] For these perspectives, attacking current paradigms and definitions of charity is ultimately a search for 'new and challenging ways of defining charity',[90] and the pursuit of 'a more just and effective definition of charity'.[91]

Social harm analysis looks to provide a genuinely alternative vision for understanding charity, which challenges its embeddedness, and aims to generate new narratives of critique of it for a complex and advanced society. These ideas need developing, and further working through, but early-stage thinking suggests that through engaging with social harm analysis, charity can be imagined differently, and that there is arguably a strong imperative for being open to this. This is built from arguing that two key problematics arise from how charity currently subsists in societal imagination; namely that this model of voluntary activity is financially unsustainable, and that it presents risks for social cohesion and instead gives life to prejudice and division. In turn, opportunities abound for these problematics

[83] Mitchell and Moody, *Foundations of Charity* (n 9) ix.
[84] Harding, 'Charity and Law: Past, Present and Future' (n 39) 575.
[85] ibid 579.
[86] Mitchell and Moody, *Foundations of Charity* (n 9)vii.
[87] ibid.
[88] ibid.
[89] ibid viii.
[90] ibid ix.
[91] ibid xi.

to be interrogated as 'harms' through further scrutiny, with initial focus likely to reflect social harm analysis' interest in 'human flourishing' – and the forces which encourage this, and those presenting risks for it.[92] As an introduction to how both identified problematics can be connected to calls for new ways to reflect on charity, a little is said on what seem to be less well known – or at least less acknowledged – origins of charity. Whilst ideas of 'do-gooding' and 'moral superiority' and in-built inequality might feel particularly out of place in twenty-first-century society, writings in cultural theology suggest these were never appropriate characterisations for charity, even at the very time that equity was looking to 'squeeze' charity somewhat uncomfortably into the existing framework of the trust.

This alternative account of charity's earliest modern origins can be seen in former Archbishop of Canterbury Rowan Williams' reflections on 'cultural bereavement'.[93] Drawing on the work of academic theologian John Bossy,[94] Williams posits that charity in 1400 was much more about love for others and connections with others, than showing grace and concern towards those in need.[95] Instead, this initial intent has changed over time to a much more financially oriented angle on giving.[96] The latter is based on asymmetry of need, and where receipt 'in some way acknowledges inferiority'.[97] This appears to be very far removed from the connections made through brotherhood, and the reciprocal nature of a mutual exchange of love pursued through coming together to celebrate love which, for Williams (and Bossy), is how charity *as an idea* appears to have originated.[98] Ideas of beneficence and asymmetrical financial and social relationships between providers and recipients of charity, together with financial incentive angles, very strongly characterise charity today. And it is from these perspectives that arguments are made that support for this current model of charity is both financially unsustainable and damaging for social cohesion.

VII. 'Alt' Narratives to Charity as a 'Force For Good': Charity Embodying Friability, Social Division, and 'Delusional Optimism'

For identifying charity's capabilities for undermining social cohesion, the historically rooted structural 'asymmetrical' dimensions of a non-reciprocal, beneficence model of charity can be conjoined with how individualism came to dominate

[92] As adopted by Pemberton (n 80), and built on theories of Doyal and Gough (see L Doyal and I Gough, 'A Theory of Human Needs' (1984) 4(10) *Critical Social Policy* 5).

[93] R Williams, *Lost Icons: Reflections on Cultural Bereavement* (Edinburgh, T&T Clark, 2000).

[94] J Bossy, *Christianity in the West 1400–1700* (Oxford, OUP, 1985).

[95] Williams, *Lost Icons* (n 93) 53–54.

[96] ibid.

[97] Chesterman, *Charities, Trusts, and Social Welfare* (n 81) 1.

[98] Williams, *Lost Icons* (n 93) 55.

the British mindset following the reformation, becoming over time synonymous with ideas of social contract, and liberties enjoyed by the 'freeborn Englishman'.[99] Individualism is a way of thinking which gives primacy and value to the individual, recognising the individual's worth within a social setting, and came to the fore in the birth of Protestantism as an alternative theology to communitarian-oriented Catholicism. Whilst individualism has been clothed with different significances in the journey towards 'modern Britain',[100] its basic ideas of autonomy and self-determination are deeply embedded, and in the context of charity, this has clearly contributed to ideas of beneficence and asymmetry – shaping regard for those *receiving* charity as being unable to self-determine, where self-determination is strongly framed by ideas of taking responsibility for one's self, as much, if not more so, than exercising choice.

Choice, though, *is* a realm for those *providing* charity, and this has become established in ways which include impositions of conditionality. Anecdotal evidence presents entirely plausible accounts of present-day church-administered Christmas provision for homeless people being conditional on attendance of church activities. If this can be substantiated, then it would appear to fit Chesterman's 1979 allusion to 'social subordination' premised on distinguishing 'deserving (deferential)' and 'undeserving poor', which was based on (then recent) sociological study from 1975.[101] Today, 1975 was 50 years ago. Moreover, this has the appearance of exposing those at the extremes of 'inequality and power imbalances within society'[102] in the *twenty-first* century, by virtue of being *homeless* to 'self-confident middle class evangelical religious and moral propaganda'.[103] This is a historian's conceptualisation of what *convicted prisoners* in the *nineteenth* century received as part of prevailing belief that institutional punishment could both punish and reform. Choice is also evident for those 'providing' charity in less direct ways, through being donors to charity; with the status of donor appearing to generate and perpetuate ideas of implied choice and demands for accountability in how donations are used by (direct) providers of charity. This can be seen in how even those charitable organisations providing what might very easily be seen as important, and even vital services to society, feel compelled to present themselves. The children's charity Barnardo's, a key partner with the State for children 'in care' feels compelled to explain the importance of providing basic safety and care for children in care in explaining how it is funded.[104] For Cancer Research UK, narratives of (pre-emptive) accountability to

[99] A MacFarlane, *The Origins of English Individualism: The Family, Property, and Social Transition* (London, Wiley-Blackwell, 1978).

[100] ibid. See also: PS Atiyah, *The Rise and Fall of Freedom of Contract* (Oxford, OUP, 1979) Chapter 10.

[101] Chesterman, *Charities, Trusts, and Social Welfare* (n 81) 352.

[102] Mitchell and Moody, *Foundations of Charity* (n 9) vii.

[103] U Henriques, 'The Rise and Decline of the Separate System of Prison Discipline' (1972) 54 *Past and Present* 61, 83.

[104] See: Barnardo's www.barnardos.org.uk/who-we-are/how-were-funded.

donors and the wider public are evident in the perceived importance of explaining 'how we spend your money'.[105]

In a different manifestation of the same idea, the lifeboat charity the Royal National Lifeboat Institution (RNLI) has experienced vulnerabilities in public support through how it is being drawn into the highly emotive and highly politicised 'small boat' journeys taken by those looking to cross the English channel seeking a new life in the UK. This organisation looks to save lives in the UK's coastal waters, remembering that mainland Britain is an island, making coastal safety a presumptive high priority. The RNLI isn't formally part of the State like HM Coastguard (the UK's national maritime emergency service), but it is closely partnered with it,[106] and has nevertheless experienced swings in donor appeal, which can threaten its very existence. This is because of perceptions that, through its sea rescue activities, the RNLI provides a 'taxi service' for illegal immigrants.[107] This is perhaps an extreme example of how support for charity amounts to public 'choice'; not direct choice in determining which 'worthy causes' are ones 'for public benefit', but choice in whether these organisations can survive or not.

There are many other illustrations of how provider, and even *donor*, perception can manifest, and distort the work of charity, and even move this away from what might be needed, to what is preferred, and what is more emotionally (or even 'morally') appealing. In times before audio books, Talking Books for blind people could struggle in attracting public support, whilst Guide Dogs for the Blind Association (complete with adorable labrador puppies) was always very popular; despite guide dog assistance not being a support model suited to everyone with impaired vision, and notwithstanding benefits of audio assistance for countering loneliness and social isolation being widely perceived. And of course all charitable organisations exist subject to public support in some way, evidently recognised by even those in very close partnership with the State. Does this suggest that a 'high civility' society could 'decide' it is no longer prepared to support children in the care of the State, or research into better treatment and cures for cancer, in ways that the RNLI case study shows are entirely possible? Here, an impetus to rethink charity and its role 'at the heart of … society' should arise from how it has become entangled with personal autonomy and encouragement to focus on what seems palatable and attractive, rather than what a 'civilised social life' might actually require.

An even greater imperative perhaps still also exists. As suggested, tax concessions are a very important face of insistence that charity requires public support and needs to command public confidence. As also signposted, there is quite a dark

[105] See: Cancer Research UK www.cancerresearchuk.org/about-us/our-organisation/how-we-spend-your-money.

[106] Indeed, HM Coastguard will often mobilise RNLI lifeboats for emergency assistance. See: HM Coastguard https://hmcoastguard.uk/what-we-do.

[107] R Hall, 'RNLI hits out at "migrant taxi service" accusations: Lifeboat charity says it is its moral and legal duty to rescue people at risk of dying as they cross Channel', *The Guardian*, 28 July 2021 www.theguardian.com/uk-news/2021/jul/28/rnli-hits-out-migrant-taxi-service-accusations.

dimension to the tax 'advantages' compact which leaves organisations to thrive or perish, without forward-looking active positive financial support. And for organisations which *are* in receipt of State support by virtue of providing highly profiled State-commissioned 'services', such as medical research and care services for children, and UK coastal safety, there is a funding gap[108] to be met by trading activities, property investment, and – mostly – public donations. This means that citizens' direct 'payment' for vital services through taxation is much less than it would be without the transfer of financial risks to meet 'funding gaps' to charitable organisations themselves. As suggested above, this system also exposes organisations providing vital services *for* citizens to the vagaries *of* donor favour. This begs the question of how sustainable this huge – and yet also highly contingent – reliance on charity for delivering a 'civilised social life' is, and whether citizens should be shielded from this reality, or be required to confront civility's true costs. For a society which wants – and actually demands – high levels of health and social care, and high levels of general amenity, then surely this also calls for honesty in how much this will cost, and an emphasis on the realities of choosing societal priorities.

VIII. Conclusion: Keeping Charity (as Social Harm) in (or Under) the Spotlight

These are clearly difficult conversations to have, but at present they are virtually absent from the public sphere. And where conversations on 'civility costs' do occur – mainly in connection with NHS funding, and social care and specialist educational needs provision – they are not connected with charity and the positivity it attracts and is looking to sustain. Instead the dominant narrative for charity continues to be that charity can achieve all that we want it to, as long as it secures the right measure of public confidence. Indeed, very recent suggestion that charity should become a 'critical friend' for government, and even a critic of it, could signal significant inroads into longstanding insistence under English charity law that charities cannot be 'political'.[109] Charity is emphasised specifically within this most current play on the importance of 'harnessing the dynamism, innovation and trusted reach' of civil society organisations,[110] reflecting the view of the newly elected Labour government that a 'fundamental reset of the relationship between

[108] See discussion in the House of Lords 29 January 2024 (vol 835) relating to Cancer Research UK's projection of a £1BN funding gap for cancer research. Lord Hunt of Kingsheath asked HM Government how it might respond to this, citing Cancer Research UK's reports that over the past five years it had experienced a 19 per cent drop in real terms in the amount it can invest in cancer research.

[109] See eg: *Southwood v Attorney General* [2000] WTLR; and Charity Commission Guidance *Campaigning and political activity guidance for charities* (updated 7 November 2022) www.gov.uk/government/publications/speaking-out-guidance-on-campaigning-and-political-activity-by-charities-cc9/speaking-out-guidance-on-campaigning-and-political-activity-by-charities.

[110] R Booth, 'Lisa Nandy announces plan to restore charities to "centre of national life", Culture secretary says civil society groups should "tell government when we're getting it wrong"',

government and civil society' is necessary for fixing 'the foundations of our country'.[111] However, this very reporting of a potentially 'foundational moment'[112] for relationships between charity and the State also noted that 'no guarantees to boost funding' would come with this. Reflections on the latter being highly salient included views that charities perceive expectations of delivering 'public services on the cheap', at a time when many were at risk of collapse 'amid rising costs, falling incomes, declines in volunteering and rising demand', and also the observation that the new government purports awareness of 'fragility in the sector'.[113]

There is, thus, some significant scepticism attaching to possibilities for a 'foundational moment', and it would instead seem that little has changed since the reform movement leading to the Charities Act 2006 (UK) was launched. This was so, also by a Labour government, with the message that 'charity law gives donors confidence that their money will be used for the purposes for which it was given', and that promoting public confidence is an 'important objective because the sector's success ultimately depends on public support'.[114] Ideas that this might be a reckless approach to delivering civility in an advanced society where citizens have high expectations, and attendant costs spiral as ever more interventions become possible, are just are not part of this presentation of charity as a 'force for good'. Neither is how this might be particularly problematic in a low tax society like the UK, where citizens' expectations do not align well with collective willingness to fund high levels of social benefit in any case. All of this casts doubt on how charity can be sustainable or even functional in present-day conditions. And yet such concerns are just not visible in pervasive insistence that the sector's success depends on public support, and neither are they so in insistence that as a society we cannot function without charity.

In launching *Private Action, Public Benefit* in 2002, then Prime Minister Tony Blair insisted that '[i]n the modern world it is simply not possible to have a dynamic and vibrant society and economy without a dynamic and vibrant voluntary sector'.[115] This was very much an idea of the time, and readily identifiable with the message of 'third way' politics, that in a globalised 'world without boundaries' it was no longer possible for governments to provide for the totality of citizens' needs.[116] As the twenty-first century has progressed, much attests to continuing complexity, and characterisations of everyday life through language of opportunity and possibility, together with exposure of perceived gaps in State provision and the 'discovery' of new 'needs' of citizens. From this, in times when

The Guardian, 19 October 2024, www.theguardian.com/politics/2024/oct/18/lisa-nandy-announces-plan-to-restore-charities-to-centre-of-national-life.

[111] ibid quoting British Prime Minister, Sir Kier Starmer.

[112] ibid quoting Sarah Elliott, the chief executive of the National Council for Voluntary Organisations.

[113] ibid.

[114] *Private Action, Public Benefit* (n 32) 3.7, 30.

[115] ibid Foreword 5.

[116] As an intellectual movement see eg A Giddins, *The Third Way: The Renewal of Social Democracy* (Cambridge, Polity Press, 1998).

it is popular to configure the growth of voluntary action as reflecting State retreat from social provision, it might also be helpful to reflect on just how much the State is delivering for its citizens – directly and indirectly – and on how unlikely it is that the State will ever be considered to be meeting demands for its interventions. In this setting voluntary action is likely to remain part of aspirations to retain high civility, together with promoting social cohesion, whilst navigating times of unprecedented need and demand.

But it does not follow from asserting voluntarism has a core role in delivering civility in conditions created by a complex, sophisticated and highly expectant society that this should be channelled through support for charity specifically. Charity is a very specific part of voluntary action which is supported by law, and financially by society in ways that other spheres of voluntarism are not. Here, it is suggested that supporting charity financially, and through perpetual repetition of the idea that it is (seemingly infinitely) capable of delivering societal needs, and that it is vital for doing so, discourages reflection on the true costs of civility, whilst also leaving organisations delivering 'specialist services' financially vulnerable, and exposed to oscillations in public opinion. It also infantilises us as a society, by denying that choices have to be made, and priorities set, and instead holds citizens in a state of 'delusional optimism'.[117] relating to what to expect, and what can be demanded. Clearly a hallmark of high levels of civility lies in government ability to provide for citizens. But an equally important one is surely government honesty, and for citizens to take responsibility for their lived experiences and responding to challenges and opportunities presented by twenty-first century living in an advanced and sophisticated society.

Clearly, questions do remain. There are questions on what might replace charity if we fundamentally rethink its presence in our lives, and the support it currently commands. There are also ones of how to harness the very considerable financial value of the charitable sector from elsewhere in society, and of what the implications of such a redistribution might be for government finances and tax burdens for individual citizens. In imagining an alternative setting where the State works differently with specialist services provision currently associated with charity, questions arise on how choices on funding priorities might be made, and by whom- and on how to ensure that this decision-making is rational and evidence-based rather than arbitrary and emotionally driven; and fair, and free from favour and corruption. These are questions which should be asked. But they are likely only to be asked where there is some discursive space for questioning charity's presumed benefits, and momentum for this. Here, it is suggested that advancing the idea of charity as social harm is a way to at least start these conversations.

[117] Borrowed from white-collar crime analysis per DO Friedrichs, 'Wall Street: Crime Never Sleeps' in S Will et al (eds), *How They Got Away With It: White Collar Criminals And The Financial Meltdown* (Columbia, Columbia University Press, 2013) 3, 6.

6

Understanding the Meaning of Charity: The Art of Doublethink

KIM D WEINERT

I. Introduction

Charity law scholars occupy a 'fortunate (or unfortunate) position of digging into a historical past to create the symmetry of a garden out of the chaos'.[1] Perhaps the first iteration of chaos for scholars is best represented by the problems with the technical legal meaning of charity. Judicial methods exhibit a range of inconsistencies that create a sense of disarray, making it difficult to determine with certainty which purposes will qualify for charitable status. Since the ambitious charity modernisation project of 2005 launched across numerous common law jurisdictions, one of the celebrated achievements was the legislative reform expanding charitable purposes and making the public benefit test less nebulous. Lifting the meaning of charity from its opaque Tudor and Elizabethan traditions was a hopeful prospect yet has led to a rolling series of disappointments.

In spite of legislative attempts to articulate the technical meaning of charity, it remains an elusive jural concept. Its elusiveness, in part, stems from its inherent link to 'goodness'. The dominance of virtue as a means of understanding charity has traditionally been represented by the value-laden 'halo effect'.[2] The effect of the halo is to create a powerful influence bias towards perceiving an entity's purpose as being morally good and the entity itself as intrinsically trustworthy, at least relative to government and for-profits.[3] In the context of charities, the halo implies an

[1] GW Paton, *A Text-Book of Jurisprudence* 2nd edn (Oxford, Clarendon Press, 1951) 1.

[2] The halo effect is defined 'as a tendency of judges to assume that once a person possesses some known as good characteristics, their other unrelated and unknown characteristics are also likely to be consistent, that is good'. JP Forgas and SM Laham, 'Halo Effects' in RF Pohl (ed), *Cognitive Illusions – Intriguing Phenomena in Thinking, Judgement and Memory* 2nd edn (Oxford, Routledge, 2016) 227.

[3] TB Ruddle et al, 'Fragile Halos: Comparing Organisational Reputation Across Sectors' (2023) 31 *J Contingencies and Crisis Management* 13, 14–15.

altruistic concern for those in need.[4] In turn, the halo simplifies morality which is often too idiosyncratic and fallible to be definable.

In determining charitable status, the halo often feels more like the narrow beam of a torch searching the darkness for an allegorical good, a pursuit driven by a desire to define and categorise purposes and actions within a virtue framework. Understanding the virtuous dimensions within the legal sphere requires an acknowledgement of the ongoing discourse between charity law today and its historical past. The past holds at its core a nuanced morality guided by the halo imagery. The juridical image of the halo reflected in a finding of charitable purpose draws attention to an implied distinctive notion of goodness encased in a judicial tone, which is one that is open-minded. This chapter will build upon and emphasise the open-textured nature of charity's empirical development by aiming to offer an analytical argument regarding the meaning of charity. The analysis offered here will utilise a narrative turn from an internal and external perspective by exploring three interrelated arguments, which hopefully offer a new and different understanding of charity's ontological meaning.

The first argument begins with the question of whether there is a uniquely best way to get to the core meaning of charity. Doctrinally understood as a jural concept with a technical meaning, charity jurisprudence reveals that 'charity' stands for and can mean something more. The first argument draws out how the purpose-centric method of the common law does its best to warn off a reductive and scientific meaning of charity. Through an exploration of a small example of strange and confusing results illustrating how equity draws and redraws the parameters of the meaning of charity, there is often a hidden and somewhat tortuous subjective axiology flowing through the cases' reasoning. If what is no longer hidden, then knowing how to make sense of this elusive jural concept as an allegorical narrative offers a helpful way to understand the inconsistent legal methods and meanings of charity.

The second argument hinges on the idea that charity manifests goodness as a grand historical narrative. Here, Iris Murdoch's *Sovereignty of Good* explores the grand narrative of goodness to cast light on an unsystematised recognition that virtues are part of the judicial method to determine whether a trust or entity is charitable. How the courts seek to find the good to suit the charity's grand narrative and its halo is illustrated by the Australian High Court's decision of *Commissioner of Taxation v Word Investments Ltd*.[5] The critical examination of the majority's reasoning in this case illustrates the invocation of goodness as a field force of imagination, to justify finding that for-profit purposes and activities

[4] Perhaps the most relatable aspect of the halo shining on those in need is manifested in illustrated in what is traditionally known as the 'poor relations' cases relating to the public benefit test and the *Pemsel* category of relieving poverty. See generally: *Dingle v Turner* [1972] AC 601; *Re Compton* [1945] Ch 123 (Lord Greene MR); *Re Scarisbrick's Will Trusts* [1951] Ch 622 (Evershed MR); *YWCA Australia v Chief Commissioner of State Revenue* [2020] NSWSC 1798 (Payne JA); *Re Central Employment Bureau for Women and Students' Careers Association Incorporated* [1942] 1 All ER 232.

[5] (2007) 243 ALR 44.

does not disqualify an organisation from having charitable status. This examination is then joined by contrasting the different ranges of affection shown towards the advancement of religion and the for-profit purposes in the minority's decision. The parallels of subjectivity in both sets of reasonings can be seen to operate on different modes of goodness and visions of how the grand narrative of charity should be represented. It is from these observations that the majority's empirical development of the meaning of charity strives to remain true to the grand narrative of charity is invested in the not-for-profit rule. Although the majority's finding is quite a contradiction in determining an investment entity to be charitable, it imbues an observation that charity's grand narrative is endlessly under renewal.

The final argument posited in this chapter explores how the technical legal and common meaning of charity is also becoming blurred. Here, the Orwellian concept of 'doublethink'[6] will be introduced to illustrate how the law is much more comfortable with holding two contradictory ideas at once in understanding charity.

II. The Indeterminacy of Charity as a Jural Concept

A classic account of indeterminacy in equity, and the focus of this part of the chapter, is on the generous degree around finding for the jural concept of charity. The courts (and now regulators) grapple with how to best answer the simple question: is an entity or trust's purpose exclusively charitable?[7] Indeed, there are instances where the question is quickly answered,[8] but not always. Determinacy in charity law is possible, albeit rare. However, such rarity does not guarantee that the court's clear methodical answer will be applied again with certainty and predictability.[9]

[6] G Orwell, *Nineteen Eighty-Four* (London, Penguin, 1949).

[7] Care must be taken by the reader of this chapter to know that 'charity' includes incorporated entities that are registered as a charity (for the sake of regulatory oversight, taxation concessions, and reputational benefits to qualify for government grants), as well as a charitable trust in its traditional sense. The Australian situation is such that an incorporated not-for-profit entity, as defined by its respective statute, has been conflated with the jural concept of charity so as to achieve federal government regulation. Despite there being contention around the constitutional validity of this regulatory arrangement, the meaning of charity is shrouded in more confusion. See s 25-5 Australian Charities and Not-for-Profit Commission Act 2021 (Cth); *cf Perpetual Trustee Company Limited v The Federal Commissioner of Taxation* (1931) 45 CLR 224. For the constitutional debate, see generally, N Aroney, 'Federal Charities Law and the Taxation Power: three constitutional problems' (2023) 51 *Federal LR* 78.

[8] For example: *Plummer v Attorney General of New South Wales* [2018] NSW 869; *Attorney-General (NSW) v NSW Henry George Foundation Ltd* [2002] NSWSC 1128; *In re The Trusts of the Arthur McDougall Fund Thompson v Fitzgerald* [1957] 1 WLR 81 (Ch D).

[9] An overlooked example of a charitable purpose is when a charity is tasked (either by statute or self-proclamation) to pursue the object concerning the regulation and disciplining of professions. It is questionable whether such an object evinces a charitable purpose with a public purpose. Across common law jurisdictions, the law remains divided. In New Zealand, statutory regulatory objects are held to be exclusively charitable, as well as in the United States of America: see *Medical Council of New Zealand* [1997] 2 NZLR 297 and *Dulles v Johnson* (1959) 273 F 2d 362. Whereas in England and Australia, regulatory objects are not charitable. The decision of the *Law Institute of Victoria v CMR*

Discovering the 'legal conception'[10] of what charity should be has always been viewed as a problem owing to the word's open-textured nature and its penumbral range. The main antagonism that indeterminacy causes in charity law is two-fold. First are the strange and confusing results apparent in judicial conclusions about what is 'charitable'. Here, oddity is located in particular cases where the purpose is striking and relatable but produces heterodox answers, as well as hard cases where answers do not always guarantee an easy understanding of the court's reasoning, such as *Word Investments* discussed below.

Second, despite the inexact nature of charity, it is often the lack of persuasive force in the varying judicial reasonings that compounds frustrations in locating a bright line that informs a finding of charity. For example, an important expansion of the meaning of charity in the 2017 Northern Territory decision of *Groote Eylandt Aboriginal Trust v Deloitte, Touche & Tohmatsu (No 2),*[11] whereby sport and housing for First Nations people and their clans (named and related beneficiaries under the trust deed) were held to be charitable. The innovative findings by the court for First Nations people and their clans manifest the evolutionary nature of charity law. Subsequently, the expansion of charity's technical meaning was illustrated in the case of *Cant v Kirby*, where Gzell J held that 'the assistance of Aboriginal persons is a charitable purpose'.[12] Whereas, in the latter case of *Aboriginal Housing Office v Jacky* Richmond J was strict in finding that housing for First Nation peoples did not assist or relieve their poverty but only improved the living standards of certain First Nation individuals which was not beneficial to the community.[13] Richmond J's formalistic reasoning in applying the *Compton*[14] test and objectively constructing the trust deed's text (specifically, clauses five and six) was to benefit 'beneficiaries consistent *with* the purpose rather than *for the* purpose'.[15] The latter decision throws into disarray how First Nation beneficiaries and their charitable trusts will come to be understood against the backdrop of drafting that reflects paternal settler state thinking and treatment of First Nations peoples. Indeed, the findings in each of these cases present different reasoning (one formalistic and the other two manifesting an unquestionable belief of providing the 'right' conclusion). The diversity in the reasoning here recognises that charity law's inescapable ephemeral nature is a source of discomfort and exasperation, but it is worthy of further exploration.

This chapter's exploration of discomfort begins by asking if there is a central question that is worthy of pursuing in the penumbral turmoil surrounding the

of State Revenue [2015] VSC 604 held that even if the tasks were performed for the public benefit or advantage, and in citing Lord Keith in *General Nursing Council for England and Wales v St Marylebone Brough Council* [1959] AC 540, 561 the purpose 'can in no sense be regarded as of a charitable nature'.

[10] *Commissioner of Taxation v Word Investments Ltd* (2007) 243 ALR 44 (Allsop J).

[11] *Groote Eylandt Aboriginal Trust v Deloitte, Touche & Tohmatsu (No 2)* (2017) 169 NTR 1.

[12] [2001] NSWSC 1193, [46].

[13] [2022] NSWSC 916 [80]. *Cf* see *Aboriginal Hostels Ltd v Darwin City Council* (1995) 33 NTR.

[14] *Powell v Compton* [1945] Ch 123; [1945] 1 All ER 198 CA.

[15] *Aboriginal Housing Office v Jacky* [2002] NSWSC 916, [78].

jural concept of charity: *Is there one best way to get to the core meaning of charity?* There need not be, for a couple of reasons.[16] First, 'best' implies and gives a sense of the need for a rigid objective act of interpretation. Of course, this proposition would aid predictability, dampen down the abstract nature of charity, and eliminate judicial discretion and choice. Assigning a hard meaning to 'charity' would bring about a legal order of neutrality for the exercise of maximal efficiency,[17] but would a single descriptive interpretative position solve the vagueness of charity? Most likely not. The 'purpose-centric' stronghold that has taken root in charity law jurisprudence ensures that charity law evolves and remains a 'moving subject'.[18] Even in jurisdictions where the *Pemsel*[19] categories of charitable purpose have been 'codified'[20] by statute,[21] the indeterminate nature of the concept has not been successfully eliminated.[22]

Further, the open texture of charity law is a necessary characteristic (despite statutory efforts) and, therefore, it logically follows that there are multiple ways, and no one best way, to find the core meaning of charity.[23] Once uncertainty and discomfort are introduced (and accepted), it allows for further reflection, which can lead to other ways of investigating the meaning of charity. It must be noted that this chapter is not proposing that the substantive application of legal principles of trusts and contracts, as seen in charity law,[24] be overlooked. The foregoing investigation and critical discussion to be found in this chapter aims to make sense of equity's wisdom. Sense-making is important to the empirical building of understanding the jural concept of charity. This is not only because the law constructs movable parameters of meaning for itself, but it also disappoints those who demand a perfect singular meaning of charity for the sake of efficiency. However, its subjectivity hides a nascent axiology which guides precedent.

If what is hidden is no more, then understanding the elusive jural concept as an allegory that emphasises virtues and values makes it seem ever so clear that there

[16] This question and responses here are posited in the fashion of A Sen, *The Idea of Justice* (London, Allan Lane, 2009).

[17] See generally, KD Weinert, 'Is it a Not-for-Profit Organisation or a For-Profit Organisation? The Case for a CIC Structure in Australia' (2014) 7 *JIALaw TA* 3.

[18] *Scottish Burial Reform and Cremation Society Ltd v Glasgow Corporation* [1968] AC 138 (HL) [45] (Lord Wilberforce).

[19] *Income Tax Special Purposes Comrs v Pemsel* [1891] AC 531 (HL).

[20] See *R (Independent Schools Council) v Charity Commission* [2011] UKUT 421 (TCC); [2012] CH. 214 [73].

[21] Charities Act 2013 (Cth) s 12 (Cth); Charites Act 2011 (UK), s 3; Charities Act 2009 (Ireland) s 3; Charities Act (Northern Ireland) 2008 s 2; Charites and Trustee Investments (Scotland) Act 2005 (Scotland); Charities Act 2005 (NZ) s 5.

[22] See, eg In *Angle Loop Ltd and Commissioner of Australian Charities and Not-for-Profits Commission* [2021] AATA 3894, the then Administrative Appeals Tribunal (AAT) agreed with the Australian Charity and Not-for-Profit Commission's (ACNC) decision to disallow charitable status. However, the AAT did not agree with the ACNC's line of reasoning and its interpretation of a 'purpose being incidental or ancillary to, and in furtherance or in aid of, charitable purpose'.

[23] Sen (n 16).

[24] See, eg *Lehtiäki v Cooper* [2020] UKSC 33; *Salvation Army (Victoria) Property Trust v City of Richmond* [1956] VLR 250; *Countess of Bective v Federal Commissioner of Taxation* (1932) 47 CLR 417.

is a moral intent to determining charitable status. Making sense of charity in this aminated way is emphasised by this chapter's antecedent that charity law today is locked in an ongoing discourse with its historical ontological commitment to the concept's characterisation begins with retrieving the communicated legal text from the Statute of Elizabeth's Preamble,[25] *Pemsel* test,[26] and the public utility test of *Oppenheim*.[27] Although these historical texts are specific to a time and place, it is the spirit of these texts that casts a long shadow on current judicial discourse. In understanding charity through its *episteme*, the judicial discretionary practices of flexibility and context-dependent, along with a choice of facts, find that the characterising of charity is underpinned by a moral and political theology. As Fullagar J observed, the precepts of charity 'possess a certain moral quality'[28] that denotes 'all good affections that a person ought to bear towards each other'.[29] The dogmatic conception of 'good' anchors the law to the words: 'advancing,' 'relieving', 'promoting', 'preventing', and 'benefit'.[30] These words expound a narrative of virtue, a high moral purpose, cast in a Judaeo-Christian tradition.

How, then, might the analytical problem of characterising charity be solved? The obvious answer is to introduce a regime to eliminate the moral (and ethical) narrative and politics that currently subsumes charity. On this positivist approach, an arbitrary meaning constructed on elements of prediction would command the law to have only one account of charity. Furthermore, if legislation were to perfect this jural concept, it may, with greater ease, facilitate cross-sectorial transactions with the government (and the market).[31] Yet, for charity law traditionalists, the main flaw in thinking about charity in this way would constrain what a charity might be, and how charity is thought about, merely for the sake of utility and intellectual tidiness. Indeed, what the jural meaning of charity 'is' or 'ought' to be has caused a particular fixation to crystalise a rational and objective meaning. This enterprise of objectivity in charity law can, however, be a rather tricky pursuit. Confronting the abstract phenomenon of charity with the rules of objectivity would stabilise the core, as seen in the broader debates in private law. But yet, time and time again, charity law shows how it refuses to be either rational, objective, or logical and thus disillusion persists within the garden.

To shore up the absence of rationality in charity law, the word 'myth' is often employed. The word is used to express frustrations and/or displeasure at how the courts produce apparently 'strange' results.[32] Teasing out the analytical morass of

[25] Charitable Uses Act 1601 (43 Eliz 1, c 4).

[26] See also the earlier decision of *Morice v Bishop of Durham* (1805) 10 Ves Jr 399; 32 ER 656.

[27] *Oppenheim v Tabacco Securities Trust Co Ltd* [1951] AC 297 (HL).

[28] *Salvation Army (Victoria) Property Trust v Fern Tree Gully Corporation* (1952) 85 CLR 159, 184.

[29] *Morice* (n 26) (Sir William Grant MR).

[30] Preamble (n 25).

[31] It would be remiss not to point out that the fuzziness that already exists between sectors would likely progress toward an indistinct haze.

[32] See: MC Cullity, 'The Myth of Charitable Activities' (1990) 10 *Tru & ELL* 7; MK Synge, 'Charity and the Myth of the Presumptions' (2016) 10 *J of Equity* 189.

charity, this chapter in asserting that the historical narrative of virtues structures itself around the answer of knowing how to solve the analytical issues concerning this jural concept. The malleable story of goodness assumes a salience that the courts use retrospectively to keep the meaning of charity moving forward. Focusing on the Australian case of *Word Investments* to illustrate how the narrative, across time, plays an important role in charity law's *raison d'etre* of always being virtuous. Of course, there is an easy temptation to assert that a narrative of 'good' is a fragile way to legitimise and stabilise the meaning of charity. However, in essence, this chapter argues that the imagery and mythological symbolism of goodness (as represented by the halo effect) occupies a central position in constructing legal dimensions to separate the traditional boundaries between charity and the other sectors. However, the inexplicit relationship charity law has with politics has meant that the deep traditional narrative and imagination of charity is becoming increasingly controlled as the ideals of modern governance are dictated to charities.

Orientating the evolution of charities to be in a close relationship with the government and the market sectors results in a charity needing to operate within a wide network of structures and institutions. Thus, as charities are inescapably drawn into a 'contract culture',[33] they are shaped into an effective and efficient institutional form. Emerging in the vision of welfarist, forward-looking quasi-public and private institutions, the intrinsic narrative of goodness is becoming a superfluous way of thinking about what charity means. From a sceptical outlook, modern charity law resembles an idea that charities are now business and state agencies in disguise (more on this later). Legislative governance standards and regulatory regimes that strive to uphold the imperative of fiscal administration have transformed charities into 'an object of economicization'.[34] Indeed, modern charity law has been a powerful force in entangling charities to behave and reshape their institutional contours to adapt and respond to market forces. Charity law's modulation for individual charities to adopt the dimensions of corporatisation evokes a different meaning of charity – one that displaces the grand narrative of good with the evils of profitability. At this stage of charity law's evolution, it feels at an organisational level that there is a hopeless struggle to grip onto its grand narrative of good.

How, then, is it the appropriate way forward to have an intellectual ontological discussion about charity? This chapter makes the argument that from an analytical perspective, the meaning of charity is to be informed by its own historical narrative while at the same time being open to the economic realities and interests that charity law now advances. In other words, it is a form of doublethink where a charity means pure good while simultaneously conforming to corporate logic.

[33] See especially: D Morris, 'Charities in the Contract Culture: Survival of the Largest?' (2000) 20 *LS* 409.

[34] R Birla, 'C=f(P): the Trust, "General Public Utility", and Charity as a Function of Profit in India' (2018) 52 *Mod Asian Stud* 132, 143.

III. Framing Grand Narrative of Goodness and its Mythical Halo

In the leading case of *National Anti-Vivisection Society v IRC*, Lord Wright remarked that charity in its legal sense is 'a word of art of precise and technical meaning'.[35] His Lordship's determination to segregate the public's framework of thought[36] of charity from the need to look at the meaning of charity as a jural concept proceeds from a place of the need for adequate and objective reasoning to guarantee some confirmation in the open text. The law's forceful isolation of the meaning of charity can make a useful contribution to the chapter's antecedent.

The doublethink posited by this chapter begins by throwing as much light on the technical legal meaning of charity as possible. By taking up the 'inside position' of analysis, charity law reveals that it operates as a boundary that claims a trust to be legitimately charitable by virtue of its legally recognised or recognisable purpose, which in turn drives an ethical utility. The pragmatic appeal of a framework of separation allows for an interpretative analysis and understanding of charity law's changing modalities that strongly shapes the definitional contour of charity. Indeed, while the garden of chaos requires a reflective prune on a regular basis to locate a shifting outer contour, it is nonetheless a task that is occupied with what charity is. By contrast, the public holds a firm understanding of what charity is for: an institutional arrangement for the good. Although a nuanced analysis of the core legal ideas may be missing in the public's sense of charity as a jural concept, at the same time, charity law has created this core set of positive ideological ideals and values for the public to think about and know about charity in this way. By the law telling the public what a charity is, cultural and social norms subsequently take over and permeate the meaning of charity through an ideal narrative.

Before further considering how an internal analysis of charity may bolster a deeper meaning of the concept from another angle, it would be useful to ask what the charity narrative is and what role a grand narrative may have in explaining the meaning of charity.[37] Narrative is a term that derives from Scottish law to mean 'that part of a deed or document which contains a statement of the relevant or essential facts'.[38] The emphasis placed on the documentary nature of the narrative calls for an analytical strategy of interpretation to elucidate the meaning of the

[35] [1948] AC 31, 41.

[36] Adam Smith's framework of public reasoning and thought is interested in how the world is seen by 'the eyes of the rest of mankind'. See A Smith, *The Theory of Moral Sentiments* (London, printed for A Millar, A Kincaid and J Bell, in Edinburgh, 1759). This chapter also comes from the Smithian quarter of openness to conceives that the meaning of charity 'to the eyes of the public' affords a moment of reflection in the doublethink paradigm. See especially the third argument of this chapter.

[37] The narrative turn undertaking in this chapter reflects Robert Cover's *Nomos and Narrative* whereby: 'No set of legal institutions or prescriptions exists apart from the narrative that locate it and give it meaning.' R Cover, *Nomos and Narrative* (1983–84) 97 *Harv LR* 4.

[38] S Keen, *Narrative Form – Revised and Expanded Second Edition* (New York, Palgrave Macmillan, 2015) 1.

authoritative written text. Although there has been much contention surrounding interpretive theories in law and the interdisciplinary turn towards narratology and literature fiction theories,[39] the enterprise of analysing the meaning of charity in an interdisciplinary space is to reveal that the jural concept is imbued with a grand narrative that extols the virtue of good. To think with clarity would signify a general propensity towards logic and objectivity, akin to a science that is broadly concerned with a procedure of proof, deductibility, and certainty. Although it is tempting to draw a fully realised story that mimics a predictive empirical explanation that the public (and even lawyers) can follow to locate determinacy in the meaning of charity, such a technique would only make the jural concept poorer and likely entail a reassessment and redefinition of the malleable nature of charity.[40] The abandonment of objectivity and logic in favour of unpredictive concepts of morality and virtues within an analysis of meaning would be a heroic ask (even in the softest of terms).

The burden of goodness carried by this concept (following a judicial determination) has mostly evaded the reach of the hard positivists' critique.[41] Feasibly, the meaning of charity is too special to be captured in precise axiomatic terms and rules. Such a claim does not mean that the courts emancipate a mechanical or objective mode of interpretation in charity law (as will be shown later in this chapter),[42] but simply raises the point that indeterminacy will always swirl around the meaning of this jural concept. How, then, does a grand narrative assist in thinking clearly about the meaning of charity? When reading the relevant deed's text, historically and over time, the case law has accumulatively revealed that there is always an independent and intuitive grand narrative playing out in the background.

In its broadest sense, the term 'grand narrative' in literary theory refers to an implicit governing story.[43] The connective threads between narrative and stories and the subsequent etymologically of story and discourse within the law and narrative scholarship embrace the main aspects of literary theory. The manifested tension between the various narrative and story approaches to finding the 'right' meaning and truth in text and utterances[44] serves an interpretive agenda, which

[39] See generally D Herman et al (eds), *Narrative Theory – Core Concepts and Critical Debates* (Columbus, Ohio State University Press, 2012).

[40] The case law regarding the fourth head of charity (within the spirit and intendment of the Preamble to the Statute of Elizabeth I) is an obvious illustration of the non-static nature of charity: *IRC v McMullen* [1981] AC 1 (HL).

[41] *cf* HLA Hart, *The Concept of Law* 2nd edn (Oxford, OUP, 1994) 182–83. Here, positivism is to be read and understood within legal formalism.

[42] In *Salvation Army (Victoria) Property Trust v Fern Tree Gully Corporation* (1952) 85 CLR159, 184, Fullagar J highlights the tensions between subjective elements in charity and determining whether a purpose or object is charitable has a technical objective sense.

[43] Keen (n 38) 118.

[44] Claims on finding the right meaning and truth within common law legal texts and utterances are contingent upon narrativity structure (a beginning, middle, and end) and/or fictionality (stories that comprise a well-organised plot, characters, themes, and tropes unfolding across space and time): R Dworkin, *Law's Empire* (Cambridge, Harvard University Press, 1986) 228–38; PJ Heald, 'The

unnecessarily induces more commotion in the garden. Rather than delving into overt theatrical storytelling in legal proceedings or comprehensively narrativity and law, this discussion focuses on how a grand narrative can accommodate an ideological vision of goodness. This allows for analysing and understanding the meaning of charity within the framework of judicial reasoning.

Besides the grand narrative offering an angle of interpretative entry point into the oblique and unperfect world of virtues, it is a self-referential method of interpreting the deed's text, facts, utterances, and the invocation of precedent. The grand narrative governing the deeply embedded historical imagination of goodness allows for choice and the comfortable use of discretionary power to reveal a story of a particular kind. By taking this story-centred approach to make sense of charity, it combines benign scepticism around virtues with the intuition extended by the courts in affirming as much goodness as possible.[45] Explaining the grand narrative of good will be an inarticulate moment in this chapter – as sometimes illustrated in charity cases. However, it is Iris Murdoch's exploration of goodness through affection and imagery which assists in explaining how the grand narrative of goodness in charity law is crafted and recrafted.

Imagination, as it will be revealed, has a useful role in understanding and making sense of the ontology of charity. In her seminal work, *The Sovereignty of Good*, her essays predominantly feature the discourse of vision and its pivotal role in shaping virtuous thoughts.[46] The correlation between goodness and imagination rests upon three core principles: realism, knowability, and concept involvement.[47] According to Murdoch, to cultivate an unclouded vision of the world, one must acknowledge its inherent properties, including kindness and mean-spiritedness, as genuine components of reality. Murdoch posits that when someone comes to know that these properties exist as a genuine part of reality, they know about reality. For Murdoch to understand these inherent properties entails gaining insights into the nature of reality itself.[48] Following realism, her vision is strengthened by knowability. The principle of knowability underscores that individuals know or come to know that the inherent properties of reality are accompanied by a sense of directive action.[49] The last principle emphasises the necessity of being cognisant of reality's properties and engaging in contemplation of the available concepts such as freedom and choice. Her portrayal of the conceptual scheme encompasses a breadth of background beliefs which can determine what aspects of reality to pick

Death of Law and Literature: An Optimistic Eulogy' (May 2009) *The Comparatist* 33; JB White, *The Legal Imagination: Studies in the Nature of Legal Thought and Expression* (Boston, Brown, 1973) and RA Ferguson, 'The Judicial Opinion as Literary Genre' (1990) 2 *Yale J L & Human* 201.

[45] See also: *Commissioner of Taxation v The Triton Foundation* (2005) 226 ALR 293.

[46] I Murdoch, *The Sovereignty of Good* (London, Routledge & Kegan Paul, 1970).

[47] ibid 64, 87.

[48] Nature by Murdoch is argued to include that the properties of kindness and others feature in the world as natural occurrences. Her broad concept attempts to reject narrow scientific interpretations of the natural world. K Setiya, 'Murdoch on the Sovereignty of Good' (2013) 13 *Philosophers' Imprint* 13.

[49] Murdoch (n 46) 34.

out or not. Across different schemes of concepts, one is free to shift in the conceptual scheme either negatively or positively.[50] Each core principle is unified by what Murdoch terms 'loving attention'.[51]

Attention is the process that facilitates an authentic apprehension of reality by looking at it lovingly and justly. The unifying force of attention enables one to have knowledge of reality, which prompts action consistent with that understanding and shaped by the conceptual schemes in which one operates. Crucially, the process of attending to the world and others in it in a loving and just manner is to aim for perfection. Perfection is a regulative ideal that permits one choice to change the concepts used. So, how does Murdoch's vision and imagery fit into the case study of *Word* and this chapter's antecedent?

A. Two Emerging Narratives from Word Investments: One about the Grandness of Goodness and the Other about Imperfection

The High Court of Australia (High Court) has always charted a singular course in charity law, its judgments fostering a legal landscape not always readily anticipated and departing from conventional expectations. This is exemplified in the landmark decisions of *Aid/Watch*[52] and *Word Investments Ltd*,[53] which redefined the scope of charitable purposes. Both decisions signify compelling examples of how the legal meaning of charity has undergone an evolution of sorts.[54] While any court's reliance on analogies is context-specific, the High Court in *Word*, perhaps in the extreme, draws attention to how the function of progression is to see an object clearly (or at least clearly enough) through a singular grand narrative of goodness.[55] The high priority of goodness revealed in *Word*'s majority judgment of Gummow, Hayne, Haydon and Crennan JJ is powerful when held up against the facts of the case.

[50] Setiya (48) 2.

[51] Murdoch (n 46) 33.

[52] *Aid/Watch Incorporated v Commissioner of Taxation* [2010] HCA 42.

[53] *Word* (n 10).

[54] That is to assert that the trajectory of charity law (in statute and at common law) is stark in contrast to the restrictive Elizabethan model of charity. In addition to legislative reform aimed at expanding charitable purposes in most common law jurisdictions, the High Court's *Aid/Watch* had a constructive part in redirecting the historical debate and clarifying the long-held uncertainty concerning the scope of the political purpose doctrine. However, there remains doctrinal complexity around advocacy and the doctrine of political purpose. See also: *Re Greenpeace New Zealand Inc* [2011] NZLR 815 (HC); *Attorney General v Family First New Zealand* [2022] NZSC 80.

[55] Although both decisions echo Murdoch's concept of 'seeing the good', the focus on *Word* in this chapter is to be able to give some distance between the chapter's antecedence and the role advocacy by charities plays in a healthy democracy as manifested by *Aid/Watch*. See also J Chia et al, 'Navigating the Politics of Charity: Reflections on *Aid/Watch Inc v Federal Commissioner of Taxation*' (2011) 35 *MULR* 353.

Incorporated as a company limited by guarantee on 8 August 1975, Word's lengthy memorandum of articles stated that one of its purposes was to provide financial support for the missionary work undertaken by Wycliffe Bible Translators (International) (Wycliffe) in developing countries.[56] Established as an incorporated entity,[57] Word paid Wycliffe to carry out Bible translations taught in developing countries.[58] Although the Commissioner of Taxation's (the Commissioner) argument emphasised that Word did not publish translated Bibles or carry out any missionary work, its objectives and activities of profit-generating were not charitable.[59] All the profits earned by Word were given to Wycliffe to enable missionaries to preach the gospel from the translated Bibles.[60] Word, in pursuing its profit-generating purpose, began to accept deposits from the Christian public to be invested at commercial rates of interest in 1996, and from 1996 to 2002, established and operated a for-profit funeral business called Bethel Funerals.[61] The shorthand facts of *Word* offered here are enough to comfortably and objectively conclude that Word was devised for commercial and not charitable purposes, but the High Court thought otherwise.

Word is a case that was not decided by the High Court simply by 'colour-matching' commercial purposes with the limited liability for-profit form. Instead, in deciding whether the profit-making purpose was charitable, the High Court deliberately shaped the profit-making purposes as part of the grand narrative of goodness. There is a worthwhile observation to make that there are two different narratives here, one about good and the other about imperfection emerging from *Word*. Each will be considered in turn. First, the grand narrative of good emerging from the majority decision is seen when contrasted against the Commissioner's argument. From the outset, the hardened tone from the majority in response to the Commissioner's characterisation of Word's money-generating as a purely commercial venture was apparent.

The preoccupation of the Commissioner's argument with form and doctrine is underpinned by the desirability to keep the contours of charity linked to its conceptual essentialism, which was not attuned to the meaning of goodness.[62] For the Commissioner, in the absence of the purpose's 'charitable quality', Word had raptured the grand narrative of goodness by characterising the purpose as one of acts of commerciality.[63] Indeed, this characterisation could be seen as a forceful interpretative act constrained by formalism. The Commissioner's main argument hinged on such a formal constraint, whereby the rules and principles of commercial

[56] *Word* (n 10) [2], [4]. Word was incorporated under Victoria's Companies Act 1961.

[57] ibid [25].

[58] ibid [2]. Whycliffe's missionary activities involved learning the local language to translate the Bible into the respective local language and then teaching people how to read the Bible.

[59] ibid [13].

[60] ibid [3].

[61] ibid [85].

[62] ibid [7], [13], [17], [23], [28], [30] and [37].

[63] ibid [13] and [24].

and trade structures and activities were emphasised. Articulating that Word's for-profit purpose and activities in its simplest form are to be seen as a business in disguise,[64] the Commissioner sought to draw a bright line that delineates acceptable for-profit conduct from charities that exist, as Kirby J noted, only to write cheques.[65] Such an argument presented by the Commissioner is not unsurprising. The simple, coherent argument is largely free from an appraisal of goodness and is rooted in the Commissioner's knowledge of commerciality. Seemingly, the main difficulty that the Commissioner's story was unable to overcome was the majority's mindset in constructing and replicating charity's grand narrative and its halo.

Behind the majority's reasoning lurks the imagery of the halo and a receptiveness to Fullagar J's remarks that a legal charity is dedicated to the desire to do good. The loving affection given to Word's for-profit purpose calls into focus the majority's principled and inner reasoning, as well as imagination. The High Court's affection begins with the refusal to distinguish between the main and other objects. Instead, all Word's purposes are seen as one recognisable group, the advancement of religion.[66] What is ultimately a formal finding, at its basic level, is a manoeuvre which removes the for-profit purpose as an obstacle. The majority's choice to do this illustrates an inner loving affection towards Word's profit-making purpose and activities. Although the High Court does not offer an account of moral discernment, but rather, in terms of familiarity with the specific *Pemsel* purpose of religion the grand narrative of goodness is unmasked. Ultimately, the advantage of this manoeuvre by the High Court silences the active critical mind and, in doing so, the enduring affection towards goodness and the imagery of the halo are seen and perfected. Indeed, while the argument is limited by its reliance on the *Pemsel* religion purpose (which presupposes ideals and conception of the good in Christian morality), it nonetheless serves as clues in tolerating the purpose-centric method and how the jural concept is shaped and reshaped, so as to unite charity with reality (the public). If charity is to be centrally understood through the grand narrative of goodness, then its unity with reality cannot be limited only to text.

Both the majority and Kirby J flag the dangers of relying on Word's written purposes.[67] For the majority, they afforded themselves the freedom (under the veil of judicial discretion) to look 'some distance beyond the expressed objects for the purpose of seeing where they lead'.[68] The freedom to grasp whatever is in the distance, along with impulses of affection as the inner substance of the meaning of charity, is a rather dangerous position for charity law (and this chapter) to occupy. However, the freedom to look far in the distance can be seen as the necessary leap needed to orientate the reshaping of the meaning of charity. Even though

[64] Justice Kirby also held the strong view that Word should be characterised as a business. ibid [169].

[65] ibid [26]–[31]. Kirby J (dissenting), [168].

[66] ibid [19].

[67] Kirby J's decision largely reflects the broad-brush strokes of the Commissioner's argument that Word was a business, not a charity. *Word* (n 10) [163], [180]–[182].

[68] *The Baptist Union of Ireland (Northern) Corporation Limited v The Commissioners of Inland Revenue* [1945] NI 99, 106.

freedom can, in some contexts, enunciate its own demands and energy to cause anarchy,[69] the majority were influential in their constraint. Constraint, according to Murdoch, is having a constructive awareness when exercising affection. Yet, one of the persistent challenges in charity law, as MacDermott J states, is to know when 'to draw the line in the right place and distinguish between what is and what is too remote'.[70] His Honour's appeal for simplicity and principled clarity singles an awareness of constraint, either as the reflexive or deliberate impulse of blinding affection. Indeed, the majority in *Word* may be heavily criticised for perhaps being blinded by too much affection towards purpose over activities, and the line drawn was too remote.[71] Nevertheless, the power of the majority to direct the narrative of goodness to yield the maximum 'natural and probable consequence of the trust'[72] had reached a point in *Word* whereby the characterisation of charity needed legitimacy.

The neutral, not-for-profit rule transforms the majority's inescapable subjective affection for Word's for-profit purpose and activities.[73] Given the general law's claim to rationality, the grand narrative of goodness is invested with the rule's force. Simply put, the lofty, grand narrative of goodness loses some of its altitude. Fading into a neutral rule of law, the majority's affection is constrained without hindering the imagination of the meaning of charity. By invoking the neutral no profit rule, the majority obscurely transforms a stated corporate purpose into directorial power[74] to prioritise profit-making, thereby endorsing Word's purpose to make and retain profits. Thus, the performative core of Word remains intact from the perspective that the director's legal obligation to help Wycliffe and other Christian organisations financially render Word's purposes as a part of reality.

B. How *Word* Anchors the Grand Narrative of Goodness

The majority's favourable outlook of Word's place, in reality, is revealed by reference to time. Living up to the conventions of honesty and fidelity,[75] which, in the

[69] Perhaps some well-deserved criticism is earned here for being rather selective and presumptive in seeing freedom as a complex liberty rather than a simple and uncontroversial principle of autonomy and value favoured by (in the words of Joseph Raz) 'all liberty lovers'. See especially: J Raz, *The Morality of Freedom* (Oxford, OUP, 1988).

[70] *The Baptist Union of Ireland (Northern) Corporation* (n 68).

[71] See especially: A Parachin, 'What Does it Mean to "Act Charitably"? in Daniel Halliday and Matthew Harding (eds), *Charity Law – Exploring the Concept of Public Benefit* (London, Routledge, 2022).

[72] *The Baptist Union of Ireland (Northern) Corporation Limited* (n 68).

[73] *Word* (n 10) [4], [5].

[74] ibid [20]. Here, the majority reads Word's memorandum to have included the Third Schedule of the Companies Act 1961 (Victoria) that allows Word 'to subscribe or guarantee money for charitable or benevolent objects, or for any exhibition, or for any public, general or useful object'. *Word* (n 10) [21].

[75] See especially David Cummings' evidence at [25] and Wycliffe's Mr Wilkerson testimony before the AAT at [43]. The majority opined that while Cummings and Wilkerson's evidence was vague, it was

eyes of the majority, Word has never faulted upon over the number of years Word pursued its purpose,[76] matters. What matters is that by complying with its legal obligation of the no profit rule, Word becomes relatable and better understood as a charity. Of course, it must be observed that the normative concept of non-distribution of profit within the textual openness of charity law imputes a path for tracking legal and moral obligations. For Word, this forensic norm was harnessed by the majority to turn its for-profit purpose and activities into a self-legitimising narrative of goodness.

C. Justice Kirby's Narrative of Imperfection

The second narrative emerging from *Word* is one of imperfection. Kirby J, forthright in his dissent, he made clear that there should be no need for any 'fresh judicial heroism'.[77] In contrast to the majority, his Honour does not bestow any loving affection towards Word's for-profit purpose and activities. Despite this, the obvious concern that Kirby J grappled with was how to speak to religion descriptively and critically. Apprehending religion was filtered and formatted into an institutional arrangement involving taxation and constitutional secularism.[78] On one level, this approach sits above the fray of the grand narrative of goodness. On another level, the formative analysis of Word as an incorporated organisational structure does not wrestle with the complexity of the meaning of charity.[79]

Resisting the choice of engaging in a discourse with the historical roots of charity, Kirby J has a different motivation. In contrast to the majority, his single-minded pursuit of determining if Word was special enough to be granted taxation privileges in legislation, which makes a claim of rationality. Although his Honour shows greater constraint in 'picking up and applying judicial elaborations'[80] of the *Pemsel* concepts, it is important to note that his reasoning can nevertheless be seen to be influenced by the halo and his ideal of goodness: his Honour's comment that his own religious tradition 'is derived from John Wycliffe, the "Morning Star" of the Christian Reformation in England …'[81] Yet, in contrast to the majority, Kirby J is brutal in his assessment of Word. In flagging that some religious institutions 'perform functions that are offensive to beliefs, values and consciences'[78] and liking Word to another 'exempt commercial bodies provide subventions for

a fatal error by the Commissioner to rely on their evidence owing to 'a much more detailed evidentiary inquiry' was needed at the AAT concerning how Wycliffe was spending Word's donated monies. Despite the imprecise evidence before the AAT, the majority was satisfied by Word by clause 4 of the memorandum of articles, which prohibits the payment of income and property to any member of Word. ibid [43], [22].

[76] ibid [28].

[77] ibid [78].

[78] ibid [92]–[94], [112].

[79] ibid [168].

[80] ibid [76].

[81] ibid [124].

overseas televangelists or for overseas madrasas teaching religion to very specialised groups'[79] are insightful hints that Word does not fit within his inner vision of the halo or the grand narrative of goodness.

Strictly understanding Word through its pragmatic value to the Christian public, an organisation that provided investment advice and a commercial funeral business for profit, is seen by Kirby J as a flaw for a charity.[82] His Honour's attention is monopolised by this one flaw. Behind this level of attention lies a fixed and static meaning of charity and a reluctance to subvert the expansion of this jural concept.[83] Indeed, the harder edge in the tone and choices made to exclude a plethora of case law leads to a clear sense of inevitability that Word is an 'unformulated faith'[84] and, therefore, that Kirby J's finding was going to be different to the majority. The obvious lack of loving affection towards Word's for-profit activities, when held up against the majority's enduring affection, creates an intriguing paradox of two visions of charity that never throw off the yoke of the grand narrative of goodness. Subjectivity and autonomy, respectively manifested in the High Court's choices, offer a great deal more than answering the restricted question of who is correct. Instead, *Word* is an unfolding account of multiplicity.

IV. The Art of Doublethink and the Meaning of Charity

Since the meaning of charity is predominantly understood as a consequence-based argument, it is often concerned primarily with the outcome. From the outside, the result gives meaning and understanding to charity. Although the results in charity law are often narrowly defined (it is or not a charity) and although *Word* delivers a legal answer, it forcefully suggests that a comprehensive understanding of charity can be assessed as something other than a good or bad entity. Indeed, a purportedly alternative understanding of *Word* signifies that charity's grand narrative of goodness can be celebrated and contrasted with the values of profit. *Word* paves the way to understanding charity in contradictory ways and believing in both meanings – a development that appears to be an Orwellian in a double sense.

The concept of doublethink in the context of charity law requires a nuanced examination of the court's reasoning in finding the meaning of charity and the modern legal framework that significantly distorts the understanding of a charity. The lucid prose of doublethink from George Orwell's novel *Nineteen Eighty-Four* (published in 1959) is defined to be:

> To know and not to know, to be conscious of complete truthfulness while telling carefully constructed lies, to hold *simultaneously two opinions which cancelled out, knowing them to be contradictory and believing in both of them*; to use logic against logic, to

[82] ibid [177], [124].
[83] ibid [123].
[84] Murdoch (n 46) 74.

> *repudiate morality while laying claim to it*, … to *forget what it was necessary to forget*, then to draw *it back into memory again* at the moment when it was needed, and then promptly to forget it again: and above all, to apply the *same process to the process itself*. That was the ultimate subtlety: consciously to induce unconsciousness and then, once again, to become unconscious of the act of hypnosis you had just performed. Even to understand the word 'doublethink' involved the use of doublethink.[85]

Elements of Orwell's definition have been used to exact themes of contradiction across varying contexts and within a moment of time. Employed as an analytical lens of inquiry across various disciplines, doublethink is used in such a way to frame paradoxical and conceptual tensions that come to signify how different and demanding opposite positions are processed and made sense of.[86] When the concept is applied to charity, doublethink manifests the complex interplay between its grand narrative of goodness and how the public makes sense of charity.

The law has always gone to great lengths to stress the difference between the technical legal understanding and the popular meaning of charity. Popular meanings are acknowledged by courts as entries in English dictionaries, thus overlooking the broader cultural and social treatment and normative activity that informs the general public's understanding of charity. The court's anxiety to separate the two meanings (like anything to do with charity) has also blurred. Despite some thoughts sitting on the fringes that there might not be a semantic distortion of the word charity,[87] Blue J makes clear that 'over time the legal and ordinary meaning of charity have interacted and informed each other'.[88] The rejection of separation invites shared values, attitudes, and expectations about the meaning of charity, which will likely manifest the contradictions in the meaning of charity through its grand narrative of goodness.

Returning briefly (as a reminder) to this chapter's antecedent, charity law today is locked in an ongoing discourse with its historical past, and much of the substantive interest to keep the conversation going promotes a highly idealised version of goodness. If the understanding of charity is to move away from its technical legal meaning, there is the risk that the public will make sense of charity not through text but through its contradictions. Contradictions within the charity sector are plentiful, and the interpretive public will strive hard not to believe in two contradictory meanings at once. Meanwhile, the law, as manifested in *Word*, is rather comfortable with contradictions. For the public, there is likely to

[85] G Orwell, *Nineteen Eighty-Four* (London, Penguin, 1949) 38–39. Emphasis added.

[86] See M Martin, 'Demystifying Doublethink: Self-deception, Truth, and Freedom in 1984' (1984) 10 *Soc Theory & Prac* 319; C Egan-Wyer et al, 'On Startups and Doublethink – Resistance and Conformity in Negotiating the Meaning of Entrepreneurship' (2018) 30 *Entrepreneurship & Regional Development* 58; D Martin-Jones, *Cinema Against Doublethink: Ethical Encounters with the Lost Parts of World History* (New York, Routledge, 2018).

[87] *Central Bayside General Practice Association Limited v Commissioner of State Revenue* (2006) 228 CLR 168, [18]; *Aid/Watch* (n 52) [23]–[24], [65]–[66].

[88] *South Australian Employers' Chamber of Commerce & Industry Incorporated v Commissioner of State Taxation* [2017] SASC 127, [81].

be one principal contradiction that will likely shroud the meaning of charity and that will be through a construct of good versus bad. The public would not be at fault for making sense of charity this way, owing to the consequential-sensitive nature of charity and, moreover, the interlinked context of the grand narrative of goodness with the public. In this context, the grand narrative of goodness also gives charity an identity, and here lies more commotion and danger. When the identity of a charity is tightly bound to the grand narrative of goodness, when a charity no longer plays to the script, and/or when the demand of pure goodness cannot be achieved (like Kirby J's vision of Word), then a charity, therefore, must be bad owing to its contradictions. Of course, this may be held out to be on the extreme side of the meaning argument. Nonetheless, the existence of opposing ideas of good and bad that are bundled up in the meaning of charity allows the law to normalise the imperfect and uncomfortable forces to play with this jural concept.

V. Concluding Thoughts

So, where does this leave us with the meaning of charity? First, there is no hope of emancipating an understanding of charity from the past. Carrying the past into the now, along with judicial efforts to keep the conversation with the past moving forward, does so with contradictory results. Agitation and general discontent around how courts answer whether a purpose is charitable tend to pursue a simple and deductive understanding of the jural concept. The automatic and natural purist of a kernel of logic, in terms of practical reasoning, denies a certain level of curiosity about goodness. When Murdoch refers to seeking an unclouded understanding of reality involving goodness, and a less perfect vision of the virtue is apparent, it offers a starting point to analyse the meaning of charity from inside its narrative.

The analytical temptation to focus on and connect formulaic rules to specific contexts is tied to a particular arrangement rather than a realisation that charity reflects goodness: it too often leads to frustrations and unsatisfying conclusions. One way of understanding the elusive concept of charity is through its narrative of goodness and affection, which will yield some sense of clarity. Indeed, the intersubjective endeavour of goodness by the majority and Kirby J in *Word* does manifest frustration. Still, proponents of different narratives, as illustrated in this Australian case, bemoan the impossibility of perfecting the meaning of charity.

What, finally, then, of the garden of chaos? The garden will always be in a state of disarray owing to hypocrisy and understanding charity in terms of affection in the light of a halo. Those looking into the garden, under the prevailing conditions of mystification, will try to communicate how the art of doublethink is the best way of understanding the meaning of charity. The public's understanding of charity will be scripted by a higher virtue – and be less tolerant towards contradictions. Suppose the public and technical legal meaning of charity is to become closer. Will this bring a sense of order by weeding out those charitable purposes that repudiate the grand narrative of goodness, or will a new season of renewal manifest new contradictions that require pruning to give the garden a semblance of order for the halo to shine – only time will tell.

PART II

Adaption and Tension

7

Discrimination as Detriment

JANE CALDERWOOD NORTON

Sometimes charities cause harm. However, courts and regulators often avoid explicitly engaging with the concept of detriment or harm in charity law. This is despite the public benefit requirement asking the decision-maker to consider not just the benefits of the entity or trust's putative purpose, but any potential detriments or harm. This chapter attempts to unpack the concept of detriment in charity law. It does so by exploring discrimination as a detriment. Put simply, discrimination is treating someone less favourably because of a protected characteristic such as race, sex or sexual orientation.[1]

With the expansion of equality law and changes in societal attitudes towards equality, discriminatory charities have received increased attention in recent years.[2] Charity law has nevertheless 'struggled' with how to respond to discrimination.[3] Judicial efforts to respond to discrimination in a charitable context have exposed the difficulties of aligning existing charity law jurisprudence with these new challenges, and in a manner that is transparent about the value judgements inherent in these decisions. The New Zealand Supreme Court's recent decision in *Family First* – concerning a conservative family values organisation – illustrates these difficulties.[4] Here, the court said that the detriments of the organisation's purposes, which it found to be discriminatory but not illegal, did not outweigh the benefits.

[1] This chapter is concerned with direct discrimination. The complexity of the concept of discrimination is noted below and addressed by others, for example below at n 95.

[2] *Attorney General v Family First New Zealand* [2022] NZSC 80; [2022] 1 NZLR 175 (*Family First*); *R (Cornerstone (North East) Adoption and Fostering Services Ltd) v Ofsted* [2021] EWCA Civ 1390; *R(Z) v Hackney London Borough Council* [2020] UKSC 40, and *LF v United Kingdom* [2022] ECHR (no 19839/21). See also J Sigafoos, 'When should Charities be Allowed to Discriminate? The Case of Single-Sex Services and Transgender People' in J Picton and J Sigafoos (eds), *Debates in Charity Law* (Oxford, Hart Publishing, 2020) and D Morris, 'Charities and the Modern Equality Framework – Heading for a Collision?' (2012) 65 *CLP* 295.

[3] M McGregor-Lowndes, 'Public Benefit and Public Policy: Keeping up with Discrimination?' in M Harding and D Halliday (eds), *Charity Law: Exploring the Concept of Public Benefit* (London, Routledge, 2022) 127. See also A Parachin, 'Why and When Discrimination Is Discordant with Charitable Status: The Problem with "Public Policy", the Possibility of a Better Solution' (2020) 6 *Can J Comp & Contemp L* 305, 309 (where the author notes that '[f]uture legal challenges are coming').

[4] *Family First New Zealand* (n 2).

It went no further, however, to explain why lawful discrimination can nonetheless be seen as a detriment in charity law and, therefore, disqualifying an organisation from charitable status.

The first part of this chapter provides an overview of charity law's approach to discriminatory charities. It explains that contrary to the Court's assertion in *Family First*, such charities are, in fact, commonplace in numerous charity sectors. It does not automatically follow, therefore, that no public benefit can be found whenever there is discrimination. The challenge, then, is how to identify discrimination that is considered detrimental (or harmful), and how to distinguish discriminatory charities that will nonetheless generate net benefit from those charities where the detriment outweighs any benefit. Are there some types of discrimination that charity law ought to consider detrimental, and lacking in public benefit, and some that it should not? And how should the court go about identifying this in a way that is coherent and avoids accusations of ideological bias?

The second part of this chapter explores this question of which discriminatory charities might lack public benefit by considering the detriment or harm associated with discrimination. It identifies two categories of harm. The first category, material harm, is well-known and generally acknowledged. While addressing material harm, this category may be seen primarily as the role of discrimination law;[5] identifying such harm could also be seen as part of assessing public benefit. This allows a distinction to be drawn between those discriminatory dispositions or organisations that should not be granted charitable status and those that should because they seek to alleviate or remedy disadvantage through, for example, affirmative action measures.

The second category of harm associated with discrimination is less considered and more controversial: expressive harm. This is a non-material or intangible harm that could be said to be caused either by the charity itself or by the government granting charitable status to organisations that discriminate. Here, the chapter argues that expressive harm may provide a reason for denying charitable status but that it should be viewed with caution.

I. Charity Law's Approach to Discriminatory Charities

First, a word about the nature of discriminatory charities. Charities might engage in discrimination in a range of ways unrelated to their purposes. Like any other employer, for example, they might discriminate against their workers in their practices. Individual employees might also discriminate when providing goods and services on behalf of the charity. In such instances, discrimination law will apply in the usual way. This chapter is interested in equality or non-discrimination norms

[5] M Harding, *Charity Law and the Liberal State* (Cambridge, CUP, 2014) 207.

operating to prevent charitable status from being granted to organisations that are engaged in otherwise *lawful* discrimination.

Charity law largely focuses on assessing the charitability of purposes, not activities.[6] This chapter is concerned, therefore, with discrimination that constitutes a charity's purpose, not discrimination that may occur in its day-to-day operations.[7] It has been suggested, however, that this focus on purposes means charity law is 'ineffective at dealing with discrimination' where it is the activities that are discriminatory but not the express purposes.[8] This focus can miss the real concern underpinning granting charitable status to certain organisations. After all, discriminatory charities will typically be for recognised and generally stated charitable purposes, such as advancement of education, rather than specifically for the purpose of discriminating against a class of persons.[9]

This chapter, therefore, considers discriminatory charities to include those that discriminate in their stated purposes *or* the projects and activities that constitute their purposes. This can include discrimination in the stipulated conditions on which a person can benefit from the goods and/or services provided by a charity. These conditions may be based on personal characteristics, or elements of human identity, that are protected from discrimination in law, such as race, sex and sexual orientation.[10]

This broader view is needed because few trusts will have explicitly discriminatory purposes. Instead, '[t]he more common problem' will be the discriminatory activities or projects – 'an institution pursues a charitable end but in a discriminatory way'.[11] This approach is also consistent with doctrine. Activities can evidence purposes.[12] They can also determine charitability both pre- and post-registration.[13] Moreover, some charities, such as the advocacy organisations discussed below, will have their activity as their purpose. As we shall see, some judicial approaches

[6] McGregor-Lowndes (n 3) 144.

[7] For a taxonomy of the different ways charities might discriminate, see Morris (n 2). Harding also draws a distinction between discriminatory purposes (which can be the concern of charity law) and discriminatory activities in pursuit of non-discriminatory purposes (which is a matter for non-discrimination law) (n 5) 206–08.

[8] I Murray, 'Charities & Discrimination: Is Charity Law Always a Better Solution than Public Policy?' (2022) 13 *Nonprofit Policy Forum* 141, 143–44.

[9] M Harding, 'Charitable Trusts and Discrimination: Two Themes' (2016) 2 *CJCCL* 227, 246 and 251.

[10] ibid 228. Parachin has called these 'discriminatorily targeted charitable trusts': (n 3) 337. Morris has taken a similar approach: (n 2) 302. See also: Francois du Toit, 'Not-for-profit Organisations and Equality Law' in M Harding (ed), *Research Handbook on Not-For-Profit Law* (Cheltenham, Edward Elgar, 2018) 232.

[11] Parachin (n 3) 324. See also Harding (n 5) 207 ('[d]iscriminatory activities in the pursuit of non-discriminatory purposes').

[12] See: the approach in New Zealand: Charities Act 2005, s 18(3) and *Family First* (n 2) [23]; J Garton, *Public Benefit in Charity Law* (Oxford, OUP, 2013) 87 (a determination of 'demonstrable public benefit … may require consideration not just of an organization's purposes but of the proposed or actual activities carried on by it'). But see: Parachin (n 3) 324 ('charity law does not typically infer purposes from activities except in rare instances').

[13] Sigafoos (n 2) 106–07.

to discriminatory charities, such as the public policy approach, allow courts to 'circumvent' the purposes/activities distinction.[14]

Although discriminatory charities have generated much attention in recent years, largely due to a few high-profile cases involving controversial organisations, discrimination by charities is not new. Some have suggested that, for the most part, 'charity law is enabling and permissive of discrimination'.[15] Given that many charities define the class of the public who can benefit from their purposes by reference to a protected characteristic (such as sex, religion, race or disability) it could even be said that 'discrimination is entrenched in charities'.[16] The concept of 'charity' itself could be seen as 'essentially founded on a legal right to positively discriminate in favour of a sector of the public'.[17] As Lord Sales has explained, 'charities focus on providing for particular groups since that is what motivates private individuals to give money'.[18] At the very least, there is no firm rule against discriminatory charities;[19] common law jurisdictions have always permitted discriminatory gifts and trusts on some grounds.[20] Equality legislation in a range of jurisdictions also anticipates that some charities will discriminate by providing exceptions for them.[21]

Despite this permissiveness and no clear common law rule against discriminatory charities, courts (at least when it comes to testamentary dispositions) have often avoided applying discriminatory conditions through 'tools' such as the

[14] As seen in *Bob Jones University v United States* (1983) 461 US 574 and discussed in Parachin (n 3) 312–13, 325–26 and 331–32.

[15] Murray (n 8) 141.

[16] Sigafoos (n 2) 104. Example: *Re Ramsden Estate* (1996) 139 DLR (4th) 746 (scholarship fund for Protestants upheld as charitable) and *University of Victoria v British Columbia* (AG) [2000] BCJ No 520 (upheld a scholarship for Roman Catholics on the basis that charitable trusts for members of a religion does not violate public policy). Both cases are discussed in A Parachin, 'Public Benefit, Discrimination and the Definition of Charity' in K Barker and D Jensen (eds), *Private Law: Key Encounters with Public Law* (Cambridge, CUP, 2013) 178–79.

[17] K O'Halloran, *Charity Law and Social Inclusion: An International Study* (London, Routledge, 2007) 160.

[18] *R(Z) v Hackney London Borough Council* (n 2) [80].

[19] Writing some decades ago, one writer observed that given the 'conflicting judicial precedent', there is 'no firm basis', under either public policy or the common law public benefit test, for a blanket statement that discriminatory trusts or institutions are non-charitable: M Galston, 'Public Policy Constraints on Charitable Organisations' (1984) 3 *Virginia Tax Rev* 291, 300.

[20] These grounds being sex, nationality, class and religion: M Harding, 'Some Arguments against Discriminatory Gifts and Trusts' (2011) 31 *OJLS* 303, 304–05.

[21] This freedom to discriminate is not unlimited and requires balancing equality objectives with charitable purposes. In the United Kingdom's Equality Act 2010 (s 193(2)), for example, the restriction must be a 'proportionate means of achieving a legitimate aim' or 'for the purpose of preventing or compensating for a disadvantage linked to the protected characteristic'. In addition to the specific exemption for charities, certain charities may also lawfully discriminate under other general exemptions such those for genuine occupational requirements. For a survey of the exemptions for charities across common law jurisdictions, see Garton (n 12) [5.40]. For a discussion of the United Kingdom exemptions, see: Morris (n 2) and Sigafoos (n 2).

cy-près doctrine or the certainty requirement.[22] This, explains Parachin, can have 'an air of artificiality'.[23] Harding has noted the frequency with which the certainty requirement is applied to invalidate discriminatory conditions 'without confronting the question of discrimination head-on'.[24] Some courts have made their reluctance more explicit by saying they will apply the certainty test more rigorously in such cases.[25] However, by using these tools the courts are able to achieve a non-discrimination goal 'stealthily' and without 'supply[ing] a reasonable account of why discriminatory gifts and trusts should be interfered with'.[26] Harding notes that even where judges in England have been willing to vary discriminatory trusts using the doctrine of *cy-près*, they have not done so because of explicit public policy concerns.[27]

In many cases, usually where the charitable trust is created by testamentary disposition, the offending condition is removed by a court at the request of the trustees.[28] Outside of these circumstances, but including where the certainty requirement is met, or the putative charity is not the result of a testamentary dispositions, trusts or organisations with discriminatory conditions or purposes can be denied charitable status on either of two bases. They could be considered to prevent charitable status from the outset because they are against public policy. Alternatively, they could be approached through a public benefit analysis: the detriment they generate could be seen as outweighing any benefit.[29] The distinction between these two bases may not always be clear.

This chapter suggests that the second approach is preferable.[30] Discrimination should be considered as part of the public benefit analysis because it allows for the reasoning to be transparent and for non-detrimental (or beneficial) discrimination

[22] Harding (n 20) 307–10 (the tools Harding refers to here are the certainty requirement and invalidating dispositions and conditions on the grounds of the public policy). See for example, *Re Lysaght* [1966] Ch 191 where the settlor had attached the 'deplorable' condition excluding Roman Catholic and Jewish students from the scholarship. The court found that racial or religious discrimination did not violate public policy and therefore was not sufficient, in itself, to invalidate the trust. The *cy-près* doctrine was applied to remove the condition when the trustees refused the gift because of it. See also use of *cy-près* in *Re Dominion Student's Hall Trust* [1947] Ch 183 and *Re Mere's Will Trust* (1957) *The Times* (4 May 1957) discussed in Harding (n 20) 305–06. More recently see *Re Canada Trust Co v Ontario Human Rights Commission* (1990) 69 DLR (4th) 321 (cf: *Kay v South Eastern Sydney Area Health* [2003] NSWSC 292 where the court said, at [18], that 'testators can be as capricious as they like and … if they wish to benefit a charity in respect of … a discriminatory group, they are at liberty to do so'). For a similar observation in the United States context. See: S Swanson, 'Discriminatory Charitable Trusts: Time for a Legislative Solution' (1986) 48 *U Pitt L Rev* 153, 158.

[23] Parachin (n 16) 175.

[24] Harding (n 20) 308.

[25] ibid.

[26] ibid 309–10.

[27] Harding (n 9) 230.

[28] Morris has also suggested that equality legislation would now typically deal with many of the cases that previously were addressed through the common law *cy-près* doctrine: (n 2) 309.

[29] McGregor-Lowndes (n 3) 128.

[30] Harding has also discussed the strengths of this approach: (n 5) 239.

to be recognised. Regardless of which approach is adopted, however, the detriment of discrimination needs to be confronted.

A. Public Policy

A public policy approach to discriminatory charities arises from a 'long-established tradition' of invalidating dispositions and trust conditions beyond the charity context.[31] Instances where discriminatory dispositions have been invalidated, or the operation of a trust thwarted, on public policy grounds are nonetheless rare.

What constitutes a public policy exclusion from charitable status is unclear. The difficulty is exacerbated in part because public policy 'changes over time'.[32] It has been described as 'a vague and malleable concept'[33] and 'shorthand for "noncharitable for inarticulate reasons"'.[34] Parachin has suggested that courts use public policy in cases where 'they instinctively perceive a discordance with charitable status … but struggle to articulate that intuition using the usual frames of reference employed in charity law'.[35]

At the very least, a public policy approach denies charitable status where purposes are seen as harmful, or otherwise contrary, to the public good. Then the question arises as to what purposes are considered so harmful that they are contrary to the public good. This does not require that the purpose is illegal. That would be a 'relatively simple' basis for invalidating a trust.[36] Rather, the question for this chapter is whether those purposes that are prima facie lawful but nonetheless inconsistent with constitutional values, such as those that are discriminatory, are contrary to public policy.

In *Family First*, where it was found that even lawful discrimination was a reason for declining charitable status, the New Zealand Supreme Court appears to take a public policy approach. In its assessment under the fourth head of charity (other purposes beneficial to the community) – which is where this issue is most likely to arise – the Court stated that a purpose to discriminate or one that includes discriminatory elements (which is what it held Family First's object of supporting the traditional family and marriage was) could not be compatible with a charitable purpose.[37]

Canada has taken a similar approach. In *Re Canada Trust Co v Ontario Human Rights Commission*,[38] the settlor's express belief in the superiority of the white

[31] Harding (n 20) 310.
[32] Swanson (n 22) 159.
[33] J Colliton, 'Race and Sex Discrimination in Charitable Trusts' (2003) 12 *Cornell J L & Pub Pol'y* 275, 297.
[34] Parachin (n 3) 307.
[35] ibid.
[36] Swanson (n 22) 159.
[37] *Family First* (n 2) [139].
[38] (1990) 69 DLR (4th) 321.

race, of British nationality, and of the Christian Protestant religion meant he had excluded people who fell outside these classes from managing or benefitting from the trust. The Court found that the trust was premised on notions of racism and religious superiority that were 'patently at variance with the democratic principles governing our pluralistic society' and offensive to 'fair-minded citizens'.[39] As such, it contravened contemporary public policy. The Court applied the *cy-près* doctrine to remove these restrictions and allow the trust to continue.

Canada Trust shows how constitutional values, such as non-discrimination, can 'give content' to the general proposition that dispositions that contravene public policy will be invalid.[40] Some have gone further to argue that it is not just public policy that demands consistency with constitutional values but the *public nature* of a charitable trust 'attracts the requirement that it conform to the public policy against discrimination'.[41] Another author has asserted that 'the very nature of charitable trusts is public' and this means '[t]heir purpose is to accomplish public goals'.[42] Charity law's notion of public benefit is seen as constraining a settlor's freedom to apply their property 'inconsistent with [constitutional] values'.[43]

The claim that charities are somehow public – such that they must advance public policy or accomplish public goal – is highly contentious. Parachin says this misunderstands charity law's internal notion of public benefit where the public aspect is concerned with that which is universal and impersonal, not 'the public' as conceived by public law.[44] Chan has made a similar observation: the public nature of charities means they are concerned with altruistic, rather than self-regarding, projects directed at 'doing good works for strangers' who are 'remote in our affections [and] to whom we are not otherwise obligated'.[45]

This debate cannot be fully addressed here but, at the very least, case law indicates that a blanket statement (such as was made by the New Zealand Supreme Court) that lawful discriminatory purposes are not compatible with charitable purpose must surely be incorrect given charity law's acceptance of some discriminatory trusts. Many existing charities, particularly religious charities, also have viewpoints identical to those of Family First, although advancing these viewpoints are typically not their charitable purpose.[46] At the very least, as Parachin has explained, it cannot be assumed that charity law's public benefit requirement

[39] ibid [39].

[40] L Weinrib and E Weinrib, 'Constitutional Values and Private Law in Canada' in Daphne Barak-Erez and Daniel Friedmann (eds), *Constitutional Rights in Private Law* (Oxford, Hart Publishing, 2002) 64.

[41] ibid 67. See also Colliton (n 33) 292 (arguing that '[c]haritable trusts are public entities by their very nature' and this is why they should not be permitted to discriminate).

[42] Colliton (n 33) 304.

[43] Weinrib and Weinrib (n 40) 68.

[44] Parachin (n 16) 183–84.

[45] K Chan, 'Not-For-Profit Organizations, Public Law and Private law' in Harding (n 10) 223 (citing the Ontario Law Reform Commission).

[46] See also Parachin (n 16) 200 ('religious charities may … teach doctrines or engage in practices that seem inconsistent … with conceptions of equality reflected in public law'). See also: E Volokh, 'Freedom of Expressive Association and Government Subsidies' (2006) 58 *Stan L Rev* 1919, 1921.

and public law's equality norms have an 'innate and obvious compatibility'.[47] Even if charity law might have 'moved in the direction of a more restrictive approach', there is no 'categorical rule' that prohibits discriminatory charitable trusts.[48]

While it may be a mistake to think that charity law and public law (specifically constitutional values) naturally cohere,[49] is there an argument for saying that public policy *ought* to prohibit discriminatory charitable trusts? While public policy exclusion is a relatively straightforward way of declining charitable status for clearly harmful purposes, for example, where the discrimination is unlawful, it is less suited to cases where the discrimination is lawful or entails benefits for one class of beneficiaries based on a discriminatory condition. Affirmative action measures such as prizes and scholarships for people from particular nationalities, races or sex, for example can be considered to generate public benefit despite being formally discriminatory. Many religious charities also entail discrimination, either through their membership restrictions or their activities (including the provision of goods, facilities or services and access to premises).[50] Moreover, cases where the sole purpose of the putative charity is to discriminate, without any benefit generated, will be rare. More often, some benefit will be sought by the discrimination.

In addition to discriminatory charities not always generating detriment, 'vague references to public policy' do not provide clear guidance about how to resolve potential conflicts between the autonomy preferences of the settlor and any interest in non-discrimination.[51] One author has said that a public policy determination can 'come down to the emotional feel and impression of each case' with discriminatory trusts invalidated 'based on the impression that enforcement of these trusts is just not the right thing to do'.[52] Another has said it 'is undisciplined, establishes little to no transferable principles to guide future decisions'.[53]

The difficulty with the public policy exclusion approach is also not just that it does not reflect the general approach to discriminatory charities or provide clear guidance, but that it avoids transparency about the detriment (or harm) posed by discrimination. It does this by circumventing the public benefit analysis entirely.[54] This risks ideological commitments masquerading as objective analysis. For Parachin, the use of public policy exclusions 'masks the true calculus going on behind the scenes and, inasmuch as it channels into charity law constitutional principles intended to restrain government action, risks moulding charities into the image of the ideal liberal state'.[55] As such, public policy should be 'a doctrine of

[47] Parachin (n 16) 173.
[48] ibid 174. In the United States, the approach to discriminatory trusts has also been described as 'fragmented and inconsistent': Colliton (n 33).
[49] Parachin (n 10) 183–84.
[50] See generally J Calderwood Norton, *Freedom of Religious Organizations* (Oxford, OUP, 2016).
[51] Murray (n 8) 141.
[52] Colliton (n 33) 299.
[53] Parachin (n 3) 308.
[54] Harding (n 5) 32.
[55] Parachin (n 3) 308.

absolute last resort' and a 'fail-safe for extreme circumstances' that cannot be dealt with using 'charity law's traditional doctrinal tools'.[56]

This next section will suggest that a public benefit approach – one that weighs the benefits and detriments of the discriminatory purposes as part of the usual assessment of charitability – is a more transparent approach to discriminatory charities, and better able to address the concerns regarding these charities. Unlike the public policy approach, however, this approach will require identifying the detriment associated with discrimination.

B. Assessing Public Benefit

The second approach to discriminatory charities assesses them through a public benefit analysis: weighing any detriment they generate against any benefit. Public policy could then be left to 'extreme circumstances'.[57]

While a public benefit analysis will have 'a more significant role'[58] when considering discriminatory charities under the fourth head of charity, it is arguably preferrable to a public policy approach because it enables more transparent reasoning.[59] It is also 'nuanced'[60] and 'contextual',[61] rather than operating as a blanket exclusion, and this allows for discriminatory trusts that generate benefit. After all, as Tarnopolsky JA explained in his concurring judgment in *Canada Trust*, some discriminatory charitable trusts are aimed at the amelioration of inequality and, therefore, 'promote, rather than impede, the public policy of equality'.[62] This could be described as 'discriminating *for* someone … rather than *against* them'.[63] It does not automatically follow, therefore, that no public benefit can be found whenever there is discrimination.

A strength of the public benefit approach to discriminatory trusts is that it 'contains resources' that may assist judges in their reasoning about the charitable status of discriminatory trusts.[64] The 'public' aspect of the assessment – and its 'stranger' requirement – could be said to be concerned with 'cultivating and

[56] ibid.

[57] A Parachin, 'What Does It Mean to "Act Charitably"? Revisiting the Purposes and Activities Distinction in Charity Law' in Harding and Halliday (eds) (n 3) 41. For example, cases of illegality or clear violations of the public interest could be disallowed using a public policy rationale. Some have suggested that a purpose that 'offends a fundamental community moral value' could also be violations of public policy: McGregor-Lowndes (n 3) 128. Appeals to morality, given their inability to be assessed empirically, have been viewed with scepticism by the courts: *National Anti-Vivisection Society v IRC* [1947] UKHL 4; [1948] AC 31.

[58] GE Dal Pont, 'Charity Law: "No Magic in Words"?' in M Harding, A O'Connell, and M Stewart (eds), *Not-For-Profit Law: Theoretical and Comparative Perspectives* (Cambridge, CUP, 2014) 105.

[59] See also Harding (n 5) 239.

[60] Harding (n 9) 249.

[61] Parachin (n 3) 333.

[62] *Canada Trust* (n 38) [104].

[63] Sigafoos (n 2) 104.

[64] Harding (n 9) 250.

promoting the belief that "others" are equal and worthy … advanc[ing] an inclusive principle of acceptance'. This still allows charitable trusts to be aimed at a narrow class of strangers (rather than all) but excludes charitable giving that 'discernibly manifests stigmatizing rejection' because it undermines inclusivity and 'the "equal worth" ethic implicit in the stranger requirement'.[65]

The 'benefit' aspect of this assessment is also helpful when considering discriminatory charities. It asks a court to assess whether the charity 'stand[s] to benefit people, as opposed to causing detriment … or having no discernible welfare implications'.[66] Included in this assessment, says Harding, could be the 'social effects of carrying out the particular purposes' and not just the purpose as generally framed.[67] He identifies two categories of effects: the direct social effects – where the purpose of the trust causes an immediate discriminatory outcomes – and indirect social effects where carrying out the purpose of the trust 'may express attitudes and beliefs about certain identity-based groups that demand members of groups'. These 'expressive effects might be felt in public culture' regardless of the impact on those directly affected.[68] In this way, charity law could be said to 'suppl[y] courts with the means through which equality-orientated considerations may (or just as easily may not)' inform any charitable status determination.[69] These expressive effects are discussed further below.

Despite the central role that the notion of public benefit plays in determining charitable status generally, Harding notes that it 'is hardly ever deployed in judicial responses to discriminatory charitable trusts'. Rather, 'invocation of … public policy is the norm' in the rare instances where these cases arise.[70] Moreover, even where the courts enlist this approach, they are more likely to find *lack of benefit* rather than identifying the detriment that discrimination entails. The applicant's failure to show how their purpose is beneficial then becomes the focus of the decision rather than the harm that might be caused by that purpose.

The *Family First* decision is again illustrative. In addition to the public policy blanket exclusion, the Supreme Court also seemed to take this second approach to discriminatory purposes and assessed them according to whether they generated public benefit. Family First's purposes were seen as discriminatory because, in pursuing support for the traditional family, it also advocated for measures that disadvantaged others.[71] These discriminatory purposes were not self-evidentially beneficial, and nor could Family First establish a benefit, or show that these

[65] Parachin (n 3) 340–41.
[66] Harding (n 9) 250.
[67] Harding (n 9). He references the example given by Lord Rigby in *Re Macduff* [1896] 2 Ch 451 that teaching the art of theft may be within the general purpose of education but nonetheless have 'undesirable social effects' and, therefore, lack benefit (at 252). Under the fourth head, this examination of social benefit is more apparent because these purposes are not seen as prima facie charitable (at 253).
[68] Harding (n 9) 254.
[69] Parachin (n 16) 205.
[70] Harding (n 9) 249.
[71] *Family First* (n 2) [136]–[137].

benefits weighed against any detriments.[72] This is interesting phrasing: rather than its purposes being detrimental, Family First could not establish a benefit. While the Supreme Court does say any benefits must be weighed against any detrimental effects, and that it is 'highly debatable' whether the benefits outweigh the detriments in this case, it does not say what constitutes detriment.[73] This decision also raises difficult questions around whether organisations with certain values will attract charitable status whereas others will not. The Supreme Court rejected that suggestion,[74] but if some discrimination is to be seen as harmful and some not, content-based assessment by the court may be unavoidable. Again, this requires identifying the detriment of discrimination.

A further example of the decision-maker (in this case the Upper Tribunal) avoiding evaluating net benefit (and, therefore, also detriment) occurred in *Independent Schools Council v Charity Commission*.[75] While this case did not concern discrimination, it involved a similarly controversial topic: fee paying schools. The Tribunal was prepared to find that there was a benefit in the provision of education but was uncomfortable with 'carry[ing] out what is an essentially political exercise' to determine whether (as suggested by the intervenor) fee-paying education generated disbenefits by being socially divisive and harmful to social mobility.[76] Such matters required a political rather than judicial resolution.[77] Any disbenefits or detriments were not recognised let alone considered.

A final example is the *Catholic Care* litigation.[78] The High Court in *Catholic Care (Diocese of Leeds) v the Charity Commission for England and Wales* stated that charitable status will only be granted if, having 'tak[en] into account any dis-benefits … its activities nonetheless yield a net public benefit'. In this case, a 'large public dis-benefit' was 'likely to flow from any unjustified, and therefore discriminatory treatment'.[79] Rather than engaging with the common law notion of public benefit, the High Court focused on statutory discrimination law and the parameters of the exemption for charities using the proportionality principle.[80] An alternative analysis could see the discrimination as causing a detriment that was not outweighed by any benefit generated (an analysis that is not inconsistent with proportionality reasoning).

[72] ibid [135] and [138]–[140].

[73] A similar approach was taken by the New Zealand Charity Commission in *Registration Decision: Exodus Ministry Trust Board* (18 August 2010) when it did not explicitly identify the harm caused by conversion therapy. Rather, it said it was unable to determine whether the purpose was beneficial (at [49]).

[74] *Family First* (n 2) [153].

[75] [2011] UKUT 421 (TCC); [2012] Ch 214.

[76] ibid [96].

[77] ibid 109.

[78] Nine decisions have arisen from this litigation, most notably *Catholic Care (Diocese of Leeds) v Charity Commission for England and Wales* [2010] EWHC 520 (Ch), [2010] PTSR 1074 and *Catholic Care (Diocese of Leeds) v Charity Commission for England and Wales* [2012] UKUT 395 (TCC).

[79] [2010] EWHC 520 (HC) [97]–[99].

[80] McGregor-Lowndes (n 3) 134.

II. Identifying the Detriment in a Public Benefit Analysis

If there is no necessary exclusion of discriminatory organisations or purposes in charity law, the challenge then is how to identify those that should receive charitable status from those that should not. It has been suggested that a public benefit analysis can provide the tools to make this distinction. A public benefit analysis requires considering the detriment or harm associated with discrimination by charities. After all, the public benefit requirement is meant to 'ensure charity status is conferred on entities that assist the community and do not … harm society'.[81] The courts have been clear that 'a trust injurious to society will not meet the standard [of benefit]'.[82]

As has been explained, however, the courts have mostly avoided identifying this detriment. Instead, they refer to lacking value or generating disbenefit.[83] This approach can enable the decision-maker to avoid passing value judgement on controversial purposes.[84] However, as with the public policy approach, it can also prevent a decision-maker from coherently and transparently identifying discrimination that causes harm.

Addressing the harm associated with discrimination may be seen as primarily the role of discrimination law.[85] Some have even warned against charity law evolving to focus on 'that for which it was not intended and is not suited', namely promoting equality and eliminating discrimination.[86] This is because charity law's function could be said to be 'facilitative': enabling and encouraging philanthropic and altruistic voluntary association' whereas anti-discrimination law is seen as 'non-facilitative (ie, constraining)'. As such, 'develop[ing] a facilitative body of law into a constraining body of law' faces 'significant challenges'.[87]

However, charity law does not need to evolve into a branch of discrimination law to respond to concerns underpinning discrimination protections. Identifying the disadvantage caused by discrimination could also be seen as part of identifying the detriment associated with discriminatory purposes and, therefore, whether they generate the public benefit necessary for charitable status (or not). It would enable the decision-maker to identify organisations and purposes that generate

[81] ibid 128.

[82] *National Anti-Vivisection Society* (n 57) 69.

[83] A possible exception is *National Anti-Vivisection Society* (n 57) where the society, whose main object was found to be the total abolition of vivisection, was denied charitable status because its object was detrimental to the public benefit because of the detriment to science and medicine if vivisection was prohibited.

[84] I have discussed this in more detail in J Calderwood Norton, 'Weighing Benefits and Detriments in the Law of Charities' in Harding and Halliday (eds) (n 3).

[85] Harding (n 5) 207. Eliminating discrimination has also been described as a 'public welfare goal … largely external to the charity law tradition': K Chan, *The Public-Private Nature of Charity Law* (London, Bloomsbury, 2016) 66.

[86] M Turnover and E Shalders, 'Commentary on Public Benefit and Public Policy: Keeping up with Discrimination?' in Harding and Halliday (eds) (n 3) 153.

[87] ibid.

public benefit and those that do not. This requires decision-makers to be explicit about the detriment associated with discrimination. Moreover, if some organisations are going to be excluded from charitable status, and risk accusations of ideological bias, 'decision-makers should reason carefully about *why* discriminatory purposes occasion detriments … and not simply assert that they do'.[88]

The claim that discriminatory charities cause harm also requires proof. The courts have been clear that if alleged disadvantages (and benefits) are to be given weight in a public benefit assessment, they need to be 'clearly demonstrated' through evidence.[89] This is the case even if it might be 'a considerable burden' for those who seek to challenge charitable status of allegedly harmful charities.[90]

However, identifying the harm of discrimination is not straightforward. As Gardner has explained, if we view discrimination as harmful, 'explain[ing] what the harm in question actually *is*' is 'a seriously obstacle'.[91] Moreover, harm has an 'overarching dependence … upon social context'; it cannot be defined in the abstract.[92] Not all discrimination is harmful – it can be benign[93] – and not all detriment is a harm that should be recognised by law.[94]

So, what could be said to be the detriment associated with discrimination for the purposes of charity law? The 'wrong' of discrimination has been extensively canvassed by others.[95] Even the meaning of the concept itself – regardless of its associated harm – generates 'considerable debate' and a 'sometimes bewildering range of legal material'.[96] Discrimination can include treatment that renders an individual worse off (which is seen as different from not providing a benefit) and that which causes them to 'be in a harmful condition' or suffer a 'bad situation … regardless of whether [they] are rendered worse off overall'.[97] A harmful condition can include refusal of a benefit, psychological harm, or harm to dignity by treating someone 'as unworthy of basic human respect … insult[ing] her

[88] Harding (n 5) 240.

[89] *Independent Schools* (n 75) [106] and Garton (n 12) 93 and [4.08].

[90] *Independent Schools* (n 75) [106].

[91] J Gardner, 'Liberals and Unlawful Discrimination' (1989) 9 *OJLS* 1, 5.

[92] ibid 8. Here Gardner is discussing liberalism's harm principle. Harm in this chapter means any detriment that might flow from a putative charitable purpose. Harm in the context of charity law may not necessarily justify state-imposed restrictions of liberty for the purposes of liberalism's harm principle.

[93] R Arneson, 'Discrimination and Harm' in K Lippert-Rasmussen (ed), *Routledge Handbook of the Ethics of Discrimination* (London, Routledge, 2018) 151.

[94] Gardner (n 91) 6.

[95] For an overview see Arneson (n 93). See also: Gardner (n 91) and D Réaume, 'Harm and Fault in Discrimination Law' (2001) 2 *Theoretical Inquiries in Law* 349; L Alexander, 'What Makes Wrongful Discrimination Wrong? Biases, Preferences, Stereotypes, and Proxies' (1992) 141 *Uni of Penn LR* 194; D Hellman, *When is Discrimination Wrong* (Cambridge, CUP, 2010); and S Moreau, *Faces of Inequality: What A Theory of Wrongful Discrimination* (Oxford, OUP, 2020). For a range of perspectives on discrimination law's theoretical foundations, see: D Hellman and S Moreau (eds), *Philosophical Foundations of Discrimination Law* (Oxford, OUP, 2013) and Lippert-Rasmussen (ed) (n 93).

[96] C McCrudden, *Buying Social Justice: Equality, Government Procurement & Legal Change* (Oxford, OUP, 2007) 512–13.

[97] Arneson (n 93) 153.

humanity … mak[ing her] the target of ridicule and abus[ing] an aspect of her identity in which she is entitled to take pride'.[98] The moral wrongfulness of discrimination could also be seen as 'primarily a problem of distributive justice or primarily a problem of relational inequality'.[99] The former is focused on harm to a people's well-being, whereas the latter focuses on a failure to relate to others in the right way (for example, through engaging in acts that are disrespectful or demeaning acts).[100] One's view of the purpose of discrimination law will depend on one's view of the wrongfulness of discrimination. In short, it could be said that a singular 'plausible, reasonably uncontroversial, normative foundation' for discrimination law has eluded scholars. Instead, it could be said to based 'on multiple foundations' – egalitarian, liberal, and dignitarian – all of which are important.[101]

These debates are for others. What I am attempting to do in this chapter is see whether some of these arguments can apply in the charity law context to identify the detriment relevant to any charitable status determination. This chapter identifies two categories of harm as most relevant to charity law: material harm and expressive harm. The first category is relatively uncontroversial; the second category is novel. Consideration of both these harms may enable us to distinguish between those discriminatory charities that provide public benefit – and therefore ought to be granted charitable status – and those that do not.

A. Material Harm

Charities generally must comply with discrimination law in their employment practices, access to premises, and delivery of goods and services.[102] However, they would not typically lose charitable status because of discrete instances of unlawful discriminatory practices. In such instances, discrimination law would apply to address any harm. By contrast, charitable purposes that discriminate (for example, by limiting who can benefit according to a protected characteristic) could cause material disadvantage and this could be a reason for denying charitable status.

The interrelated material, socio-cultural, and political disadvantages (detriments) associated with discrimination are well-known and have been recounted in detail by others.[103] Khaitan, for example, explains that '[s]ocio-cultural disadvantage is … the prevalence of prejudice against and (certain)

[98] Reaume (n 95) 361.

[99] S Moreau, 'Equality and Discrimination' in J Tasioulas (ed), *The Cambridge Companion to the Philosophy of Law* (Cambridge, CUP, 2020) 177.

[100] ibid.

[101] T Khaitan, *A Theory of Discrimination Law* (Oxford, OUP, 2015) 8. See also M Foran, 'Grounding Unlawful Discrimination' (2022) 28 *Legal Theory* 3, 5.

[102] Morris (n 2) 300.

[103] Khaitan (n 101) 51–56. This chapter just uses the term material disadvantage because that is what is most relevant to charities, and because the term encompasses the full breadth of tangible harm in contrast to the expressive harm discussed below.

stereotypical assumptions about the members of a group' such as that they are judged less worthy than others.[104] These socio-cultural disadvantages can then easily lead to political and material disadvantages.[105] Material disadvantage occurs when a person is prevented from 'securely accessing … goods necessary to live a good life' such as education and health that are available to others.[106] According to Raz, '[d]epriving a person of opportunities or of the ability to use them is a way of causing him harm'.[107] Writing in the charity law context and basing his concerns on the value of autonomy expounded by Raz, Harding has explained how discrimination can limit or interfere with the adequate range of options individuals need to shape their lives.[108] Due to this concern for material harm, discrimination law aims to ensure everyone has 'equal access to … basic social institutions' provided not only by the state but by those with power over people's access to these institutions.[109]

For the most part, it is relatively easy for charity law to deal with instances where a discriminatory purpose would cause material harm. This will typically be addressed by discrimination legislation. Material disadvantage could also be an easily recognisable detriment for the purpose of any public benefit analysis. Charities should not be exacerbating this material disadvantage. However, despite the argument that preventing discrimination is the role of discrimination law and not charity law, charities can also play a role in reducing these advantage gaps where the goods and services they provide are needed to live a good life. While this could be an argument against permitting discriminatory charities, given that charity law protects 'the ability of individuals to formulate their own benevolent projects', and that charitable benefits do not need to be available to all,[110] it is difficult to make the case that excluding an individual from these benefits would harm their ability to live a good life such that these charities should be prohibited over and above the application of general discrimination law. Unlike the government, charities do not need to be concerned with the interests of the whole political community but 'may legitimately focus on the needs of a community defined by geography, religion, or a particular affiliation'.[111]

Where this focus on the material detriment of discrimination is most useful in charity law is where it allows us to distinguish between those discriminatory charities that should be granted charitable status and those that should not. If we take a material harm approach to detriment, affirmative action measures could be said not to entail this detriment as they are orientated towards remedying

[104] ibid 53.
[105] ibid 54.
[106] ibid 54; See also Moreau (n 99) 175.
[107] J Raz, *The Morality of Freedom* (Oxford, OUP 1986) 413.
[108] Harding (n 5) 227.
[109] Moreau (n 99) 172.
[110] Chan (n 85) 75.
[111] ibid 77–78.

these disadvantages.[112] Equal treatment may mean 'providing different or special treatment … discrimination may bring with it public benefit, when it is necessary to overcome some disadvantage or social exclusion'.[113] This contrasts with those purposes that aim to perpetuate this disadvantage. For example, Family First sought to taking rights away from certain groups of people and limit their access to a range of legal and economic benefits.

The more challenging cases are where the discrimination is associated with a charitable purpose – or entails benefits – that itself may attract human rights protection such as charities for the advancement of religion that help to give effect to religious freedom.[114] Here it could be argued that the concerns underpinning those protections – or the value placed on these goods – do not extend to granting charitable status to organisations that may perpetuate disadvantage. This will require a difficult balancing exercise.

B. Expressive Harm of Discrimination

The second type of harm associated with discrimination is less considered and more controversial: expressive harm. This is a non-material or intangible harm. Can charities or, alternatively, government association with a charity, cause expressive harm and should this be considered a detriment in any public benefit analysis? This matters because some discriminatory charitable trusts that might be granted charitable status due to the net benefit they generate (despite entailing some material detriment) might not receive this status if an expressivist view is taken.

Two expressive wrongs[115] could potentially arise with discriminatory charities: the first is the expressive wrong that occurs when an organisation discriminates or expounds discriminatory views (and they may expound these regardless of charitable status, but charitable status may give them additional funding streams and credibility to do so). The second expressive wrong could be that caused when government grants charitable status to these same organisations. With this second expressive wrong, the argument is that charitable status gives these views the

[112] *Canada Trust* (n 38) [97]–[98] (concurring judgment of Tarnopolsky JA). See also: Colliton (n 33) 297 ('trusts discriminating in favour of traditionally disadvantaged groups may be justified as attempts to rectify past discrimination or to correct economic and opportunity imbalances').

[113] Morris (n 2) 303.

[114] I have discussed this elsewhere: *Freedom of Religious Organisations* (n 50). For a discussion of freedom of association as a shield to be used by discriminatory charities against attempts to revoke tax-exempt status on public policy grounds, see D Brennen, 'Charities and the Constitution: Evaluating the Role of Constitutional Principles in Determining the Scope of Tax Law's Public Policy Limitation for Charities' (2002) 5 *Florida Tax Review* 779, 831–44.

[115] Philosophers tend to distinguish between harm (which makes someone worse off or has other adverse consequences) and wrongs (where something can be wrong without causing harm). To the extent that we understand expressive concerns to be non-consequentialist, some have suggested that 'problematic' expression is more aptly termed an expressive *wrong* rather than an expressive *harm*: K Voight, 'Relational equality and the expressive dimension of state action' (2018) 44 *Social Theory and Practice* 437, 446. 441. This chapter uses the term 'wrong' to include harm.

moral imprimatur of state support – it confers 'legitimacy'[116] – and this causes harm that would not be caused if the expression were that of a private individual or organisation.

i. *What is Expressive Harm?*

The expressivist notion of law arises predominantly from North American case law and literature, and typically in the constitutional rights context.[117] The general idea is that when the state acts (or not) it 'will inevitably express messages'.[118] All of us, including the state, 'are required to express the right attitudes towards people'.[119] In a liberal democracy, these attitudes come from 'the values that inform [our] constitutional order, such as the principles that political liberalism require or that specific constitutional provisions guarantee'.[120] Adopting Dworkin's principle, this means that 'state action must express "equal concern and respect" for all persons' regardless of their racial, ethnic, and religious differences.[121] A state can, therefore, 'injure citizens through … law or government conduct' that does not express this principle 'even where immediate material or otherwise intangible burdens are absent'.[122]

Expressive harm occurs, therefore, because a person 'is treated according to principles that express negative or inappropriate attitudes towards her'.[123] This 'bad' attitude can even be expressed negligently, inconsiderately, or recklessly and can cause expressive harm unintentionally.[124] Expressive harms 'are not tied to material injuries specific individuals'[125] and differ from 'nonexpressive harms to their material and liberty interests, their psyches, and their social reputations'.[126] These non-expressive or tangible harms can accompany this expressive harm but need not.[127] While the concern is not with material wellbeing – and instead with

[116] O'Halloran (n 17) 126.
[117] E Anderson and R Pildes, 'Expressive Theories of Law: A General Restatement' (2000) 148 *U Penn L R* 1503. See also: D Hellman, 'The Expressive Dimension of Equal Protection' (2000–01) 85 *Minn L R* 6 and C Sunstein, 'On the Expressive Function of Law' (1996) 144 *U Penn L R* 2021. For a critique of this approach and that of others see: M Adler, 'Expressive Theories of Law: A Skeptical Overview' (2000) 148 *U Penn L R* 1363.
[118] C Brettschneider, 'When the State Speaks, What Should it Say? The Dilemmas of Freedom of Expression and Democratic Persuasion' (2008) 6 *Perspectives on Politics* 1005, 1009.
[119] Anderson and Pildes (n 117) 1514.
[120] ibid 1570.
[121] ibid 1520.
[122] R Levy, 'Expressive Harms and the Strands of Charter Equality: Drawing Out Parallel Coherent Approaches to Discrimination' (2002) 40 *Alberta L R* 393, 394.
[123] Anderson and Pildes (n 117) 1527.
[124] ibid 1529.
[125] ibid 1539.
[126] ibid 1530.
[127] Khaitan (n 101) 149 (giving the example of a national census which does not allow an atheist to self-identify as such under the religion column; or a state which provides all the material benefits of marriage to same-sex couples but describes their relationship as a 'civil partnership').

acting on a bad or unjustified attitude – expressive acts can also cause or worsen disadvantages by endorsing existing prejudices and harmful stereotypes.[128]

An expressive theory of law considers, therefore, the attitudes or messages that implicit in, and expressed by, state action.[129] In the context of rights jurisprudence in the United States of America, for example, an expressivist explanation for the Establishment Clause prohibition on displaying a cross in a public school classroom is that it avoids sending the message that the state endorses Christianity. This is a different concern from one based on how displaying the cross affects the interests of individual students.[130] Anti-discrimination law could be seen as 'express[ing] disapproval of the inegalitarian treatment of citizens'.[131] On Anderson and Pildes' account, all state action – not just the passing of legislation – must express 'equal concern and respect' for all individuals and therefore 'avoid actions that express the view that some individuals have lesser status when it comes to community membership'.[132] Expressive theories of law based on this egalitarian commitment 'seek to identify the expressive content of particular policies' and then assess whether it is 'consistent with a view of all individuals as equals and the idea of an inclusive, egalitarian community'.[133]

Under most expressivist accounts the consequences or substantive harm caused by the expressive dimension of state action, while important, is not the primary concern.[134] Rather, actions (such as policy and laws) are evaluated 'according to how well they express attitudes we ought to have towards people'.[135] Harm can, therefore, be 'inherent in the principle on which the laws are enacted'.[136] For example, if they are 'adopted out of contempt or hostility'[137] towards a protected minority group, this is intrinsically harmful 'regardless of their direct material, social, psychological consequences'.[138] This deontological expressive harm has been termed a 'failure of recognition' because it is 'not just a failure to give certain things to people – resources, jobs, opportunities, even increases in well-being – but a failure to recognise their equal standing as fellow members of society'.[139]

[128] ibid. See also Harding (n 5) 232.
[129] Voight (n 115) 441.
[130] Brettschneider (n 118) 1009.
[131] ibid 1010.
[132] Voight (n 115) 442.
[133] ibid 444.
[134] Anderson and Pildes (n 117) 1513–14. But see: Levy (n 122) 396.
[135] ibid 1513.
[136] ibid 1542 and 1534.
[137] ibid 1533.
[138] ibid 1542. See also: 1531 and 1534.
[139] Moreau (n 99) 178 and 180. Some have suggested that, at its heart, expressive harm is harm to dignity: T Khaitan, 'Dignity as an Expressive Norm: Neither Vacuous nor a Panacea' (2012) 32 *OJLS* 1, 4. Dignity can entail many different notions, but generally speaking its focus is on 'one's feelings of general self-respect or worth' rather than material harms: Levy (n 122) 402. See also: *Egan v Canada* [1995] 2 SCR 513 and *Vriend v Alberta* [1998] 1 SCR 493.

ii. Expressive Harm Caused by Charities

This account of expressive harm could inform an assessment of the public benefit (or not) of discriminatory charities. While so far we have been talking about expressive harm in terms of state action (ie the expressive harm contained in policies or law), the first possible expressive harm is that which is contained in the actions of the discriminatory charity itself. As already explained, charities that discriminate in the provision of goods and services will most likely already be covered by discrimination legislation and therefore a common law public benefit analysis may be unnecessary. Expressive harm will be most relevant in determining the public benefit of advocacy organisations (such as Family First) whose purposes expound discriminatory or inegalitarian views.[140]

We should be cautious, however, of recognising a non-governmental organisation's advocacy as a detriment in charity law because it is expressively harmful for two main reasons. First, if charitable status is declined because of the expressive content of an organisation's advocacy, this may have 'serious implications for … freedom of expression'.[141] Denying charitable status – with the financial and operational implications for an organisation that brings – could be said to place a sanction on certain speech and cross the line into coercion.[142] Weighty reasons are needed for sanctions on speech, and mere offence is not enough.[143] Within a very narrow group of exceptions, we also cannot demand that private individuals or bodies avoid expressive harms in horizontal relationships (ie those between private persons).[144]

That being said, I have expressed scepticism previously about whether denial of charitable status to advocacy organisations violates freedom of expression on the basis that speakers are not entitled to a platform.[145] Brody and Tyler have also noted that 'tax exemption is not a constitutional right'.[146] Others have also drawn a distinction between state coercion and denial or withdrawal of funding or privileges. Coercion gives someone no choice, whereas financial incentives – such as tax privileges – encourage a particular choice which they are still free to reject.[147]

[140] The Supreme Court found that it is engaged in propaganda and not education, and that its purposes included advocacy for specific causes. It does not provide a service, and it is not turning people away from that service because of their sexual orientation or marital status.

[141] Khaitan (n 139) 15.

[142] Brettschneider (n 118) 1014.

[143] Khaitan (n 139) 15.

[144] ibid 16.

[145] J Calderwood Norton, 'Charities and Freedom of Expression' [2019] *New Zealand Law Journal* 174. This argument was accepted in *Family First* (n 2) [159]–[160]. See also: Harding (n 5) 186 and *Regan v Taxation Without Representation* (1983) 461 US 540. But see: *Citizens United v Federal Electoral Commission* (2010) 558 US 310 where, outside the charity law context, the Supreme Court found that regulating the means and structures used for political expression can constitute an impermissible burden on free speech.

[146] E Brody and J Tyler, 'Respecting Foundation and Charity Autonomy: How Public is Private Philanthropy' (2010) 85 *Chi-Kent L Rev* 571, 610.

[147] C Brettschneider, *When the State Speaks What Should it Say* (Princeton, Princeton University Press, 2012) 111–12.

The state generally has no duty to subsidise the exercise of constitutional rights.[148] Conferring or withdrawing charitable status and its associated tax privileges have even been seen as 'a legitimate tool of democratic persuasion' to encourage 'the ideal of free and equal citizenship'.[149]

There is also a question of whether viewpoint neutrality is appropriate for charity law, given this area of law is inherently value driven through its concept of public benefit. Charity law is 'manifestly non-neutral'.[150] The granting of charitable status, therefore, is not analogous to the American concept of a 'public forum', which requires viewpoint neutrality where the state creates spaces for a variety of viewpoints to be heard, such as public university campuses.[151] This reasoning is, of course, open to abuse. Charitable status might be denied or withdrawn not to promote democratic values but to undermine them by suppressing opposition to the government.[152] At the very least, conditions placed on subsidies, including regarding compliance with equality norms and other constitutional values, should be applied even-handedly.[153] All this is to say that freedom of expression jurisprudence does not easily map onto the law of charities.

The second reason why we should be wary of an expressive harm argument applying to the actions of charities is that it is usually only consequential (rather than deontological or intrinsic) harms that are relevant to charity law. This is because, as explained earlier, charity law typically weighs or assesses detriment based on *evidence*. Moral benefits have been accepted, at least in principle,[154] but detriments must be demonstrable or tangible and capable of proof; intrinsic 'wrongness' is not usually relevant to charity law. Instead, the courts will find that benefit is lacking (as opposed to a positive finding of harm) in instances where there may be intangible but unprovable harm.

The concerns behind the expressive harm generated by advocacy organisations may also, in fact, be best explained as concerns about material harm. After all, advocacy by charities is not typically valued for its intrinsic worth – it is valued because of the tangible contribution it makes to a vibrant democratic culture[155] and/or the ends sought. When recognising the harm of advocacy, therefore, the focus may need to be on the material consequences of the expression. This would be consistent with the approach that sees Family First's advocacy as harmful because it aims to deprive certain groups of individuals (gay people, single parents, women) of advantages or access to certain state benefits.

[148] Volokh (n 46) 1922.
[149] Brettschneider (n 147) 128.
[150] A Parachin, 'Charity, Politics and Neutrality' (2015–16) 18 *Charity Law & Practice Rev* 23, 44.
[151] *Rosenberger v University of Virginia* (1995) 515 US 819.
[152] Brettschneider (n 147). This regularly occurs under authoritarian regimes: M Sidel, 'Authoritarian regimes and the nonprofit community' in K Kearns and W Wang (eds), *Elgar Encyclopedia of Nonprofit Management, Leadership and Governance* (Cheltenham, Elgar, 2023) and H Li, S Tang and C Lo, 'Nonprofit Policy Advocacy under Authoritarianism' (2017) 77 *Public Administration Review* 103.
[153] Volokh (n 46) 1922–23.
[154] *National Anti-Vivisection Society* (n 57).
[155] Harding (n 5) 190.

iii. Expressive Harm of Charitable Status

It could also be argued that *granting charitable status* to organisations that discriminate (or expound discriminatory views) – or at least those that do not have the right attitude based on equal concern and respect for all people – can be an expressive wrong committed by the state separate from that done by the organisation itself. It could also be seen as more harmful than any expressive wrong done by the charity because 'what the state expresses matters a good deal more to our self-esteem than many other bodies and persons'.[156] While the underlying bad attitude may come from the organisation and not the state, the state could be said to express this bad attitude by granting charitable status. Given the role of the Attorney-General in supervising charities and the 'incentivising privileges' that the state provides them (such as tax concessions and allowing charitable trusts to continue in perpetuity), charitable status entails 'some form of government support'.[157] This support – and the associated government-granted status as a charity – could be viewed as endorsing the underlying discriminatory attitude because, as Parachin has observed, granting charitable status is not just an act of toleration but recognition that the trust is 'achieving something worthwhile'.[158] It is a 'stamp of approval' that the charity 'enrich[es] the texture, health and general good of society'.[159] Granting charitable status to discriminatory a charity, therefore, contains a message that contempt or hostility towards certain groups of people is worthwhile or contributes to the good of society even if it is not the state demeaning these groups directly.

This recognition of expressive harm has the potential to disqualify some charities that have otherwise been found to generate public benefit. For example, in *Kay v South Eastern Sydney Area Health* – where a gift to a hospital for treatment of 'white babies' was held to be a valid charitable trust – the focus was on the material harm (or lack of) and not the expressive harm.[160] The outcome might have been different had weight been placed on the potential detriment arising from 'the state – through the courts – being perceived to endorse racial discrimination by enforcing a racially discriminatory trust'.[161]

The argument that the state can cause harm through its association with charity is not entirely new. The state is already aware of this when engaging charities for services that it would otherwise be providing. With increasing reliance on outsourcing service provision, this means that the government regularly uses its

[156] Khaitan (n 139) 209.

[157] Murray (n 8) 150. See also: A Parachin, 'The Role of Fiscal Considerations in the Judicial Interpretation of Charity' in Harding, O'Connell, and Stewart (eds) (n 58) 123.

[158] Parachin (n 16) 194.

[159] O'Halloran (n 17) 25.

[160] *Kay v South Eastern Sydney Area Health* (n 22). The decision emphasized a 'pragmatic approach' in that 'a fund to benefit white babies could just mean that more of the general funds of the hospital would be available to treat non-white babies' (at [19]).

[161] Murray (n 8) 144.

contracting function to advance, or ensure consistency with, its policy agenda.[162] It 'may generally choose the message it wishes to express'.[163] This usually includes ensuring – through the terms of the contractual or grant arrangement – that any charity it enlists complies with equality norms.[164] Where the charity is performing a public function, the argument for compliance with equality norms – the same norms that apply to any other public body – is also clear and relatively uncontroversial. This is not to say that whether the charity is considered a public body is always an easy question, but rather, where that is the case, it is generally accepted that equality and other human rights norms apply to its activities.[165]

I have suggested that granting charity status to discriminatory charities could be viewed as endorsement of the charity's views and that this has the potential to cause harm. As such, this gives the state reason to deny charitable status. After all, the state 'may legitimately provide and prefer institutional arrangements which contribute to' its underlying values.[166] It has no reason to promote that which is harmful or not worth pursuing. As noted earlier, it would be highly problematic, however, if government conditioned charitable status (as opposed to contracts or grants) on advancing *particular* policies or supporting *particular* governments. Independence from government is a central feature of charities – it allows them to hold government to account, amongst other things – and they should not be seen as simply an extension of the state.[167] The argument I have advanced here is concerned not with charities complying with particular policies of whatever government is in power but with the potential harm that may flow from charities that hold attitudes inconsistent with our fundamental constitutional values. Granting charitable status to such organisations, I have suggested, may be expressive harm. This expressive harm could be part of any public benefit assessment when determining charitable status.

[162] McCrudden (n 96) 1–3.

[163] Brody and Tyler (n 146) 610.

[164] McCrudden (n 96) 6–7; Morris (n 2) 396.

[165] For the complexities around the distinction between government and charities, and the 'porosity in the relevant concepts', see Dal Pont (n 58) 101–02. See also: M Freedland, 'Charity Law and the Public/Private Distinction' in S Moody and C Mitchell (eds), *Foundations of Charity* (Oxford, Hart Publishing, 2000) 119 (charitable activity is now 'intractably equivocal in terms of the public/private distinction'); D Brennen, 'Charities and the Constitution: Evaluating the Role of Constitutional Principles in Determining the Scope of Tax Law's Public Policy Limitation for Charities' (2002) 5 *Florida Tax R* 779, 783 (noting that it is much discussed whether charities are public bodies, private actors, or 'something in between'); and the discussion in Chan (n 110) of hybrid public authorities in *R(Weaver) v London & Quadrant Housing Trust* [2009] EWCA Civ 587 where the fact that a housing trust was 'acting in the public interest and [had] charitable objectives' supported the conclusion that its functions were public (at 76).

[166] Gardner (n 91) 19. Here Gardner is referring to the value of autonomy and draws on the work of Joseph Raz. Harding has given a similar account: (n 5) 235–36. This explains why some institutions are precluded in society – they fail to contribute to these values: Gardner (n 91) 20.

[167] M Synge, *The University-Charity: Challenging Perceptions in Higher Education* (Exeter, self-published, 2023) 288–89. Although the distinction can 'become blurred' when the public purse funds charitable projects: Chan (n 110) 188.

III. Conclusion

This chapter has attempted to unpack the concept of detriment in charity law by looking at discriminatory charities. It identified two categories of detriment or harm – material harm and (the more controversial) expressive harm. Identifying the detriment of discrimination will not, of course, be the end of the matter when decision-makers are faced with discriminatory charities. This detriment will need to be balanced against any putative benefit. Although this chapter attempted to provide some guidance, this assessment is not easy where it 'depend[s] on value judgments influenced by social and political agendas'.[168] The extent to which discriminatory charities are permitted will necessarily involve value judgements and therefore will continue to pose challenges for any charity decision-maker.

[168] *Independent Schools* (n 75) [107].

8

Disability Injustices, Charities, and Repair: Towards Reparative Charity Law

LINDA STEELE

I. Introduction

Disability service providers (that is, organisations delivering services to disabled people to support their daily living needs, including accommodation, personal care, transport, supported employment, and recreational activities) have a key role in violence against disabled people. Violence includes physical and sexual assault, the use of restrictive practices, labour exploitation, and neglect in personal and medical care. Disabled people and their families and communities continue to be marked by the lasting effects of this violence, experiencing physical and socioeconomic impacts as well as trauma, grief, anger, and loss which have gone unrecognised and unresolved.

Many disability services have charitable status (disability service charities), thus bringing violence against disabled people within the realm of charity law. However, the role of charity law in enabling violence, and in facilitating accountability and redress in response to that violence, has to date been overlooked in public inquiries, policymaking, and scholarship. Even the recent Australian Royal Commission into Violence, Abuse, Neglect and Exploitation of People with Disability (Disability Royal Commission) in the volume of its *Final Report* devoted to disability services gave only cursory attention to charity law, despite recognising many disability services involved in violence against disabled people have charitable status (including disability service charities being the subject of three of the four case studies by the Disability Royal Commission).[1] Instead, the primary focus has been on the National Disability Insurance Scheme (NDIS) regulatory framework. The NDIS's regulatory framework should play a role in violence prevention and accountability

[1] Royal Commission into Violence, Abuse, Neglect and Exploitation of People with Disability, *Final Report* Volume 10, Disability Services' (Canberra, Commonwealth of Australia, 2023).

because the NDIS is an important source of funding for disability service charities. However, the NDIS regulatory framework will never be comprehensive as not all disabled people using disability service charities are funded through the NDIS, and disability service charities can and do operate outside of the NDIS. Moreover, disability service charities receive economic benefits from their charitable status, notably in relation to taxation, fundraising, accessing public and philanthropic funds, and brand reputation.[2] Viewing disability service charities through a charity law lens can illuminate an alternative understanding of responsibility and accountability, as well as relationships between disability services, disabled people, and the state.[3] Indeed, that charity law can have an important role in redressing and preventing violence in charities is demonstrated by the recent introduction of the Australian Charities and Not-for-Profits Commission *Governance Standard*[4] requiring entities to take reasonable steps to participate in the National Redress Scheme (government redress scheme for survivors of historical institutional child sexual abuse[5]).

Charity law scholars have yet to engage with disability let alone the specific issue of the complicit role of charities in violence against disabled people.[6] Absence of disability in charity law scholarship is curious given disability has always been present in charity law, as reflected in the 1601 Preamble to the Statute of Elizabeth which – four hundred years later – has travelled through to the Charities Act 2013 (Cth). Engagement with disability is sorely needed, not only to facilitate violence prevention and redress for disabled people, but also to consider charity law's ongoing role and existence. Contrary to the assumed reciprocation at the heart of charity law – charities receive economic benefits by giving public benefit – the systemic problem of violence in disability service charities highlights an alternative transactional logic facilitated by charity law – charities receive publicly subsidised economic benefits while (and maybe even for) perpetrating social harm. Violence against disabled people in disability service charities thus illuminates relationships between charity law and disability, and foundational questions about 'whether law should continue to constitute legal charity as it has done historically, or now allow legal charity to wither and die in favour of other modes of social action'.[7]

[2] M Harding, 'What Is the Point of Charity Law' in K Barker and D Jensen (eds), *Private Law: Key Encounters with Public Law* (Cambridge, CUP, 2013) 154.

[3] See a similar method of using charity law as a lens, in the context of application of charity law to regulation of universities: M Synge, 'The University-Charity: Challenging Perceptions in Higher Education' (2023) 87(1) *MLR* 240.

[4] Australian Charities and Not-for-Profits Commission Regulations 2022 (Cth), cl 45.30.

[5] Department of Social Services, 'National Redress Scheme' www.nationalredress.gov.au.

[6] Scholarship by Barr et al on charities providing mental health-related housing support does not question the relationship between disability and charity law, instead beginning from the assumption charities should play this role: W Barr, 'Social Housing – Charities and Vulnerable Groups' in J Picton and J Sigafoos (eds), *Debates in Charity Law* (Oxford, Hart Publishing, 2020).

[7] M Harding, 'Charity and Law: Past, Present and Future' [2020] *Singapore Journal of Legal Studies* 564.

The invitation for charity law scholars to engage with disability is timely. While charity law scholarship is mainly characterised by historical and doctrinal analysis and 'under-theorisation',[8] some scholars are considering charity law's philosophical and socio-legal dimensions, including charity law's relationship to social harm and accountability.[9]

This chapter calls for a critical engagement with charity law's relationship to violence and disability. It makes this call in two interrelated ways. The first is by bringing together longstanding critiques by Disability Justice activists and critical disability scholars on the role of charity in disabled people's oppression and critical scholarship on historical-structural injustice and repair. The second is by viewing disability service charities through a charity law lens. This chapter identifies areas for further exploration of charity law at two scales. One scale focuses on charity law doctrine's role in enabling and redressing violence against disabled people, particularly related to charity law's definition of charity and approach to accountability. The second scale focuses on the future of charity law, particularly related to processes of reckoning, repair and abolition, and ultimately re-imagining socio-legal relations of disability support.

This chapter provides new lines of critical inquiry for charity law scholars related to disability and, more broadly, to charity law's intersection with violence, historical-structural injustice, accountability, and redress. For disability socio-legal scholars and Disability Justice activists, this chapter illuminates charity law as an important site of critical intervention and political resistance central to building non-violent *and* economically and socially just futures for disabled people.

Section II begins with an overview of violence against disabled people in Australian disability service charities, particularly by reference to the Disability Royal Commission. Section III analyses charity law with a focus on its definition of charity and approach to accountability by reference to longstanding critiques by Disability Justice activists and critical disability scholars of the role of charity in disabled people's oppression and critical scholarship on historical-structural injustice and repair. The chapter concludes in Section IV by encouraging charity law scholars to reckon with charity law's role in violence against disabled people, including by orienting towards questions of repair, abolition and disability socio-legal futures without charity law.

[8] Harding (n 2) 1.

[9] JL Beard, 'The Significance of Christian Charity to International Law' in P Slotte and JD Haskell (eds), *Christianity and International Law* (Cambridge, CUP, 2021); Harding (n 2); M Harding, *Charity Law and the Liberal State* (Cambridge, CUP, 2014). See also, chs 5 and 6 of this collection, specifically S Wilson, 'Re-imagining Charity in English Imagination: Advocating a Social Harm Critique of Charity as a Cornerstone for the 'Organization of a Civilized Social Life in Twenty-First Century Britain' and KD Weinert, 'Understanding the Meaning of Charity: The Art of Doublethink'.

II. Australian Disability Services and Violence

A. Disability Service Charities, Past and Present

Charity law scholars John Picton and Jennifer Sigafoos observe '[t]hroughout the common law world, charities are embedded in the daily lives of citizens'.[10] This rings true in relation to disabled people in Australia. In a contemporary context, disability service charities provide support to disabled people in many aspects of their daily living, including accommodation, personal care, transport, supported employment, and recreational activities. Some disabled people might pay for this support from disability service charities through private funds, including older disabled people ineligible for the NDIS or people who have received compensation payments for disablement. For many other disabled people, their use of disability service charities is funded through the NDIS. For example, as of March 2024, 649,623 disabled people had approved plans for NDIS funding,[11] and over the past decade, the NDIS has contributed to the increase in size of the disability service charity sector (in terms of numbers of charities and revenue of charities).[12]

The NDIS has profoundly re-shaped disability service charities. The scheme provides funding directly to eligible disabled people to spend on reasonable and necessary support relating to their daily living, health, and community participation. This approach aims to give disabled people greater 'choice and control' in their support and break away 'from previous welfare approaches'.[13] Prior to the NDIS, funding was provided as a 'block' to disability service charities, which resulted in a concentration of control in charities and 'a one-size-fits-all approach' offering a 'limited range of services [that] couldn't respond to the diverse needs of people with disabilities'.[14]

The main policy aim behind the NDIS was to move to an individualised funding arrangement, which has been celebrated for facilitating greater autonomy and person-centredness in disability support. However, the NDIS has also been criticised for having some perverse economic impacts that result in the commodification of disabled people. The move to greater 'consumer' choice has resulted in the 'marketisation' of disability services. Disability services 'compete' in the 'NDIS marketplace' to supply the demand of NDIS participant 'consumers'.[15] These market

[10] J Picton and J Sigafoos, 'Fault Lines in Charity Law' in J Picton and J Sigafoos (eds), *Debates in Charity Law* (Oxford, Hart Publishing, 2020) 1.

[11] National Disability Insurance Agency, 'NDIS Quarterly Report to Disability Ministers' (National Disability Insurance Agency 2024) Q3 2023–24. 14.

[12] N Cortis et al, 'Australia's Disability Charities' (Sydney, Centre for Social Impact and Social Policy Research Centre, 2015).

[13] P Ramcharan, 'Understanding the NDIS: A History of Disability Welfare from "Deserving Poor" to Consumers in Control' (*The Conversation*, 5 July 2016) www.theconversation.com/understanding-the-ndis-a-history-of-disability-welfare-from-deserving-poor-to-consumers-in-control-58069.

[14] ibid.

[15] Royal Commission into Violence, 'Abuse, Neglect and Exploitation of People with Disability', *Final Report*, Volume 10, Disability Services (n 1) 4. For a critique see G van Toorn, *The New Political*

dynamics are 'a deliberate design feature of the NDIS, intended to give people with disability maximum choice and control over the services they receive.'[16] Increased funding for disability services through the NDIS, coupled with the exit of state governments from frontline disability service provision and related land transfers of former government run facilities to disability service charities, has resulted in the growth of the non-government disability service sector.[17]

Charities have a long involvement with disabled people in Australia. Charities were brought to Australia as part of settler colonial invasion and occupation of Australia.[18] During the nineteenth century, benevolent society charities were involved in providing community-based and institutional 'care' to disabled people.[19] In the late nineteenth and early twentieth centuries, charities with a specific focus on particular impairment types began to emerge. In the mid-twentieth century, families of disabled people formed organisations to provide community-based accommodation, employment, and recreational opportunities outside of large residential settings.[20] The history of nineteenth and early to mid-twentieth century Australian disability is commonly understood as oppressive and harmful to disabled people, characterised by institutionalisation, segregation, exclusion, and violation.[21] However, many older disability service charities continue to exist today in the NDIS context with multi-million dollars of annual revenue, having recently re-branded and re-named to fit within an NDIS paradigm of disability focused on inclusion and empowerment (a practice which also disconnects these organisations from harmful pasts). Disability service charities are deeply entrenched in Australia's history and present, entwined with disabled people's lives, and resilient and responsive to social shifts, public policy developments and public exposure of their role in violence and social harm.

B. Contextualising Violence in Disability Service Charities

Three preliminary points are important to understanding the current issue of violence against disabled people in Australian disability service charities.

Economy of Disability: Transnational Networks and Individualised Funding in the Age of Neoliberalism (London, Routledge, 2021).

[16] ibid 36.

[17] Cortis et al (n 12).

[18] A O'Brien, *Philanthropy and Settler Colonialism* (London, Palgrave Macmillan, 2015) 1–35.

[19] L Hallahan, 'Disability in Australia: Shadows, Struggles and Successes' (Royal Commission into Violence, Abuse, Neglect and Exploitation of People with Disability, 2021) 29–38 https://disability.royalcommission.gov.au/system/files/2021-11/Research%20Report%20-%20Disability%20in%20Australia%20-%20Shadows%2C%20struggles%20and%20successes.pdf.

[20] Hallahan (n 19); Cortis and others (n 12).

[21] G Goggin and C Newell, *Disability in Australia: Exposing a Social Apartheid* (Sydney, UNSW Press, 2005); Hallahan (n 19).

First, disability service charities in Australia largely operate in contexts of segregation, institutionalisation, and control in the 'deinstitutionalised' community.[22] Disability service charities often provide support services in segregated settings – group homes, day centres, supported employment, and transport. In these settings, disabled people are congregated and are separated from non-disabled people in closed environments where disabled people lack control over their circumstances and have limited freedom to leave.[23] Disabled people in these settings are exposed to violence including physical and sexual violence, restrictive practices, and non-consensual sterilisation and long acting reversible contraception. This violence is 'linked to segregated settings and institutional practices'. In part, this is because 'services continue to be designed and delivered in ways that maintain a power imbalance between providers and participants, with institutional cultures and practices that limit choice and control'.[24] Other factors associated with violence include normalised staff practices involving dehumanisation and violation, economic efficiency and risk management in staffing and resourcing of services, and cultures of ableism.[25] Disabled people in segregated employment settings are additionally subjected to labour exploitation, including through payment of subminimum wages.[26] Disabled people subjected to violence in contemporary segregated and institutional settings operated by disability service charities also have less access to redress because of such factors as gatekeeping, normalisation of violence and disabled people's lack of awareness of rights, as well as the legality of much of this violence.[27]

[22] C Spivakovsky, L Steele and P Weller, 'The Lasting Legacies of Institutionalisation: Questioning Law's Roles in the Emancipation of People with Disabilities' in C Spivakovsky, L Steele and P Weller (eds), *The Legacies of Institutionalisation: Disability, Law and Policy in the 'Deinstitutionalised' Community* (Oxford, Hart Publishing, 2020).

[23] Disabled People's Organisations Australia, 'Segregation of People with Disability Is Discrimination and Must End' (2020) https://dpoa.org.au/wp-content/uploads/2020/11/Segregation-of-People-with-Disability_Position-Paper.pdf.

[24] Royal Commission into Violence, Abuse, Neglect and Exploitation of People with Disability, *Final Report* Volume 3, Nature and Extent of Violence, Abuse. Neglect and Exploitation' (Commonwealth of Australia 2023) 262.

[25] Senate Community Affairs References Committee, *Violence, Abuse and Neglect against People with Disability in Institutional and Residential Settings, Including the Gender and Age Related Dimensions, and the Particular Situation of Aboriginal and Torres Strait Islander People with Disability, and Culturally and Linguistically Diverse People with Disability* (Canberra, Parliament of Australia, 2015) www.aph.gov.au/Parliamentary_Business/Committees/Senate/Community_Affairs/Violence_abuse_neglect/Report; C Spivakovsky, L Steele and D Wadiwel, 'Restrictive Practices: A Pathway to Elimination' (Royal Commission into Violence, Abuse, Neglect and Exploitation of People with Disability 2023).

[26] L Steele, 'Law and Disability "Supported" Employment in Australia: The Case for Ending Segregation, Discrimination, Exploitation and Violence of People with Disability at Work' (2024) 49(2) *Mon LR* 43.

[27] D Wadiwel, C Spivakovsky and L Steele, 'Complaint Mechanisms: Reporting Pathways for Violence, Abuse, Neglect and Exploitation' (Royal Commission into Violence, Abuse, Neglect and Exploitation of People with Disability 2022) https://disability.royalcommission.gov.au/system/files/2023-02/Research%20Report%20-%20Complaint%20mechanisms%20Reporting%20pathways%20for%20violence%2C%20abuse%2C%20neglect%20and%20exploitation_0.pdf.

Second, while the NDIS is popularly understood as a break from a harmful history of segregation and institutionalisation, the NDIS largely funds segregated services. The NDIS will not fund 'mainstream and community supports' because '[t]hese are the supports available to everyone, whether or not they have a disability'.[28] Moreover, the NDIS's market-based model and funding for group-based supports financially incentivises economic efficiency in service provision that undermines individuality, choice and wellbeing. The NDIS also regulates, rather than prohibits, the use of restrictive practices in NDIS funded services, thus enabling disabled people to be detained, tied down, supervised, and otherwise restricted in ways often associated with the purportedly bygone era of institutionalisation.[29] However, the NDIS legislative framing in terms of 'choice and control' and human rights[30] cloaks these oppressive dimensions of the NDIS in discourses of inclusion, participation and autonomy. Ultimately, the NDIS is juxtaposed to a 'dark past'[31] of institutionalisation when it is in fact a continuation of it.

Third, disability service charities have only been in Australia following white invasion and occupation.[32] Prior to this, disability service charities did not exist in Australia and, as profoundly deaf Worimi scholar Scott Avery notes, there was a culture of inclusion towards disabled people.[33] In a contemporary context, First Nations disabled people are subjected to violence in disability service charities, as well as barriers to accessing such services.[34] Thus, disability service charities' introduction and ongoing existence in Australia can be understood as part of the ongoing 'logic of elimination'[35] of settler colonialism.

C. Disability Service Charities in the Disability Royal Commission

The Disability Royal Commission was established in 2019 to investigate how to prevent and better protect disabled people from violence, abuse, neglect, and exploitation, as well as best practice in responding to violence, abuse, neglect, and

[28] National Disability Insurance Scheme, 'What Are Mainstream and Community Supports?' https://ourguidelines.ndis.gov.au/how-ndis-supports-work-menu/mainstream-and-community-supports/what-are-mainstream-and-community-supports.

[29] Spivakovsky, Steele and Wadiwel (n 25).

[30] One of the objects of the National Disability Insurance Scheme Act 2013 'in conjunction with other laws, give effect to Australia's obligations under the Convention on the Rights of Persons with Disabilities': National Disability Insurance Scheme Act 2013 (Cth), s 3(1)(a).

[31] N Altermark, *Citizenship Inclusion and Intellectual Disability: Biopolitics Post-Institutionalisation* (London, Routledge, 2019).

[32] O'Brien (n 18) 1–35.

[33] S Avery, *Culture Is Inclusion: A Narrative of Aboriginal and Torres Strait Islander People with Disability* (First People's Disability Network (Australia), 2018).

[34] Royal Commission into Violence, Abuse, Neglect and Exploitation of People with Disability, *Final Report* Volume 9, First Nations People with Disability' (Canberra, Commonwealth of Australia, 2023).

[35] P Wolfe, 'Settler Colonialism and the Elimination of the Native' (2006) 8 *Journal of Genocide Research* 387.

exploitation and how to promote a more inclusive society for disabled people.[36] Violence, abuse, neglect, and exploitation in disability service settings, and the roles of disability service providers, their management and staff, in perpetrating and responding to violence, abuse, neglect, and exploitation were a strong focus throughout the Disability Royal Commission's public hearings. Of the four public hearings designated for in-depth exploration of case studies, three were on case studies of disability service providers with charitable status and Public Benevolent Institutions (PBIs): Sunnyfield, Life Without Barriers (LWB), and Australian Foundation for Disability (Afford).

Public Hearing 13 on 'Preventing and responding to violence, abuse, neglect and exploitation in disability services (a Case Study)' focused on Sunnyfield.[37] Sunnyfield was established in 1962 'by a group of parents of children with disability as the "Sunnyfield Association" in response to a lack of supports and services for people with disability'.[38] These days, Sunnyfield has an annual revenue of $81,309,758[39] and on a daily basis 'deliver[s] nearly 2,000 support services for people with disability'.[40] Sunnyfield promotes itself to prospective clients and their families as offering disabled people a better future, its homepage broadcasting: 'Welcome, we're glad you're here. Working together with families, friends and dedicated staff, Sunnyfield is your trusted NDIS service provider that supports a brighter future for people with disability'.[41] Public Hearing 13 presented a different side to Sunnyfield, through the experiences of three residents: Melissa, Carl, and Chen. Melissa, Carl, and Chen experienced violence and abuse at the hands of their Sunnyfield disability support workers. Carl 'was subjected to hair pulling; being tipped out of a lounge chair, pushed and kicked; being dragged by a vehicle harness strap; and being purposely frightened by a support worker' and Melissa 'was dragged by her wrists down a hall while she was naked'.[42] Moreover, their families then received defensive and hostile responses when they complained to the service, including Melissa being issued with an eviction notice.[43] The Disability

[36] Royal Commission into Violence, Abuse, Neglect and Exploitation of People with Disability, *Final Report* Executive Summary, Our Vision for an Inclusive Australia and Recommendations' (Royal Commission into Violence, Abuse, Neglect and Exploitation of People with Disability, 2023) x–xi htps://disability.royalcommission.gov.au/publications/final-report-executive-summary-our-vision-inclusive-australia-and-recommendations.

[37] Royal Commission into Violence, Abuse, Neglect and Exploitation of People with Disability, 'Public Hearing 13': Preventing and Responding to Violence Abuse Neglect and Exploitation in Disability Services (a Case Study)' (Royal Commission into Violence, Abuse, Neglect and Exploitation of People with Disability 2021) Public Hearing Report https://disability.royalcommission.gov.au/system/files/2022-04/Report%20-%20Public%20hearing%2013%20-%20Preventing%20and%20responding%20to%20violence%2C%20abuse%2C%20neglect%20and%20exploitation%20in%20disability%20services%20%28a%20case%20study%29_0.pdf.

[38] ibid 22.

[39] 'Sunnyfield' (*Australian Charities and Not-For-Profits Commission*) www.acnc.gov.au/charity/charities/06fe133a-39af-e811-a95e-000d3ad24c60/profile.

[40] 'Services' (*Sunnyfield Disability Services*) www.sunnyfield.org.au/services/.

[41] (*Sunnyfield Disability Services*) www.sunnyfield.org.au/.

[42] Disability Royal Commission Final Report (n 1).

[43] 'Transcript of Proceedings, Public Hearing 13, Day 1' https://disability.royalcommission.gov.au/system/files/2021-10/Transcript%20Day%201%20-%20Public%20hearing%2013%2C%20Sydney.pdf.

Royal Commission recommended Sunnyfield management and board 'meet with Melissa, Carl and Chen, or their families, to: apologise for Sunnyfield's failures to prevent the violence and abuse they endured; and discuss what redress and/or additional supports and assistance they require'.[44]

Public hearing 20 on 'Preventing and responding to violence, abuse, neglect and exploitation in disability services (two case studies)'[45] focused on LWB. LWB was established in 2002. With an annual revenue of $413,120,000,[46] LWB provides a range of services including disability, aged care, and foster care.[47] Its stated purpose is to 'partner with people and change lives for the better'[48] and it focuses on removing barriers to better futures:

> We believe what unites us are the rights we have and should all enjoy as human beings. Yet the opportunity to live freely, without significant barriers, is not afforded to all Australians. This drives us, a collective of diverse and passionate people to partner through relationships and change lives for the better.[49]

Public Hearing 20 focused on the experiences of four disabled people who lived in group homes operated by LWB, including two women (Sophie and Natalie) who lived in the same group home and had experiences related to sexual violence. Sophie was not supported by LWB after she was sexually assaulted in 2017 in a public park by a man with whom she was on a date. She was also physically assaulted by a LWB worker during an investigation by the service and 'was not given an opportunity to report the incident to the police'.[50] In the four years preceding the sexual assault, LWB had not supported Sophie's expressed desires for sexual expression and intimate relationships, including not providing sex education and not allowing her to have men in her room without supervision (including her fiancé at the time).[51] During 2012–14, Natalie was subjected to indecent assault by a disability support worker during provision of personal care, but managers failed to report and promptly remove the worker and he was permitted to continue

[44] Royal Commission into Violence, Abuse, Neglect and Exploitation of People with Disability, 'Public Hearing 13: Preventing and Responding to Violence Abuse Neglect and Exploitation in Disability Services (a Case Study)' (n 37) 8.

[45] Royal Commission into Violence, Abuse, Neglect and Exploitation of People with Disability, 'Public Hearing 20: Preventing and Responding to Violence, Abuse, Neglect and Exploitation in Disability Services (Two Case Studies)' (Royal Commission into Violence, Abuse, Neglect and Exploitation of People with Disability 2023) https://Public Hearing Report 20 disability.royalcommission.gov.au/system/files/2023-05/Report%20-%20Public%20hearing%2020%20-%20Preventing%20and%20responding%20to%20violence%2C%20abuse%2C%20neglect%20and%20exploitation%20in%20disability%20services%20-%20two%20case%20studies.pdf.

[46] Australian Charities and Not-For-Profits Commission 'Life Without Barriers' www.acnc.gov.au/charity/charities/feed745e-38af-e811-a960-000d3ad24282/profile.

[47] Life Without Barriers, 'Life without Barriers' www.lwb.org.au/.

[48] ibid.

[49] ibid.

[50] Disability Royal Commission Final Report (n 1) 62.

[51] Royal Commission into Violence, Abuse, Neglect and Exploitation of People with Disability, 'Transcript of Proceedings, Public Hearing 20, Day 1' https://disability.royalcommission.gov.au/system/files/2021-12/Transcript%20Day%201%20-%20Public%20hearing%2020%2C%20Virtual_0.pdf.

working in Natalie's home for 2.5 weeks after management was notified. Natalie, who was incontinent, was also 'hospitalised after crying and exhibiting significant pain'[52] in 2020 due to a bowel obstruction and was required to undergo a manual disimpaction under a general anaesthetic, being close to rupturing her bowel. This followed months of staff failures to document Natalie's bowel movements.[53] The Disability Royal Commission recommended LWB 'should consider making an ex gratia payment to Natalie as compensation for the conduct of LWB Worker'.[54]

Public hearing 23 on 'Preventing and responding to violence, abuse, neglect and exploitation in disability services (a case study)' focused on Afford. Afford was established in 1952 and was originally named the Poliomyelitis Society of Australia and provided care and rehabilitation to people living with polio.[55] It now has an annual revenue of $140,332,288[56] and provides a range of services to disabled people including in relation to accommodation, community support and employment.[57] Afford's website states they are 'here to provide you with accommodation and housing, community connection, disability supports and employment services so that you can live the life you choose and feel connected in your community' and their 'impact also goes beyond our delivery of disability services – we partner across the sector to ensure the voices of people living with disability are heard and valued'.[58] Public Hearing 23 focused on the experiences of three disabled people (Jason, Toby, and Simon) at a Sydney-based day program operated by Afford (one of its 44 day programs). Jason, Toby, and Simon were abused by a disability support worker while receiving 1:1 unsupervised support.[59] For example, the worker 'recorded intimate images and videos of several day program participants, including of Jason during personal care in the bathroom at Jason's home and in public toilets' and 'shared those images with others'. He also

[52] Disability Royal Commission Final Report (n 1) 10.

[53] Royal Commission into Violence, Abuse, Neglect and Exploitation of People with Disability (n 51).

[54] Royal Commission into Violence, Abuse, Neglect and Exploitation of People with Disability (n 45) 13.

[55] Royal Commission into Violence, Abuse, Neglect and Exploitation of People with Disability, 'Public Hearing 23: Preventing and Responding to Violence, Abuse, Neglect and Exploitation in Disability Services (a Case Study)' (Royal Commission into Violence, Abuse, Neglect and Exploitation of People with Disability 2022) Public Hearing Report 13 https://disability.royalcommission.gov.au/system/files/2023-05/Report%20-%20Public%20hearing%2023%20-%20Preventing%20and%20responding%20to%20violence%2C%20abuse%2C%20neglect%20and%20exploitation%20in%20disability%20services%20-%20a%20case%20study.pdf.

[56] Australian Charities and Not-for-Profit Commission, 'Australian Foundation For Disability', *Australian Charities and Not-For-Profits Commission* www.acnc.gov.au/charity/charities/2c2eac96-38af-e811-a963-000d3ad244fd/profile.

[57] The Australian Foundation for Disability, 'Afford's Disability Supports Services' www.afford.com.au/services/.

[58] The Australian Foundation for Disability, 'Welcome to the Australian Foundation for Disability (Afford)' (18 May 2020) www.afford.com.au/.

[59] Royal Commission into Violence, Abuse, Neglect and Exploitation of People with Disability, 'Transcript of Proceedings, Public Hearing 23, Day 1' (16 May 2022) https://disability.royalcommission.gov.au/system/files/2022-05/Transcript%20Day%201%20-%20Public%20hearing%2023%2C%20Sydney.pdf.

'assaulted Jason by blowing e-cigarette smoke into his face and slapping him'.[60] Simon's mum also expressed concerns her son and other participants in the day program 'were not being shown age-appropriate content and were watching television designed for children' and 'were not being supported to develop their independent living skills, such as brushing their hair and cleaning their teeth'.[61] The Disability Royal Commission 'also heard that some participants were not being encouraged or supported to use non-verbal forms of communication, or augmented or alternative communication devices'.[62] While the Disability Royal Commission did not find Afford responsible for the abuse by the staff member itself, it did find Afford had not responded appropriately to the abuse, including not providing redress.[63] The Disability Royal Commission attributed this in part to Afford pursuing 'a strategy of significant organisational growth' and its 'commercial approach' which 'included financial incentives and rewards to Afford staff', this being incompatible with 'providing safe and high-quality services to people with disability'.[64] While not a focus of Public Hearing 23, the Disability Royal Commission also noted in its Public Hearing report Afford management's response to the 2019 death of Merna Aprem, a disabled woman who 'drowned at Afford's group home'. Ms Aprem 'could not be revived after she was found unconscious with her nose and mouth submerged in a bathtub of water and vomit'.[65] The Disability Royal Commission observed:

> immediately after Ms Aprem's death, the CEO report to the Board only briefly referred to her death as 'a tragedy with a client at our Woodbine Group Home while bathing' … While it stated that counselling services had been offered to the 'client's family, staff and other clients', it made no reference to how Ms Aprem's family was being otherwise supported by Afford. There was no suggestion of any apology to Ms Aprem's family, of conducting an investigation or root cause analysis, or any other action by Afford or its Board. The report then moved swiftly to discuss Afford's budget, its expansion in Queensland, its efforts to bring down the debts owed to Afford, and its financial performance.
>
> In the following CEO report, Mr Herald wrote '[a]ll in all, a very good year', an apparent reference to Afford's financial performance. He made no mention at all of Ms Aprem's death or of any action taken, or even suggested, in response.[66]

Volume 10 of the Disability Royal Commission's *Final Report* ('Volume 10') was on disability services. It notes the Disability Royal Commission 'heard evidence

[60] Disability Royal Commission Final Report (n 1) 62.
[61] ibid 67.
[62] ibid.
[63] Royal Commission into Violence, Abuse, Neglect and Exploitation of People with Disability (n 55) 31.
[64] ibid 10.
[65] J Gramenz, 'NDIS Provider's Failures in Bathtub Death Cost $400,000' *Australian Associated Press Pty Limited* (14 June 2023).
[66] Royal Commission into Violence, Abuse, Neglect and Exploitation of People with Disability (n 55) 83.

about violence, abuse, neglect and exploitation in disability services at five disability service provider hearings and several other hearings' and '1,745 additional accounts of violence, abuse, neglect and exploitation in disability services were presented in submissions and private sessions'.[67] Volume 10 identifies violence extending to 'physical assaults, sexual assaults and verbal abuse involving support staff, volunteers, community members and other residents in group homes'. While noting this violence is 'not unique to the disability services sector':

> the relationship between those providing disability services and supports and the people with disability receiving those services and supports creates a particular risk of violence and abuse. … support workers and service providers can hold significant power within the relationship, notwithstanding the move towards greater choice and control for people with disability through the NDIS.[68]

Volume 10 also identifies neglect or 'slow violence' – 'service provider or disability support worker fails to provide the conditions necessary for the physical, emotional, social and cultural wellbeing and development of a person with disability to whom they are providing services'.[69] Attitudinal and systemic barriers to accessing supports and services – such as LWB's failure to support Sophie's goal of pursuing intimate and sexual relationships – are characterised by the Disability Royal Commission as 'structural and systemic' forms of neglect.[70] The Disability Royal Commission notes restrictive practices are a form of violence particularly experienced by 'people with disability who have high support needs, including those living in supported accommodation settings'.[71]

Volume 10 contains recommendations about disability services developing complaints and redress processes in the context of NDIS regulation. It recommends the National Disability Insurance Scheme Quality and Safeguards Commission (NDISQSC) develop 'model procedures' for NDIS providers including complaints handling that 'address the need to consider the impact or harm caused to a participant and provide guidance on forms of redress',[72] and guidelines on 'accessible and responsive complaint handling and investigative practice'.[73] It also recommends amending NDIS legislation to require NDIS providers to 'consider redress and forms of support to an NDIS participant' where the NDISQSC has found the provider 'bears responsibility for the violence, abuse, neglect or exploitation experienced by the NDIS participant' and the NDISQSC should 'provide practical advice on suitable forms of redress'.[74]

[67] Royal Commission into Violence, Abuse, Neglect and Exploitation of People with Disability (n 1) 45.
[68] ibid 61.
[69] ibid 66.
[70] ibid 68.
[71] ibid 65.
[72] Recommendation 10.14: ibid 18.
[73] Recommendation 10.15: ibid.
[74] Recommendation 10.16: ibid 19.

There are five observations of the Disability Royal Commission's engagement with violence in disability service charities. First, the Disability Royal Commission recognised the systemic problem of violence in disability service charities and its ongoing impacts on disabled people and their families. Second, it linked this systemic problem to persistence of segregation and control in disability service charities. Third, it recognised the impact of financial imperatives on violence in disability service charities. Fourth, the Disability Royal Commission identified profound problems with how disability service charities respond to violence in their services, notably failures of accountability and redress. Fifth, the Disability Royal Commission identified a key role for the NDIS legislative framework and NDISQSC in regulating and developing redress and accountability practices of disability service charities.

D. Charity Law's Absence from the Disability Royal Commission

While disability service charities were a key focus of the Disability Royal Commission, the *charitable status* of these organisations was not an area of exploration and in turn *charity law* was completely absent in the Disability Royal Commission's work.

All three organisations discussed in the case studies above had charitable status and were PBIs. However, in each public hearing report the Disability Royal Commission only noted the organisations' charitable status, and did not consider their charitable status as a source of regulation and accountability. Similarly, Volume 10 cursorily acknowledges: 'Most of the disability service providers that have been the subject of detailed evidence during our public hearings have been medium to large, not-for-profit and NDIS-registered'.[75] Yet, it was NDIS registration – not charitable status – that attracted in-depth consideration. The only further reference in Volume 10 to charity law as a potential source of regulation and accountability, is noting some disability services are 'charitable organisations registered with the Australian Charities and Not-for-Profits Commission in accordance with the *Australian Charities and Not-for-profits Commission Act 2012* (Cth)'.[76] A research report by the Australian Government Solicitor commissioned by the Disability Royal Commission on key elements of the legislative framework affecting disabled people did not discuss charity legislation.[77] This is not only a limitation of the Disability Royal Commission. For its part, the Australian Charities and Not-for-Profits Commission did not engage with the Disability Royal

[75] ibid 109.

[76] ibid 110.

[77] Australian Government Solicitor, 'Report on the Key Elements of the Legislative Framework Affecting People with Disability' (Royal Commission into Violence, Abuse, Neglect and Exploitation of People with Disability, 2020).

Commission process either in written submissions or appearing in public hearings, in contrast to the active participation by the National Disability Insurance Agency and NDISQSC.

The Disability Royal Commission was a missed opportunity to consider the role of charitable status and charity law more broadly in enabling, responding to and preventing violence against disabled people in disability service charities. In failing to critically engage with charity law, the Disability Royal Commission legitimated charity law's role in disabled people's lives and contributed to the idea of the self-evidence of charities as the appropriate legal framing of social action towards disabled people.

III. Charity Law, Disability, and Violence

A. Disability, Charity, and Ableism: Critical Connections

This section situates analysis of charity law and disability in Disability Justice activists' and critical disability scholars' critique of the role of charity in disabled oppression. Activists and scholars reject understanding disabled people's circumstances through a medical model of disability. In that model disabled people have pathological deficits internal to them which make them dependent and burdensome and thus naturally unequal. In rejecting the medical model, disabled people's circumstances are instead understood as a structural problem of oppression. Rather than being naturally lesser and unequal, disabled people are situated in a social hierarchy of ableism – a 'system of assigning value to people's bodies and minds based on societally constructed ideas of normalcy, productivity, desirability, intelligence, excellence, and fitness'.[78] Disabled people's positioning on this social hierarchy justifies denying to them equality, means to flourish, and legal and social protection from violence. Disabled people are dehumanised. Interventions in their bodies and lives are rationalised as necessary. These interventions are not understood socially, nor often legally, as violent and unjust and individuals and organisations (often in health, social care, and disability sectors) involved in these interventions are seen as benevolent and innocent.[79]

In ableist hierarchies, disabled people are positioned as surplus and an economic burden on their families, communities, and the nation on the basis that they are incapable of productive labour. Their high needs for care and support are considered superfluous because any care and support will ultimately be sustaining

[78] Talila A Lewis, 'Working Definition of Ableism – January 2022 Update' (1 January 2022) www.talilalewis.com/blog.html. See also Dan Goodley, *Dis/Ability Studies: Theorising Disablism and Ableism* (London, Routledge, 2014).

[79] C Chapman and AJ Withers, *A Violent History of Benevolence: Interlocking Oppression and Moral Economies of Social Working* (Toronto, University of Toronto Press, 2019).

bodies and lives that are not contributing to society. The socially assigned status of disabled people as excluded from productive labour supports the economic devaluing of their bodies and the emergence of other, violent ways of achieving economic gain from their dehumanised bodies. Economic gain might instead be realised through underpaid labour (eg, in sheltered employment), unpaid labour (eg, in volunteer social enterprise programmes), or harmful interventions in disabled people's bodies and lives that result in financial gain to others (eg, provision of services that amount to warehousing).[80]

Within this approach to disability and ableism, 'charity' – both as a term to refer to a form of behaviour involving giving to those in need and as a term to refer to legal entities delivering services – is central to disabled people's oppression. Provision of support to disabled people is viewed through a charity lens as behaviour involving giving to those in need, in which disabled people are seen as passive recipients of care provided by benevolent non-disabled people concerned with relieving the suffering arising from disabled people's disability. Imbuing the medical model with a 'moral element',[81] the charity lens shapes dual subjectivities: the disabled 'beneficiary' of charity as suffering, grateful and passive and the non-disabled as innocent, morally virtuous, generous and active.[82] These subjectivities lock disabled people in paternalistic power relations in which violence is illegible because it is incongruous with alleviation of suffering at the heart of charity.[83]

Disability Justice activists and critical disability scholars approach 'charity' – in the sense of legal entities delivering services – as oppressive towards and extractive of disabled people. Disability service charities access revenue through monetising subjugated representations of 'disabled people's identities as individual and tragic, rather than social and positive'.[84] Despite hinging their revenue on exploitation of discursive representations of disabled people, disability service charities do not then use all their funds on direct support to disabled people but are instead structured to utilise some of their funds to grow their asset bases and future revenue. Disability service charities are governed and managed by people (often non-disabled people) who hold the power to make significant decisions impacting disabled people's lives and bodies but are guided by organisational imperatives and interests distinct to disabled people's lived experiences and needs.[85]

[80] L Ben-Moshe and J Stewart, 'Disablement, Prison and Historical Segregation: 15 Years Later' in Ravi Malhotra (ed), *Disability Politics in a Global Economy: Essays in Honour of Marta Russell* (London, Routledge, 2017) www.routledge.com/Disability-Politics-in-a-Global-Economy-Essays-in-Honour-of-Marta-Russell/Malhotra/p/book/9781138590946; J Graham, 'Socialism Needs Disability Justice' (*Midnight Sun*, 8 February 2023) www.midnightsunmag.ca/socialism-needs-disability-justice/; D Wadiwel, 'Critical Disability Studies and the State' (2023) 12 *feminists@law* 1.

[81] AJ Withers, *Disability, Politics and Theory* (Halifax, Fernwood Publishing, 2012) 58.

[82] P K Longmore, *Telethons: Spectacle, Disability, and the Business of Charity* (Oxford, OUP, 2016) 71–101; Withers (n 81) 56–57.

[83] Chapman and Withers (n 79).

[84] Withers (n 81) 58.

[85] ibid 58–61.

The extractive nature of disability service charities results in financial benefit to the organisations while causing socio-cultural and material detriment to disabled people. For example, disabled activist and writer El Gibbs notes that the disability service 'economy' is growing with the NDIS but this money remains largely concentrated within disability service charities and non-disabled people. She explains '[s]o much money has come into disability services' but 'there are no requirements for any of these organisations to employ us in order to get that money'. 'Instead', she argues 'much of this money has gone to increasing the size of the separate disability sector' and '[d]isabled people are still separated from the rest of the community, particularly for people with an intellectual disability, instead of the dream ten years ago that fuelled the campaign for the NDIS of being more included in the community'. She asks: 'Where is our share? I am sure you can hear that I am cranky about this. So much money has poured into the disability economy, yet over half of disabled people still live in poverty.'[86]

The UN Convention on the Rights of Persons with Disabilities (CRPD) is said to have brought about a paradigm shift in the socio-political status of disabled people from charity to equality,[87] and the NDIS legislation is framed by the CRPD. Many disability service charities market their services by reference to discourses of inclusion, empowerment and hope (rather than paternalism and suffering), as demonstrated in Section II.C in relation to the websites of Sunnyfield, LWB, and Afford. However, these charities co-opt these disability human rights concepts because the existence and operation of these disability service charities causes segregation, discrimination, exploitation, and violence that undermines equality, non-violence and liberation and renders impossible ever achieving these aspirations.[88] These discursive representations effect an ontological violence[89] where disabled people's futures are tethered to disability service charities. Indeed, the co-option of these disability human rights concepts demonstrates the resilience of disability service charities to political shifts in the status of disabled people. This is a core problem that the Disability Royal Commission failed to identify and explore but which has profound implications for ongoing failure to recognise and respond to violence in disability service charities. The Disability Royal Commission's call for the 'critical need for disability providers to foster a culture that puts the human rights of people with disability at the forefront of service delivery', which 'requires an evolution

[86] El Gibbs, 'Getting Our Fair Share of the Disability Economy' (*El Gibbs*, 5 June 2022) https://elgibbs.com.au/getting-our-fair-share-of-the-disability-economy/.

[87] See, eg, AS Kanter, *The Development of Disability Rights Under International Law: From Charity to Human Rights* (London, Routledge, 2014).

[88] Altermark (n 31); J Levinson, *Making Life Work: Freedom and Disability in a Community Group Home* (Minneapolis, University of Minnesota Press, 2010); C Spivakovsky, 'Governing Freedom through Risk: Locating the Group Home in the Archipelago of Confinement and Control' (2017) 19 *Punishment and Society* 366.

[89] A Kafer, *Feminist, Queer, Crip* (Bloomington, Indiana University Press, 2013); E Kim, *Curative Violence: Rehabilitating Disability, Gender, and Sexuality in Modern Korea* (Durham, Duke University Press, 2017).

from benevolent or charitable approaches and service provision that perpetuates outdated models, to approaches based on autonomy and social inclusion that drive innovation'[90] is arguably impossible where the concept of charity and charitable organisations are inextricably undermining liberation and enabling violence.

Disability Justice activists argue for dismantling charities and creating alternative, emancipatory means of providing support. AJ Withers calls for 'creatively and collectively demand[ing] and build[ing] successful alternatives to the charity industry'. This includes 'build[ing] strong communities that are inclusive of disabled people that acknowledge disabled people as equals, rather than as objects of pity or inspiration', 'creat[ing] accessible and inclusive spaces and work to ensure that people's needs are met publicly with collective, public (rather than private) resources' and 'creat[ing] interactions between disabled and non-disabled people based on mutual aid and respect'.[91] Leah Lakshmi Piepzna-Samarsinha proposes 'care webs'. These resist 'the model of charity and gratitude', and instead 'are controlled by the needs and desires of the disabled people running them' and 'work from a model of solidarity not charity – of showing up for each other in mutual aid and respect'.[92] These practices are already happening in Australia. The Australian Disability Justice Network has the byline of 'solidarity not charity' and operates a mutual aid fund 'for disabled people in crisis situations whose needs are not being met by the state'.[93] Moreover, Avery has argued for First Nations led disability support in order to facilitate self-determination.[94]

B. Disabling Charity Law

Charity law scholar Matthew Harding observes: 'Legal charity is an artifice of law; as a mode of action, it would not exist but for the law that creates and sustains it'.[95] Thus, it can be assumed charity law is in fact central to the structural conditions discussed in Section III.A (even if not the central focus of Disability Justice activism and critical disability scholarship). This section surfaces intersections of disability, violence and law in the legal definition of charity and charity law's approach to accountability, drawing on the critiques of charity discussed in Section III.A.

[90] Royal Commission into Violence, Abuse, Neglect and Exploitation of People with Disability (n 1) 82.

[91] Withers (n 81) 79. See also INCITE! Women of Color Against Violence (ed), *The Revolution Will Not Be Funded: Beyond the Non-Profit Industrial Complex* (Durham, Duke University Press, 2017).

[92] LL Piepzna-Samarasinha, *Care Work: Dreaming Disability Justice* (Vancouver, Arsenal Pulp Press, 2019) 26. See also D Spade, *Dean Spade: Building Solidarity During This Crisis (and the Next)* (London, Verso, 2020) 1.

[93] Disability Justice Network, 'About' disabilityjusticenetwork.com/about/.

[94] Avery (n 33).

[95] Harding (n 7) 565.

i. Legal Definition of Charity

'Charity' is defined in the Charities Act 2013 (Cth) as an entity, among other things, having 'charitable purposes that are for the public benefit'.[96] This definition includes references to disability resonating with ableist understandings of disabled people, and as such charity law scholars could further interrogate the socio-cultural understandings of disability underpinning and promoted by charity law and how these enable and legitimate violence against disabled people in disability service charities.

'Charitable purposes' is defined as including 'the purpose of advancing social or public welfare'.[97] This purpose includes 'relieving the poverty, distress or disadvantage of individuals or families'[98] and 'caring for and supporting … the aged; or … individuals with disabilities'.[99] A further purpose is 'advancing health'.[100] That purpose 'includes the purpose of preventing and relieving sickness, disease or human suffering'.[101] These purposes include language positioning givers of charity as active and disabled people as passive ('caring for', 'relieving'), and understandings of disability as individual misfortune ('relieving sickness, disease or human suffering'). None of the purposes specifically refers to facilitating the self-determination, emancipation, and equality of disabled people, nor recognising and redressing disability when caused by structural oppression. The hierarchy between givers and receivers of charity effected by the legal concept of 'charitable purpose' also contributes to the public reputation of charities as morally virtuous, resonating with the critique of charities in Section II.A. For example, Harding argues 'the pursuit of charitable purposes generates a multiplicity of goods'[102] and 'the charity sector is distinctively a site for altruism insofar as charity law orients that sector towards altruism by demanding that charity founders form altruistic purposes'.[103] It is acknowledged that 'promoting or protecting human rights' is also a charitable purpose.[104] While this might not carry the same ableist language as the other purposes earlier discussed, it is a problematic and even perverse purpose to apply to disability service charities given criticisms of their governance and operations in Sections II.B and III.A.

The 'charitable purpose' must be for 'public benefit'. The charitable purposes discussed in the preceding paragraph – preventing human suffering, relieving poverty and distress and caring for and supporting people with disability[105] – are

[96] Charities Act 2013 (Cth) s 5 'charity'.
[97] ibid s 12(1)(c).
[98] ibid s 15(1).
[99] ibid s 15(2).
[100] ibid s 12(1)(a).
[101] ibid s 14.
[102] M Harding, 'Independence and Accountability in the Charity Sector' in J Picton and J Sigafoos (eds), *Debates in Charity Law* (Oxford, Hart Publishing, 2020) 15.
[103] ibid 18.
[104] Charities Act 2013 (Cth) s 12(1)(g).
[105] ibid s 7(d).

assumed to be for 'public benefit', '[i]n the absence of evidence to the contrary'.[106] Assuming these purposes are for public benefit results in what charity law scholar Kim Weinert refers to as the legal concept of charity having an 'inherent link to goodness'.[107] This gives rise to a 'halo effect' that shapes public perception of charities fulfilling ableist purposes as inherently benevolent and innocent and thus incomprehensible as perpetrators of harm: 'The effect of the halo is a powerful influence on perceiving an entity's purpose as being morally good and the entity itself as intrinsically trustworthy.'[108]

In a context where 'charitable status is normally determined by reference to an organisation's purposes, rather than its activities',[109] the incidence of violence in specific disability service charities is beside the point for the legal definition (ie, it does not matter if some charities' activities reflect a better track record in how disabled people are treated). Rather, the problem is that existence of the legislation and bestowing charitable status pursuant to that legislation sustains ableist understandings of disability that – as discussed in Section III.A – render disabled people violable and charities beyond accountability.

Many disability service charities are PBIs, including Sunnyfield, LWB, and Afford discussed in Section II.C. Pursuant to the Australian Charities and Not-for-Profits Commission's interpretation of PBI, the 'benevolent' aspect of PBIs means the entity is 'organised, promoted or conducted for the relief of poverty or distress (sickness, disability, destitution, suffering, misfortune or helplessness)',[110] that is, the entity is 'specifically targeted at people in need and provided to relieve the needs of those people'.[111] In the Australian Charities and Not-for-Profits Commission's interpretation, disability per se as an example of 'distress' sustains an ontology of disability as individual experience of misery and pain which is compounded by its association with other pejorative conditions ('sickness', 'destitution', 'suffering', 'misfortune', 'helplessness'). According to the Australian Charities and Not-for-Profits Commission, an entity's services must not merely be targeted towards a group in need but 'must be actually directed towards *relieving* the poverty or distress experienced by the people it assists'.[112] The emphasis on 'relief' positions PBIs as active and disabled people as passive which entrenches paternalistic power relations. 'Relief' focuses on reducing severity of an inherently negative experience rather than on transformative and emancipatory action. Moreover, the Australian Charities and Not-for-Profits Commission's interpretation provides

[106] ibid s 7.
[107] Weinert (n 9).
[108] ibid.
[109] M Synge, 'Universities: A Question of Charity' (2022) 16 *J of Eq* 103, 106. See also M Harding, 'Distinguishing Government from Charity in Australian Law' (2009) 31 *Sydney Law Review* 559, 562.
[110] Australian Charities and Not-For-Profits Commission, 'Commissioner's Interpretation Statement: Public Benevolent Institutions' (Australian Charities and Not-For-Profits Commission, 2016) CIS 2016/03 5 citing *Perpetual Trustee Co Ltd v Commissioner of Taxation* (1931) 45 CLR 224.
[111] ibid.
[112] ibid 8.

benevolence does not extend to supporting people through 'ordinary human experience' (such as people going through marriage difficulties).[113] This requirement for relief outside of ordinary experience situates disability ontologically as inherently outside of what it means to exist as a normal human, in turn as per Section III.A legitimating inequality of disabled people and their segregation and violation.[114]

Preliminary analysis of ableism threaded through the legal definition of charity highlights discrimination embedded within charity law per se and the legal status of charity itself, irrespective of discriminatory purposes or activities of individual charities. Scholarship on the relationship between equality law and charity law has focused on the latter, particularly in the context of charities excluding marginalised groups (eg, racial minorities, women, transgender people).[115] In this scholarship discrimination is argued to only be for a charitable purpose where it advances substantive equality[116] or where overall the benefits outweigh harm of discrimination by reason of the public benefit requirement of charities.[117] However, overlooked in this scholarship is the issue of when discrimination relates not to *exclusion* of disabled people as a group from a specific charity,[118] but rather where *inclusion* of disabled people as beneficiaries of a disability service charity relates to discrimination embedded within charitable purposes themselves. The complexity of this issue is compounded by exemption of charities from the Disability Discrimination Act 1992 (Cth) where these confer 'benefits' on disabled people.[119] This reference to 'benefits' in discrimination legislation is likely to be locked in the ableist interpretive loop discussed in relation to charitable purpose such that services that are segregating or coercive will likely be seen as beneficial and thus beyond scope of legal understandings of disability discrimination.

The analysis in this chapter of the legal definition of charity highlights how charity law entrenches oppressive disability power relations, an issue yet to be explored in scholarship on charity law and political advocacy. In her own research

[113] ibid 7 citing *Marriage Guidance Council of Victoria v Commissioner of Pay-roll Tax (Vic)* 90 ATC 4770.

[114] Cf Harding's argument that charity law serves the value of autonomy by promoting goods that are 'autonomy-enhancing': Harding (n 2).

[115] J Sigafoos, 'When Should Charities Be Allowed to Discriminate? The Case of Single-Sex Services and Transgender People' in J Picton and J Sigafoos (eds), *Debates in Charity Law* (Oxford, Hart Publishing, 2020); D Morris, 'Charities and the Modern Equality Framework – Heading for a Collision?' (2012) 65 *CLP* 295; A Parachin, 'Public Benefit, Discrimination and the Definition of Charity' in K Barker and D Jensen (eds), *Private Law: Key Encounters with Public Law* (Cambridge, CUP, 2013); M Harding, 'Some Arguments Against Discriminatory Gifts and Trusts' (2011) 31 *OJLS* 303.

[116] Sigafoos argues in the context of transgender people that charities should only be able to discriminate when advancing equality: 'charitable discrimination should be acceptable only when it is advancing equality in a substantive way, by redressing disadvantage, challenging stigma and stereotype, enhancing voice and participation, or achieving social change': Sigafoos (n 115) 105.

[117] Parachin (n 115); Morris (n 115).

[118] 'when should it be acceptable for charities to exclude potential beneficiaries based upon a protected characteristic, and when should this be unlawful discrimination?': Sigafoos (n 115) 103.

[119] Disability Discrimination Act (Cth), s 49. In the UK context, see Sigafoos (n 115) 105–09.

on the public aspects of charity law over time, Jennifer Beard argues political advocacy is within charitable purposes when it advances the work of the charity in relation to its beneficiaries, including when their beneficiaries are disabled people.[120] However, disability service charities are regularly involved in resisting law reform that would enhance disability rights (and reduce their revenue). One such example is Disability Trust (a disability service charity which featured in the case study of a man who was sexually abused as a child while in the care of the organisation in the Royal Commission into Institutional Responses to Child Sexual Abuse[121]). Disability Trust formed part of a group of disability service charities that advocated to the Australian Fair Work Commission not to make changes to the wage award framework that would result in increases to disabled people's wages in disability supported employment settings where disabled people can be legally paid below the minimum wage. They argued these changes would impact on the financial sustainability of their organisations.[122]

ii. Accountability of Charities

Charity law's approach to accountability legitimates violence against disabled people in disability service charities because it provides no explicit or direct pathways to accountability and redress for violence. Accountability is not a strong feature of charity law, with its focus instead on charitable status, and rules around taxation, fundraising, and property. For example, a 547-page Australian textbook on charity law devotes two pages to the topic of accountability, and a further 10 pages to options for accountability reform.[123] These limitations in charity law are particularly disturbing noting the focus in the three Disability Royal Commission case studies (discussed in Section II.C) on disability service charities' failures to respond to and redress violence. Indeed, this failure was particularly stark in relation to Afford where there was a recognised focus by Afford on celebrating revenue from disabled people over recognising death of disabled people.

Harding identifies three dimensions of charity accountability to the state: constitutive, stakeholder, and governance.[124] 'Constitutive accountability' is 'accountability that is embedded in the fundamental state requirement that charities have purposes that satisfy the legal definition of charity [and] the public

[120] J Beard, 'Charities, Election Campaigning and the Australian Constitution' (2019) 43 *Melbourne University Law Review* 462, 474–76.

[121] Royal Commission into Institutional Responses to Child Sexual Abuse, 'Case Study 41: Disability Service Providers' (*Royal Commission into Institutional Responses to Child Sexual Abuse*) www.childabuseroyalcommission.gov.au/case-study/27150f40-1e84-4b27-9f8bc25fc162a561/case-study-41,-july-2016,-sydney.

[122] Illawarra Forum, 'Letter to Vice President Hatcher, Fair Work Commission' (31 October 2017) www.fwc.gov.au/documents/sites/awardsmodernfouryr/am2014286-corr-if-011117.pdf. For critiques see: Steele (n 26).

[123] GE Dal Pont, *Law of Charity* 2nd edn (Sydney, LexisNexis Butterworths, 2017) 516–28.

[124] Harding (n 102).

benefit test'.[125] This mode of accountability has limited utility in relation to disability service charities where charitable purposes themselves are sustaining injustice by setting up power dynamics and subjectivities that normalise violence against disabled people. 'Stakeholder accountability' refers to 'accountability that the state demands when it deals with charities as a stakeholder, for example via grant funding or through contracts by which funding is provided for the delivery of agreed outcomes'.[126] This mode of accountability is also of limited utility because the NDIS regulatory framework, which is a key source of stakeholder accountability for disability service charities receiving NDIS funds, enables segregated accommodation and supports and use of restrictive practices. Moreover, NDIS complaints processes are recognised of limited use for individuals because they are harmful and do not provide for recognition and redress.[127]

'Governance accountability' is 'accountability of charity managers and controllers in matters bearing on the application of charity assets to charitable purposes'.[128] Governance accountability is in part directed by the Australian Charities and Not-for-Profits Commission governance standards.[129] There are three governance standards particularly relevant to violence against disabled people. Governance Standard 1 requires an entity to demonstrate it has and is complying with a charitable purpose.[130] This standard is stuck in the same vicious loop as discussed in relation to constitutive accountability, because charitable purposes enable violence against disabled people. Governance Standard 3 is 'Compliance with Australian laws'.[131] This standard requires a registered entity to not engage in conduct amounting to an indictable offence.[132] While registered entities are expected to comply with all Australian laws, only a serious infringement can potentially result in enforcement action.[133] This is of limited use because governance accountability conforms to how criminal law defines and organises wrongfulness of violence and harm and many forms of violence against disabled people are lawful under criminal law.[134]

One further governance standard holds some promise for eliciting accountability for violence against disabled people. Governance Standard 6[135] requires entities to take reasonable steps to participate in the National Redress Scheme.[136] The object of this requirement is 'to maintain and enhance public trust and

[125] ibid 23.
[126] ibid 22.
[127] Wadiwel, Spivakovsky and Steele (n 27).
[128] Harding (n 102) 22.
[129] Australian Charities and Not-for-Profits Commission Regulations 2022 (Cth).
[130] ibid cl 45.5(2)(a), (c).
[131] ibid cl 45.15.
[132] ibid cl 45.15(2).
[133] ibid cl 45.15, Note 3.
[134] L Steele, 'Disability, Abnormality and Criminal Law: Sterilisation as Lawful and "Good" Violence' (2014) 23 *Griffith Law Review* 467; C Spivakovsky and L Steele, 'Disability Law in a Pandemic: The Temporal Folds of Medico-Legal Violence' (2022) 31 *Social & Legal Studies* 175.
[135] Australian Charities and Not-for-Profits Commission Regulations 2022 (Cth) cl 45.30.
[136] ibid cl 45.30(2).

confidence in the Australian not-for-profit sector by ensuring a registered entity's governance enables it to be accountable for its past conduct relating to institutional child sexual abuse'.[137] This standard will apply to disability service charities who provided services to children, such as Disability Trust mentioned in Section III.B.i. One could consider whether a further standard could be introduced requiring disability service charities to recognise and redress violence against disabled people of any age. However, this will depend on willingness of government to introduce a disability redress scheme, noting Governance Standard 6 was introduced to incentivise participation in the National Redress Scheme (Australian government redress scheme for survivors of historical institutional child sexual abuse) following recommendations from the Royal Commission into Institutional Responses to Child Sexual Abuse.[138] While redress schemes like the National Redress Scheme are a common policy response in many nations and will extend to institutional child sexual abuse in disability service charities,[139] redress schemes specific to disabled people are not similarly common and the Disability Royal Commission did not recommend a redress scheme.

Thus, overall charity law does not provide direct means of facilitating accountability of charities for violence against disabled people to the state or to disabled people themselves. Charity law becomes a mode of denial, through which charities can be narrated as benevolent and the violence at their core largely sits outside recognition and accountability.

C. Charity Law, Disability and Historical-Structural Injustice

Preliminary analysis in Section III.B highlights the need for charity law scholarship to explore charity law's role in enabling and redressing violence against disabled people. This is urgently needed to ensure charity law is responding to the contemporary systemic issue of violence in disability service charities. In this section, I propose such scholarship is also necessary by reason of the longer-term role of disability service charities in oppression of disabled people in Australia (discussed in Section II.A), coupled with charity law's role in Australian settler colonialism.[140]

'Historical-structural injustice' refers to the lasting impact of widespread injustice on structural conditions in the present. Widespread injustice cannot be frozen in time nor locked in the past because longer-term structures in society 'outlive unjust (past) events' and exist within a 'continuum between past and present'.[141] 'Historical-structural injustice' is 'a type of injustice that has been reproduced

[137] ibid cl 45.30(1).

[138] The Treasury, 'Incentivising Charities to Join the Redress Scheme – New Governance Standard FAQs' (Australian Government) treasury.gov.au/sites/default/files/2020-12/faqs.pdf.

[139] S Winter, *Monetary Redress for Abuse in State Care* (Cambridge, CUP, 2023).

[140] O'Brien (n 18).

[141] A Nuti, *Injustice and the Reproduction of History: Structural Inequalities, Gender and Redress* (Cambridge, CUP, 2019) 8. See similarly IM Young, *Responsibility for Justice* (Oxford, OUP, 2011).

in such a pervasive way that we cannot fully understand (some) existing injustices without accounting for the dynamic presence of history'.[142] Scholarship on structural harm provides concepts to situate charity law's current role in violence against disabled people in longer trajectories of structural harm, and to understand how the conditions for these harms in part evolve and endure through legal and justice systems. Charity law scholars could explore how structural injustice experienced by disabled people is sustained through charity law, albeit evolving over time with shifts in doctrinal and social approaches to charity and disability. While such analysis is beyond the scope of this chapter, in future scholars could situate the rich historical analysis that is a key feature of charity law scholarship in critical conversation with questions of violence, accountability and historical injustice. Such scholarship is timely given developments in the USA and UK related to the role of philanthropy in slavery and racial segregation,[143] and apologies by some Australian charities related to their involvement in Stolen Generations and eugenics.[144] Indeed, it is likely charity law is a key vehicle of historical-structural injustice given this jurisdiction is said to have changed little over 400 years old – despite the Charities Act 2013 (Cth) being driven by modernisation of charity law[145] – with charitable purposes originating in the Preamble to the Elizabethan Statute of Charitable Uses 1601.[146]

The enduring legal definition of charity could be understood by reference to the concept of 'injuries of normality'. 'Injuries of normality' refers to 'systematic harm inflicted on people categorized as abnormal, deviant, deficient or inferior with respect to norms and standards of health, fitness, functionality, productivity and usefulness'.[147] 'Injuries of normality' might not be recognised where there is a failure to acknowledge the underlying biopolitical rationality of normality enabling those acts – this rationality being considered 'normal rather than wrong'. In turn injuries go unremedied and the biopolitical rationality continues to operate in the present to enable harm.[148] Future charity law scholarship can explore whether consistency over centuries of the legal language of charitable purposes does not simply reflect the archaic and conservative nature of charity law, but rather a failure to recognise and unseat ableism underpinning charity law.

[142] Nuti (n 141) 9.

[143] See, eg, A Florant et al, 'A Reparations Roadmap for Philanthropy' (*Stanford Social Innovation Review*, 27 September 2023) ssir.org/articles/entry/a_reparations_roadmap_for_philanthropy; The Charity Commission, '[Withdrawn] Charity Commission Finds National Trust Did Not Breach Charity Law' (*GOV.UK*, 21 March 2021) www.gov.uk/government/news/charity-commission-finds-national-trust-did-not-breach-charity-law.

[144] See, eg, The Benevolent Society, 'Our History' www.benevolent.org.au/about-us/our-history; 'Apology for Forced Medical Procedures Linked to Racism in Australia' (*MSI Australia*, 3 August 2022) www.msiaustralia.org.au/apology-for-forced-medical-procedures-linked-to-colonisation-and-racism-in-australia/.

[145] Charities Act 2013 (Cth) Preamble.

[146] Dal Pont (n 123) 17, 77–117. See also Beard (n 9).

[147] K Braun, *Biopolitics and Historic Justice: Coming to Terms with the Injuries of Normality* (Bielefeld, transcript-Verlag, 2021) 22.

[148] ibid 26.

Situating in a longer temporal view of charity law the contemporary systemic problem of violence against disabled people enlivens questions of disability service charities' accountability for the past in the present. Charity law remains – as Weinert describes – 'tethered' to its past.[149] Yet disability service charities are increasingly distanced from their pasts with the paradigm shifts of the NDIS and CRPD providing a springboard for re-naming and re-branding in ways that superficially rejects the charity paradigm and its harmful connotations in disability social history. The fact the legal framework giving these charities their organisational legal status and identity remains relatively consistent across time provides a point of tension and rupture in disability service charities' self-representation. Indeed, we might not only see charity law's relationship to its past as one of 'tethering' but also 'haunting' – charity law remains haunted by a particular understanding of disability that is inherently violent and continues to undermine both the possibility for disability service charities to advance equality and self-determination,[150] and our ability to see and respond to harm in those charities.

As a critical concept, 'haunting' refers to surfacing 'the living effects, seething and lingering'[151] of harm associated with 'repressed or unresolved'[152] social violence that is otherwise represented as concluded and irrelevant to the present. Haunting is an 'inheritance' of sorts,[153] that is, something we now hold possession of and are actively responsible for.[154] It can inspire action through 'transformative recognition' of our role in social violence.[155] If we know charity law contributes to social harm, our responsibility as scholars is to reckon with how to address that. 'Reckoning' 'involves trying to discern how we can best contribute to changing or altering those social conditions and arrangements that leave some more vulnerable to violence or suffering than others'.[156] It also involves 'working to address the injustices we inherit, a coming-to-terms with what they mean in and for our everyday lives in the present'.[157] Reckoning therefore involves confronting and transcending present ways of knowing charity law and our place in it, and transforming social relations and everyday existence through that process.[158] Reckoning with charity law is central to a more just future for disabled people,

[149] Weinert (n 9).

[150] See similarly Weinert's critique of *Aboriginal Housing Office v Jacky* [2002] NSWSC 916 as 'reflect[ing] paternal settler state thinking and treatment of First Nations peoples': ibid 5. Cf Harding's observation of courts' and legislatures' willingness 'to abandon even the public benefit requirement in response to pressure to accommodate charities serving Indigenous communities in post-colonial settings'. M Harding, 'Charity and Law: Past, Present and Future [2020] *Sing JLS* 564, 574–75.

[151] AF Gordon, *Ghostly Matters: Haunting and the Sociological Imagination* 2nd edn (Minneapolis, Minnesota University Press, 2008) 195.

[152] ibid xvi.

[153] ibid 200.

[154] A Dean, *Remembering Vancouver's Disappeared Women: Settler Colonialism and the Difficulty of Inheritance* (Toronto, University of Toronto Press, 2015) 7.

[155] Gordon (n 151) 8.

[156] Dean (n 154) 142.

[157] ibid 141.

[158] Gordon (n 150) 202.

because without confronting our own (often invisible) implication in violence, we will repeat the past and present in the future.[159] Thus, to reckon with charity law is to grapple with the doctrinal content and lived experiences of charity law *and* our place as scholars engaged with charity law and the violence it allows or ignores.

IV. Conclusion: Reckoning, Repair, and Abolition?

Violence against disabled people in disability service charities is a systemic problem. This chapter has shown charity law is integral to this violence. Charity law sustains socio-cultural ideas about disability that justifies dehumanisation, segregation, and violation of disabled people, and fails to deliver accountability and redress when disabled people experience violence in disability service charities. Preliminary analysis of charity law suggests disability and violence are inextricably connected at the heart of charity law and the longevity of this connection requires situating contemporary violence against disabled people in longer-term historical-structural injustice associated with disability service charities and charity law.

Returning to Harding's question quoted in Section I of the future of charity law in social action,[160] this chapter suggests the need for radical re-evaluation of charity law's role in disabled people's lives and their access to support. Disability Justice activists argue imagining and building more just and equitable communities involves rendering harmful systems and practices unthinkable.[161] Disability law abolitionist scholar Jamelia Morgan argues transforming conventional approaches to legal thought and analysis is a necessary dimension of this strategy.[162] Reckoning with charity law's role in violence against disabled people is a necessary foundation for re-imagining socio-legal relations of disability support and ultimately building non-violent, and economically and socially just futures.

[159] Dean (n 154) 73.
[160] Harding (n 7).
[161] T Lewis, 'Disability Justice Is an Essential Part of Abolishing Police and Prisons' (7 October 2020) https://level.medium.com/disability-justice-is-an-essential-part-of-abolishing-police-and-prisons-2b4a019b5730; The Abolition and Disability Justice Collective, 'Cripping Abolition' abolitionanddisabilityjustice.com/opening/.
[162] J Morgan, 'Responding to Abolition Anxieties: A Roadmap for Legal Analysis' (2022) 120 *Michigan Law Review* 1199.

9

Assessing Charity Commission Regulation: An Empirical Investigation into Statutory Inquiries 2021–24

JENNIFER SIGAFOOS

I. Introduction

The Charity Commission for England and Wales (Commission or Charity Commission) is the principal regulator for a diverse and economically important segment of the UK economy. Due to the nature of charities and charitable purposes, the sector's efforts are focused on people who are particularly vulnerable. These elements make it important to understand how the Commission performs as a regulator. There is little literature, however, focusing on Commission regulation in a systemic way. In this first comprehensive empirical investigation of the most serious regulatory interventions by the Commission, I will use data from the most recent 3.5 years of reported statutory inquiries to investigate the Commission's performance as a regulator.

There are around a half a million non-profit organisations in the United Kingdom (UK), of which around 80 per cent are charities.[1] According to the Commission, as of 31 March 2024, there were 170,056 registered charities in England and Wales.[2] Charities with an annual income below £5,000 are not required to register with the Commission unless they are set up as charitable incorporated organisations (CIOs). The Charity Commission also regulates these more than 100,000 smaller unregistered charities, which includes groups such as those that run village halls and playing fields.[3] In addition, there are more than 80,000 exempt charities, who

[1] Charity Excellence Framework, 'How Many Registered Charities are there in the UK?' (2024) www.charityexcellence.co.uk/how-many-charities-in-the-uk/.

[2] Charity Commission, *Annual Report and Accounts, 2023–2024* (London, The Stationery Office, 2024) www.gov.uk/government/publications/charity-commission-annual-report-and-accounts-2023-to-2024/charity-commission-annual-report-and-accounts-2023-to-2024.

[3] Charity Commission, 'A snapshot of charities in Wales' (Publication, 2009) https://assets.publishing.service.gov.uk/media/5a7c4d2eed915d338141de4d/walesreport.pdf.

have another principal regulator but can still receive some regulatory functions from the Commission.[4] As well as being numerous, the sector is economically significant, with the Charity Commission being responsible for the regulation of £96 billion of charity income and £94 billion of charity spending in the fiscal year 2023–24.[5]

The sector relies on public trust and confidence, both to ensure sufficient charitable donations and to inspire willingness to volunteer in crucial roles, including that of charity trustee.[6] In England and Wales, trustee roles are generally voluntary, and trustees are only compensated for reasonable expenses. The Commission says that 'The concept of unpaid trusteeship has been one of the defining characteristics of the charitable sector, contributing greatly to public confidence in charities.'[7] There is a statutory power for charities to pay trustees for goods or services provided beyond those of being a trustee, subject to conditions.[8] In addition, some charities compensate their trustees for the performance of trustee duties where the charity's governing document allows for it and it is considered by the board to be in the best interests of the charity. The Commission notes that suitable authority to authorise these payments is 'relatively uncommon' in charity governing documents, and the Commission may authorise such payments where the trustee board presents a 'reasoned case' that it is in the best interest of the charity and there is no suitable alternative that would not involve the trustee compensation.[9] This is presented by the Commission in its guidance as a means of enabling individuals who could not otherwise afford to do so to serve as trustees by compensating them for their loss of income due to taking on the trustee duties.[10] It nevertheless remains uncommon for trustees to be compensated for services performed as trustees, and these individuals' voluntary contributions of their time and energy prop up the sector, while at the same time exposing the trustees themselves to personal reputational and sometimes financial risks if things go wrong.

Public trust and confidence in the charity sector is also crucial considering the nature of the services it provides and the beneficiaries it serves. Many charities now play an important role in the delivery of key public services. The

[4] Exempt charities are those listed in Schedule 3 of the Charities Act 2011 (UK), common funds that only accept deposits from exempt charities, and those made exempt by other pieces of legislation. Exempt charities can receive advice and guidance from the Commission and can be investigated by the Commission via a Statutory Inquiry at the request of their principal regulator. The Commission can also authorise trustee actions in certain situations, such as the making of ex gratia payments. The Commission must consult the principal regulator for the exempt charity in these situations. Charity Commission, 'CC23: Guidance, Exempt Charities' (Publication, 2023) www.gov.uk/government/publications/exempt-charities-cc23/exempt-charities.

[5] Charity Commission (n 2).

[6] N Hyndman, 'Editorial: The Charity Sector – Changing Times, Changing Challenges' (2017) 37(3) *Public Money & Management* 149–53.

[7] Charity Commission, 'Guidance: Trustee expenses and payments' (Guidance, 2024) www.gov.uk/government/publications/trustee-expenses-and-payments-cc11/trustee-expenses-and-payments, s 1.

[8] Charities Act 2011 (UK), s 185.

[9] Charity Commission (n 7) s 6.4; 8.1.

[10] ibid s 8.1.

government – both national and local – spends approximately £17 billion on grants and contracts with the charity sector annually, an amount that has plateaued in recent years.[11] Health and social care is by far the biggest sector in which voluntary and community sector organisations and social enterprises (VCSEs) win government contracts, worth £11.6 billion in 2021.[12] Although these represent only a small fraction of the overall public spend on public services, in some sectors charitable providers are particularly dominant: 69 per cent of government contracts for homelessness services and 64 per cent of contracts for services for survivors of domestic violence and sexual abuse were won by VCSEs over the period 2016–20.[13] The VCSE sector is also the largest provider of NHS-commissioned mental health services.[14] The nature of these services, along with the tenor of charitable purposes – set out historically in *Pemsel*[15] to be purposes for the relief of poverty, the advancement of education and the advancement of religion – mean that the beneficiaries of the services are likely to be particularly vulnerable people.[16] It is therefore important that the sector regulation is sufficiently robust to ensure safeguarding and protection of charitable service users.

In light of the above, the Charity Commission is potentially under resourced to meet the considerable task of regulating the sector, having suffered drastic funding cuts in the early 2010s. Although recent budgets have been more positive, with £32.254 million in the 2023–24 budget, funding has still not reached previous levels, even without taking inflation into account.[17] As of 31 March 2024, the Commission reported 488 staff.[18] Forced to do more with less, the Commission retrenched in its strategic plan in the 2010s, deciding to focus on only two of its

[11] NCVO, 'UK Civil Society Almanac 2023' (Article, 2023) www.ncvo.org.uk/news-and-insights/news-index/uk-civil-society-almanac-2023/financials/what-are-the-trends-in-income-from-government/.

[12] Tussell, 'UK Public Procurement through VCSEs, 2016-2020: Report for the Department for Culture, Media and Sport (Tussell, 2021) https://assets.publishing.service.gov.uk/government/uploads/system/uploads/attachment_data/file/1069635/UK_Public_Sector_Procurement_through_VCSEs.pdf; N Sykes, 'Understanding the ecosystem: charities and public services: Evidence for the Law Family Commission on Civil Society' (Pro Bono Economics, 2021) www.probonoeconomics.com/understanding-the-ecosystem-charities-and-public-services.

[13] ibid.

[14] N Sykes, 'Understanding the ecosystem: charities and public services' www.probonoeconomics.com/understanding-the-ecosystem-charities-and-public-services.

[15] *Special Commissioners of Income Tax v Pemsel* [1891] AC 531 (HL). The fourth *Pemsel* 'head' of charity was other purposes beneficial to the community.

[16] The concept of vulnerability is contested. Vulnerability is a universal human condition, but it is also particular, as how vulnerability is experienced by an individual is conditioned by that individual's access to resources. MA Fineman, 'The Vulnerable Subject: Anchoring Equality in the Human Condition' (2008–09) 20 *Yale J L & Feminism* 1. I use the term 'particularly vulnerable people' here to account for this paradoxical nature of vulnerability. L Peroni and A Timmer, 'Vulnerable Groups: The Promise of an Emerging Concept in European Human Rights ConventionLaw' (2013) 11(4) *International Journal of Constitutional Law* 1056–85.

[17] At peak spending, in FY2007–08, the Charity Commission reported spending £33.5m. Charity Commission, 'Annual Report and Accounts, 2007–08' (London, The Stationery Office, 2008) https://assets.publishing.service.gov.uk/media/5a7c930440f0b626628ad067/0574.pdf.

[18] Charity Commission (n 2).

five statutory objectives, accountability and compliance.[19] Despite arguments that the Commission's lighter touch regulatory approach avoided driving out potential charitable activity,[20] the Commission moved away from the previous friend to the sector element of its role and focused more on delivering accountability for charity to the public.

The Commission's 2018–23 Strategy continued its focus on public trust: 'Our purpose is to ensure charity can thrive and inspire trust so that people can improve lives and strengthen society.'[21] In its new 2024–29 Strategy, the Commission identified five strategic objectives for the period:

1. We will be fair and proportionate in our work and clear about our role.
2. We will support charities to get it right but take robust action where we see wrongdoing and harm.
3. We will speak with authority and credibility, free from the influence of others.
4. We will embrace technological innovation and strengthen how we use our data.
5. We will be the expert Commission, where our people are empowered and enabled to deliver excellence in regulation.[22]

Perhaps in response to criticism from the sector, in the new strategy the Commission suggests that it will take a more balanced approach to its dual functions of supporting and enforcing the sector: 'This means that we place equal emphasis on being a source of support to trustees, but also a tough enforcer.'[23] It is a difficult balance to strike, as too onerous a regulatory regime would surely discourage individuals from taking up charity trusteeship, but a regime that is too light touch would expose the sector, and the particularly vulnerable people it serves, to unacceptable risk.

It is also complicated by the diversity of the sector, both in aims and income. In terms of organisational aims, the Charities Act 2011 (UK) codified 12 charitable purposes, as well as a catch all category, ranging from the prevention and relief of poverty to promoting the efficiency of the military or police, fire, rescue

[19] Charity Commission, 'Charity Commission Strategic Plan 2012–2015' (2011) https://data.parliament.uk/DepositedPapers/Files/DEP2012-0103/DEP2012-0103.pdf. The Charity Commission's five statutory objectives are: (1) increase public trust and confidence in charities, (2) promote awareness and understanding of the operation of the public benefit requirement; (3) promote compliance by charity trustees with their legal obligations in exercising control and management of the administration of their charities, (4) promote the effective use of charitable resources, and (5) enhance the accountability of charities to donors, beneficiaries, and the general public.

[20] A Hind, 'Increasing Public Trust and Confidence in Charities: On the Side of the Angels' (2011) 31(3) *Public Money & Management* 201–05.

[21] Charity Commission, 'Charity Commission Statement of Strategic Intent 2018–23' (Corporate Report, 2018) www.gov.uk/government/publications/charity-commission-strategy-2018-2023/charity-commission-statement-of-strategic-intent-2018-2023#fn:7.

[22] Charity Commission, 'Charity Commission Strategy, 2024–2029' (Corporate Report, 2024) www.gov.uk/government/publications/charity-commission-strategy-2024-2029/charity-commission-strategy-2024-2029.

[23] ibid.

and ambulance services.[24] The organisations that comprise the sector are also varied in terms of income. In 2020–21, the overwhelming majority were classified by the NCVO as 'micro' (47 per cent – incomes less than £10,000) or 'small' (33 per cent – incomes from £10,000 to £100,000).[25] Only 0.04 per cent were classified as 'super-major', with annual incomes more than £100 million.[26] The Commission's regulatory regime must be sufficiently flexible to effectively regulate the hugely divergent circumstances in which charities operate.

The Commission approaches this balancing act by adopting an explicitly 'risk-led' approach.[27] It aims to be proactive in identifying and preventing risk, to address harm effectively, and to focus its resources on the highest risks.[28] Through the evaluation of risk, the Commission aims to meet the standards of best regulatory practice, as is required of it by the Charities Act 2011 (UK), 'including the principles under which regulatory activities should be proportionate, accountable, consistent, transparent and targeted only at cases in which action is needed'.[29] How well this risk-led approach achieves the desired balance, avoiding both too onerous and too permissive regulation, is an important question.

There have been criticisms of the Charity Commission's performance as a regulator.[30] In 2013 the National Audit Office (NAO) published a report on the regulatory effectiveness of the Commission.[31] At that time, its annual income was £22.3 million and there were approximately 163,000 main registered charities. The NAO noted that it was reporting in a time of considerable public and parliamentary interest in the performance of the Commission in light of the Cup Trust scandal, a large-scale tax evasion scheme masquerading as a charity. The NAO also identified the large funding cuts that had taken place at Commission, with a fall of 40 per cent in real terms from 2007–08 to 2013–14, at a time when the size of the sector had remained relatively stable. However, four reports of the NAO, over the previous 26 years, had also criticised the Commission's regulatory performance. In its previous investigation of the Commission, in 2001, the NAO found that the use of the Commission's statutory powers was in decline, and in 2013 the use was found to have declined further, although there were potential signs that the trend

[24] Charities Act 2011 (UK), ss 3(1)(a–m).

[25] NCVO, 'UK Civil Society Almanac 2023: Profile' (Profile, 2023) www.ncvo.org.uk/news-and-insights/news-index/uk-civil-society-almanac-2023/profile/how-many-voluntary-organisations-are-there/.

[26] ibid.

[27] Charity Commission, 'Regulatory and Risk Framework' (Policy Paper, 2016–2020) www.gov.uk/government/publications/risk-framework-charity-commission/regulatory-and-risk-framework; M Webster and R Teele Langford, 'Comparison of Enforcement Powers of the Charity Commission for England and Wales and the ACNC' law.unimelb.edu.au/__data/assets/pdf_file/0006/4277625/Webster-Langford-CCEW_ACNC-Comparison.pdf.

[28] ibid s 1.3.

[29] Charities Act 2011 (UK), s 16(4).

[30] D Morris, 'The Charity Commission for England and Wales: A Fine Example or Another Fine Mess?' (2015) 91(3) *Chicago-Kent Law Review* 965–90.

[31] National Audit Office, *The regulatory effectiveness of the Charity Commission* (London, The Stationary Office, 2013) www.nao.org.uk/wp-content/uploads/2013/11/10297-001-Charity-Commission-Book.pdf.

was reversing.[32] In 2015 and again in 2017, the NAO followed up to its report and found that the Commission was making good early progress at addressing the concerns raised in its earlier report.[33] One of these concerns was about the small number of statutory inquiries opened by the Commission annually, as well as progress toward concluding and closing ongoing inquiries.

Despite this reported progress, these early signs may not have amounted to much overall. There does seem to have been a surge in reported resolutions of statutory inquiries in 2016 and 2017, but this has since tailed off again. A key criticism by the NAO was the perception that the Commission remains a reactive, rather than proactive, regulator. There is speculation that problematic charity cases are unlikely to come to the Commission's regulatory attention absent media coverage, parliamentary interest or complaints. The Commission gained new investigation and enforcement powers under the Charities (Protection and Social Investment) Act 2016. There is little in the way of literature considering the Commission's use of these new powers, or its current use of previous powers.

There also have been recent criticisms of the Commission's regulation from the perspective of safeguarding of particularly vulnerable people. In May 2024, the Parliamentary and Health Service Ombudsman (PHSO) released a report into its investigation of a complaint by a whistleblower, Lara Hall, about the Charity Commission's response to alleged sexual exploitation by a charity, reported to be the British Pakistani Christian Association (BPCA), now called British Asian Christian Association (BACA).[34] Ms Hall, who was both a beneficiary of the charity's services overseas and a volunteer, is referred to in the report as Miss A but is reported to have previously waived her anonymity.[35] Ms Hall had made allegations of serious safeguarding concerns regarding the conduct of a charity trustee, who had engaged in a sexual relationship with her. Ms Hall was a previous survivor of human trafficking and sexual abuse and she reported that the sexual relationship was abusive and had been reported to the police. The complaint to the Commission also alleged

[32] National Audit Office, *Giving confidently: The role of the Charity Commission in regulating charities* (National Audit Office, 2001); National Audit Office (n 31) 3.21.

[33] National Audit Office, *Report: Value for Money, Follow-up on the Charity Commission* (London, National Audit Office, 2015) www.nao.org.uk/reports/follow-up-on-the-charity-commission/; National Audit Office, *Charity Commission: Progress Report* (London, National Audit Office, 2017) http:www.nao.org.uk/wp-content/uploads/2017/11/Charity-Commission-progress-report.pdf.

[34] H Whitehead, 'Charity Commission criticised over its communication with vulnerable whistleblower', *Civil Society* (London, 20 May 2024) www.civilsociety.co.uk/news/charity-commission-criticised-over-its-communication-with-vulnerable-whistleblower.html; Parliamentary and Health Service Ombudsman, 'An investigation into the Charity Commission: Miss A's complaint' (London, Parliamentary and Health Service Ombudsman, 2024) www.ombudsman.org.uk/sites/default/files/Miss%20A%20complaint%20WEBSITE%20VERSION_0.pdf.

[35] Parliamentary and Health Service Ombudsman, 'Ombudsman rules Charity Commission failed to properly handle safeguarding concerns related to sexual exploitation' (London, Parliamentary and Health Ombudsman Service, 18 May 2024); Whitehead (n 34); A Rickets, 'Regulator told to pay compensation to whistleblower who suffered 'maladministration'', *Third Sector* (London, 20 May 2024) www.thirdsector.co.uk/regulator-told-pay-compensation-whistleblower-suffered-maladministration/governance/article/1873481.

financial improprieties. The Commission opened a regulatory compliance case to investigate and ultimately issued an Official Warning to the BPCA in February 2021, about failures in safeguarding procedures and wider governance concerns.[36] The regulatory compliance case was reported to be closed in 2022.[37] The PHSO criticised the Charity Commission's handling of the case, including its failure to guarantee Ms Hall's welfare, as she was a vulnerable adult, and said that the Commission's failings led to 'a significant and serious exacerbation of her vulnerabilities and emotional ill health.'[38] The PHSO recommended an apology and financial compensation from the Commission, as well as ensuring that steps are taken to prevent future occurrences. It was reported that the Charity Commission was initially resistant to the findings and threatened to judicially review the PHSO for making a substitute regulatory decision but has subsequently agreed to accept the findings.[39]

In light of the size and significance of the charitable sector, as well as the risks to the public, including particularly vulnerable people, if the sector is ineffectively regulated, it is important to better understand the Charity Commission's regulation. There have not been systematic studies focusing on the outcomes of Commission regulation.[40] In this paper I will consider the most recent 3.5 years of reported statutory inquiries published by the Commission. Statutory inquiries are the most serious level of investigation by the Commission and are warranted when preliminary investigations indicate 'serious cases of abuse and regulatory concern' that merit further investigation in line with the Commission's Risk and Regulatory Framework.[41] I have built a dataset of these statutory inquiries, along with other reports of the cases, which I will use to investigate the Charity Commission's performance as a regulatory body. The UK's Legislative and Regulatory Reform Act 2006 sets out the Better Regulation Commission's five principles of good regulation, which are echoed in the Charities Act 2011 (UK): transparent, accountable,

[36] Charity Commission, 'Charity Commission case exposes failures at British Pakistani Christians Limited' (Press Release, 2022) www.gov.uk/government/news/charity-commission-case-exposes-failures-at-british-pakistani-christians-limited.

[37] ibid.

[38] Parliamentary and Health Service Ombudsman (n 35) para 5.

[39] M Gillard, 'Charity Commission failed whistleblowers raising sex abuse allegations, says watchdog' *The Times* (London, 17 May 2024).

[40] Although this is true of academic literature, specialist charity solicitors sometimes release updated year in review-type reports focused on charity trustee audiences. Examples read while producing this projects are: L Rhodes, 'Charity Commission Inquiries: top takeaways for charities' (Bates Wells, 2024) https://bateswells.co.uk/updates/charity-commission-inquiries-top-takeaways-for-charities/. Also identifying the key theme of the dominant trustee: S Clune, 'Charity Commission: 2023 review of statutory inquiries' (Article, 2023) www.stoneking.co.uk/literature/e-bulletins/charity-commission-2023-review-statutory-inquiries; Stone King, 'Charity Commission Inquiries: themes from recent cases' (Article, 2023) www.stoneking.co.uk/literature/e-bulletins/charity-commission-inquiries-themes-recent-cases. There are also more commonly reports from charity solicitors and other sector-facing entities such as accountants that report on the outcomes of particular inquiries.

[41] Charities Act 2011 (UK), s 46; Charity Commission, 'Guidance: Statutory inquiries into charities: guidance for charities' (Guidance, 2024) www.gov.uk/government/publications/statutory-inquiries-into-charities-guidance-for-charities-cc46/statutory-inquiries-into-charities-guidance-for-charities s 1.1; Charity Commission (n 27).

proportionate, consistent, and should be targeted only at cases in which action is needed.[42] I will consider to what extent the Charity Commission is able to meet these goals for good regulation, as well as the implications for both the regulator and the regulated. I will argue that the Commission is a reactive regulator, rather than proactive, and question whether it is sufficiently transparent. I will show that the Commission commonly exercises its powers to appoint Interim Managers and to disqualify trustees, at least in these most serious regulatory cases. However, in light of the size of the sector as compared to the number of statutory inquiries reported annually, my findings raise concerns that the Commission does not have an adequate regulatory reach.

II. Methodology

I read and analysed every published statutory inquiry report from the Charity Commission for 2024 (January–July), 2023, 2022 and 2021. There are not large numbers of published statutory inquiries, but the resulting dataset included 227 reported statutory inquiries in total. Of these, only 65 were reports of inquiries independent of the 'Double Defaulters' statutory class inquiry that the Commission opens annually for selected charities that are in default of their statutory obligations to meet reporting requirements by failing to file their annual documents for two or more years in the past five years. It is possible that the global Covid-19 pandemic delayed the progress and publication of inquiry reports for some of the included years, but these numbers are comparable to the numbers in previous years. In order to ensure inquiries were not omitted, I also looked at every published news item for the Charity Commission on the www.gov.uk website. I coded each inquiry report for a number of different elements, including form and type of charity, income, potential triggers for the investigation, the types of misconduct investigated, the powers exercised and the enforcement actions taken. I then searched in online databases for the charity's name and trustees (if named in the inquiry report) and analysed and coded the resulting media articles and other hits. I also found public comments discussing cases on the Facebook pages of some of the charities, or other social media, which I also coded. As the project progressed, I identified other potential themes such as the existence of a dominant individual controlling the charity, operating overseas, issues involving charity land[43] and the appointment of Interim Managers. As each potential theme was identified I returned to the earlier reports and coded those reports for the new themes, as well.

I focused on statutory inquiries as they are at the pinnacle of potential regulatory action by the Charity Commission. They are the types of regulatory intervention

[42] Legislative and Regulatory Reform Act 2006 (UK), s 42; Charities Act 2011 (UK), s 16(4).

[43] Earlier research by Debra Morris into charitable disputes also identified these as common causes of these disputes. D Morris, 'Disputes in the Charitable Sector' (Liverpool, Charity Law & Policy Unit, 2003) www.liverpool.ac.uk/media/livacuk/law/2-research/clpu/ADRReport03.pdf.

where the Commission would exercise its new powers under the 2016 Act. They are also discrete, and it is clear when a case has been opened as an incidence of regulatory intervention, as opposed to a soft regulation or ongoing casework intervention, where the regulator might engage more informally. I also focus on statutory inquiries because other systematic data on regulatory interventions are simply unavailable for assessing the performance of the Commission.

One potential limitation to the study is that the Charity Commission may not publish every statutory inquiry report. The Commission sets out circumstances in which it might not publish an inquiry or that an inquiry has not been opened, when to do so would:

- be detrimental to a particular individual or group of individuals, for example a risk to someone's personal safety;
- contravene or prejudice requirements for confidentiality or commercial sensitivity, or risk National Security;
- cause severe prejudice to the charity and/or its beneficiaries;
- contravene the Commission's duty to use its resources in the most efficient, effective and economic way;
- make regulation less effective and damage public confidence in charities; mean that public interest in not publishing outweighs the public interest in publishing.[44]

The Commission also states that it may delay publication of a report to avoid prejudicing investigations by law enforcement or a regulator or to give trustees time to compete certain actions. One potential explanation for the decline in reports again after the surge in 2016 and 2017 is that the Commission is holding back from publishing a larger number of reports. The Commission does report larger numbers of inquiries opened each year in its annual report. For example, in the 2019–20 Annual Report, the Commission reports 181 concluded Statutory Inquiries, with 155 concluded in 2018–19.[45] This far exceeds the number of published concluded inquiries, despite the fact that those cases should have been concluded and reported by the end of the period of data collected.

Given the pressure on the Commission to be seen to be performing, however, it seems unlikely that the number of reports that are altogether unpublished would be particularly numerous. I also read all of the Commission's published statements on live cases, which do not suggest that there are numerous inquiries going unreported.[46] It is likely that many inquiries are unreported because they are concluded but essentially put into a holding pattern while trustees are expected to comply with regulatory advice. Then if the regulatory follow up finds that trustees

[44] Charity Commission, 'Collection: Inquiry Report: Charity Commission' (Collection, 2024) www.gov.uk/government/collections/inquiry-reports-charity-commission#inquiry-reports-published-in-2022.

[45] Charity Commission, 'Annual Report 2019-20' (Report, 2020) https://assets.publishing.service.gov.uk/government/uploads/system/uploads/attachment_data/file/901690/Charity_Commission_Annual_Report_and_Accounts_2019_to_2020.pdf p 14.

[46] Charity Commission, 'Collection: Statement on Live Cases' (Collection, 2024) www.gov.uk/government/collections/statements-on-live-cases-charity-commission.

have not complied the Commission reopens the case. This aligns with one of the Commission's stated reasons for delaying publication, and in the reported inquiries we can see this happened frequently, reported retrospectively as now a new inquiry has been opened after the trustees failed to complete the actions to the satisfaction of the Commission.

The Commission also appears to be quite slow in reporting the outcome of some inquiries, which it occasionally attributes to discretion and concerns about impeding the investigation. In most cases, it seems to be more related to the pace of investigations, rather than necessarily reflecting delay due to this sort of discretionary decision.

This project has used a mixed methods approach, also called multi-strategy.[47] A mixed or multi-methods approach aims to utilise the relative strengths of various research techniques to increase reliability.[48] This complementarity allows for a fuller understanding of complex phenomena.[49] The data included in the dataset are both quantitative and qualitative. The quantitative data will be presented below as descriptive statistics to present a full empirical picture of these regulatory interventions by the Commission. It is inspired by a core philosophical principle underpinning the Empirical Legal Studies movement, that 'it is better to have more systematic knowledge of how the legal system works rather than less, regardless of the normative implications of that knowledge'.[50] Using a comprehensive dataset will allow for structured investigation of these most serious regulatory interventions by the Commission. The qualitative data were analysed for themes using a thematic analysis assisted by NVIVO software.[51] The qualitative data develop deeper insights into how the regulatory system is working, helping to explain the patterns revealed in the quantitative analysis.

III. Analysis

A. A Systemic Picture of Commission Statutory Inquiries

The dataset includes 227 statutory inquiries from 2021 to mid-2024. 71 per cent of these were reported through the Double Defaulters statutory class inquiries, and

[47] A Bryman, *Social Research Methods* (Oxford, OUP, 2004); A Bryman, 'Integrating Quantitative and Qualitative Research: How Is It Done?' 6(1) (2006) *Qualitative Research* 97.

[48] JW Creswell and VL Plano Clark, *Designing and Conducting Mixed Methods Research* 3rd edn (London, Sage Publications, 2018); C Teddlie and A Tashakkori, 'Major Issues and Controversies in the Use of Mixed Methods in the Social and Behavioural Sciences' in A Tashakkori A and C Teddlie (eds), *Handbook of Mixed Methods in Social and Behavioural Research* (London, Sage Publications, 2003) 3.

[49] A Bryman, *Quantity and Quality in Social Research* (London, Routledge, 1998); Teddlie and Tashakkori (n 48); T Clark et al, *Bryman's Social Research Methods* 6th edn (Oxford, OUP, 2021).

[50] T Eisenberg, *The Origins, Nature, and Promise of Empirical Legal Studies and A Response to Concerns* (Cornell Law Faculty Publications, 2011) 974 https://scholarship.law.cornell.edu/facpub/974.

[51] V Braun and V Clarke, 'Using Thematic Analysis in Psychology' (2006) 3(2) *Qualitative Research in Psychology* 77–101.

only 29 per cent were independent statutory inquiries. In the case of some of the charities initially included in the four Double Defaulters statutory class inquiries (2021–24), the casework involved with the Double Defaulters inquiry revealed potential mis- or malfeasance that led to the Commission opening an independent statutory inquiry. These charities were included in the dataset when the report of the independent inquiry was released separately, rather than with the Double Defaulters inquiry.

Of the 65 independent statutory inquiries, 68 per cent of the charities involved operated in England and Wales, 20 per cent operated overseas and 12 per cent operated in England and Wales as well as overseas. The most common charitable purpose was the advancement of education, with 47 per cent of charities, followed by prevention or relief of poverty at 46 per cent and 40 per cent with advancement of religion. These were followed by the provision of overseas aid (32 per cent),[52] community development (22 per cent) and health (17 per cent). The remaining charitable purposes were represented in smaller percentage of cases. Most charities report multiple charitable purposes, so the percentages add up to more than 100 per cent. It is difficult to directly compare this to data for the overall population of charities, but Damm and Kane's Charity Field Classification project estimates that 42 per cent of charities meet a tag for education, 22 per cent for religion and 18 per cent for social welfare (which includes poverty in that classification system.)[53] This would suggest that religious and poverty charities are overrepresented in the independent inquiries group.

The charities in the independent inquiries group are over representative of larger income size charities. At the top of the income bands, 11 per cent of the independent inquiries sample had an annual income greater than £10 million, where this is true of only 1 per cent of all charities.[54] Combining the top three income bands, charities with incomes over £1 million are 23 per cent of the inquiries group, but only 1.9 per cent of the overall charity population.[55] On the other end of the income bands scale, charities with annual incomes less than £25,000 make up 18 per cent of the inquiries charities, but are 59 per cent of the overall population.[56] Charities with larger annual incomes are therefore more likely to be subject to a statutory inquiry than those with smaller annual incomes. I ran a chi-square test of independence between these two variables and this result was highly significant, p-value of <.00001.[57]

[52] Overseas aid is not an enumerated standalone charitable purpose in the Charities Act 2011 (UK) but is commonly listed on the Register. It is a sub-set of the relief of poverty.

[53] C Damm and D Kane, *Charity Field Classification: Main Project Report* (Sheffield Hallam University Centre for Regional Economic and Social Research, 2021) http:charityclassification.org.uk/data/charity-classification-report.pdf.

[54] Charity Commission, 'Charities by Income Band – 27 August 2024' (Register, 2024) register-of-charities.charitycommission.gov.uk/sector-data/charities-by-income-band.

[55] ibid.

[56] ibid. Again combining three income bands.

[57] X^2 (1, N = 65) = 84.95, $p = < .00001$. The result is significant at $p < .05$.

This finding is reinforced by the direction of the expected error for how precisely I was able to pinpoint the charities' annual income. I included the reported income for the charity in the year that appeared to trigger the SI. In some cases, this was included in the report, especially where the report alleged inaccurate accounts. In most cases the income was not included in the report. For these charities, I looked up their reported income for the year on the Charity Commission website. There were some charities for which the triggering year was too long ago for accounts to still be available on the Commission website. In these cases, I have included the income from the closest available year. This is likely to mean that a few charities are reported at below the appropriate income band, because charities are frequently removed from the register and wound up as a result of the inquiry, so their reported income in these cases is likely to be lower than was the case in the year before the inquiry. There also was a group of seven statutory inquiries in 2021, all connected to two common trustees and by common registered details. These charities made up 33 per cent of the included charities with annual incomes less than 25 per cent, again causing the smaller charities to appear more frequently than they would otherwise have done. It seems likely that these smaller related charities were identified proactively because of the suspected fraud on the part of the two common trustees in the larger charity.

This finding that charities with larger incomes are more likely to be subject to a statutory inquiry is in line with what might be expected, given the Commission's explicitly risk-led regulatory approach. Charities with larger incomes will present a greater risk for loss of charitable funds. They also will present greater risks in terms of reputational damage to public trust and confidence. This aligns with statutory goal of proportionate regulation.[58]

B. The Charity Commission as a Reactive Regulator

The Charity Commission is a reactive, rather than proactive regulator. In only two of the statutory inquiries was there no evident external triggering event that led to the inquiry. In both of those cases, the inquiry was reported to be triggered proactively due to the charity operating overseas in a high-risk area (Iraq and Pakistan, respectively). In the remaining reported inquiries, there was at least one 'trigger', and in most cases there were several. The presence of several triggers in most inquiries means that a meaningful quantitative analysis of which sort of potential trigger is more likely to result in an opened inquiry is not possible. Some common triggers are set out below.

[58] Charities Act 2011 (UK), s 16(4).

i. 'Double Defaulter' Charities

Numerically speaking, the most common triggers for an inquiry was consistent failure to file the required accounts and trustee report.[59] On 20 September 2013, the Commission launched a 'class statutory inquiry' into what it calls 'double defaulters', organisations that are late filing accounts on two or more occasions in five years. The Commission adds new double defaulters to the class inquiry each year. Before a formal inquiry is launched the Commission engages in what it calls the pre-inquiry stage of case work, where it issues a 'final warning' to the charity, notifying it that it is at risk of being added to the inquiry. Only if the charity then fails to come into compliance is the charity added to the inquiry. In 2019, the inquiry was amended to include additional factors that enable the regulatory decision making to be 'risk-based and proportionate'.[60] The specific factors are not identified, but the Commission's Regulatory and Risk Framework identifies that the Commission should weigh its decisions in light of the likelihood of the risk and the severity of the harm if it should come to pass.[61] The Commission also reports on the number of charities that are brought current during this pre-inquiry stage, and the amount of charity funds that are now accounted for. Analysis indicates that the size of the charity is again a factor in this risk-based assessment. In 2021, the Commission reported that 23 charities were brought current, with a combined income of £14 million, and in 2022 35 charities and £40 million in income were accounted for. As most charities are small, it appears that it is mostly larger charities that are caught up in the risk-based regulation of the double defaulters.

ii. Regulator/Police Reports

Inquiries were commonly triggered by notifications from other regulatory bodies or police. A number of inquiries were launched into charities with a purpose of

[59] The Charity Commission website notes:

> All registered charities must provide information annually to the Charity Commission ('the Commission'). The rules vary according to the charity's size and structure. Registered charities with:
>
> - income up to £10,000 should complete the relevant sections (income and expenditure) of the annual return
> - income above £10,000, and all Charitable Incorporated Organisations ('CIOs'), must prepare and file an annual return
> - income above £25,000, and all CIOs, must also file copies of their trustees' annual report and accounts.

Charity Commission, 'Decision: double defaulter charities between April 2020 and March 2021' (Publication, 2021) www.gov.uk/government/publications/charity-inquiry-double-defaulter-charities-between-april-2020-and-march-2021/charity-inquiry-double-defaulter-charities-between-april-2020-and-march-2021.

[60] ibid.

[61] Charity Commission (n 27).

education after Ofsted or Department for Education investigations found failings in the schools run by or linked to the charities, such as inadequate educational standards or failings in safeguarding. There were also several inquiries triggered by police investigations, such as into individuals suspected of links to funding terrorism.

An example of an inquiry being triggered by an intervention by another regulator, the Richmond Psychosocial Foundation International inquiry[62] was triggered by a Coroner's Report attributing the death of a resident to serious governance failures.

iii. Trustee/Auditor Reports

Several inquiries were triggered by reports of serious incidents (RSI) filed by charity trustees. Reports by independent examiners of charity accounts also triggered investigations. There were also inquiries triggered by what appeared to be schisms in trustee boards. Finally, inquiries were triggered by a lack of filing reports. Persistent failure to comply with reporting requirements was another common trigger (beyond the Double Defaulters discussed above).

An example of an RSI by the trustees triggering an inquiry is Human Appeal,[63] where the RSI was made, reporting that several of the charity's trucks carrying flour had been stopped and held for several hours by an armed group and that on a separate occasion its warehouse in Syria had been seized by a terrorist organisation linked to Al-Qaeda. The inquiry was triggered by the fact that the trustees had taken eight and four months, respectively, to report such serious incidents to the Commission, and that the trustees had failed to make a report under s19 of the Terrorism Act 2000 (UK) (TACT), as was required.

iv. Media/Parliamentary Interest

Inquiries appear to have been triggered by complaints by members of the public or donors to the Commission, to MPs, or by MPs who were patrons of charities. In its service standards aspirations, the Commission identifies that it will attempt to respond to letters from MPs within 20 days, so this is a frequent enough occurrence to merit a specific performance measure. Many of the cases that resulted in inquiries also merited considerable coverage in local press, and a handful in national press. Lock argues that media pressure can force the Commission into

[62] Charity Commission, 'Decision Charity Inquiry: Richmond Psychosocial Foundation International (Decision, 2021) www.gov.uk/government/publications/charity-inquiry-richmond-psychosocial-foundation-international/charity-inquiry-richmond-psychosocial-foundation-international. An operational case had been opened by the Commission after the death, then closed to allow for other regulatory and statutory agencies to investigate. This was followed by the regulatory compliance case to investigate complaints.

[63] Charity Commission, 'Decision Charity Inquiry: Human Appeal' (Decision, 2021) www.gov.uk/government/publications/charity-inquiry-human-appeal.

launching regulatory interventions against its preferences.[64] In some of the cases in this study, it appeared that media interest was the main trigger, but on examination there had been a prior trigger and the media interest came later. An example is Care4Calais, where the Commission reports that lack of compliance with previous Commission regulatory engagement, including a prior action plan, led to the initiation of the inquiry.[65] The considerable media coverage of the charity's decision to bring judicial review proceedings against the then government over its plans to deport people seeking asylum to Rwanda came after the inquiry had already been initiated. The Commission concluded that this was acceptable political activity for the charity.[66]

v. Prior Regulatory Intervention

Finally, another common trigger was a prior regulatory intervention by the Commission. In these cases, the Commission had established a future review date and had reengaged with the charity as a result.

C. Poor Financial Controls is the Most Common Allegation Investigated

Most inquiries presented a series of interlinked problems, connected to poor governance. The inquiry reports therefore present results of investigation into several allegations of mis- or malfeasance. The most common allegation investigated can be broadly defined as poor financial controls. There were some common themes within this grouping for the situations that the Commission considered to be sufficiently serious to open an inquiry. Some of these are set out below, along with some examples of how that issue presented in an inquiry or inquiries.

i. Insufficient Financial Controls/Managing Conflicts of Interest

Financial mismanagement was a common matter for investigation in inquiries, often with a strong element of potential private benefit to trustees or linked individuals. It was common in these scenarios for there to be too much control by a single trustee, or a founder, discussed further below. The individual was then very closely associated with the charity, to the point where other trustees deferred, or

[64] RS Lock, 'The Regulatory Role of the Charity Commission' (1998) 13(7) *Managerial Auditing Journal* 403–10.

[65] Charity Commission, 'Charity Inquiry; Care4Calais' (Inquiry, 2023) www.gov.uk/government/publications/charity-inquiry-care4calais/charity-inquiry-care4calais.

[66] ibid.

the provision for the charity was too closely interlinked with the provision for this controlling member.

An example is The Retreat Animal Rescue,[67] where the charity held what purported to be a lease to part of Brickyard Farm. Two of the trustees occupied a house and garden on the farm. The trustees had purchased the property, and the charity had previously been permitted to use the land rent-free. After several years, a significant donation was made to the charity, at which point in time the trustees used the donation to pay off part of the loan with which the property had been purchased, and a 25-year leasehold interest was carved out of the freehold and granted to the charity. The inquiry found that at the time of the lease the charity was without the proper number of trustees and could not validly decide to enter a lease. In addition, as the charity took the form of a trust it had no separate legal personality, meaning both sides of the lease were held by the same individuals. The inquiry found that the charity had failed to manage conflicts of interest appropriately and that there were insufficient financial controls. It issued an Action Plan (section 15 Charities Act 2011 (UK)) to the charity to regularise the lease. The Commission also gave notice of its intention to issue an Official Warning[68] to trustees A and B. However, trustee B resigned, so the Official Warning was only issued to trustee A as Official Warnings can only be issued to current trustees.[69]

The subjects of some inquiries had such extreme conflicts of interest that they appeared to be sham charities that could never have been properly in the public benefit, such as the inquiry opened in 2019 into 'seven charities connected by two common trustees and common registered details'.[70] In that inquiry, one trustee operating under two aliases was involved in all seven charities. One of these charities had 13 other trustees and was able to adequately explain itself and establish that it was operating in the public benefit to the Commission. It was offered advice and withdrawn from the inquiry. The other six charities appeared to be controlled by this single individual or one other. They all had other listed trustees, but these did not respond to the Commission or replied to say that they were not involved. The Charity Commission removed the six charities from the register and used its power under section 181(a) of the Act to disqualify the two trustees, one for 15 years and the other for five years.

[67] Charity Commission, 'Decision Charity Inquiry: the Retreat Animal Rescue' (Decision, 2021) www.gov.uk/government/publications/charity-inquiry-the-retreat-animal-rescue/charity-inquiry-the-retreat-animal-rescue.

[68] The Charities (Protection and Social Investment) Act 2016 (UK) added a new s 75A to the Charities Act 2011 (UK) that gave the Charity Commission a new power to issue official warnings when it considers there has been a breach of trust or duty or other misconduct or mismanagement in a charity.

[69] Charity Commission (n 67).

[70] Charity Commission, 'Charity Inquiry: seven charities connected by two common trustees and common registered details' (Decision, 22 July 2021) www.gov.uk/government/publications/charity-inquiry-seven-charities-connected-by-two-common-trustees-and-common-registered-details.

ii. Insufficient Financial Controls/Cash Couriers

The Commission has published regulatory alerts warning against the use of cash couriers to transport money to international charity sites.[71] The Commission notes that the practice carries significant risks, including that it is associated with terrorist or criminal activity, and that it carries safety risks to both the courier and the funds. It is also difficult to audit and to maintain adequate records of income and expenditure in line with charitable purposes. Several inquiries involved cash couriering, likely linked to the fact that approximately one third of the inquiries charities had a purpose of overseas aid and one third operated overseas. These inquiries illustrated another element of the risk identified by the Commission: that funds are at risk of being seized and held by the police under the Proceeds of Crime Act 2002 (UK) (POCA) or the TACT.

An example is the Human Aid UK Inquiry, where two volunteers and the charity's Director of Operations was stopped at Heathrow Airport and found to be in possession of $9,774 (USD) and £9,200 (GBP) in cash. As the individuals failed to properly account for the cash, it was seized by the police under section 294 of POCA and detained for six months.[72] The Commission had already been engaged with the charity after police reports that the charity was operating in high-risk areas and was insufficiently vetting its domestic and overseas partners. The inquiry noted failings in financial management and overall governance, as well as misconduct or mismanagement specifically related to the cash couriering. The trustees then took positive steps in response to the regulatory intervention and had taken on board the regulatory advice. Although the Commission exercised its power under section 76(3)(f) of the Act to make an Order restricting the trustees from transferring charity assets out of the UK without prior authorisation, as well as an Order preventing trustees from transferring or applying charity funds or property in Turkey or Syria, after the positive engagement by the charity trustees, the Orders were discharged in July 2020.[73]

iii. Insufficient Financial Controls/Professional Fundraising

Several inquiries involved the use of suspect professional fundraising arrangements by charities. In most of these there were also strong elements of payments to connected companies or individuals.

In the inquiry into the Alternative Animal Sanctuary, there was a financial arrangement with a professional fundraiser, which involved a poor return for the charity, with only 18 per cent of the amounts raised received as income by the

[71] Most recently in May 2022. Charity Commission, 'Regulator renews its message warning charities against the use of cash couriers' (News Story, 3 May 2022) www.gov.uk/government/news/regulator-renews-its-message-warning-charities-against-the-use-of-cash-couriers.

[72] Charity Commission, 'Decision Charity Inquiry, Human Aid UK (Decision, 2021) www.gov.uk/government/publications/charity-inquiry-human-aid-uk/charity-inquiry-human-aid-uk.

[73] ibid.

charity (£1.8 million of £10.6 million over 12 years) and the rest being expended on costs and fees under the agreement.[74] The inquiry considered that the arrangement was also unfavourable because there was no opt out clause before seven years and the arrangement was intended to generate the primary source of income for the charity. In addition, the fundraising solicitations did not contain a sufficient solicitation statement[75] or information about the arrangement or the proportion of funds that would be devoted to charitable purposes. The inquiry considered that this lack of transparency exposed the charity to an unacceptable level of risk to its reputation.

In this case, the inquiry had been triggered by the charity's auditors over concerns about lack of adequate controls and management of conflicts of interest, outside of these fundraising arrangements, as well as the fact that the charity was insolvent on its balance sheet. The Commission had used its temporary protective powers under section 76(3)(g) of the Act to appoint an Interim Manager to the charity. The charity was eventually wound up pursuant to an Order under section 337(6) of the Act, as it was concluded that it was not feasible to address significant underlying issues at the charity, even with a new board of trustees, especially as the charity operated out of the Chair's property. The Charity appealed the order to the First Tier Tribunal (Charity) but the appeal was dismissed. Its £407,000 in assets were distributed to ten different local charities with similar purposes. Two of the charity's trustees were disqualified under section 181(A) of the Act, for periods of 15 and 10 years, respectively. Another trustee made a voluntary undertaking that they would not act as a trustee for five years.[76]

Similar issues were raised in the Support the Heroes inquiry.[77] There, trustees had again failed to manage conflicts of interest, and the fundraising was conducted by a professional fundraising company with strong personal ties to the founder. Over a three-year period only approximately 17 per cent of the total funds raised (£223,000 of £1,318,039) were applied to charitable purposes. Again, there was insufficient disclosure in the solicitation statement and the Commission was concerned about the reputational risk to the charity. Complaints had been raised by member of the public to both the Commission and the charity and there had been an investigative programme on the BBC, as well as national media coverage.[78]

[74] Charity Commission, 'Decision Charity Inquiry: The Alternative Animal Sanctuary' (Decision, 2 September 2021) www.gov.uk/government/publications/charity-inquiry-the-alternative-animal-sanctuary.

[75] Under s 60 of the Charities Act 1992 (UK) and The Charitable Institutions (Fund-Raising) Regulations 1994 (UK) professional fundraisers and commercial partners are required to make a solicitation statement disclosing information about how much will go to which charity whenever they are asking for donations and representing that a contribution will be made to a charity.

[76] ibid.

[77] Charity Commission, 'Decision, Charity Inquiry: Support the Heroes' (Decision, 2022) www.gov.uk/government/publications/charity-inquiry-support-the-heroes.

[78] ibid.

D. Mismanagement in Administration of Financial Affairs can Merit Inquiry

In several inquiries the Commission concluded that failures to make payments on time, or to consider the affordability of loans or other expenditures is mismanagement of the charity's financial affairs on the part of trustees. The Commission considered that this might result in loss in confidence in the charity or its trustees.

One notable example is the cautious inquiry report into the investigation of the failure of Keeping Kids Company.[79] Operating as Kids Company, the charity was a high-profile failure, with considerable critical media coverage, especially as the charity had received substantial income from government sources, including £17 million over the three years prior to its collapse. This led to published investigations by the NAO in 2015 and the Public Administration and Constitutional Affairs Committee (PACAC) in 2016.[80] The Official Receiver (OR) in 2017 issued an application pursuant to section 6 of the Company Directors Disqualification Act 1986 (UK) (CDDA) for a disqualification order for acting as directors or being involved in the management of a company against the trustees of the charity. The OR also sought to disqualify the CEO on grounds that she was a 'de facto' director. The OR's allegation against the trustees and the CEO was that they 'had caused and/or allowed Kids Company to operate an unsustainable business model'. The High Court's judgment was that the allegation was not made out against any of the trustees. Although the model was high risk it was not unsustainable in practice. The judgment was critical of the OR and its understanding of how charities operate. The judgment also found that the trustees were ultimately in charge and that the CEO was not a de facto director. The judgment also suggested that the Charity Commission was ultimately the correct arbiter for these situations in the case of charities.[81]

The Commission's Inquiry had been paused during the earlier investigations and court proceedings. Its report was published approximately a year and a half after the judgment. Although it took note of the findings in the High Court, the Commission nevertheless criticised the trustees for operating a demand-led model that was so dependent on fundraising and a main fundraiser (in the CEO). The report noted that although the model was not unusual for the sector, what made it high risk was the size of the charity, and that it was unusual for a charity

[79] Charity Commission, 'Decision Charity inquiry: Keeping Kids Company' (Decision, 10 February 2022) www.gov.uk/government/publications/charity-inquiry-keeping-kids-company/charity-inquiry-keeping-kids-company.

[80] National Audit Office, 'Investigation: the government's funding of Kids Company' (Report, 2015) www.nao.org.uk/reports/investigation-the-governments-funding-of-kids-company/; House of Commons Public Administration and Constitutional Affairs Committee, 'The collapse of Kids Company: lessons for charity trustees, professional firms, the Charity Commission, and Whitehall' (Fourth Report of Session 2015–16, 2016) publications.parliament.uk/pa/cm201516/cmselect/cmpubadm/433/433.pdf.

[81] *The Official Receiver v Atkinson & Ors* [2021] EWHC 175 (Ch).

of this size. Trustees are responsible for identifying and balancing risks associated with their operating model. This can include financial planning and recording and maintaining a reserves policy. The report also noted that funding shortfalls had resulted in the charity missing payments such as PAYE payments to HMRC, and other payments to HMRC, and that payroll was one day late in November 2014 due to funds not having cleared. This constituted mismanagement on the part of the trustees and could have undermined confidence. The trustees also should have ensured checks and balances to prevent power imbalances and considered limiting the terms for key roles such as trustees and the chair.[82] In March 2025, the High Court heard arguments in a judicial review brought by Michael-Karim Kerman, Kids Company's former clinical director, to challenge the Commission's Inquiry Report.[83]

E. A Dominant Individual is a Warning Sign for Potential Board Failings

Analysis of inquiries published in 2023 highlighted the issues that can arise when a charity is dominated by an individual.[84] I then went back though the previous reports to code for this variable. Sometimes the reports discuss this directly, but oftentimes where it was unclear I used media reports and Facebook comments to confirm. The individual is often a trustee or chief executive, but frequently is the religious leader in the case of a religious charity. This individual's dominance in decision making leads to the trustee board being insufficiently independent in its decision making.

The issue of a dominant individual leading to poor governance is common in the reported inquiries. In my sample, I identified this in 62 per cent of the independent statutory inquiries.[85] This suggests that it is a very important factor to consider for charities and the regulator. In the inquiry into Rheema Church London, the dominant individual was the Pastor, who held the principal administrative role in the charity.[86] There was a history of regulatory intervention by the Commission after a whistleblower complaint raised concerns about how trustees were applying charitable funds and led to a regulatory compliance case in 2010 that

[82] Charity Commission (n 79).

[83] E Moss, 'Kids Company report could have "chilling impact" on charity sector, court hears', *Civil Society Media* (2025) www.civilsociety.co.uk/news/kids-company-report-could-have-chilling-impact-on-charity-sector-court-hears.html.

[84] Rhodes (n 40) also identifies this trend in the year's reports. Earlier research from Debra Morris also identified this a major trigger of charitable disputes. Morris (n 43).

[85] It is not possible to test for the statistical significance of this as there is no numerical value available for the number of charities not subject to a statutory Inquiry that are dominated by an individual. The figure is nevertheless so large as to allow conclusions to be drawn with confidence even in the absence of significance testing.

[86] Charity Commission, 'Decision Charity Inquiry: Rheema Church London' (Decision, 30 March 2023) www.gov.uk/government/publications/charity-inquiry-rhema-church-london.

was closed in 2012, with the issuance of advice and guidance to trustees. Another whistleblower complaint led to Commission reengagement in 2014 and an inquiry was opened in 2015. There were strong elements of potential private benefit to the dominant individual, with charitable funds being misappropriated or misapplied. The inquiry found that there was insufficient control by the trustees, who met only once per annum. Poor financial controls resulted in a tax liability of £543,286 as the charity had been reporting incorrectly and was unable to demonstrate that its spending was for charitable purposes. An interim manager was appointed, who suspended and eventually dismissed the dominant individual. A challenge in the Employment Tribunal was dismissed. The Interim Manager (IM) eventually paid the charity's extensive liabilities and wound it down.[87]

F. Lack of Compliance with Obligations to Prepare and File Charity Accounts

Inquiries even beyond the double defaulters class inquiry suggest that a failure to file annual accounts and trustee statements is symptomatic of deeper governance problems at charities. The double defaulters inquiries begin from failures to comply with this duty to be accountable to the public and to beneficiaries, but it was common across the independent inquiries, as well. The basic failure to comply with annual reporting requirements was symptomatic of deeper problems in the charities that made it to the final inquiry stage for double defaulters. Possibly the charities that came into compliance after having received the notice that they were at risk of being added to the inquiry had fewer systematic issues.

G. Commission Pleases Neither Side in Political Battles Over Charities

Numerous recent attempts have been made to leverage Charity Commission regulation to stifle voices from across the sector, and some incidence of this can be seen in the inquiries sample. The then-Culture Secretary, Oliver Dowden warned in 2021 against charities 'hijacked by a vocal minority seeking to burnish their woke credentials' and stated he had issued an instruction directing officials selecting the new Charity Commission Chair to 'ensure that the new leader of the Commission will restore charities' focus to their central purpose'.[88] The Culture Secretary, who has the power to appoint the chair, said, 'candidates will be tested on how they

[87] ibid.

[88] Department for Digital, Culture, Media and Sport and O Dowden, 'Culture Secretary Oliver Dowden op ed on recruitment of new Charity Commission chair' (News Story, 12 September 2021) www.gov.uk/government/news/culture-secretary-oliver-dowden-op-ed-on-appointment-of-new-charity-commission-chair.

will harness the oversight powers of the Commission to commence this rebalancing [away from the perceived 'woke' agenda]. And ministers will only select a candidate that can convince on these criteria.'[89] The Good Law Project issued judicial review proceedings in response, arguing that this was an impermissible and improper attempt by the Secretary of State to 'direct and control the exercise of the new Chair's regulatory functions … [seeking] to ensure that the selected candidate exercises the oversight powers of the Commission in a particular way, consistent with the secretary of state's political agenda'.[90] The eventual appointee subsequently withdrew after reports of complaints in previous appointments and the case was dropped.[91]

In recent years, multiple complaints were made by Conservative Members of Parliament (MP) against charities working in ways of which they disapproved. Complaints were made against the Runnymede Trust, a race equality thinktank, for an open letter it joined, criticising the report of the Commission on Race and Ethnic Disparities (Cred).[92] A group complained about a blogpost from the children's charity Barnardo's that offered parents tips on how to discuss 'white privilege' with children.[93] The National Trust has come under repeated criticisms after it published a report that investigated links between its properties and their historical associations with colonialism and slavery.[94] In each case, the Commission opened a regulatory compliance case in response and concluded that the activities complained of had not breached charity law.[95] As discussed above, in the inquiries covered in this analysis, the Commission considered the appropriateness of the political activities of Care4Calais in bringing judicial review proceedings against

[89] ibid.

[90] Bindmans LLP, 'Letter sent pursuant to the pre-action protocol for judicial review – The Good Law Project v The Secretary of State for Digital, Culture, Media and Sport' (London, Bindmans, 17 September 2021) https://drive.google.com/file/d/1vTKyD-RrrtClaXYH4WaGKGrePyWME_OG/view paras 20–21.

[91] The Good Law Project, 'Case Update: Why it's 'job done' with the Charity Commission' (London, The Good Law Project, 23 February 2022) goodlawproject.org/update/job-done-charity-commission-chair/.

[92] N Parveen and A Mohdin, 'Tory MPs demand inquiry into equality thinktank over race report criticism' *The Guardian* (London, 20 April 2021) www.theguardian.com/world/2021/apr/20/tory-mps-demand-inquiry-runnymede-trust-thinktank-race-report-criticism-charity-commission.

[93] P Butler, 'Barnardo's blogpost on white privilege did not breach charity laws' *The Guardian* (London, 4 Aug 2021) www.theguardian.com/world/2021/aug/04/barnados-blogpost-on-white-privilege-did-not-breach-charity-laws.

[94] P Butler, 'National Trust report on slavery links did not break charity law, regulator says' *The Guardian* (London, 11 March 2021) www.theguardian.com/uk-news/2021/mar/11/national-trust-report-uk-slavery-links-did-not-break-charity-law-regulator-says.

[95] Charity Commission, 'Charity Commission finds National Trust did not breach charity law' (Press Release, 11 March 2021) www.gov.uk/government/news/charity-commission-finds-national-trust-did-not-breach-charity-law; R Hargrave, 'Charity Commission clears Barnardo's over white privilege blog' (London, Civil Society Media, 4 August 2021); Charity Commission, 'Charity Commission concludes compliance case involving The Runnymede Trust' (London, Charity Commission, 1 September 2021) www.gov.uk/government/news/charity-commission-concludes-compliance-case-involving-the-runnymede-trust.

the then-government over its plans to offshore asylum seekers to Rwanda and concluded they were acceptable.[96]

The Commission has been a potentially equal disappointment to MPs and others complaining from the left side of the political spectrum. In March 2024, the Good Law Project made a complaint to the Commission on behalf of Dr Andrew Purkis OBE, a former Commission Board member and three MPs (representing the Scottish National Party, the Green Party and the Liberal Democrats). It stated that the trustees of the Institute for Economic Affairs, which calls itself 'an educational charity and a UK-based free-market thinktank promoting free thought',[97] had fallen foul of Commission guidance for education charities and think tanks and that concerning acceptable political activity.[98] The Commission responded quickly and rejected the complaint. It noted that charity thinktanks made a positive contribution to intellectual debate and, barring active endorsements of political parties or other unacceptable political activity, the Commission 'will not be used as a weapon to stifle their important thinking in this regard, and thus will rarely intervene when allegations of political bias are made, from whatever angle'.[99] The Good Law Project has responded by filing a complaint and request for reconsideration of the decision in May 2024.[100]

The Commission was similarly resistant to a complaint in May 2022 from a large coalition of politicians, writers, scientists and others organised by Extinction Rebellion, who argued that the Global Warming Policy Foundation, UK was not an educational charity but rather a fossil fuel lobby group.[101] The Commission opened a regulatory case in response, which it closed on 30 July 2024. The Commission reported months of engagement with the charity's trustees, concerning 'the educational value of the charity's research, its funding sources and its relationship with a wholly owned trading subsidiary and with a sister organisation'.[102] The Commission reported that the charity's trustees had agreed to changes, including

[96] Charity Commission (n 65).

[97] Institute for Economic Affairs, 'What we do' (London: Institute of Economic Affairs, 2024) https://iea.org.uk/what-we-do/.

[98] The Good Law Project, 'Complaint re: Apparent breach of duties by trustees of the Institute of Economic Affairs Limited (Charity No 235351)' (London, The Good Law Project, 13 March 2024) https://drive.google.com/file/d/1BcTqbzRNjmDGj8kGTdHwIItBZSUqo0Ne/view.

[99] Charity Commission, 'Letter to the Good Law Project' (Letter, 25 March 2024) http:drive.google.com/file/d/1eQnpbU7F2zZgUXWpHdTAxgZ1nlUjhZf4/view.

[100] The Good Law Project, 'Complaint re: Apparent breach of duties by trustees of the Institute of Economic Affairs Limited (Charity No 235351)' (London, The Good Law Project, 10 May 2024) https://drive.google.com/file/d/1eTe69mL7eiYIOMmDMREbp51tDA801qw_/view.

[101] Extinction Rebellion, 'Charity what charity? Letter of complaint about the Global Warming Policy Foundation's charity status' (London, Extinction Rebellion, 23 May 2022) https://extinctionrebellion.uk/2022/05/23/charity-what-charity-letter-of-complaint-about-the-global-warming-policy-foundations-charity-status/.

[102] Charity Commission, 'Regulator concludes case into climate change think tank following changes' (Press Release, 30 July 2024) www.gov.uk/government/news/regulator-concludes-case-into-climate-change-think-tank-following-changes.

a pre-print process for external review of its publications, as well as publishing a wider range of sources of information on its pages, including those advancing different views. In addition, the wholly owned trading subsidiary changed its name to better distinguish its non-charitable campaigning from the activities of the charity itself. The Commission was satisfied that there were sufficiently robust processes for managing conflicts of interest presented by the charity's relationship with its American sister organisation.[103] The case was closed, with the Commission noting 'We expect the trustees to now fully implement the proposed changes. On that basis, we are satisfied the concerns raised are now resolved.'[104]

The Commission has thus shown itself to be resistant to political pressure from both sides attempting to use its regulatory power to stifle charities advancing opposing views. In 2024, Commission Chair Orlando Fraser KC confirmed that the Commission had withdrawn a regulatory alert to thinktanks issued in 2018, during the period between the referendum on leaving the European Union but before the European Union (Withdrawal Agreement) Act 2020 (UK) received Royal Assent in January 2020.[105] That alert warned that charitable thinktanks must ensure that the charity's outputs were 'balanced and neutral' and be careful about political campaigning.[106] Fraser noted that the alert had been issued in 'febrile times', and reiterated that the Commission will 'rarely intervene' in situations alleging political bias, although

> We expect their research to be open-minded and their conclusions not to be predetermined. But we are unlikely to consider that a progressive think tank is in breach of charity law by the fact that it may favour left-of-centre solutions, and likewise with others elsewhere on the political spectrum.[107]

The extent to which the conclusions drawn in these regulatory compliance cases and inquiries are equivalent is debatable. Likewise, this position from the Commission seems to be a departure from previous guidance and case law, but a further discussion is beyond the scope of this chapter. I conclude only that while we can see that the Commission is a reactive regulator, on this particular front the evidence shows it has proved resistant to being pushed into particular regulatory conclusions by political pressure. Most of these regulatory compliance cases opened in response to political pressure were not escalated to statutory inquiries. The Commission's regulatory neutrality advances its strategic aims of being fair

[103] ibid.

[104] ibid.

[105] H Whitehead, 'Charity Commission chair rejects calls for think tanks to lose charity status' *Civil Society Media* (London, 13 March 2024) www.civilsociety.co.uk/news/charity-commission-chair-rejects-calls-for-think-tanks-to-lose-charity-status.html.

[106] Charity Commission, 'Regulatory alert issued to charitable think tanks' (News Story, 7 December 2018) www.gov.uk/government/news/regulatory-alert-issued-to-charitable-think-tanks?utm_source=8ba60208-0ced-4f78-aa0a-88754742eb48&utm_medium=email&utm_campaign=govuk-notifications&utm_content=immediate.

[107] O Fraser, 'Yes, political think tanks deserve their charitable status' (London, The Charity Commission, 14 March 2024).

and proportionate and to 'speak with authority and credibility, free from the influence of others'.[108]

H. The Appointment of Interim Managers is a Commonly Used Power

As was seen in the case of Rheema Church London, the Commission appoints IMs using a risk-led approach in some inquiries under section 76(3)(g) of the Act.[109] In the sample of cases, the exercise of this power to appoint an IM was exercised in 29 per cent of independent inquiries. In some cases, the IM has the power to work to the exclusion of the powers of the trustees, and sometime is appointed to work alongside trustees. The Commission sets out the circumstances in which it might be appropriate to appoint an IM: when the Commission has concerns about a charity's ability to operate; when trustees are unable to act; when there is a significant risk to the charity's assets, income, services, beneficiaries, volunteers or employees, or to its reputation; or a risk to the reputation of charity more generally.[110] An Order appointing an IM is appealable to the FTT (Charity).

The cost of the IM is usually the responsibility of the charity, although the Commission will occasionally indemnify this cost. The IM in some inquiries was a large expense to the charity. For example, in Achiezer,[111] the IM concluded that the charity needed to be wound up, which necessitated the sale of the charity's property portfolio. This realised £623,000. The cost of the IM, including fees of £133,500 and related professional fees of £92,243.25, meant that the funds remaining to charity were £429,819.22, which were distributed to three charities with similar objects.[112]

I. The Power to Disqualify Trustees is Commonly Used

The Commission has the power to disqualify trustees under section 181A Charities Act 2011 (UK). In order to make an order for disqualification, the Commission must be satisfied that one or more of the six conditions in section 181A (7) are met, that the individual is unfit to be a charity trustee; and that the making of the

[108] Charity Commission (n 22).
[109] Charities Act 2011 (UK), s 76(3)(g).
[110] Charity Commission, 'Charity Commission power to appoint an Interim Manager for a charity' (Policy paper, 5 July 2022) www.gov.uk/government/publications/how-the-charity-commission-appoints-interim-managers/charity-commission-power-to-appoint-an-interim-manager-for-a-charity#fn:1.
[111] Charity Commission, 'Decision Charity Inquiry: Achiezer' (Decision, 19 August 2022) www.gov.uk/government/publications/charity-inquiry-achiezer/charity-inquiry-achiezer.
[112] ibid.

order is 'desirable in the public interest in order to protect public trust and confidence in charities'.[113] The Commission has the discretion to decide the length of the disqualification (up to 15 years) and whether the disqualification applies to all charities or to a particular charity or class of charities. In the independent inquiries this power was commonly exercised by the Commission, and can be seen in 45 per cent of reported cases, often for multiple trustees. In a further 6 per cent of cases the Commission reported that one or more trustees made voluntary undertakings not to act as a trustee, presumably to avoid official disqualification.

IV. Conclusion

The Commission's 2018–23 strategy states that 'Regulation is a means to an end; it is not an end in itself.'[114] As set out above, the Better Regulation Commission established five principles of good regulation, which are incorporated into the Charities Act 2011: it should be transparent, accountable, proportionate, consistent, and targeted only at cases in which action is needed.[115] The small number of published inquiry reports indicates potential concerns with a number of these principles. If the Commission is not publishing most inquiry reports, then there are concerns about the transparency of its workings. As it is, most of the Commission's case work is undertaken as regulatory cases, rather than inquiries. These are more opaque to scrutiny, as only a small number of case concluding statements are published, which may be appropriate in terms of shielding charities and trustees in these cases where less serious regulatory intervention is indicated.

The Commission has set itself the goal to be more transparent about its regulatory work. It has occasionally published statistics for this work, such as the number of inquiries and the types and size of charities they represent, or the number of times that it exercised various powers in a particular year. These are not regularly published, however, and sometimes conflict with other published accounts. For example, the Commission published a spreadsheet on the number of Statutory Inquiries launched in 2018–19, which listed a total of 90, with an additional five for unregistered charities.[116] However, as noted above, the Commission's annual report for 2019–20 states that 155 had been opened in 2018–19. The workings of the Commission for its regulatory functions therefore remain frustratingly non-transparent and the regulator could do more, even if it is not the case that it is withholding publication of most of its inquiry reports.

[113] Charities Act 2011 (UK), s 181A(6).
[114] Charity Commission (n 21).
[115] Legislative and Regulatory Reform Act 2006 (UK), s 42; Charities Act 2011 (UK), s 16(4).
[116] Charity Commission, 'Inquiry, operational compliance and monitoring case statistics; Inquiry case statistics: 1 April 2018 to 31 March 2019' (2019).

If it is the case that most inquiry reports are not published, I am not satisfied with the circumstances in which the Commission says it might not publish. As set out by the Commission, above, they certainly seem to be a reasonable limit on transparency. It would not be reasonable regulation to expose an individual or a group to a risk to their personal safety, or to harm national security. As the reports that are published contain information that is certainly considerably prejudicial to charities and beneficiaries, the standard for what must be held back as 'severely prejudicial' would seem to be very high indeed. The same argument suggests that any claimed public interest in not publishing might well be merited. However, the very reasonableness to the criteria set out raises questions about why these particular inquiry reports were not published, as it seems unlikely that a majority of reports in a year could fall foul of them. The small number published limit the extent to which the Commission can be accountable to a key stakeholder – the public.

In the published reports, the Commission seems to be proportionate and consistent in its response. In many cases, trustees were reported to have engaged productively with the inquiry and to have been offered some regulatory advice and guidance to improve their governance arrangements. It was in situations where the Commission perceived there to be unmanageable conflicts that measures such as an IM were implemented. There was little indication from the reports that the Commission was acting in an unjustified way. On the other hand, these are the reports of only the most significant regulatory cases that the Commission undertakes, so the seriousness of the allegations will perhaps inevitably lead to a perception of proportionate investigation.

Were these inquiries targeted only at the cases that needed it? The analysis above has revealed the Commission to be largely a reactive regulator. All but two cases had a trigger or triggers that led to the Commission's investigation. The mechanism of the Double Defaulters Class Inquiry that the Commission established in 2013 has been a positive step towards expanding its regulatory net and places it on a more proactive footing. There is nevertheless the impression that a charity that files its account on time and refrains from political activity is unlikely to rise to the Commission's attention. The cases reported in these inquiries merited serious investigation. Every inquiry report indicated real issues with the charity's performance or governance, and I am confident that regulatory intervention was needed here. The worry instead is that the small numbers indicate that regulatory interventions might also be needed elsewhere.

10

A Normative and Dimensional Analysis of the Chinese Legislative Framework for Charitable Organisations

SHAOMING ZHU

I. Introduction

In recent years, charitable organisations have become an important force in China. Trusted by many to provide public welfare and social aid, charitable organisations (along with philanthropy generally) have emerged as a professionalised industry in China.[1] This industry within China's legal system is highly regulated, and ways in which charitable organisations are regulated has also evolved since 2016. The regulatory framework in which charities operate now involves a range of instruments, including the Charity Law[2] which establishes the legal basis for regulating charitable organisations, other relevant laws,[3] regulations issued by different Ministries,[4]

[1] S Ni, 'The Organisational Features and Functional Advantages of Modern Charitable Trusts – Comparison with Charitable Foundations' (2014) 46 *Academic Monthly* 86, 87.

[2] Which was promulgated and implemented in 2016.

[3] Following its general provisions, the Charities Law (2016) provides the definition, form, conditions, registration, governance and termination of charitable organisations. The importance of importance of legal definition of charitable organisations. In addition to the Charities Law (2016), other laws with superior legal effect include the Public Welfare Donation Law (1999), the Red Cross Society Law (2017), the Enterprise Income Tax Law (2018), and the Civil Code (2021), which together constitute the fundamental legal positioning and rights and obligations of charitable organisations.

[4] Under the law, provisions regulating and guiding the specific behaviour of charitable organisations are mostly found in departmental regulations and amount to hundreds. Amongst the most important and relevant departmental regulations include the Interim Regulations on the Registration and Administration of Private Non-Enterprise Units (1998), Regulations on the Administration of Foundations (2004), Accounting System for Private Nonprofit Organisations (2004), Management of Social Organisation Evaluation Measures (2011), Interim Provisions on the Management of Foreign Chambers of Commerce (2013), Regulations on the Registration and Administration of Social Organisations (2016), Measures for the Recognition of Charitable Organisations (2016), Notice on Registration of Charitable Organisations and Other Related Issues (2016), Measures for the Administration of Public Solicitation by Charitable Organisations (2016), Measures for Information Disclosure by Charitable Organisations (2018), and Measures for the Management of Credit Information of Social Organisations (2018), Implementation Opinions of the Ministry of Civil

as well as the normative documents issued by the State Council.[5] Also within this regulatory framework is a significant body of rules to regulate and adjust the identity and activities of charitable organisations, covering all aspects of registration, recognition, taxation, fundraising, and information management of charitable organisations.

According to the Ministry of Civil Affairs' press conference in the fourth quarter of 2020, as of the end of September 2020 there were 7,825 registered and recognised charitable organisations in China. Since the promulgation of the Charity Law, charitable organisations' annual growth rate has decreased year by year, from 437.04 per cent in 2017 to 41.91 per cent in 2019.[6] In other words, the current legal system of charitable organisations does not appear to effectively motivate relevant charitable entities to register or transform their legal status into charitable organisations.

After carefully examining the relevant provisions of the current legal system of charitable organisations, this chapter concludes that while the status of 'charitable organisation' is an appealing name, it lacks practical appeal. Specifically, the problems can be summarised in the following two aspects. First, the concept of charitable organisations under the Charity Law remains unclear and appears to be inconsistent within the wider legal, regulatory framework. The Charity Law defines the scope of charitable organisations to be: 'charitable organisations may take the form of foundations, social groups, social service institutions and other organisations'.[7] However, the current regulatory system governing charitable organisations, also includes the concepts of 'non-profit legal persons (fei ying li fa ren)', 'non-profit organisations (fei ying li zu zhi)', and 'public welfare organisations (gong yi xing she hui tuan ti)'. These concepts cannot be seamlessly integrated with the term 'charitable organisations'. For example, the Civil Code uses the concept of 'non-profit legal persons', which includes institutions, social organisations, foundations, and social service organisations. The Law on Public Welfare Donations and the Implementing Regulations of the Enterprise Income Tax Law use the concept of 'public welfare social organisations'. The Circular of the Ministry of Finance and the State Administration of Taxation on the Management of Tax-Exempt

Affairs on Further Strengthening and Improving the Registration and Management of Social Service Organisations (2018), Interim Measures for the Management of Investment Activities of Charitable Organisations for Value Preservation and Enhancement (2019).

[5] Normative documents issued by the State Council include Guiding Opinions on Promoting the Healthy Development of Charities (2014). The first normative document issued by the State Council concerning charities explicitly encouraged the establishment of charitable organisations. Further, the State Council has also issued the Opinions of the General Office of the State Council on Promoting the Disclosure of Government Information in the Field of Social Welfare Construction (2018), which does not directly adjust the positioning and rights and obligations of charitable organisations but has implications concerning the disclosure of information by charitable organisations.

[6] J Jin, 'The Development of Charitable Organisations and the Improvement of the Legal System' in *Report on the Evaluation of the Implementation Effect of the Charity Law of the People's Republic of China* (Chinese Social Security Society, 2020) 23.

[7] Art 8, para 2 of the Charity Law.

Qualifications of Nonprofit Organisations consider that institutions, social groups, foundations, social service organisations, religious activity sites, religious institutions and other non-profit organisations identified by the Ministry of Finance and the State Administration of Taxation can be non-profit organisations.

Second, there needs to be more incentive policies offered to charitable organisations in Charity Law and China's legal system. As the fundamental legislation for regulating charitable organisations' rights, obligations and activities, the Charity Law affirms the legislative purpose of supporting and encouraging the development of charitable organisations. However, the 2016 Charity Law only contains 22 empowering and protective articles for charitable organisations,[8] covering aspects such as charitable organisations, recognition criteria, fundraising, trust, charitable services and volunteers, and taxation. The 2023 Amendment added six articles in this regard.[9] In contrast, the number of articles aimed at regulating charitable organisation significantly exceeds those aimed at empowering and protecting. For the empowering articles to fulfil its purpose of promoting and supporting the development of charitable organisations, there also needs to be a timely supporting policy for charitable organisations to flourish. Unfortunately, supporting policies which will enable charitable organisations to enlarge their role in employment, land management, finance, and investment have not been provided – seven years after the Charity Law came into effect.

By way of an example, China's tax policy could potentially offer greater incentives to adopt the charitable organisation form, as defined under the supreme law. Furthermore, the respective tax policy could be more consistent across the criteria used to identify a charitable organisation and the criteria for identifying tax-exempt organisations. At present, a situation can easily arise where a charitable organisation that meets the conditions for identification under the Charity Law is, nevertheless, not a public welfare or non-profit social organisation under tax law. The criteria of public benefit or non-profit social organisations recognised under tax law can be found in the Notice of the Ministry of Finance and the State Administration of Taxation on Issues Relating to the Administration of Tax-Exempt Qualifications of Nonprofit Organisations (2018) and the Notice of the Ministry of Finance, the State Administration of Taxation and the Ministry of Civil Affairs on Matters Relating to Pre-tax Deduction for Public Benefit Donations (2020). Among them, the Notice of the Ministry of Finance and the State Administration of Taxation on Issues Relating to the Administration of Tax-Exempt Qualifications of Nonprofit Organisations (2018)[10] on the tax-exempt

[8] See Arts 5, 7, 23, 26, 28, 35, 41, 46, 53, 59, 61, 67, 77, 79, 80, 82, 84, 85, 86, 87, 89, 91 of the 2016 Charity Law.

[9] See Arts 71, 85, 88, 95(2), 96, 102 of the 2023 Charity Law.

[10] The qualified non-profit organisations identified in the Circular of the Ministry of Finance and the State Administration of Taxation on Issues Relating to the Administration of Tax-Exempt Qualifications of Nonprofit Organisations must also meet the following conditions: (a) establishments, social organisations, foundations, social service institutions, places of religious activities, religious institutions and other non-profit organisations identified by the Ministry of Finance and the State Administration of

status of non-profit organisations allows non-profit organisations to use their property for reasonable salary and wage expenses. However, the Measures for the Recognition of Charitable Organisations[11] prohibits the distribution of the organisation's property among the organisation's members. In other words, there needs to be more consistency between the regulatory measures that recognise charitable and non-profit organisations and those dealing with tax-exempt status. Furthermore, according to the Announcement of the Ministry of Finance, the General Administration of Taxation and the Ministry of Civil Affairs on Matters Relating to Pre-Tax Deduction for Public Welfare Donations, public welfare social organisations are charitable organisations, other social organisations and mass organisations that are established or registered according to law and qualified for pre-tax deduction for public welfare donations according to the prescribed conditions and procedures.[12] But according to this announcement, charitable organisations do not naturally have the right to 'public welfare donations pre-tax deduction qualification'. In other words, the criteria of 'public welfare donation pre-tax deduction eligibility' and the criteria of charitable organisations are

Taxation in accordance with the relevant state laws and regulations or registered; (b) engaged in public welfare or non-profit activities; (c) the income obtained, except for the expenses related to the organisation and reasonable, all for the public welfare or non-profit purposes specified in the registration approval or charter; (d) the property and its fruits are not used for distribution, but does not include reasonable salary expenses; (e) in accordance with the registration approval or charter, the remaining property of the organisation after cancellation is used for public welfare or non-profit purposes, or by the registration and management authorities to take the transfer to the organisation of the same nature and purpose of the organisation and other means of disposal, and announced to the public; (f) the input person does not retain or enjoy any property rights to the property invested in the organisation, the input person referred to in this paragraph refers to legal persons, natural persons and other organisations in addition to the people's government at all levels and its departments; (g) staff salaries and welfare expenses controlled within the prescribed ratio, not disguised allocation of the organisation's property, of which: the average salary and wage level of staff shall not exceed twice the average salary level of similar organisations in the same industry in areas above the prefecture and city level (including prefecture and city level) where the tax registration is located, and staff benefits shall be implemented in accordance with the relevant state regulations; (h) the taxable income obtained and its related costs, expenses and losses shall be compared with the tax-exempt income and its (H) the taxable income and its related costs, expenses and losses shall be accounted for separately from the tax-exempt income and its related costs, expenses and losses.

[11] Art 4 of the Measures for the Recognition of Charitable Organisations: foundations, social organisations and social service institutions applying for recognition as charitable organisations shall meet the following conditions: (a) have the corresponding conditions for registration as a social organisation at the time of application; (b) to carry out charitable activities as the purpose, the scope of business in line with the provisions of Art 3 of the Charity Law; the annual expenditure and management costs of charitable activities in the previous year at the time of application in line with the State Council Civil Affairs Department on the provisions of charitable organisations; (c) not-for-profit, the proceeds and operating balances are all used for charitable purposes specified in the charter; property and its fruits are not distributed among the promoters, donors or members of the organisation; the charter has provisions on the transfer of surplus property to other charitable organisations with the same or similar purposes; (d) a sound financial system and a reasonable remuneration system; (e) the laws and Administrative regulations provide for other conditions.

[12] See: Art 3 of the Announcement of the Ministry of Finance, the General Administration of Taxation, and the Ministry of Civil Affairs on Matters Relating to Pre-Tax Deduction for Public Welfare Donations, Ministry of Finance Announcement (2020) No 27, May 21, 2020.

different and intertwined. A social organisation may not necessarily be charitable even if it is eligible for pre-tax deduction of public welfare donations in the sense of tax law. This follows from the scope of social organisations being broader than that of charitable organisations. However, when a charitable organisation that meets the requirements of the Charities Law turns out not to be necessarily considered a social organisation of public benefit in the tax law sense, it shows that relevant supporting laws and policies do not support the Charities Law.

Although the Charity Law clarifies the legal right of charitable organisations to enjoy tax benefits, the relevant tax preferential policies need to be faster to respond and adjust. For example, the revision of the Circular of the Ministry of Finance and the State Administration of Taxation on Issues Related to the Administration of Tax-Exempt Qualification Recognition of Nonprofit Organisations in 2018 did not grant significant tax benefits to non-profit organisations compared to the original 2014 version. The only noticeable changes made were to delete the restrictive provision about the conclusion of the annual review on the criteria for the recognition of non-profit organisations, and to add a three-month extension of the application period for review of the eligibility for tax exemption benefits for non-profit organisations. Another example in the current tax system that does not support the Charity Law is that the receipt of housing donations by charitable organisations requires the donor or recipient to pay a tax on the deed, which significantly discourages real estate donations to charitable organisations and detracts from the effectiveness of the Charity Law.[13]

The foregoing discussion of this chapter suggests although the Charity Law provides a fundamental guarantee and foundation of the legal system governing charitable organisations, there still remain numerous obstacles to its efficiency, such as inadequate supporting legal measures and conflicts with other laws and regulations. These problems are an important reason for the limited increase of charitable organisations despite the significance of promulgating and implementing the Charity Law. In fact, the maximum effect of implementing the Charity Law depends not only on the legislative quality of the Charity Law itself, but also on the coordination and support of relevant supporting legal measures. Therefore, a comprehensive study of the relevant legislative[14] system for charitable organisations is necessary to solve the problem that the existing legal system needs to motivate the relevant entities to register as charitable organisations effectively.

[13] G Zheng, 'The Implementation Effect of the Charity Law and the Improvement of the Legal System' in *Report on the Evaluation of the Implementation Effect of the Charity Law of the People's Republic of China* (2020) 15.

[14] In this chapter, 'legislation' is broadly interpreted as the activities of relevant subjects in formulating and changing normative legal documents. Thus, the object of study includes not only the activities of the National People's Congress and its standing committee in formulating laws but also the activities of relevant ministries and commissions in formulating ministerial regulations.

II. Existing Perspectives on the Study of Legislation on Charitable Organisations

Currently, most research concerning charitable organisations' legislation in China cannot be separated from policy, which is concerned with the legal positioning, nature and objectives of charitable organisations and their related concepts. There are different research perspectives, such as the perspectives of public law (administrative governance law) and private law (special civil law theory), the perspectives of regulatory law and promotion law, the perspectives of organisational law and behavioural law, and the perspectives of its social nature and property nature.

From the perspectives of public law (administrative governance law) and private law (special civil law), there are different claims about the functions of legislation for charitable organisations. Some scholars believe that charity organisations belong to the private law system. It thus follows that China should construct a legal system with the Civil Code as the command and leading law and a separate single law for charity organisations as a supplement.[15] Other scholars advocate that the administrative law function of Non-Governmental Organisation (NGO) laws and define the status of various types of NGOs in administrative law by the degree of their autonomous power and the degree of autonomy held by the NGOs.[16] Scholars who advocate strengthening the construction of a supervisory system for philanthropy do not directly state that administrative law rationality include charity organisation legislation, but they argue that the operation of public welfare assets by charities requires an external governance constraint.[17] In addition to these arguments, some scholars advocate that the hybrid public-private law function of the charity legislation, involves both the intervention of state power and social autonomy,[18] of which private law relations are the contents and public law relations are the means.[19]

The research perspectives of regulatory law and promotional law reflect different claims of scholars as to whether charity organisation legislation is regulatory or empowering. While most scholars advocate for a promotional institutional design for charitable organisation legislation. Others argue from a legal functionalist perspective that good law charitable organisation legislation should reflect

[15] Z Wu, 'Principles, Models and Structure of the Legislation for Nonprofit Organisations in China' (2014) 6 *Comparative Study on Economic and Social System* 103.

[16] W Wei, 'The Classification of NGOs and the Positioning of Administrative Law' (2013) 2 *Journal of Baoji College of Arts and Sciences* (Social Science Edition) 179.

[17] J Yao and D Huang, 'Reflections on the Construction of the Supervision System of Charity with Chinese Characteristics' (2004) 9 *Soc Sci (Shanghai)* 59.

[18] G Zhang, 'Institutional Space, Organisational Competition and Elite Decision Making: An Agenda-Setting Dynamic Analysis Perspective' (2020) 9 *Chinese Administration* 72; J Chen and L Liu, 'Self-serving and Benevolence in Conflicting Unison: A Marketization Analysis of China Charity Law Reform' (2018) 2 *Law & Economy* 20; T Jiang, 'The Legal Construction of Government Intervention in Charitable Activities During Major Emergencies' (2020) 6 *Economic and Trade Law Review* 151.

[19] J Ma, 'The Legal Definition of Charity' (2016) 7 *Academic Exchange* 92.

the goal of promoting charitable causes,[20] whereas other scholars believe that the administrative nature of charity organisation legislation is necessary and that administrative law should be improved to build a legal system that effectively promotes the cultivation, development, and management of non-profit organisations, including the legal status of the organisation, tax benefits, supervision and management, personnel system, information disclosure, social security, government support and other aspects of supporting measures.[21] Moreover, charity organisation legislation should reflect the idea of management rather than restriction at a public administrative level.[22]

Defining and understanding a charitable organisation with greater meaning can be assisted by organisational and behaviour law (private law). From the perspective of organisational law and behavioural law, academic writings on behavioural law are significant, and studies on the positioning of organisational law are relatively few. The function of organisational law is to assert the legal personality of an organisation, describe its characteristics and internal structure, set its goals and organisation's capacity to act and prescribe rights, stipulate the mutual relationship between the organisation and its members, and provide for an organisation's decision-making mechanisms, as well as the implementation of this mechanism.[23] Within organisational law, the characteristics of charity legislation are the key to establishing the primary attributes and governance mechanisms of charitable organisations. However, the fundamental rights and obligations of charitable organisations still need to be established in the form of behavioural law. Therefore, among the existing literature, the analysis of relevant charitable acts has occupied almost the vast majority of the charitable jurisprudence, including charitable trusts,[24] charitable donations,[25] charitable services,[26] and other specific

[20] L Cai, 'The Goodness of the Charity Law: A Jurisprudential Interpretation of the Legislative Objectives' (2016) 4 *Jianghuai Forum* 26; X Gao and H Yang, 'The Risk of Power Orientation in Rights-Oriented Legislation: A New Perspective on the Charity Law' (2016) 6 *Tsinghua Law Journal* 190.

[21] M Wang and X Jia, 'Some Issues with the Legal Policy of NGOs in China' (2003) Suppl 1 *Journal of Tsinghua University* (Philosophy and Social Science Edition) 106; Y Li, 'Study on Interpretation and Suggestion to Perfection of Charity Law' (2017) 3 *Journal of Beijing University of Aeronautics and Astronautics (Social Sciences Edition)* 35.

[22] D Yang and Y Li, 'A Review and Reflection on the Sixty Years of Chinese NGO Legislations' (2011) 1 *Journal of Shanxi Normal University (Social Science Edition)* 21.

[23] Y Zhu, 'A Preliminary Investigation of the General Rule of Organisation Law' (2020) 27 *Law Expo* 55.

[24] Y Liu, 'Legal Transplantation and Localization of Public Trusts in China' (2015) 1 *Chinese and Foreign Law* 151; J Wang et al, 'The Operation Mechanism of the Legal System of Charitable Trust and the Obstacles to its Development in China' (2011) 4 *Global Law Review* 108; X Lv, 'From Public Interest Trusts to Charitable Trusts: Transnational Transplantation and Its Local Construction' (2019) 10 *Social Science Front* 199.

[25] G Gao and J Gao, 'Analysis of the Development Trend of China's Charitable Giving Mechanism' (2009) 12 *Soc Sci (Shanghai)* 52; J Gao, 'The Implications of the External Monitoring Mechanism of Charitable Giving in the United States' (2010) 7 *Exploration and Controversy* 67.

[26] B Li, 'Exploring the Development of Community-based Philanthropy in China' (2007) 3 *Academic Exchange* 121; Y Zhang, 'Reflections on the Sustainable Development of Voluntary Philanthropy in China' (2004) 5 *Journal of Jinan University* (Social Science Edition) 78.

acts that charitable organisations must carry out or may carry out. Many scholars advocate that charitable or non-profit organisation legislation should adopt the model of unifying the law of organisation and the law of conduct.[27] In the legislative process of charity law, there is also a tilt from the organisational law's initial positioning to the behavioural law's positioning.[28]

The organisational law and behavioural law orientation are inseparable from the social and property nature of charitable organisation legislation. For example, one scholar has analysed the property considerations of charitable organisation legislation from the perspective of the substance of charitable organisation behaviour, arguing that how charitable organisation behaviour is essentially the donor giving the trust property (donated materials) to the trustee (the charitable organisation) for management or disposal, the trustee acquiring the right to dispose of that property, and the trust benefits accruing to the beneficiaries (the individual or collective receiving the donation), all three of whom do not enjoy complete ownership rights.[29] Other scholars have argued from the perspective of organisational law that the organisational position of non-profit organisations has other functions besides providing organisational entities with the value of competent subjects beyond contractual acts (ie, clarifying the attribution and division of organisational responsibility from the perspective of property law).[30] The vital marker distinguishing charitable organisations from other organisations' property is that their property is nominally attributed to charitable organisations but has social public attributes and value. Therefore, some scholars believe it is more reasonable to position the property of charitable organisations as the property of charitable legal persons.[31] Moreover, charity law is supposed to have the fundamental value of promoting distributive justice.[32]

The perspectives adopted in the above literature are different, and they have some significance in analysing the core content of legislation on charitable organisations in their perspective frameworks. However, most of these studies do not break through the 'subject-behaviour-responsibility' framework of traditional legal relations theory (ie, the subject qualification of charitable organisations, behaviour requirements, and responsibility constraints). The theoretical framework of subject-behaviour-responsibility is more applicable to evaluating single legal rules or analysing judicial practice in China. For a comprehensive legislative system of charitable organisations, this framework cannot solve the problem of

[27] Wu (n 15) 103.

[28] Ma (n 19) 92.

[29] X Yu, 'Analysis of the Behavior of Charitable Organisations and Its Implications for the Development of Charity in China' (2006) 4 *Productivity Research* 171.

[30] H Hansmann and R Kraakman, 'The Essential Role of Organisation Law' (2000) 110 *Yale LJ* 387.

[31] S Yang, 'Legal Characterization and Legislative Regulation of Property of Charitable Organisations' (2016) 5 *Journal of East China University of Science and Technology* (Social Science Edition) 115.

[32] X Lv, 'Distributive Justice: the Fundamental Value of Charity Law' (2018) 5 *Zhejiang Social Science* 41.

harmonising the rules from different laws and regulations and conforming to the legislative intent of the Charity Law. The legislative system of charitable organisations is concerned with the state of the world as it should be and is more suitable for top-level design using a normative analysis.

III. Introduction to the Systematic Normative Analysis Method

For a long time, jurisprudential research in China has focused on law implementation (ie, justice and law enforcement).[33] Therefore, although normative analysis is a basic method of legal research, it has not been applied in the study of the legislative system, nor has it been able to be further extended and developed in the practice of the legislative system in China.

In Chinese jurisprudence, normative jurisprudence is often used in legal interpretation and argumentation to provide arguments for justice,[34] especially in interpreting and arguing single rules. In these fields, some scholars believe that the object of normative analysis is the institutional fact, the trinity of value carrier, operational effect, and normative system, including legal norms, legal application, especially judicial precedents, formal legal interpretation, and legal organisational facilities;[35] and that normative analysis reveals the value dimension, factual dimension, and technical dimension of the legal norms under study,[36] to realise the legal concepts and legal provisions for the function of describing, annotating and interpreting legal concepts and legal texts, and ultimately resolving legal disputes.[37] This approach is in line with Bales' emphasis in his book, *Principles of Law*, that the book's scope is limited to discussing what courts should make in the face of the parties to a dispute.[38]

However, some scholars have tried to go beyond the value-empirical dimension, social-empirical dimension, and normative-empirical dimension of normative analysis to expand its object of action and application value. They argue that the aim of normative analysis reveals an existing and effective legal system (ie, a positive law system), which upholds the position of 'value neutrality', and it is a methodological system composed of logical and linguistic analysis,[39] with the

[33] H Ge and X Li, 'Legislation: a Perspective of Legal Theory Research' (2013) 8 *Learning and Exploration* 76.

[34] X Tan, 'The Methodological Composition and Scope of the Application of Normative Jurisprudence' (2012) 4 *Legal Science* (Journal of Northwest University of Political Science and Law) 37.

[35] H Xie, 'On Three Empirical Methods of Normative Analysis' (2008) 5 *Journal of Jianghai* 137.

[36] H Xie, 'On the Method of Normative Analysis' (2009) 2 *Chinese Jurisprudence* 38.

[37] Tan (n 34) 38.

[38] MD Bales, *Principles of Law: a Normative Analysis* (Dordrecht, Kluwer Academic Publishers, 1987) 2.

[39] L Rao, 'On the Core Meaning of Normative Analysis Method – Based on the Perspective of Jurisprudence' (2014) 6 *Journal of Guangxi Academy of Political and Legal Management Cadres* 8.

goal of constructing a logical structure of the positive law, revealing the meaning of norms, dividing the hierarchy and types of norms, and refining the legal norms into a coherent system to guide their application.[40]

Judicial decision-making involving the value, factual, and technical dimensions can reflect the rights and obligations, relations regulated by the law, and their effects and legality. However, concerning legislative issues, these three dimensions reveal a legislative system's organic nature and internal logic. The scientific nature of legislation does not lie in the grasp of universal laws, but in the process of 'rational legislation'.[41] Rational legislation should respond to the value guidance of the legislative system, the integrity of the structure, the organic connection of the content, and the dynamics of the process.

The value dimension measured by a legal system does not merely refer to the inquiry concerning the legality and illegality of certain behaviours but to the value orientation of the legislation, and the value expectation of justice, order and predictability to which the law is directed. The technical dimension measured by a legislative system does not merely refer to an analysis of rights and obligations imposed by a particular legal rule, but rather it is the approach adopted by legislation in terms of mode and manner – a unique technical field that distinguishes legislation from justice and law enforcement. The analysis of the rights and obligations of the law, which the technical dimension shoulders in the traditional method of normative analysis, should belong to the dimension of content in the normative analysis of legislation. To combine the content of the legislation organically, the structural dimension must also be included in the normative analysis of a legislative system. Therefore, based on the previous research, this chapter proposes to construct and apply a normative analysis framework of a legislative system employing the four dimensions of 'value-structure-content-technique'.

First, the value dimension should consider the background of a specific piece of legislation. The significance of considering its background can be contextualised as a necessary response and application, as well as addressing whether the legislation is indigenous or borrowed. No law can exist or operate in isolation from the context of its time or the fabric of society. Therefore, an adequate and reasonable assessment and understanding of the legislative background are among the most fundamental steps of legislative activity. Legislative jurisprudence refers to applying legal philosophy to legislation to reflect the fundamental values represented by the laws enacted. It is a codified analysis and expression of the nature and role of the sectoral laws enacted within the

[40] T Wu, 'On the Value and Application of Normative Analysis Method in Intersectional Jurisprudence' (2013) 1 *Legal Methods* 93.

[41] C Hong, 'Jurisprudential Exploration of Scientific Legislation: an Analysis Based on the Transmutation of the Concept of Rationality' (2017) 6 *Local Legislation Research* 101.

framework of legal philosophy. It is the basis and inner force of legislation, the reflection of the core attributes of the adjusted objects and legal relations, the carrier of the national legal culture, and the crystallisation of the rational spirit of the times. Only when the legislative jurisprudence is determined, is it only then possible to ensure that the application of the enacted laws is consistent with the lawmaker's original intent when encountering uncertainties in the law enforcement and judicial processes.

Second, the structural dimension is used to measure the systematicity and coherence of a legislative framework. It can be divided into two parts: an external structure and an internal structure. In a modern legal system,[42] due to the intersection and overlap of different legal departments, legal sources and legal adjustment objects, the legal science is intricate and complex. Therefore, clarifying the external and internal structures of sectoral laws is the basic premise to determine their scope and objectives. In particular, the external structure refers to the position of the sectoral law, which is dedicated to regulating certain subjects or legal relations as a part of the legal system in the field to which it belongs. The internal structure refers to the rational or scientific arrangement of the legislative process for the legal objects it regulates, according to its internal relations. After the internal and external relations of the legislative structure are clarified, the content of legislation can be presented more clearly.

Third, the content dimension points to specific legal norms or legal rules. The legislative purpose, general principles, and basic rules are particularly important to specific legal norms and rules. Among them, the statement of legislative purpose colours the content, is closely linked to the background of legislation, and has an essential role in the interpretation of the law and judicial and law enforcement inspiration. It is a provision that all Chinese legislation would normally contain. General principles reflect and embody the legislative jurisprudence of a law, and its general principles and basic content should be guided by legislative jurisprudence and committed to the values it espouses. The basic rules, on the other hand, directly regulate the legal relations regulated by the law, and only when they are definite, specific, relevant and enforceable,[43] can they provide a direct basis for the realisation of the purpose and principles of the law.

Fourth, the technical dimension depends, to a large extent, on the structure, content, and effectiveness of the legislation. Regarding the structure, the technical dimension answers the question of the mode of legislation. In terms

[42] The modern legal system in China refers to the comprehensive framework of laws and regulations established in the late twentieth century, following economic reforms initiated in the late 1970s. It encompasses various legal branches, including civil, criminal, administrative, and economic laws, and is characterised by the integration of statutory laws and regulations to guide governance, economic activities, and social behaviour within the country. The modern legal system supports China's transition to a market-oriented economy while maintaining social order and political stability.

[43] Art 6 (2) of the Legislative Law.

of content and its effectiveness, the technical dimension answers the question of the legislative model. Legislative models can be divided into three types: centralised, decentralised, and mixed. In the field of charity, more and more countries have adopted the model of centralised legislation, and some countries that used decentralised legislation but have begun to adopt or consider adopting centralised legislation to meet the legal needs of charity development.[44] The legislative approach, on the other hand, answers the question of what legislative approach to use and at which level of effectiveness to develop the legal norms. Presently, legislatures mainly adopt a decentralised approach, meaning that more legal rules are enacted through administrative regulations and sectoral rules. In addition, legislative interpretation also constitutes a dynamic complement to the legislative approach in China, that is, when the provisions of the law need to clarify the specific meaning further, or when new circumstances arise after the law is enacted. The basis for applying the law needs to be clarified; the Standing Committee of the National People's Congress can make a legislative interpretation.

Building a legal system around the four dimensions of 'value-structure-content-technique' differs from considering legal norms in the three dimensions of 'subject-behaviour-responsibility'. The former is helpful for legislators to establish a legal system that starts from the legislative background, which is based on legislative jurisprudence, influences the legislative structure with the appropriate legislative model, develops the legislative content in the proper level of effectiveness, and includes the legislative interpretation to assist the dynamically changing legal needs, and thus makes up for the lack of a comprehensive legal system in the 'subject-behaviour-responsibility' framework. In this way, it makes up for the lack of consideration of the overall structure and value dimension in the framework of 'subject-behaviour-responsibility', avoids the problem of structural imbalance and value deficiency, and achieves the optimal arrangement of the legislative contents.

The legislative system of charitable organisations as an organic whole, reflecting the level of social development and the development of the rule of law in China today, carries a rich connotation and values. The standardised legislative process pursues the rationality of legislative subjects, legislative matters, legislative procedures, and legislative results to achieve democratic, scientific, and fair legislation.[45] By analysing and constructing the legislative system of China's charitable organisations by the four dimensions of 'value-structure-content-technique', especially the supporting legal system of the Charity Law, we may realise the rationality requirement for charitable organisations' legislation.

[44] G Zheng (ed), *Research on Philanthropy Legislation* (Beijing, People's Publishing House, 2015) 7.

[45] T Shen, 'Research on the Rationality of Legislation' (2012) 12 *Journal of Jinan (Philosophy and Social Science Edition)* 48.

IV. Analysis and Construction of the Systemic Norms of the Supporting Measures of the Charity Law

A. Value Dimension: Consideration of Legislative Background and Legislative Jurisprudence

Amongst the relevant sectoral regulations issued and revised after promulgating the Charity Law in 2016, only a few regulations clearly state that their purpose is to 'promote the sustainable and healthy development of charitable organisations'.[46] The reason that the relevant supporting measures of the Charity Law do not adequately or timely reflect and/or express the legislative intent of the Charity Law, is that the current legislative system of charitable organisations does not express either a unified and precise language of the value orientation of the legislation for charitable organisations, nor is the legislative background to which they respond, and the basic jurisprudence they adopt. This is also related to the current model of charity legislation overall, which adopts a decentralised approach to legislation. The value orientation of the legislation cannot be precisely and wholly stated in one law. This is coupled with the fact that the legislative practice of sectoral law in China has interacted less with jurisprudence for a long time. Sectoral law legislation has emphasised rules over principles, important elements over values, and logic over jurisprudence. The view exists that the overall effectiveness of the combined normative system can be produced through the logic of each legal norm.[47]

The lack of value dimension makes the current legal regulation of charitable organisations more fragmented in an already scattered legislative model. Therefore, the supporting legal policies of the Charity Law urgently need a value construction with guiding and systemic significance. As mentioned above, this can be considered from the two aspects of legislative background and legislative jurisprudence.

From the perspective of a legislative background, charitable organisations are increasingly taking centre stage in social governance. As a specific vehicle for the implementation of the Charity Law, the supporting legal policies of the Charity Law should, further explain the positioning of charitable organisations concerning social governance, as well as the needs of charitable organisations to expand their charity work and improve the ecology of the charity sector, and to realise their value rationality and instrumental rationality. In terms of value rationality, the supporting legal policies of the Charity Law should further answer the question of the autonomy of charitable organisations and the charity sector, as well as their local attributes and values as an important part of China's social governance system. Therefore, the relevant supporting legal policies should first clarify that

[46] Art 1 of the Interim Measures for the Management of Investment Activities of Charitable Organisations for Value Preservation and Enhancement (2019).

[47] L Li, 'Composition of the Chinese Legal System' www.iolaw.org.cn/showArticle.aspx?id=523.

charitable organisations (and other charitable subjects) are necessary players and stakeholders in the national governing system and can fundamentally serve society beyond charity itself. In terms of instrumental rationality, the relevant supporting legal policies need to specify the role and functions of charitable organisations in a particular perspective of modern social governance in response to the specific issues and needs of contemporary times under their jurisdiction.

From the perspective of legislative jurisprudence, although the Charity Law points out the purpose of charity and gives the status and role of charitable organisations from the legislative level, the relevant supporting measures of the Charity Law do not transcend the limitations of regulatory and lagging legislation, and truly liberate the forms and behaviours of charitable organisations. One of the main features of modern public charity is that charity primarily relies on the scale and efficiency of the public charity organisations' behaviours.[48] Today in China, charitable organisations carrying out their missions has gone far beyond individual-style donations or aid; instead, they seek to mobilise a deeper and wider range of stakeholders, including government, corporations, and other social resources, through organisational platforms and behaviours. As a form of existence parallel to enterprises and government, charity organisations seek to grow, innovate, and gain influence. Therefore, the supporting legal policies of the Charity Law need to stand on a higher ground to gain insight into the meaning of existence and the development direction of charitable organisations. The old way of legislative thinking, such as focusing on governing and supervising, which results in a situation where the rules are primarily focused on registration and supervision, needs to transcend into the thinking of guiding and promoting charitable organisations.

Therefore, it is recommended that charitable organisations be given the legal status of autonomous participation in social governance directly in specific supporting measures, and that policy and regulations limiting charitable organisations' vitality be lifted by de-administrating and improving the diversity and quality of regulation. In specific sectoral regulations, this means embedding and reflecting the three needs that the legislative system of charitable organisations should respond to: first, the need for charitable organisations to increase their social influence to supplement the deficiencies of government and enterprises in social governance; second, the need for more diversified types of behaviours and activities of charitable organisations so that they can attract and invest more resources for charitable causes, translate into a wider range of charitable effects, and become a catalyst for social and economic development; and third, the need for different degrees of differentiated regulation in response to varying types of charitable organisations based on their market targets and sources, capacity, and internal governance requirements.

[48] G Deng, *Introduction to Public Welfare Charity* (Jinan, Shandong People's Publishing House, 2015) 228.

B. Structure Dimension: Consideration of the External and Internal Structures of the Legislative System of Charitable Organisations

As the relevant Ministries directly or indirectly involved in the management of charitable organisations issued their own regulations, there needs to be more communication and connection between them, thus creating a confusing situation in the internal and external structure of the legislative system of charitable organisations. Although the Charity Law seeks to clarify the scope of charitable organisations, there remain ambiguities in the legal system. The relevant provisions must be more comprehensive and coordinated, forming an effective division and legislative echo with other sectoral laws. Therefore, clarifying the internal and external structures of the legislative system of charitable organisations is of great significance. In particular, the purpose of clarifying the external structure of the system is to understand the basic requirements of the law for charitable organisations compared to other types of entities that participate or do not participate in charity, given that the current legal regulations still need to be fully harmonised. The purpose of clarifying the system's internal structure is to clarify the distinctions and boundaries between different types of charitable organisations and how the specific legal rules fit into them.

In the external structure of the legislative system of charitable organisations, there is a layering of different relationships between charitable organisations and other types of organisations, other types of non-profit organisations, and other types of charitable subjects. One of the most important layers of external relations is the distinction between charitable organisations as non-profit and for-profit organisations. Its core significance lies in the confirmation of the tax-exempt status of charitable organisations; that is, the qualification of charitable organisations and tax-exempt status should be unified.

In the United States of America, the incorporation of a non-profit organisation is closely tied to obtaining tax-exempt status. A non-profit organisation becomes a separate entity by registering and applying for tax-exempt status under federal tax law. The purpose of registration as an entity is precisely to obtain tax-exempt status; without tax-exempt benefits, many private organisations organised by citizens on their initiative and established for a certain purpose would exist and operate in large numbers without registration. However, the current legal system related to charitable organisations in China cannot achieve an effective connection between recognising charitable organisations and recognising tax-exempt status. When a charitable organisation meets the requirements of the Charity Law, it is not necessarily a public welfare social organisation under the tax law; it shows that the legal system is not friendly to the tax preference system of charitable organisations. Therefore, the tax preference policy should be determined as the core content of the legislative system of charitable organisations.

Regarding an internal structure, charitable organisations have emerged in an increasing number of forms depending on the groups they cater to, their charitable content, and their charitable approach. In the United States, section 501(c)(3) of the tax code[49] provides for seven types of organisations: religious, educational, charitable, scientific, literary, public safety testing, promotion of amateur sports competition, and the prevention of child or animal abuse. However, the legislative system for charitable organisations in China needs to adequately distinguish the boundaries that exist between charitable organisations of different natures, thus resulting in the existing legal system that does not correspond to the logic of governance and growth of various charitable organisations. There is also an imbalance in the proportion of different types of charitable organisations. From 2016 to 2019, among the charitable organisations registered and recognised nationwide, 4,803 were foundations, accounting for over 70 per cent, 1,542 were social groups, accounting for less than 23 per cent, and 427 were social service organisations (private non-enterprise units), accounting for only about 6 per cent.[50] Since the existing internal structure needs to cover and be linked to existing groups of social organisations that can carry out charitable work, it cannot achieve the effect of liberating the diversity of charitable organisations or promoting their development. Consequently, the results that the current Charity Law has to combine multiple roles of organisational law, behaviour law and promotion law,[51] the legislative regime is unable to unleash the functions and values of each role completely, and further causes the relevant legal content to be incomplete.

Therefore, to improve the legislative system of charitable organisations, it is necessary to enrich the internal composition and improve the external interaction among all relevant supporting policies of the Charity Law. First, in terms of clearing the external structure, it is necessary to grant relevant rights and obligations to charitable organisations in other coterminous laws. For instance, the Enterprise Income Tax Law could clarify a charitable organisation's preferential tax policies in labour, land, finance, trust, and so on. Further, in terms of the internal structure, separate laws such as the Law on Charitable Trusts and the Law on Volunteer Services could be enacted to set up boards within the legislative system of charitable organisations that clarify different types of charitable organisations and the different ways they conduct business; at the same time, the Law on the Promotion of Charitable Organisations or the Law on the Organisation of Nonprofit Organisations could be changed to the situation that the legislative structure remains too scattered. The hierarchy of other regulations supporting charitable organisation development needs to be higher.

[49] United States, Internal Revenue Code: Section 501(c)(3). 26 USC § 501(c)(3), US Government Publishing Office, 2018.

[50] Office of the Social Construction Committee of the National People's Congress, Briefing of the Social Construction Committee of the National People's Congress, No 212 of the 13th, 2020.

[51] Jin (n 6) 36.

C. Content Dimension: Consideration of Legislative Purpose, General Principles and Basic Rules

The content dimension of the legislative system of charitable organisations considers the specific presentation of the legal provisions of charitable organisations. The legislation concerning charitable organisations is not only an organisation law but also a law of behaviours. From the perspective of its legislative purpose, it is both a regulatory law and a promotional law concern. The current ministerial regulations regulating charitable organisations focus on the registration and supervision of charitable organisations rather than on the empowerment and promotion of charitable behaviour. Thus, the basic rules need to reflect the social benefits of expanding charitable behaviour, improving the environment, or protecting the fundamental rights and interests of stakeholders through legislation.

The importance of cultivating and developing charitable organisations has been self-evident. Therefore, in the specific construction of the content of the legislative system of charitable organisations, including legislative purpose, general principles and basic rules, it could be clarified that the relevant legal supporting measures should contain two significant goals. The first goal is cultivation and development, and the second is supervision and management. The logic of the former goal is the growth needs of charitable organisations, and the latter goal ensures the order and management of the social system. The two goals determine the basic principles of the relevant supporting measures and coordinate the specific contents of these measures (as shown in Table 10.1 below) of the legislation of charitable organisations.

Table 10.1 Legislative Content for Charitable Organisations

Purpose of Legislation	**Nurturing Development**	**Supervision and Management**
General Principles	Promote and monitor the development of charitable organisations	
Basic Rules	Legal Positioning	Registration, Qualification
	Organisational Form	Internal Governance
	Business and Activity Scope (Fundraising, donations, investments, trusts, charitable services, volunteers, religious activities)	Information Disclosure
	Tax Benefits	Financial Management
	Other Promotion Measures	Assessment
		Legal Liability

Second, the content of legislation directly affects the motivation and direction of charitable subjects' behaviour and its repetition. Thus, the basic content of legislation on charitable organisations should be reinforced positively to establish a recognition of the profound meaning and value of the social environment. Therefore, under the current situation where regulatory measures are more than promotion measures, the distribution of the content of the legislative system of charitable organisations could be balanced by further strengthening the promotion measures. A few things can be done to that end. First, expand the empowering provisions in the supporting policies. For example, the law could enumerate the positive and negative lists, further open up the qualifications and channels for charitable organisations to participate in finance, trusts, impact investment, and social enterprises, and give legal status to charitable organisations to mobilise social resources to participate in public welfare and social governance to create efficient charitable outputs. Second, the incentive provisions in the supporting policies should be increased. The scale effect of charitable organisations in carrying out charitable activities is far beyond that of individuals and enterprises. Therefore, social resources and charitable wealth could be guided into charitable organisations through a means of tax preferences to provide financial support for the establishment and development of charitable organisations. Simultaneously, more incentive policy preferences could be given to the personnel who work in charitable organisations to increase the attractiveness of operating a charitable organisation.

D. Technical Dimension: Consideration of Legislative Models and Legislative Approaches

Under the current legislative activities on charitable organisations, the legislature has adopted a decentralised legislative model; that is, instead of enacting a charitable organisation law, the legislature has enacted more legal rules through administrative regulations and ministerial rules, which is the reason why there are fewer laws at the congressional level and more rules at lower levels among the existing normative documents regulating charitable organisations. Currently, as the charity sector in China is rapidly evolving, decentralised legislation helps respond to new approaches, situations, and issues that arise. The decentralised legislative technique also has obvious disadvantages, including the need for systematisation, the inability to constitute a complete system of rules, the possibility of conflicts among related rules, and the inability to demonstrate the basic principles of long-term stable legal interpretation.

Many other elements concerning a decentralised legislative model need to be clarified regarding charitable organisations' scope and related concepts. The problems caused by the technical dimension have been visualised in the structural dimension.

Since the Charity Law has already been enacted, implemented and amended, and most of its content is directed at regulating charitable organisations,[52] the possibility or necessity of enacting a separate Charitable Organisations Law may be insignificant. Therefore, it is not practical to solve the problem of defining the scope and harmonising the concept of 'charitable organisations' by altering the decentralised legislative model. However, a legislative approach in the technical dimension can make up for the shortcomings of the legislative model (ie, the Standing Committee of the National People's Congress can make up for the weaknesses of the decentralised legislative model by making a legislative interpretation). Through legislative interpretation to supplement and amend the deficiencies in the existing legislation of charitable organisations, the advantages of the decentralised legislative model can be considered. and solved, such as the lack of systematisation, consistency, and stability of the legislation. Moreover, owing to the effect of legislative interpretation being equivalent to the law itself, doing so can directly address the defects of the low hierarchy of other relevant rules. It can provide a clear basis for formulating and amending other supporting regulations and rules, not coordinated with the Charity Law – without causing further conflicts of effect and structural confusion. In practice, few legislative interpretations are issued by the Standing Committee of the National People's Congress, and the more common ones are judicial interpretations made by the Supreme People's Court or the Supreme People's Procuratorate. However, the validity of judicial interpretations is always controversial and is not considered to have the same validity as the law itself. Therefore, legislative interpretation can provide a clear basis for clarifying charitable organisations' scope and legal status.

However, in the absence of judicial interpretation, legislative interpretation can be used as an effective supporting measure for the implementation of the Charity Law, and the concept of 'non-profit organisations' in the scope of charitable organisations in Article 8 of the Charity Law can be explained and clarified through legislative interpretation. On the one hand, through legislative interpretation, it is indicated that China's charitable undertakings are in a stage of rapid development. New forms and methods of charitable organisations are constantly emerging, which may precede the laws and regulations. Therefore, the law uses the term 'other non-profit organisations' to provide an expansive and inclusive definition of charitable organisations. On the other hand, through legislative interpretation, the relationship between 'non-profit legal person', 'charitable organisation', 'non-profit organisation' and 'public benefit social organisation' can be clarified, which would

[52] The 2016 Charity Law mentions 'charitable organisations' 141 times, while 'donors', 'volunteers', 'beneficiaries', and 'the government' are mentioned 38, 24, 24, and 23 times, respectively. After the amendment, the 2023 Charity Law mentions 'charitable organisations' 156 times, 'donors' 38 times, 'volunteers' 27 times, 'beneficiaries' 28 times, and 'the government' 47 times. This indicates that the Charity Law places significant emphasis on charitable organisations' status, rights, and obligations over other stakeholders.

encourage the amendment of concepts no longer suitable for the current legal system under the Civil Code, the Charity Law, and this legislative interpretation.

V. Conclusion and Discussion

Although there are many micro issues in the legal system concerning charitable organisations, only under a systematic normative analysis perspective can we find the appropriate measures to repair and create a vital legislative system, which will provide a supportive legal environment needed for the development and healthy growth of charitable organisations in China. The four dimensions of 'value-structure-content-technology' are used to analyse the supporting legal policies of the Charities Law to improve the overall legislative system of charities and to achieve a more significant effect of its implementation.

In the legislative system of charitable organisations, the problems are reflected in these four dimensions, and their corresponding solutions are interdependent rather than independent of each other. As the technical dimension has adopted a decentralised legislative model, it has led to the issuance of separate regulations by each sector and the lack of consistency in defining relevant basic concepts. As is the case where decentralised legislation has been adopted, the legislative system has not been balanced and coordinated through the structural dimension, leading to confusion about the internal and external structure of the legislative system due mainly to the lack of structural clarity and that the legislative system is unable to provide a comprehensive and coordinated legal basis for charitable organisations in terms of content. Further, due to the lack of clarity in the structure, the legislative system is unable to provide a comprehensive and coordinated legal basis for the behaviour of charitable organisations, and due to the imbalance in the content, the legislative system is inadequate for the measures related to the cultivation and development of charitable organisations, resulting in the failure of the basic value of the legislative system of charitable organisations to be manifested; and due to the lack of the construction of the value of the legislation of charitable organisations, the decentralised legislative model lacks the guidance of unified basic principles, forming a vicious cycle. This cycle cannot be improved through the revision of a single legal rule.

In civil law countries, the presentation of the law is centred on the legislative text. Using a scientific and rational normative analysis framework in the legislative process relates to the effect of the legislative activity and the legal system's overall normativity. The promulgation of the Charity Law has not had the remarkable impact of promoting charitable organisations in China as expected, which indicates that the quality of its legislation needs to be improved, and the quality requirements of the legislation should be a concern of the legislative and academic communities. This phenomenon has also occurred in Western countries. Since the beginning of the twentieth century, Western countries have entered the era of large-scale legislation codification, one after another, and a so-called 'legislative orgy' phenomenon has emerged. However, with the exponential increase in the amount of written legislation, the quality of legislation becoming lower and lower, and legislation often deviated from its intended purpose.[53] It is for this reason that Western scholars have begun to explore legislative jurisprudence to respond to, and even solve, the growing problem of the expansion of the quantity but the decline in the quality of legislation in European countries,[54] and address the need to adopt scientific research methods at the legislative level to improve the rationality of legislative decisions,[55] and establish a rational legislative theory of good law.

In China, however, scholars need to be more involved in analysing legislative theory and the legislative system. The four dimensions of 'value-structure-content-technology' proposed in this chapter are aimed at the normative consideration of the legislative system of charitable organisations, especially the support of legal policies of the Charity Law. However, it still belongs to the theoretical framework of legislative jurisprudence. Therefore, the proposal of the four dimensions of 'value-structure-content-technology' tries to make up for the limitations of the existing literature, which mostly takes the subject qualification, behaviour requirements and responsibility constraints of charitable organisations as the framework of analysis, and to go beyond the analysis of the nature and function of the legislation of charitable organisations, and concern the consideration of the internal rules of the legislative system of charitable organisations. In terms of legislative practice, it could possibly build a unified and normative framework and discourse system for the Charity Law and related laws and policies, so that the rules from different legal documents can coordinate with each other, reduce conflicts, and achieve common goals and intentions.

[53] B Wang (ed), *Legislative Jurisprudence: Frontier Theories of Legislation* (Beijing, Law Press, 2019) preface.

[54] LJ Wintgens, *Legisprudence – A New Theoretical Approach to Legislation* (Oxford, Hart Publishing, 2002).

[55] J Cohen, 'Towards Realism in Legisprudence' (1950) 59 *Yale LJ* 886.

11

Governing Animal Rescues Through Charity Law

SARAH SINGH AND MARIE FOX*

I. Introduction

This chapter offers a socio-legal analysis of Charity Law's role in governing animal rescue and rehoming organisations in England and Wales, focusing specifically on charitable organisations that pursue the purpose and undertake the activities of rescuing and rehoming companion animals.[1] In doing so, our chapter seeks to bring Animal Law into conversation with Charity Law. In recent years, Animal Law has emerged as a separate legal discipline, taught in a growing number of UK law schools, which has produced an expanding body of scholarship.[2] Within socio-legal scholarship, too, more attention is being devoted to animals[3] – though they remain a marginal concern. However, Animal Law to date has primarily focused on questions of animal status, criticising how animals are legally understood as property or commodities, debating the case for according them legal rights and examining the use of animals in particular contexts, for example science. There is

* We would like to acknowledge the research assistance of Kate Sandford, and the helpful feedback and input of Bleddyn Davies and Jennifer Sigafoos on this chapter. We are grateful to Research England for funding the empirical study and to our collaborators Battersea Dogs and Cats Home, Causeway Coast Dog Rescue and the UK Kennel Club. Most of all we thank our participants for giving their time to take part in our study.

[1] There is considerable variation in terminology given inconsistency in referring to animal rescues, shelters, sanctuaries etc. The Animal Welfare (Licensing of Activities Involving Animals) Scotland Regulations 2021 refers to animal rehoming centres. However, in this chapter, we have for the most part adopted the terminology of 'animal rescue', which reflects the fact that there may often be no physical centre for many of these organisations.

[2] See, for instance: S Brooman (ed), (2018) 39 *Liverpool Law Review (Special Issue): Animal Law in the United Kingdom: Academics, Conferences, A-LAW and Student Engagement* 1; R Fasel and S Butler, *Animal Rights Law* (Oxford, Hart, 2023).

[3] H Carr, 'Caring at the Borders of the Human: Companion Animals and the Homeless' in R Harding, R Fletcher and C Beasley (eds), *ReValuing Care in Theory, Law and Policy Cycles and Connections* (London, Routledge, 2018); D Wyatt, J Maher, D Allen, N Clarke and D Rook, 'The Welfare of Wildlife: an Interdisciplinary Analysis of Harm in the Legal and Illegal Wildlife Trades and Possible Ways Forward' (2022) 77 *Crime, Law and Social Change* 69.

a general acceptance within the field that enforcing animal welfare provisions is a particular concern,[4] but relatively little attention has been devoted to how this issue can be addressed. Interestingly, while animal welfare is a long-established charitable purpose, and a number of regulatory inquiries by the charity regulator have involved animal charities, animal welfare has attracted little attention within Charity Law.[5] Our contribution aims to address this blind spot by exploring the novel issue of how Charity Law can contribute to the governance of animal rescues.

In the following section, we will explain the pivotal role such organisations, many of which are charities, play in facilitating animal welfare. Our key argument is that animal rescue organisations address crucial gaps in state provision of animal care and should be better regulated and supported by law. Yet, as we demonstrate, this is part of a general failure to govern the rescue of animals adequately. In the absence of a dedicated statutory regime, activities involving the rescuing of animals are subject to piecemeal regulation via a diverse range of legal provisions drawn from criminal law, public law, environmental law, and, as we will show, Charity Law. For the purposes of this chapter, we will focus on the legal position of organisations that rescue and rehome companion animals in England and Wales.[6] However, it should be noted that our empirical data is mainly limited to dogs and covers the entire UK. Having explained the crisis in animal rescue across the UK and why this issue is important, we set out our methodology, before briefly discussing how animal welfare has featured in Charity Law jurisprudence. We then focus on the more specific issue of the extent to which charitable status is important for rescues and how it contributes to their viability. This is largely in terms of making charities accountable for their finances, thereby ensuring their sustainability and ability to provide services, as well as offering public reassurance that they have a legal basis. We then explore the Charity Commission's investigations into animal charities, suggesting that they can play a role in revealing animal neglect and cruelty. In effect, we argue that, in highlighting poor governance and managerial practices, these Charity Commission inquiries often flag broader animal welfare concerns.

However, while animal rescues may benefit from seeking charitable status, our empirical data shows how common misunderstandings may deter organisations from doing so. Moreover, the Charity Commission's inquiries suggest that trustees in this sector frequently do not understand and/or comply with the legal duties

[4] M Radford, *Animal Welfare Law in Britain: Regulation and Responsibility* (Oxford, OUP, 2001) Part IV.

[5] Interpretations of public benefit in the context of advancing animal welfare as a charitable purpose are discussed briefly in treatises such as, W Henderson et al (eds), *Tudor: Charities* 11th edn (Sweet & Maxwell, 2023) 273–78; H Picarda, *The Law and Practice Relating to Charities* 4th edn (London, Bloomsbury Professional, 2010). See also P Jamieson, 'On Charities Edge: The Animal Welfare Trust' (1987) 13(1) *Mon LR* 1. The focus has been largely on animal welfare as a charitable purpose.

[6] In Scotland the Office of the Scottish Charity Regulator (as established under and applying Charities and Trustee Investment (Scotland) Act 2005) regulates charities, while in Northern Ireland the Charity Commission for Northern Ireland was established under and applies the Charities Act Northern Ireland 2008 (as amended in 2022).

their role entails. Consequently, for animal rehoming charities to function more effectively there is a need for better education concerning trustee roles and more effective enforcement. In summary, we argue that Charity Law could be more effective in ensuring good governance and thus promoting animal welfare. However, ultimately, given the different aims of Charity and Animal Welfare Law and the challenges the Charity Commission faces in seeking to govern such a diverse range of charities, we conclude that Charity Law has a limited role to play in promoting animal welfare and that dedicated statutory regulation of the animal rehoming sector is desperately needed.

II. Context: Animal Rescue in Crisis

Animal rehoming organisations were first established in the Victorian era when social attitudes to animals changed, and pet-keeping became popular.[7] These cultural changes were reflected in the establishment of charitable trusts for the advancement of animal welfare (as well as private purpose trusts for the maintenance of particular animals, usually the testator's pets).[8] Over time, the animal rehoming sector has grown, with an estimated 1,000 organisations now operating in England alone, although no registration or accurate record keeping is required.[9] As with many third sector activities, animal rescues have come to assume a pivotal role in providing services, which over the course of the twentieth century had largely come to be seen as the responsibility of local government.[10] In recent decades, however, deep cuts to local authority budgets have resulted in a loss of key officials, including dog legislation officers and dog wardens, as well as fewer local authority owned kennels for stray dogs.[11]

[7] E.g. H Ritvco, *The Animal Estate: The English and Other Creatures in Victorian England* (Cambridge, Harvard University Press, 1989). D Flindt, 'The Legal Meaning of Charity and how the Public Benefit Test Affects Animal Protection Organisations' (2013) 22 *Journal of Animal Welfare Law*, 22.

[8] E.g. *Re Dean* [1889] 41 Ch D 552.

[9] WH Deb, 26 February 2019, vol 699, *Animal Rescue Homes* (David Rutley MP), https://hansard.parliament.uk/commons/2019-02-26/debates/EC70319B-914E-408C-A987-7C4DE9D98F1E/AnimalRescueHomes. Judging from similar debates in Scotland preceding a licensing regime this is likely to be a notable underestimation. Despite lack of awareness raising in Scotland, Scottish local authorities have already seen significantly more licensing applications than the 25 animal rescue centres and four to five sanctuaries that were estimated to exist when Parliament was discussing the likely impact of a licensing regime (although it had been conceded that numbers were likely to be higher). The Government of Scotland, 'Business and Regulations Impact Assessment: Animal Welfare (Licensing of Activities Involving Animals) Scotland Regulations 2021' (Government of Scotland, 2020) 16.

[10] The Environmental Protection Act 1990 (UK), ss 149–51 imposes duties on local authorities to deal with stray dogs and appoint officers for those purposes.

[11] M Heath, *Improving the Effectiveness of Animal Welfare Enforcement* (All-party Parliamentary Group on Animal Welfare, 2022) https://apgaw.org/wp-content/uploads/2022/08/Improving-Animal-Welfare-Enforcement-Report.pdf; See also: Environment Food and Rural Affairs Committee, *Written Evidence; Dog Control and Welfare* (United Kingdom Parliament, House of Commons, 2012) https://publications.parliament.uk/pa/cm201213/cmselect/cmenvfru/writev/dogcontrol/dog.pdf.

This situation was compounded by the initial demand for pets during the Covid-19 pandemic, especially dogs, which fuelled an increase in dog breeding and imports, followed by increased relinquishment of animals in its wake. This period also saw an increase in the movement of dogs into the UK, partly to respond to demand but also because animals were displaced by war.[12] Prior to the pandemic, in 2019, it was estimated that around 130,000 dogs entered UK rescues each year.[13] However, upon the resumption of pre-pandemic lifestyles, austerity and a cost-of-living crisis have meant that the number of unwanted animals has soared. August 2022 represented an all-time high in the number of dogs surrendered since records began, with Dogs Trust reporting that 4,370 enquiries were received in that month alone. The unprecedented demand for dog adoption during the pandemic led many rescues to adapt their service models to allow them to assume functions previously carried out by local authorities, including caring for seized and stray dogs. The role of animal charities has also expanded in other ways, with some adopting social enterprise models in an attempt, wherever possible, to keep animals in their homes. Thus, many now provide traditionally private services, such as reduced-price veterinary care and grooming. Expanding breed-specific legislation to encompass the XL bully type[14] has also added to the pressure on 'general' (ie, non-breed specific) rescues. In the run up to the introduction of the Dangerous Dogs Order in December 2023, there was an influx of dogs surrendered to general rescues by individual owners unwilling or unable to apply for an exemption or have their dog euthanised. These burdens were exacerbated by the Government's significant underestimation of the numbers of this type of dog in England and Wales.[15]

Yet notwithstanding the Government's assumption of more onerous responsibilities for protecting animal welfare, England and Wales have no statutory regulation of animal rescues.[16] Consequently, any individual or group can self-define as a rescue or sanctuary, thereby placing owners who need to surrender much loved pets and animals themselves in a vulnerable position. The problem of identifying good rescues is compounded by the fact that they can take a host of legal forms. Rather than pursuing charitable status, as we explore in section V below, some organisations elect to carry out their activities as private individuals

[12] E.g. as a result of the relaxation of rules around the import of animals from Ukraine. See eg: K Sandvik, 'The Ukrainian Refugee Crisis: Unpacking the Politics of Pet Exceptionalism' (2022) 61(4) *International Migration* 292.

[13] A Carter and J Martin, 'Demographic Changes in UK Rescue Centre Dog Population' (2021) 24(4) *J Appl Anim Welf Sci* 347; C Clark et al, 'Number of Cats and Dogs in UK Welfare Organisations' (2012) 170(19) *The Veterinary Record* 493.

[14] The Dangerous Dogs (Designated Types) (England and Wales) Order 2023 amended the Dangerous Dogs Act 1991 (UK) to add the type of dog known as the XL Bully as a banned type.

[15] For a critique from a rescue's perspective see V Waddon, 'Is the XL bully ban working?' (Hope Rescue, December 2024) www.hoperescue.org.uk/news/is-the-xl-bully-ban-working#:~:text=This%20is%20having%20a%20significant,increased%20demand%20for%20their%20services.

[16] Scotland introduced a licensing regime for rescues and sanctuaries in 2021 (The Animal Welfare (Licensing of Activities Involving Animals) (Scotland) Regulations 2021).

or not-for-profit organisations. Accordingly, and in the absence of a dedicated statutory regime which might entail licencing or registration (as in Scotland), it is impossible to ascertain precisely how many rescues exist or what proportion of them are registered charities as opposed to not-for-profits. For members of the public wishing to surrender or adopt dogs, it is tricky to distinguish reputable rescues from those that are fronts for animal breeding, trafficking and/or hoarding.[17] Moreover, even those organisations that are registered charities have very diverse structures. For instance, larger organisations are often incorporated under the Companies Acts or as a Charitable Incorporated Organisation, whereas smaller rescues may take the form of a charitable trust or an unincorporated organisation. Additionally, operating practices and conceptions of their role may also differ. Such variation heightens trustees' difficulties in understanding and complying with their duties under Charity Law. In light of this, a general sentiment emerging from our focus groups was that: 'While events in recent years have increased the pressures on rescues, the failure to enact legislation to regulate and support rescues is an enduring one.'[18]

III. Methodology

The situation outlined above, which suggests a prima facie case for regulatory reform, prompted us to undertake a pilot study into the attitude of rescue organisations to law reform initiatives in the UK. To date, high profile, large-scale national rescues have set the agenda in pressing for regulatory reform, which is generally in the interests of large, mainly English organisations, that are well resourced and well placed to comply with potential regulatory requirements.[19] We, therefore, aimed specifically to canvas the views of smaller rescues, which may face very different challenges, and whose views often go unheard in debates about regulation. Our research was undertaken in collaboration with one large charity (Battersea Dogs and Cats Home), who have an established track record of supporting smaller rescues, one small regional charity (Causeway Coast Dog Rescue) and the UK Kennel Club, all of whom facilitated access to a range of smaller rescues.

[17] Hoarding is a psychiatric disorder, recognised under the DSM V, characterised by the accumulation of a large number of animals, coupled with a failure to provide for their basic welfare needs including appropriate diet, environment and healthcare.

[18] From analysis of focus groups, as discussed in M Fox and S Singh, 'Puppy Pandemic: Legal Regulation of Dog Rescues in the UK in the Wake of the Covid-19 Pandemic – A Social and Legal Studies Workshop' (2022) https://socialandlegalstudies.wordpress.com/2022/10/31/puppy-pandemic-legal-regulation-of-dog-rescues-in-the-uk-in-the-wake-of-the-covid-19-pandemic-a-social-and-legal-studies-workshop/.

[19] This empirical research – 'Legal Governance of Dog Rescues: Addressing Post-Pandemic Challenges in a Period of Austerity' – was carried out 2023–2025 and was funded by *Research England*. Ethics approval was granted by the School of Law and Social Justice Ethics Committee (ref 11483; granted 18.7.22, modified 17.5.23 (to accommodate focus groups)).

The empirical data set comprises 24 semi-structured interviews with rescues across all four UK jurisdictions.[20] The interviews were supplemented by two focus groups, in which 26 Kennel Club breed specific rescues participated. These sessions examined attitudes to the regulation of rescues, including views on the benefits, burdens and limitations of having charitable status.[21] We then undertook a thematic analysis of the interviews. This theoretically un-bounded method of qualitative analysis allowed us first to identify themes through general coding (for example, perceptions of charitable status, of the regulator, etc) and then to code for broader themes as and when they emerged.[22] In this chapter, we draw on this qualitative data to inform our views about regulation, including the role Charity Law has to play in ensuring good governance.

Our arguments are also informed by our experiences as trustees of a small dog rescue – a regional, breed-specific charity based in the North of England. This equipped us with an insider's perspective into the challenges facing dog rescues and the likely obstacles to regulatory reform for smaller rescues.[23] An analysis of Charity Commission inquiries into animal rescue charities supplements our examination of Charity Law's potential. These inquiries are published on the Charity Commission's website when it has been deemed by the regulator that there are generally applicable lessons to be heeded. Once two years have elapsed, the Charity Commission's inquiries are archived and harder to locate, but for the purposes of this chapter, we have examined 14 inquiries from 2005–24,[24] which offer some insight into the issues that particular animal charities have posed for the regulator. Inevitably, our data will have limitations. Not all Charity Commission investigations are publicly available. In our empirical research, the focus has been on dogs, rather than companion animals in general. Although we endeavoured to recruit a representative range of rescues,[25] in practice most of those which participated were registered charities and, in the case of the focus groups, all but two were breed specific.

However, before turning to our specific focus on these organisations, we begin by exploring how Charity Law has engaged with animals and the promotion of

[20] Seven interviews were in person; the remainder were conducted via Zoom. Ten were with breed specific rescues; the other fourteen were general rescues. All interviews were undertaken by the authors; in most cases, by both of us. They ranged in length from one to two hours. The interviews were transcribed and anonymised, as were our focus groups.

[21] The focus groups were both carried out at the Kennel Club's London premises on the 27 June 2023.

[22] V Braun and V Clarke, 'Using Thematic Analysis in Psychology' (2006) 3(2) *Qualitative Research in Psychology* 77–101.

[23] Both co-authors have been trustees of North West English Springer Spaniel Rescue (M Fox, December 2016–March 2024 and S Singh, September 2019–March 2025).

[24] Plus one warning: (Charity Commission, 'Official Warning to the UK German Shepherd Angels' (Charity Commission, 12 June 2023) https://apps.charitycommission.gov.uk/SCHEMES/069301.PDF, and one regulatory investigation into the RSPCA (Charity Commission, 'Regulator concludes regulatory case into governance at the RSPCA' (www.gov.uk, 18 December 2020) www.gov.uk/government/news/regulator-concludes-regulatory-case-into-governance-at-the-rspca.

[25] Recruitment was facilitated by our collaborators, but we also used personal contacts from volunteering with a number of rescues.

animal welfare more generally, showing both that animal welfare cases lie at the heart of questions over what constitutes 'public benefit' and how Charity Law is inherently anthropocentric.

IV. Conceptualising Animal Welfare as a Public Benefit

An entity must have been established for charitable purposes only and provide public benefit for it to be validly charitable. Advancement of animal welfare is a well-established charitable purpose with a rich history. From the late nineteenth century animal welfare was recognised as falling under the fourth *Pemsel* head, 'other purposes beneficial to the community'.[26] It has, since the Charities Act 2006 (UK), been included as a standalone charitable purpose, now enshrined in section 3(1)(k) of the Charities Act 2011 (UK). It is notable, however, that, in contrast to other jurisdictions, such as Ireland, where the welfare of animals is deemed a good in itself,[27] in England and Wales the acceptance of charitable trusts for the welfare of animals has always been premised on the understanding that improving the welfare of animals enriches human lives, and thus can be for public benefit.[28] Purported benefit to humans can be direct, as, for example, in *London University v Yarrow*.[29] In this case, a facility that provided medical treatment to 'animals useful to man', and which educated the public about caring for said animals was understood as being for public benefit and thus charitable.[30] Less obvious public benefit is demonstrated in cases such as *Re Wedgewood*,[31] which held that organisations which benefitted animals were charitable because such activity 'raises the morality of mankind to care for animals'.[32] Such rulings reflect the anthropocentric approach of law in general. In UK Animal Law, the property status of animals has meant that the welfarist approach has had the most traction, underpinning key statutes, most significantly the Animal Welfare Act 2006 (UK). This sets welfare standards that both prohibit cruelty and require the animal's needs

[26] In *IRC v Pemsel* [1891] AC 531, three charitable purposes or 'heads' of charity were recognised. These were relief of poverty, advancement of education and advancement of religion. This case also recognised a fourth, residual category of 'any other purposes beneficial to the community' which allowed for development of further charitable purposes. Many of these purposes were codified under the Charities Act 2006 (UK) (now replicated in the Charities Act 2011 (UK), s.3 (1)). See Flindt (n 7) 22.

[27] *Armstrong v Reeves* (1890) 25 LR Ir 325; Picarda (n 5) 211.

[28] Jamison (n 5) 1–36.

[29] *London University v Yarrow* (1857) 1 DE G & J 72.

[30] For further discussion regarding public benefit which confers a practical benefit to animals 'useful to mankind' see: *Re Grove-Grady* [1929] 1 Ch 557 per Lord Hanworth at para [570]. The usefulness of dogs to man is also pivotal in *Re Douglas* (1887) 35 Ch D 472 CA; and this reasoning was applied in *Adamson v Melbourne and Metropolitan Board of Works* [1929] AC 142. See also: *McGuvie Smith Institute v Campbelltown Municipal Council* [1965] VR 238. See generally: Flindt (n 7) 22–24.

[31] *Re Wedgwood* [1915] 1 Ch 113.

[32] This sentiment was repeated in *Re Moss* [1949] 1 All ER 495 and influenced reasoning on the charitable status of gifts to promote animal welfare in the Australian case of *Cat Protection Society of Victoria* [1971] VR 801.

to be met; however it permits harm to animals if this is outweighed by perceived benefit to humans.[33] A similar utilitarian approach is evident in Charity Law, as demonstrated by the fact that a gift to promote the humane destruction of animals was held to be charitable.[34]

The potential clash between human and animal interests is apparent in the seminal case of *National Anti-Vivisection Society v IRC*.[35] The issue here was whether the NAVS was entitled to exemption from Income Tax on the grounds that it was a body established for charitable purposes only. A majority of the House of Lords overturned an earlier ruling in *Re Foveaux*[36] that anti-vivisection campaigning could be deemed charitable. In *NAVS v IRC*[37] it was held that benefits to the public from animal research outweighed any moral benefit conferred by campaigning against vivisection on animal welfare grounds. As Calderwood-Norton notes, the repercussions of this case extend far beyond the animal welfare context, getting to the crux of questions about what constitutes proof of 'benefit' in assessing public benefit, and demonstrating how regulators should approach balancing competing benefits, or rather benefits which may also imply an element of detriment.[38] Until this ruling, moral benefit had been sufficient to evidence public benefit, but in *NAVS v IRC* it was held that any moral benefit potentially had to be weighed against scientific evidence of the material benefits of vivisection, a task that the court avoided by finding the evidence of moral benefit lacking.[39] As the Special Commissioners for Tax who initially heard the case made clear, in Charity Law, human interests (and the promotion of human happiness) will *always* trump the interests of animals. While it is no longer necessary to establish that animal welfare is a valid charitable purpose, when striving for greater legal protection of animal welfare, the requirement to show tangible (provable) benefits to humans continues to be central.

While public benefit is largely uncontentious when it comes to animal rescue organisations, it is interesting that the traditional constructs of direct and indirect benefits to humans continue to be reflected today. Thus, for instance, the Charity Commission's model charitable objects clauses recommend that organisations use wording such as 'for the benefit of the public, these rescues are operated …' or 'to promote human behaviour towards animals …'.[40] However, the tension between human and animal interests which was at the heart of *IRC v NAVS* will

[33] Animal Welfare Act 2006 (UK), s 4.

[34] *Re Wedgwood* [1915] 1 Ch 113.

[35] *National Anti-Vivisection Society v IRC* [1948] AC 31.

[36] *Re Foveaux* [1895] 2 Ch 501.

[37] *National Anti-Vivisection Society* (n 35).

[38] J Calderwood-Norton, 'Weighing Benefits and Detriments in the Law of Charities' in Daniel Halliday and Matthew Harding (eds), *Charity Law: Exploring the Concept of Public Benefit* (London, Routledge, 2022) 199.

[39] ibid 202.

[40] See: www.gov.uk/government/publications/example-charitable-objects/example-objects-animal-charities.

inevitably arise for animal welfare charities, since on occasions promoting animal interests will impact negatively on humans or other animals. Competing animal interests came to the fore in 2013 when the Charity Commission entered 'talks' with the RSPCA after MPs complained about the organisation spending £320,000 on litigation to enforce the Hunting Act 2004 (UK).[41] Media reports alleged that as a consequence of the charity spending funds on lawsuits, it was forced to euthanise many companion animals, thus prioritising the organisation's political beliefs over public benefit.[42] As in the case law outlined above, this raises important questions about what constitutes public benefit in this context. Implicitly negative media coverage suggested that pet welfare was more important than protecting wild animals, or at least those cast as pests. Media discourse glossed over the fact that money is just one of a constellation of factors which impacts upon an organisation's capacity to rescue and rehome an ever-increasing number of surrendered, abandoned or seized animals. While the RSPCA received no formal sanction, the repercussions from this inquiry have been far-reaching. On the 28 January 2021, the RSPCA announced that they were 'exploring the transfer of our animal welfare prosecuting role to the Crown Prosecution Service to focus on our frontline work rescuing and caring for animals and investigating cruelty'.[43]

While the RSPCA's decision is in keeping with a trend of charities no longer taking private prosecutions,[44] it will likely lead to a drop in prosecutions for animal cruelty, given the RSPCA's remarkable prosecutorial record, with a reported 98 per cent success rate in prosecutions taken.[45] Interestingly, charity case law also indicates tensions around the RSPCA's role in enforcing animal welfare law. In *Re Herrick, Colohan v Att Gen*[46] a charitable trust was upheld for 'policemen' bringing animal cruelty cases to justice. However, a similar bequest was not upheld in *Re Hollywood, Smyth v Att Gen*[47] as the gift specified that RSPCA officers were to be excluded from consideration.[48]

[41] K Youde, 'Charity Commission to Hold Talks with RSPCA after Prosecution Row' (Third Sector, 14 January 2013) www.thirdsector.co.uk/charity-commission-hold-talks-rspca-prosecution-row/governance/article/1166608.

[42] V Martindale, 'The RSPCA: Can it Destroy and Protect Animals and the Same Time?' *The Independent* (London, 28 January 2013) www.independent.co.uk/voices/comment/the-rspca-can-it-destroy-and-protect-animals-at-the-same-time-8470469.html.

[43] The RSPCA, 'We're Reviewing Our Prosecutor Role to Focus on Frontline Cruelty' (*RSPCA*, 28 January 2021) www.rspca.org.uk/-/news-reviewing-prosecutor-role-to-focus-on-frontline-cruelty.

[44] Other charities which have relinquished prosecutorial powers include the NSPCC, and, pertinently to the animal welfare context, the RSPB.

[45] The RSPCA has a 98 per cent prosecutorial success rate. V Martindale, 'The RSPCA: Can it Destroy and Protect Animals and the Same Time?' *The Independent* (London, 28 January 2013). www.independent.co.uk/voices/comment/the-rspca-can-it-destroy-and-protect-animals-at-the-same-time-8470469.html.

[46] *Re Herrick, Colohan v Att Gen* (1918) 52 ILT 213.

[47] *Re Hollywood, Smyth v Att Gen* (1917) 52 ILT 51.

[48] Jamieson (n 5) 30.

V. Rehoming Companion Animals and the Role of Charity Law

In contrast to inherently controversial issues like vivisection or hunting, the Charity Commission appears to accept that rescuing and/or rehoming companion animals is a less contentious issue. However, we are mindful that while this may be perceived as a relatively apolitical focus for organisations seeking to promote animal welfare, many of the larger and well-known animal rescue and rehoming bodies have explicitly political origins. For example, the Canine Defence League (now Dogs Trust) was established in response to concerns over using dogs and cats in vivisection.[49] Moreover, today, larger nationwide rescues typically have well established auxiliary limbs which are overtly political. For example, the RSPCA's 'political animal' resources are explicitly aimed at parliamentarians and their staff.[50] In creating alliances such as the Dog Control Coalition (DCC), many large, often multi-site/nationwide rescues have established working relationships with government departments such as DEFRA and thus play a key role in advising the government on animal-facing issues.[51]

Moreover, depicting the process of rescuing and rehoming companion animals as a politically neutral and thus inherently beneficial act[52] may be misleading, given this activity entails grappling with tricky questions, such as determining when the import of dogs is an act of rescue or trafficking. Our focus group participants raised similar concerns, citing 'rescues' that purchase puppies from puppy farms as a key component in the pet breeding industry: 'We know a fellow who calls himself a rescue, he's a registered charity who buys litters, says he's rescued them from a breeder, seen the bitch and then "rescued" them from the nasty breeder.'[53]

Moreover, as is the case throughout the third sector, relations with Government are increasingly complex. Many rescues are contracted to deliver local authority services. For instance, cuts to local authority funding have resulted in a decline in council owned or funded kennels, meaning that councils often have to enter into contracts with animal rescues to take stray dogs or those

[49] H Kean, 'Animal Protection in Britain' in Andrew Linzey (ed), *The Global Guide to Animal Protection* (Champaign, University of Illinois Press, 2012) 9–10.

[50] https://politicalanimal.rspca.org.uk/.

[51] The Dog Control Coalition comprises several large rescues (Battersea Dogs and Cats Home, Blue Cross, British Veterinary Association, Dogs Trust, Hope Rescue, PDSA, RSPCA, SSPCA, the Kennel Club and the USPCA) who often advise DEFRA/DAERA on issues such as the pandemic, XL bully ban, etc.

[52] Significantly, 'public benefit' has not been discussed in any sustained way in formal Charity Commission inquiries or reported cases involving rescues or sanctuaries. The issue was noted briefly in the collapse of the Big Cats Sanctuary; however this was because the coordinator was charging for opportunities to see the cats and, thus, the sanctuary was not sufficiently accessible to an appreciable section of the community.

[53] Focus Group 1.

seized by the police. However, the contracting out of essential state services to third sector providers is fraught with risk. Research in the wake of the collapse of 'Kids Company'[54] indicated that public anger was due to reliance on the third sector to fulfil what were understood to be state obligations, rather than any failure on the part of the regulator.[55] In the animal welfare context, anecdotally, we are aware that the increased use of private and charitable boarding facilities has given rise to similar concerns about the public procurement process, and particularly the squeezing out of smaller rescues. In addition, diminishing numbers of public-facing animal welfare professionals, such as dog wardens and dog legislation officers (DLOs), mean that members of the public have become increasingly reliant on rescues when they encounter stray dogs, suspect animal cruelty or require advice on matters of dog law, further stretching their limited resources.[56] The increasing role animal rescues play in delivering local authority services therefore entails risks; risks in terms of animal welfare, but also for the reputation of both the charitable and animal rescue sectors. In lieu of a specific regulatory regime, Charity Law is one of the only means of regulating these services. In our interviews and focus groups, we therefore sought to explore our participants' expectations of, and frustrations with, charitable status. Analysis of inquiries then allowed us to explore the relationship between the governance requirements imposed by Charity Law and how this (albeit indirectly) aligns with good welfare standards.

Obtaining charitable status benefits individual rescues, the public who donate to rescues and the rescue sector as a whole. For individual rescue organisations, the main benefits of charitable registration and status are reputational and fiscal. Charitable status exempts organisations from income and capital gains tax liability, allowing them to claim gift aid on donations. In terms of reputation, charitable status is an important hallmark in terms of fundraising as 'just knowing that an organisation is a charity is often enough to give the public confidence to donate money to it'.[57] Surveys indicate that in England and Wales, the public has higher levels of trust and confidence in charities than in the church or the legal system, showing the significance of charitable status in reassuring the public.[58] While the Covid-19 pandemic placed an unprecedented strain on rescues, the sector defied the downturn in charitable giving during the pandemic, with animal welfare

[54] *Re Keeping Kids* [2021] EWHC 175 (Ch). This case is notable for its leniency towards trustees as noted in Henderson et al (n 5) vi.

[55] J Picton and J Sigafoos, 'Charity Law and Policy: Looking Forward' in John Picton and Jennifer Sigafoos (eds), *Debates in Charity Law* (Oxford, Hart, 2020) 304.

[56] This is well illustrated by the extensive public education activities undertaken by various rescues regarding new restrictions around XL bully type dogs – see e.g. the campaign work of the Dog Control Coalition – for instance: www.thekennelclub.org.uk/media-centre/2023/september/the-kennel-club-and-dog-control-coalition-response-to-changes-to-the-dangerous-dogs-act/.

[57] Cabinet Office, 'Private Action, Public Benefit: A Review of Charities and the Wider Not-For-Profit Sector, strategy unit report' (Cabinet Office, September 2002) 14.

[58] ibid.

consistently remaining the most popular cause for charitable giving across the UK every year since 2021.[59]

In the absence of statutory regulation, which could provide for a register of rescues, it is difficult for the public to determine which rescues are legitimate. Increasingly, membership of an umbrella body, the Association of Dogs and Cats Homes (ADCH), is used as a badge of legitimacy by those charities that are members. More generally, charitable status can provide some reassurance regarding the financial management of an organisation and, to a lesser extent, its compliance with record keeping requirements. Not only does this foster public confidence, but it benefits the sector. Requiring annual financial reports helps to ensure the longevity and sustainability of organisations. In turn, this helps to protect animal welfare, which may be compromised when organisations lack adequate resources or, worse, have to close their doors. Ensuring that organisations remain solvent allows them to provide the lifetime assurance that ideally should be given upon adoption, meaning that the rescue will take the animal back into its care at any point should the adopter no longer be able to care for the animal. Given these advantages, the ADCH has recently encouraged not-for-profit organisations to become charities, including by enlisting pro-bono solicitors to assist would-be ADCH members with their applications for charitable status.

Yet, notwithstanding the advantages that legal charitable status holds (and the importance of recent reforms which sought to clarify the registration process),[60] it is important to understand why not all rescues will seek, or be granted, charitable status. Our focus groups indicated various reasons for this. For example, participants observed that the registration process was 'long and drawn out', and noted that organisations with very low income which are not incorporated need not be registered (but remain subject to Charity Law and benefit from the same tax advantages with HMRC):[61] 'Some don't register as charities because you can only go for the big registration and the small charities are unregistered, you know?'[62]

Those rescues which had not sought charitable status sometimes misunderstood the level of oversight the Charity Commission has over a charity's day-to-day activities. Others were apprehensive about onerous reporting requirements: 'Doing a CIO application isn't easy to do and it doesn't help so what you do is people avoid by going the nonprofit route … and they're not regulated.'[63]

Furthermore, when balancing the benefits and burdens of registration, some participants noted, in line with Hogg's findings, that while charitable status is generally assumed to be key to ensuring public confidence, in practice, there may not be such a strong correlation between charitable status, public confidence and

[59] Charities Aid Foundation, 'UK Giving Report' (CAF 2024) www.cafonline.org/docs/default-source/uk-giving-reports/uk_giving_2023.pdf, 6.

[60] Under the Charities Act 2006 (UK), now Charities Act 2011 (UK).

[61] Income less than £5000 per annum.

[62] Focus Group 1.

[63] Focus Group 2.

charitable giving.[64] Further, not-for-profit rescues suggested that public confidence instead derived from their longstanding reputation: 'We're not a registered charity, we are the oldest breed club in existence. We have a lot of people of an older generation that when they pass away, we get some really major bequests; houses and things like that.'[65]

Participants representing registered charities have also voiced concerns that the Charity Commission takes a very prescriptive and granular approach to charitable purposes. For instance, this issue was raised by breed specific rescues who worried that assisting crossbreeds would contravene their charitable purposes, putting their charitable status at risk. Furthermore, budget cuts have resulted in the Charity Commission undertaking less proactive advisory activities,[66] having to direct its minimal resources reactively into investigating breaches in compliance. Being an under resourced regulator with broad investigatory powers means that it is more likely to act upon any complaints or reports concerning emotive issues, such as animal welfare, since these are more likely to be taken up in the media. There is, however, a risk that this reinforces misconceptions of the Commission as a regulator with teeth. We now turn to an analysis of Charity Commission inquiries, which offers further insight into how these misconceptions and misunderstandings result in breaches of Charity Law, which, in turn, may be the first indicator that animal welfare has been compromised.

VI. Insights from Commission Inquiries

As Jennifer Sigafoos explores in greater detail in chapter nine, inquiries may be triggered on a number of grounds. In the context of animal rescues, they are often in response to another regulatory intervention – for example if the police or RSPCA have investigated a rescue following a public complaint. In common with the Charity Commission's investigations across the charity sector, inquiry reports indicate that most interventions are triggered by chronic financial mismanagement. Typically, the charity in question will have attracted the regulator's attention by going far beyond its 'double default' rule, failing to meet several annual financial reporting deadlines and/or failing to act on previous warnings. Other inquiries are instigated because of complaints by the public, fellow trustees or – more commonly – independent auditors. Paradoxically, given concerns that some focus group participants expressed regarding the Charity Commission's heavy-handed approach, others were frustrated by their perception that the charity regulator's approach was both light touch and too fiscally orientated. Specifically, it

[64] E Hogg, 'Licking their Own Lollipops: What do Charities and the Public Think about the Regulation of Charitable Activities?' in Picton and Sigafoos (n 55).

[65] Focus Group 2.

[66] Hogg (n 64) 226.

was suggested by some participants that rescues which they suspected of failure to meet welfare standards had nevertheless been accorded or managed to retain charitable status. This view is, to some extent, borne out by our analysis of Charity Commission inquiries. For instance, one intervention by the RSPCA, which led to the removal of animals from the charity 'People and Pets Animal Welfare' prompted a Charity Commission inquiry. This entailed, amongst other things, liaising with the police and RSPCA to clarify concerns over the accommodation provided for animals. Ultimately, the Charity Commission agreed to monitor the rescue, since it concluded that the trustees had begun to display a better understanding of their roles and to comply with its recommendations on structural aspects, such as the redistribution of key duties.

Significantly for our purposes, Charity Commission inquiries have indicated that evidence of poor governance and inadequate financial oversight is often linked to compromised welfare. In this way, failures in governance can act as the 'canary in the coal mine' by flagging animal welfare concerns, even though these are not the regulator's primary focus. For instance, 'Capricorn Rescue' went well beyond a 'double default' situation, which meant the charity had ignored its legal responsibility in filing its annual accounts with the Charity Commission; the charity had been late each year between 2007–15, despite regulatory advice and guidance from the Charity Commission. Notwithstanding this, the Charity Commission's inquiry into this charity's managerial and governance practices was initiated following public complaints, which garnered such negative media coverage that it attracted parliamentary interest. Such cases suggest that the Charity Commission may be more likely to respond to emotive issues such as animal cruelty – since they are acutely aware that failure to address such concerns risks bringing the charitable sector into disrepute. Following the recommendations of an interim manager, the Charity Commission concluded that in this case closure was necessary, with the RSPCA stepping in to rehome 137 animals from squalid conditions.[67]

Similarly, an inquiry into the 'Alternative Animal Sanctuary', triggered by concerns from the charity's auditors, exposed both financial mismanagement and animal cruelty. In this case, the inquiry was opened in 2017, and an interim manager, appointed in 2019, ultimately concluded that the charity should be wound down and two trustees, including the chair, should be disqualified from serving as trustees (for 15 and 10 years, respectively). Over this two-year period the RSPCA issued a number of warrants following the breach of numerous improvement and statutory notices; however, the rescue coordinator continued to take in animals to replace those seized. Subsequently the rescue coordinator was

[67] Charity Commission, 'Charity inquiry; Capricorn Animal Rescue and Sanctuary' (Charity Commission, 2022) https://webarchive.nationalarchives.gov.uk/ukgwa/20221223045747/https:/www.gov.uk/government/publications/charity-inquiry-capricorn-animal-rescue-and-sanctuary-inc-aston-hawarden-animal-aid.

convicted of 16 animal cruelty offences and banned from keeping animals, which resulted in closure of the organisation.

This particular inquiry demonstrates the limitations of a system which does not focus directly on animal welfare. Although this case did involve the Charity Commission and RSPCA working together, even then extreme cruelty may not be quickly and effectively addressed, resulting in approximately 400 dogs and cats being euthanised due to neglect. These inquiries reveal the costs to animals where rescue goes wrong; but the costs to the police and other animal welfare organisations are also high, with the RSPCA bearing the cost of prosecution while also treating and rehoming any remaining animals.[68] Additionally, such cases can entail costs to the Charity Commission itself, since the regulator must meet the costs of appointing interim managers if the remaining funds of the charity do not cover this expense.[69]

Our analysis of inquiries into animal rescues, coupled with insights from the focus groups, also suggests that trustees often misunderstand their potential liability under civil and criminal law. This is further complicated by the fact that, as noted above, even where rescues have sought and been granted charitable status, they may still take a variety of legal forms which affect how far trustees may be held liable for regulatory breaches.[70] Typically, Charity Commission inquiries involve small, one-site organisations that have missed multiple reporting deadlines. They then usually reveal a failure to manage conflicts of interests (often due to the rescue being based at one of the trustee's homes, a particular feature of the animal welfare sector),[71] a lack of oversight of finances,[72] and a failure to manage this

[68] Although, of course, any system of regulation will entail costs.

[69] Charity Commission, 'Charity inquiry; Capricorn Animal Rescue and Sanctuary' (Charity Commission 2021) www.gov.uk/government/publications/charity-inquiry-the-alternative-animal-sanctuary/charity-inquiry-the-alternative-animal-sanctuary; Matty Hewitt, 'Police Raid Animal Sanctuary Near Boston for Third Time' *Lincolnshire Live* (Lincoln, 8 January 2020) www.lincolnshire-live.co.uk/news/local-news/alternative-animal-sanctuary-raided-rspca-3716200.

[70] www.shoosmiths.com/insights/past-webinars/the-spectre-of-personal-criminal-liability-for-charity-trustees.

[71] E.g. the inquiry into Muffin Pug Rescue revealed trustees using charity money to make mortgage payments, thus paying for their family home. This was also the case at King Charles Cavalier Rescue, where appropriate steps had not been taken regarding the rescue being based at the rescue co-ordinator's home (as well as other evidence that donations had been used for personal benefit). Charity Commission, 'Charity inquiry: Muffin Pug Rescue' (Charity Commission, 2024) www.gov.uk/government/publications/charity-inquiry-muffin-pug-rescue/charity-inquiry-muffin-pug-rescue.

[72] Inquiries into Action Aid for Animals and King Charles Cavalier Rescue each found evidence of breaches of trustee duties due to one trustee having access to finances with no oversight from other trustees. Similarly, the inquiry into White Horse Stables' found evidence of two trustees signing off one another's expenses with no oversight from other members of the executive committee. Charity Commission, 'Charity inquiry: Action Aid for Animals' (Charity Commission 2019) www.gov.uk/government/publications/charity-inquiry-action-aid-for-animals/action-aid-for-animals; Charity Commission, 'Charity inquiry: Cavalier King Charles Spaniel Rescue & Welfare (Charity Commission, 2016) https://assets.publishing.service.gov.uk/media/5a800fe3ed915d74e33f8391/cavalier_king_charles_spaniel_rescue_and_welfare.pdf.

by recruiting a sufficient number[73] of trustees from an adequately wide pool (e.g. trustees often being family members).[74]

Most inquiries in this field have addressed smaller charities; however, a six-year regulatory case[75] into the RSPCA suggests that the larger nationwide rescues may experience the opposite problem – for instance, having too many trustees who were entrusted with too much involvement in day-to-day operational matters. Common problems which transcend the size of the organisation include trustees having insufficient skill sets/experience and serving long terms of office unopposed.[76] Sanctions for financial mismanagement usually include monitored compliance with action plans and/or trustee disqualification. However, even if organisations are sanctioned by removal from the Charity Registry for their failure to comply with Charity Law, they can continue to operate as a self-professed not-for-profit rescue or rehoming organisation.

The aforementioned 'Alternative Animal Rescue' inquiry also revealed a lack of understanding of the duties involved in investing money and fundraising, which can render organisations vulnerable to fraudulent third parties. For example, auditors reported that between 2009–16 this particular charity raised £8.1million from the public via a third-party fundraiser. However, the charity only received £950,000, and the third party retained the rest.[77] Aside from the financial and reputational damage done to organisations, cases such as *Charity Commission v Wright and another* also reveal that trustees are unaware of the ramifications of not complying with the Charity Commission's directions following an inquiry. In this case trustees were held in contempt of court, having failed to comply with the Charity Commission over a sustained period.[78]

The inquiry into 'Chichester and District Dog Rescue Society' exhibited several typical features: a very small trustee board dominated by a married couple and a lack of financial oversight and reporting, resulting in £300,000 being

[73] Following a Charity Commission inquiry, UK German Shepherd Rescue Angels received an official warning, having not filed accounts on time for five years and failing to have the required number of trustees. Charity Commission, 'Official Warning to UK German Shepherd Rescue Angels' (Charity Commission, 2023) https://apps.charitycommission.gov.uk/SCHEMES/069301.PDF.

[74] E.g: the Retreat Animal Rescue were investigated having missed several reporting deadlines. The inquiry found a small pool of trustees who were either married to or siblings of the founder resulting in a failure to manage conflicts which had impacted the organisation's finances. Charity Commission, 'Charity inquiry: The Retreat Animal Rescue' (Charity Commission, 2021) www.gov.uk/government/publications/charity-inquiry-the-retreat-animal-rescue/charity-inquiry-the-retreat-animal-rescue.

[75] As distinct from an inquiry.

[76] A Ricketts, 'Charity Commission Closes Six-year Case into the RSPCA' (Third Sector, 5 January 2021) www.thirdsector.co.uk/charity-commission-closes-six-year-case-rspca/governance/article/1703273.

[77] The fundraising regulator was established in 2016 but has a relatively low take up, particularly amongst smaller organisations and has only undertaken 13 investigations to date.

[78] *Charity Commission v Wright and another* [2019] EWHC 3375 (Ch) (8 November 2019) (Morgan J).

unaccounted for.[79] This organisation was ultimately re-registered following a change in trustees who implemented the Charity Commission's recommendations. This inquiry remains notable as the Charity Commission observed that the organisation reportedly paid vet fees on behalf of owners who could not afford them, a practice which the Charity Commission noted was not entirely aligned with 'rescuing and rehoming'. This indicates that animal welfare charities should be mindful to frame their charitable objectives relatively broadly so as to allow for operational changes in response to changing social conditions. As we have shown, rescues constantly have to evolve, with many of our participants reporting that they are refocusing activities to keep animals in their homes due to a shortage of kennel space or potential new homes. This can entail such measures as contributing towards vet bills and/or providing food and basic medications (eg flea and worming treatment).

In summary, our analysis of the Charity Commission inquiries shows that, although they frequently result in little more than directions as to how to improve, disqualification of trustees and/or (much more rarely) removal from the registry, they can nevertheless make a contribution to animal welfare by exposing welfare breaches. While rarely discussed in inquiries, these interventions may, in practice, force organisations to close as a result of seizure of assets if the organisation is no longer deemed to be operating for the public benefit. While the Charity Commission inquiries are inevitably limited in protecting animal welfare, this exploration of recent inquiries suggests that they can usefully function as what Margaret Somerville terms 'ethical canaries'[80] in flagging more serious issues, showing that Charity Law still has some role to play in regulating this sector.

As a final point, we would note that it is important for trustees to be mindful that their actions are ultimately circumscribed by criminal law. Anecdotally, law firms claim to be seeing more criminal prosecutions against individuals (particularly senior figures/managers of charities), which can include the imposition of custodial sentences for those directly involved in serious health and safety breaches.[81] Any offence for which a charity could be found liable will be closely linked to the principal operational activities of the charities concerned. Thus, for a charity dealing with the rehoming of dogs, it is important that those involved understand the risks in accepting a dog for rehoming which is either potentially dangerous, for example, with a bite history or is of or similar to a banned type, even if exempted.

[79] Charity Commission, 'Charity inquiry: Chichester and District Dog Rescue Society' (Charity Commission 2020) https://webarchive.nationalarchives.gov.uk/ukgwa/20201231114338/https:/www.gov.uk/government/publications/charity-inquiry-chichester-and-district-dog-rescue-society.

[80] M Somerville, *The Ethical Canary: Science, Society and the Human Spirit* (Toronto, Penguin, 2000).

[81] www.shoosmiths.com/insights/past-webinars/the-spectre-of-personal-criminal-liability-for-charity-trustees.

VII. Finding a Way Forward

Ultimately, this chapter has shown that Charity Law, while imperfect, nevertheless has a key role to play in protecting animal welfare, both by reacting to complaints and potentially uncovering some of the most egregious welfare breaches committed by rescues. It is also important not to underestimate the importance of striving to ensure that rescues are financially sustainable. However, it is concerning that while serious welfare breaches likely occur in many charities, they may well avoid triggering an inquiry provided they file financial reports and thus elude scrutiny. We have seen that the Charity Commission inquiries may be prompted by complaints from the public or other regulatory bodies (for example, the RSPCA or the police). Nonetheless, the fact remains that many rescues operate in remote rural locations or are based in private homes, which makes it easier for them to evade public scrutiny. And, of course, many not-for-profit rescues will completely evade any regulatory oversight unless they are guilty of perpetrating extreme cruelty. For all these reasons, the capacity of Charity Law to govern the rescue sector is limited. Ultimately, it is perhaps unrealistic to expect Charity Law to play a more expansive role in promoting animal welfare, given the breadth of the regulator's role, its limited resources and the diversity of charitable purposes. When this is coupled with the different understandings of animals at play, and the variation in animal rescues that we have traced, we suggest that it is untenable to expect Charity Law to offer anything other than very light-touch regulation. Therefore, while the Charity Commission will continue to play a vital role in the absence of a dedicated governance regime, our analysis of Charity Law underlines our general argument that sector-specific regulation of animal rescues is needed.

Even within this particular subcategory of the charitable purpose of advancing animal welfare, the diversity in rescue policies, practices and governance creates tensions in how regulation could and should work. Currently, the lack of an agreed animal welfare benchmark which charities are expected to meet hinders the ability of Charity Law to increase resilience by fostering cooperation across the sector. For example, while the Charities Act 2006 made it easier for organisations to merge,[82] the diversity in animal welfare standards across rescues continues to impede cooperation within the sector:

> There are people who work for the bigger organisations and the bigger charities that I would never see eye to eye with so I wouldn't necessarily want to get involved. I would rather be confident that I was doing what I felt was right for our charity rather than be bundled into this, you know, cauldron of regulations.[83]
>
> It comes down to trust and that charity knowing you as an individual – as we're talking about mickey mouse rescues; how does that charity know the difference between? So you come back to some kind of [additional] registration don't you?[84]

[82] Charities Act 2006, s 44, as discussed in D Morris, 'Charities and the Big Society: a Doomed Coalition?' (2018) 32(1) *LS* 132.

[83] Interview Participant 17.

[84] Focus Group 1.

A further reason that Charity Law is limited in its ability to effectively regulate this sector is that regulation relies on perceptions of risk. However, this is calculated very differently in Charity Law and animal rescue domains. In Charity Law terms, the larger the organisation, the larger the risk posed since the conceptualisation of risk is, to some extent, fiscal. Thus, Picton and Sigafoos have suggested that the 'Charity Commission would do well to focus its regulation on larger entities' particularly in times of austerity.[85] However, in the context of risks posed to animal welfare, we draw the opposite conclusion from our empirical research, that is, that greater scrutiny should be focused on smaller organisations since they are more likely to breach welfare standards. This position is borne out by the Charity Commission inquiries examined above, where concerns about neglect or cruelty involved smaller charities.

Participants in our focus groups generally favoured better governance, but were also understandably wary about the impact of further regulation, particularly given the lack of effective enforcement in both charity and welfare law as noted above: 'We don't necessarily need to have big regulation on animal welfare. What you need to do is have an organisation that takes money from the public to be regulated or accountable in some way: that's more the issue.'[86]

This tension is also evident when considering the take up of voluntary welfare orientated codes to which rescues may choose to adhere. Both the Kennel Club and ADCH have 'opt-in' schemes which require members of the schemes to report on welfare issues. For instance, they are asked to record how many animals were in their care at the start and end of each regulatory period, the proportion that were euthanised, and so on. Since the Kennel Club facilitated our focus groups, it is unsurprising that all our participants had 'opted in' to the Kennel Club's breed specific rescue scheme. However, the focus groups revealed a relative lack of take up of other opt-in, welfare-orientated mechanisms, including the ADCH minimum welfare standards. Therefore, it appears that a desire for better practice is coupled with wariness about statutory and other forms of regulation and the associated burdens, particularly for smaller organisations, which typically must prioritise animal-facing activities.

Moreover, as a regulator focused on setting a minimal welfare standard, the ADCH has little fiscal oversight, prompting its requirement for applicants to have already secured charitable status. Some of our participants cited this as a barrier to engaging with this more proactive and welfare-orientated body:

> It's a sort of catch 22 you know, if you haven't got this, you can't do that. We just took one look at it and said 'that doesn't fit us'. We haven't got charity status and we haven't got this and we haven't got that, we haven't got premises, whatever it was, there was loads we didn't have and yet we still feel we provide a really good service.[87]

Significantly, however, the desire to join what they perceived as a more welfare-orientated regulatory body did motivate some participants who might otherwise

[85] Picton and Sigafoos (n 55).
[86] Focus Group 2.
[87] Focus Group 1.

not have sought charitable status: 'We applied to the ADCH but were rejected as we're not a charity. We're now in the process becoming a charity.'[88]

Of course, the position is complicated by the involvement of multiple regulatory bodies, which are subject to multiple regulatory regimes and have very different objectives. During the Covid-19 pandemic, rescues were subject to (sometimes contradictory) advice from multiple sources. For instance, generic guidance issued to charities sometimes conflicted with more specific and detailed advice coming from bodies such as ADCH and the Kennel Club. As Breen acknowledges, 'multiple emerging regulators may dilute compliance for those unable to keep up with the regulatory burden.'[89] Any regulatory change which demands increased bureaucracy can deter volunteers, as was seen by the resignation of many volunteers following more stringent charity reporting requirements introduced in 1993.[90] Once again, this is particularly likely to be a consideration for smaller organisations already struggling to comply with such requirements or lacking awareness of them.[91] Such rescues are often run entirely by volunteers, who typically are primarily motivated by more animal-focused activities. As with all animal-welfare orientated interventions, enforcement will be key as research indicates that 'those who work in smaller charities often indicate their view on what regulation should entail by simply not complying.'[92]

VIII. Conclusion

In focusing specifically on dog rescue and rehoming as one facet of the charitable purpose of 'advancement of animal welfare',[93] this chapter has questioned the extent to which protection of animal welfare can truly sit comfortably within Charity Law, an anthropocentric legal framework which inherently prioritises human benefit. It is arguable that the rationale for recognising animal welfare as charitable has shifted, since the benefits of the human-animal interactions have become widely accepted/celebrated.[94] This can, however, perpetuate further species distinctions by elevating the status of companion animals over wild or farmed animals, although both have been a growing focus of animal welfare charities, both nationally and internationally.

[88] Focus Group 2.

[89] Oonagh Breen, 'Redefining the Regulatory Space? The First Forays of the Irish Charities Regulatory Authority' in Picton and Sigafoos (n 55).

[90] Eddy Hogg, 'Licking their Own Lollipops: What do Charities and the Public Think about the Regulation of Charitable Activities?' in Picton and Sigafoos (n 55) 216.

[91] ibid.

[92] ibid 218.

[93] Charities Act 2011 (UK), s 3(1)(k).

[94] See e.g. M Fox and M Ray, 'No Pets Allowed? Companion Animals, Older People and Residential Care' (2019) 45 (2) *BMJ Medical Humanities* 211–22; N Jenkins et al (eds), *Multi-Species Dementia Studies: Towards an Interdisciplinary Approach* (Bristol, Bristol University Press, 2025).

Using UK animal rescue as a lens to interrogate English and Welsh Charity Law reveals the extent to which good governance is critical to ensuring animal welfare. This is clear from our interview data. For instance, many requirements can be derided as 'bureaucracy', yet having an adequate number of diversely skilled trustees, for example, is integral to ensuring the proper governance and financial sustainability of organisations. In turn, this is key to ensuring that welfare standards are maintained. As Charity Commission inquiries into rescues show, while adequate financial reporting by no means signals high animal welfare standards, the absence of such compliance can put animals at risk. Analysis of these inquiries, together with our findings, highlight the need for greater education of charitable trustees to ensure that they understand the duties that the role entails. As we have seen, many Charity Commission inquiries recommend educating trustees about their basic duties. Moreover, our interviews highlighted the need for broader education in the not-for-profit sector to dispel misconceptions that registration and reporting duties mandated by Charity Law are arduous. As we have outlined above, this lack of awareness leaves animals vulnerable to neglect and rescues, and trustees vulnerable to both civil and criminal liability.

While not peculiar to Charity Law, the continuing framing of animals as property (in this context as donatable or sellable products) causes dissonance in the rescue sector, compounding the legal ambiguities that plague day-to-day rescue activities and rendering rescues vulnerable to legal action. For instance, the law's categorisation of animals as property or commodities is at odds with how rescues understand them as living beings more akin to family members. This is particularly apparent in law's failure to adequately categorise adoption donations (the main source of income for many small rescues) as a contribution towards the organisation's charitable purposes. Legal rulings indicate that adoption donations are instead understood as fixed fees for tax purposes, thus framing the donation as payment for a particular dog rather than a donation towards the organisation's general activities.[95] These radically different understandings of animal status and human relationships with animals are reflected in the plethora of welfare-orientated clauses participants cited as central to their adoption agreements (often regarding specific of care/return of animals). While well intentioned, in practice, these would likely be legally unenforceable. On a practical level, this raises questions about the obligation of a rescue to return a donation should the adoption fail and the dog be returned. It leaves rescue organisations at risk of legal action if adopters seek to claw back adoption donations in the county courts. Thus, our own organisation successfully defended one case where an adopter argued that the dog placed in his care was a 'faulty product' under the Consumer Rights Act 2015 (UK).[96]

[95] *Three Counties Dog Rescue v HMRC* [2011] UKFTT 817 (TC).

[96] *Ogden v North West English Springer Spaniel Rescue (NWESSR)* [2018], (Unreported) Manchester County Court, Claim No E29YJ500, 16 August 2018. Cases such as *Gables Farms Dog and Cats Rescue v Revenue & Customs Commissioners* [2008] 1 WLUK 16 show HMRC grappling over whether there are different tax implications for dogs surrendered from owners compared to stray dogs brought into

As we have seen, the increasing role rescues play in the delivery of day-to-day services is fraught with risk. Where rescues fail, this impacts not only the animals directly in their care but also the sector as a whole, since larger (often national) rescues are called upon to take in and treat any surviving animals. Moreover, as 'rescue' is seen by many as synonymous with 'charity', where a rescue is used as a front for trafficking or hoarding this impacts public confidence in both rescue and the charity sector more broadly. As highlighted above, the Charity Commission are attentive to this issue given the reputational damage that welfare busts have for both the animal rescue and charity sectors. This sensitivity to media coverage regarding rescues is, however, a double-edged sword since it can, for instance, allow MPs to evade being held to account by animal welfare organisations simply by accusing them of expending too much resource on lobbying.

It is significant that, perhaps to a greater extent than media campaigns and political lobbying from animal welfare organisations, it is high profile charity scandals which have ultimately prompted regulatory reform in this area. The fall-out from the Capricorn Rescue inquiry, for instance, led the Welsh government to implement a voluntary code of practice for rescues and sanctuaries. Similarly, an SSPCA cruelty bust at Scottish charity the Ayrshire Ark, involving the deaths of 15 dogs and a cat (which garnered public and media reaction), prompted the introduction of the statutory licensing scheme in Scotland. The introduction of a similar regulatory framework is on the parliamentary agenda to different extents in England, Wales and Northern Ireland. Notwithstanding its limitations, until a more proactive regulatory approach is adopted, charitable status will remain at the heart of animal rescue. By helping to secure the financial sustainability of the rescue sector Charity Law can play a vital, albeit limited, role in ensuring that animal rescues have the necessary stability so they can continue to rescue, rehabilitate and rehome vulnerable animals, while also flagging breaches of animal welfare.

rescue by a dog warden. While, ultimately, it was recognised that the source of intake has no tax implications, this illustrates the complexities facing rescues who are constantly having to evolve to ever changing social conditions. The status of adoption contracts has recently been tested in the High Court (of England & Wales). In this case a rescue organization (Paws on Hearts Rehoming) became aware that an adopter was seeking euthanasia of their dog (Mr Bones) due to a recurring infection in his leg which they believed could have been treated, if necessary, by amputation. In response to a clause regarding euthanasia in the organization's adoption agreement the High Court granted dual ownership to the rescue organization and granted an interlocutory injunction to stop Mr Bones being euthanized until a further veterinary assessment could be made (Dogs Today, 'Court Upholds Rescue's Rights; So How Was Mr Bones Still PTS?', *Dogs Today*, (Issue 365, December 2024).

INDEX

A

abolitionist movement 18

accountability
- animal welfare organisations 241
- Charity Commission oversight 176
- charity law 5, 7, 167–169, 170, 171
- constitutive 167–168
- disability service charities 147–148, 149, 159, 167–169, 170, 171, 172
- donors, to 96–97, 99
- governance accountability 168–169
- stakeholder 168
- subscriber organizations 16

accounts
- preparation and filing 193

Achiezer 197

administrative costs 91

advocacy groups
- animal welfare organisations 231, 232, 244
- charitable status 6, 64
- discriminatory practice 123, 125, 132, 141–142
- political advocacy 4, 166–167

affirmative action 10

AgeUK 91

alms-houses 16

Alternative Animal Sanctuary 189–190, 236–237, 238

ambulance service efficiency, promoting 177

animal law
- animals framed as property 223, 229, 243
- discipline of 223

animal welfare organisations
- accountability 241
- adopter's rights 243
- adoption donations 243
- Animal Welfare Act 229–230
- anti-vivisection campaigning 230
- breed specific 228, 235
- charitable objectives, framing 235, 239
- charitable status, obtaining 233–235, 238
- Charity Commission investigations 224, 228, 235–239, 241, 243
- charity law's role 223–225, 227–244
- companion animals 223, 224, 228, 232–244
- conflict of interests 237
- Covid-19 crisis 226, 233, 242
- criminal prosecutions 239
- diversity 240
- expanding services 226, 235, 239
- financial mismanagement 236, 238–239
- financial reporting 238, 240, 243
- funding cuts 225
- gaps in state provision 224, 232–233
- historical background 24, 225
- import of dogs into UK 226, 232
- incorporated 227
- legitimacy 233–235
- local authority provision 225, 232
- monitoring 236, 238
- number in UK 225, 227
- political advocacy 231, 232, 244
- public benefit, as 229–231
- puppy farms 232
- regulation 12, 226–227, 234, 238, 240–244
- rehoming sector 223, 224, 225–226, 232–244
- Scotland 227, 244
- state outsourcing to 232–233
- trustees 225, 238–239
- United Kingdom 223–244
- voluntary codes 241–242

Association of Dogs and Cats Homes (ADCH) 234, 241–242

auditors
- reports by 186, 190

Australia
- charitable purposes 111
- *cy-près* doctrine *See cy-près* doctrine in Australia
- disability injustices *See* disability injustices
- Disability Justice activism 149, 160, 161, 163, 172
- Disability Royal Commission 147, 149, 153–160, 162–163, 167, 169
- economic footprint of religion 73, 74
- National Disability Insurance Scheme 11, 147–148, 154, 158, 159, 168

National Redress Scheme 148, 168–169
Public Benevolent Institutions 154, 159, 165–166
settler colonialism 151, 153, 169
Stolen Generations 170
Australian Charities and Not-for-profits Commission (ACNC) 7, 55, 159–160, 165–166
Governance Standard 148
Australian Foundation for Disability (Afford) 154, 156–157, 162, 165, 167
autonomy
government contracts and 5
Avery, Scott 153, 163
Ayrshire Ark 244

B
Bales, MD
Principles of Law 209
Barnardo's 84, 96, 194
Battersea Dogs and Cats Home 227
Beard, Jennifer 167
Belgium
religious charities 68, 71
beneficiaries
disabled *See* disability injustices
paternalistic power relations 161, 162
safeguarding interests of 3
bequests *See* **testamentary gifts**
Beveridge Report 37
Blair, Tony 99
Blue J 117
Bossy, John 95
Boyle, William
A Practical Treatise on the Law of Charities 24
Bramwell LJ 31–32
Breen, Oonagh 242
Bridgeman, Richard 22
British Asian Christian Association 178–179
Brody, E and Tyler, J 141
Brougham, Henry 27–29

C
Calderwood-Norton, J 230
Canada
economic footprint of religion 73–74
Cancer Research UK 96–97
Canine Defence League 232
Capricorn Rescue 236, 244
Captain Tom Foundation 91–92
Care4Calais 187, 194–195
cash couriers 189
Causeway Coast Dog Rescue 227
certainty requirement 127
Chan, K 129
Chancery, Court of 16, 20, 23, 24–27, 28, 30
cy-près doctrine 36
charitable status
advocacy groups 6, 64, 123, 125, 132, 141–142
animal welfare organisations 233–234, 238
boundaries of 6
charitable purposes, definition 164–167
determining 101–119
exploitation of 6, 31
grant of, as expressive harm 138–139, 141–142, 143–144
legitimacy conferred by 139
charities
accountability *See* accountability
asymmetrical and non-reciprocal model 95–96
benefits enjoyed by 58, 60, 87–90, 143, 148
boundaries of charitable status 6, 81, 87
charitable character, recognised 81–82, 87
contemporary concept of 87, 108–109
controversial 70–72
court enforcement 61, 83
discriminatory *See* discriminatory practice
doublethink in understanding of 10, 103, 107, 116–118
economic significance of sector 57, 64–65, 72–76, 85–88, 174
educational *See* educational institutions
exclusive institutions 6, 32
halo effect 10, 101–103, 107, 108–119, 165
indeterminacy of, as jural concept 102, 103–107, 108, 109
infantilisation of society 100
legal definition 8, 19–23, 30–32, 77, 80–81, 83, 101–102, 103, 104, 117, 149, 164–167, 170
legal personality 17, 188
legal recognition 4–5, 58, 59–60, 61–62, 79–82, 86–87, 143, 202, 203–204, 205, 215
liberality and benevolence 21–22
malleable nature 109
meaning 102–119
moral intent 106
number of Chinese 202
number of UK 85, 173

place in UK culture 77–100
pluralistic nature 8
popular meaning 117
presumed social benefits 79–83, 86–89, 92, 93–94
private entities, as 3
public benefit *See* public benefit rule
public purpose, gifts for 22–23, 31–32
public trust and confidence in 3–4, 85, 89–92, 97–98, 99, 101, 174–175, 176
purposes 30–32, 41, 61–65, 80–82, 83, 101–102, 105, 111, 175, 176; *See also* public benefit rule
registration *See* registration
religious *See* religious charities
role 4, 78, 79–83, 85
sham 188
social change, support for 88
social conception of 77–89, 108–109
state support 79, 80, 82, 84, 85, 89, 93, 94, 98, 138–139, 143
status as *See* charitable status

Charity Commission for England and Wales
accountability 179, 198–199
animal welfare organisations 224, 228, 235–239, 241, 243
complaints to 186–187
consistency 180, 198–199
cy-près jurisdiction 39, 40, 50–51
disqualification of trustees 92, 180, 188, 190, 197–198, 236, 238, 239
dual function 176
establishment 27–29, 83, 88
factors triggering investigations 184–187, 235
fiscal orientation 235–236
funding 175–176, 177
generally 7, 11, 12, 90
incorporated charities 173
interim manager, power to appoint 190, 193, 197
media pressure for investigations 186–187
number of registered charities 173
Official Warnings 188
political pressures 193–197
powers 29–30, 39, 40, 181
reactive nature of inquiries 184–187
regulatory role 173–199
reports 181–182, 198–199
risk-led approach 177
statutory inquiries 11, 179–199, 241
statutory objectives 175–176
strategic objectives 176, 198
transparency 179, 180, 198–199
unregistered charities 173

charity commissioners
Australia *See* Australian Charities and Not-for-profits Commission (ACNC)
historic role 20, 24, 27–28
UK *See* Charity Commission for England and Wales

charity law *See also* **regulation**
adaptability 13
animal welfare organisations 223–225, 227–244
asymmetrical and non-reciprocal model 95–96
changing social norms 3–4, 5, 6, 70–72
charitable character, recognised 81–82, 87
charitable purposes 30–32, 41, 61–65, 80–82, 83, 101–102, 105, 111, 175, 176; *See also* public benefit rule
common law 46, 61–62, 81, 83, 102
compliance, oversight 176
contemporary concept of charities 87
contemporary realities 10, 13, 62, 78–79
definition of charity 8, 19–23, 30–32, 77, 80–81, 83, 101–102, 103, 104, 117, 149
disability service charities 147, 149, 159–172
disabling 163–172
discriminatory charities 124–132
dual mandate 3, 4–7, 8
enabling injustice 126, 147, 149, 153, 163, 169–170
equity 6, 46, 83–84, 86
evasion 21
evolving role 4, 13, 62–63, 64, 77–78, 79–83, 105
facilitative function 134
foundational statute 3, 13, 20, 24, 61, 82–83
historical background 7–8, 12–13, 15–33, 82–87, 95, 102
historical-structural injustice 149, 169–172
Hodgson Review 82–83, 85, 92
legal recognition of charities 4–5, 58, 59–60, 61–62, 79–82, 86–87, 143, 202, 203–204, 205, 215
limits 29–33
Medieval contributions to 83–87, 88–89
modernisation of English law 81–82, 85, 88–90, 99, 101, 107
moral foundations 10, 102, 161

nineteenth-century England 23–33, 78, 88
PASC Report 82–83, 85
Pemsel test 30–31, 61–62, 83, 87, 105, 106, 113, 128, 175, 229
politics, relationship with 107
positive ideological ideals and values 108
presumed social benefits 79–83, 86–87, 92, 93–94
principles of good regulation 179–180, 198–199
public benefit *See* public benefit rule
public confidence and 3–4, 85, 89–92, 99, 174
reforms, resistance to 167
reporting duties 243
social harm critique 80, 93–95
statute law 61–62, 81–82
third sector 9, 87
treatises 24
trusts 87

Chesterman, M 96

Chichester and District Dog Rescue Society 238–239

China, charitable/non-profit organisations
decentralised legislative model 218–219, 220
development direction 214
distributive justice, promotion 208
diversity 214
forms 216
government policy 206
importance of sector 201, 214, 217
incentive policies 202, 203–204, 218
judicial interpretations 219
legislative approaches 212, 218–220
legislative framework 11–12, 201–221
legislative purpose 211, 217–218
legislative quality 220–221
non-profit legal persons 202
normative analysis 209–221
number of 202
professionalisation of sector 3–4, 7, 189–190, 201
public benefit 203
public welfare organisations 201, 202, 204–205
rational legislation 210, 213–214
recognition 203–204, 205, 215
registration in 202, 216
research perspectives 206–209
social influence 214
social organisations 202–205
structure of legislative system 210–212, 215–216, 220
supporting measures 205, 213–220
tax treatment 201–205, 215
trustees 208
types 203, 216
unclear and inconsistent concept 202–203
value 208, 209, 210, 213–214, 220

Christ's Hospital 16

civil society
supporting machinery or harmony of 62–63

class interests 28–29

coercion, state 141

Coke CJ 17

colonialism 194
Australia 151, 153, 169

commercialisation
commercial governance 17
doublethink 107
for-profit subsidiaries 6
generally 107
hybrid non-profit business models 6
investments 6
market-based service provision 153
moral foundations of charity law 10
public benefit and 5, 6, 7, 10
revenue generation 6
scope of charitable purposes 111–116

common law
charity law 46, 61–62, 81, 83, 102
discriminatory charities 126
equity 83–84, 86
meaning of charity 102

conflict of interests, regulation 12, 13, 89–90, 187–188, 190, 196
animal welfare organisations 237

Coram, Thomas 17

corporate oversight 7, 10

Crennan J 111

Cup Trust 177

custom 20, 23

***cy-près* doctrine**
amalgamations 41–42
amendment of charitable purpose 40–41
'appropriate considerations' 39, 46, 47–48
'as near as possible' 36–37, 39–42, 45
Australia *See cy-près* doctrine in Australia
cessation ground 38
Charity Commission jurisdiction 39, 40, 50–51
Court of Chancery 36

discriminatory trusts 127, 129
donor intent 36–39, 41–42, 50
English reforms 35, 36–43, 45–46, 48, 49, 50
grounds or occasions 36, 37–38, 41–42, 43, 46–47
history and evolution 35, 36–42
impossibility/impracticability 36, 42, 43, 45
incorporated charities 41, 55
interpretation 40
Nathan Report 37–38, 42–44, 51
New Zealand 42
perpetual charitable trusts 8, 35, 36, 41–42, 51, 55
precedent, doctrine of 50–51
purpose 35, 37, 40
small charitable trusts 40
'spirit of the gift' 38–39, 43–45, 46, 47, 48–49
'suitable and effective' purpose 45, 48–50
total return investment 54

***cy-près* doctrine in Australia**
donor intent 50
educational endowments 8–9, 54
generally 9, 30, 35–36, 42–43, 51
grounds or occasions 43–46, 52, 53
impossibility/impracticability 42, 43, 45
Nathan Report 42–44, 51
precedential value of English cases 48–51
public benefit 51
reform 36, 51–55
similarity requirement 52–53
small charitable trusts 51, 52, 53
'spirit of the gift' 43–45, 46, 48–49, 53
statutory regime 42–55

D

dehumanisation of disabled people 152, 160, 172
deserving and undeserving poor 96
detriment
benefits weighed against 123, 130, 131–133, 138
discrimination as 123–145
expressive 124, 138–145
historical-structural 169–172
injuries of normality 170
material 124, 136–138, 142, 145
potential 123
proof of 135–136, 142
public benefit rule 123–124, 142
unintentional 139

Dickens, Charles
Bleak House 7–8, 15, 24
disability injustices
accountability 147–148, 149, 159, 167–169, 170, 171, 172
attitudinal and systemic 158, 159, 160
Australian NDIS 147–148, 150–153, 154, 158, 168
Australian Royal Commission into 147, 149, 153–160, 162–163
Australian service charities 11, 147–172
benefits, charities conferring 166
charitable purposes, definition 164–167
charity law and 147, 149, 159–172
complaints process 158
contraception 152
dehumanisation 152, 160, 172
Disability Justice activism 149, 160, 161, 163, 172
disabling charity law 163–172
discriminatory practices 166
economic exploitation 161, 162
enabling 147, 149, 153, 163, 169–170
equality 160, 162, 164, 166, 171
financial imperatives, impact 152, 159
governance/management of services 161–162, 168–169
historical-structural 149, 169–172
human rights 153, 162–163, 164
individualised funding arrangements 150–151
institutionalisation 151, 152–153
labour exploitation 147, 152, 154, 158, 161
market-based service provision 153
medical model of disability 160, 161
neglect 153–154, 157–158
paternalistic power relations 161, 162
physical abuse 147, 149, 152, 154, 157–159, 162
public benefit rule 164
re-imagining disability support 149, 172
redress 147, 148, 149, 152, 158, 159, 168–169
reforms, resistance to 167
relieving distress, services directed towards 165–166
restrictive practices 147, 153
rights awareness 152
segregation and exclusion 151, 152–153, 159, 162, 166
self-determination 96, 163, 164, 171

sexual abuse/exploitation 147, 149, 152, 155–159, 162, 167, 168–169, 175, 178–179
social hierarchy of ableism 160–161, 162, 170
socio-cultural understandings of disability 164
sterilisation 152
Disability Trust 167
discriminatory practice
advocacy organisations 6, 123, 125, 132, 141–142
affirmative action 10
assessment 123–134
benefit sought by 123, 130, 131–133, 138
benign 135
certainty requirement 127
changing social attitudes 123
charitable status, granting 138–139, 141–142, 143–144
charity law's approach 124–132, 166
common law and discriminatory charities 126
cy-près doctrine 127, 129
detriment, as 123–145
distributive justice 136
educational institutions 133
enabling 126, 147, 153, 163
expressive harm 124, 136, 138–145
failure of recognition 140
ideological bias 124, 135
lawful 123–132
material harm 124, 136–138, 142, 145
proof of harm caused 135–136, 142
proportionality principle 133
protected characteristics 123, 125, 126, 136
public benefit analysis 10, 123–124, 125, 126, 127–128, 129–138, 141–144
public policy approach 128–131
purposes/activities distinction 125–126
relational inequality 93, 95, 123–145
religious organisations 6, 10, 68, 129–130
social effects 132
socio-cultural disadvantage 136–137
testamentary dispositions 126, 127
Dog Control Coalition (DCC) 232
Dogs Trust 226, 232
domestic violence services 175
donations, registration 25
donors *See also* **fundraising**
accountability to 96–97, 99
complaints by 186–187
conditionality, imposition 96
cy-près doctrine and donor intent 36–39, 41–42, 50
donor-securement tactics 91
generally 174
incentives for 6
intent 24, 36–39, 41–42, 50, 95
vagaries of donor favour 97–98
Dowden, Oliver 193–194
Duke, George
The Law of Charitable Uses 22

E
ecclesiastical courts 36
Edelman J 35, 42
educational institutions
charitable purposes 30, 61, 83, 175
Charity Commission investigations 186
cy-près doctrine 8–9, 54
discriminatory practice 133
exclusive 6, 32
Independent Schools Council v Charity Commission 82
misappropriation of funds 27–29
public benefit rule 31–32
regulation 27–29, 30
Eldon, Lord 22, 26–27, 30, 31
Elias CJ 70, 71
emotionally driven decision-making 100
endowments
conditions or restrictions 8
decline of endowment charities 23–24
reallocation *See cy-près* doctrine
England and Wales *See* **Charity Commission for England and Wales**
equality
compliance, charitable activities 144
disabled people 160, 162, 164, 166, 171
discrimination as social detriment 93, 95, 123–145
discriminatory practices 136
Norwegian religious entities 66–68
equity
development of doctrine 83–84, 86
indeterminacy 102, 103
jurisdiction of conscience 86
modern expectations of 6
eugenics 170
Extinction Rebellion 195

F
fee-based services 6

financial control
accounts, preparation and filing 193
cash couriers 189
conflict of interests 187–188, 190
insufficient 187–190, 193
professional fundraising 189–190
trustees' responsibility 192
financial integrity 3, 5, 91–92, 192–193
financial mismanagement 191–192
animal welfare organisations 236, 238–239
financial performance, over-emphasis on 7
financial privileges
donor incentives 6
exploitation 6, 31
gift aid 6
tax exempt status 3, 5, 6, 31, 87–90, 97–98, 143
financial sustainability 94–95, 98–100, 191–192
fire service efficiency, promoting 176
Firmin, Thomas 17
founders
preserving autonomy of 3
voluntary initiative 4
Foundling Hospital 17
France J 65
Fraser, Orlando 196
Friendly Societies 17, 24
Fullagar J 106, 113
fundraising *See also* **donors**
aggressive 91
dependence on 191
professional 189–190

G
Gardner, J 135
gift aid 6
Gladstone, William 19
Global Warming Policy Foundation 195–196
globalisation 99
Good Law Project 194, 195
Gorsky, Martin 23
governance
accountability 168–169, 170, 171
administrative costs 91
animal welfare organisations 236
China's legislative framework 11
contemporary transformation 6–7
corporate governance principles 7, 10
dominant individual as warning sign 192–193
evolution 6–7
financial mismanagement 91–92, 191–192
high-profile failures 3
international organisations 7
professionalisation 3–4, 7, 189–190, 201
strategic management 3
structures, generally 3
visitors 30
governors 17
Grant, Sir William MR 18, 21–22
Greenwich Hospital 16
Guide Dogs for the Blind 97
Gummow J 111
Gzell J 104

H
Hall, Lara 178–179
halo effect 10, 101–103, 107, 108–119, 165
Halsbury LC 31
Hammond, PE 58
Harding, M 46, 127, 132, 163, 164, 167, 172
Hardwicke, Lord 17, 18, 20, 25, 29
harm *See* **detriment**
Haydon J 111
Hayne J 111
hierarchical patronage 24
Hillyard, P 80
Hodgson Review 82–83, 85, 92
Hogg, E 234–235
homelessness services 175
Human Aid UK 189
Human Appeal 186
human rights
compliance, charitable activities 144
disabled people 153, 162–163, 164
promoting or protecting 64, 71, 128–129, 138, 164

I
impact assessment 4
inclusivity 6
incorporated charities
animal welfare organisations 227
cy-près doctrine 41, 55
financial mismanagement 91–92, 191–192
registration 173
scope of charitable purposes 111–116
injuries of normality 170
injustice *See also* **disability injustices**
historical-structural 169–172
international organisations 7
investments, commercialisation 6

J
Jehovah's Witnesses
 Belgium 68, 71
 New Zealand 69
 Norway 67–68, 69
joint stock companies 17
Jones, Gareth
 History of the Law of Charity 1532–1827 8, 15

K
Kennel Club, UK 227, 228, 241, 242
Kenyon, Lord 27
Kerman, Michael-Karim 192
Khaitan, T 136–137
Kids Company 91, 191, 233
Kirby J 60, 113, 115–116, 118

L
Ladies' Charitable Society 17
Leeming JA 42, 45–46, 49
Lewison LJ 47–48, 50
Life Without Barriers (LWB) 154, 155–156, 158, 162, 165
Lock, RS 186–187

M
MacDermott J 114
McGregor-Lowndes, Myles 50–51
Macnaghten LJ 30, 31, 83, 87
Mallon J 60
market forces 3
membership
 religious organisations 6
 restricted 6
mental health services 175
merging charities 240
middle class philanthropy 18
military efficiency, promoting 176
mis-selling 91
misappropriation of funds 27–29
mission drift 5, 7
Mitford, John 26
Moore, Francis 20, 21, 22
Moore, Tom 91–92
Morgan, Jamelia 172
Morritt LJ 47
mortmain restrictions 18–19, 21–23, 24, 31
Mulheron, RP 40
Murdoch, Iris
 The Sovereignty of Good 102, 110–111, 114, 118
mutuality 17, 24

N
Nathan Report 37–38, 42–44, 51
national charities 24
National Trust 194
New Zealand
 cy-près doctrine 42
 Destiny Church 59
 Exodus Ministries 69–71
 Jehovah's Witnesses 69
 public benefit rule 62–65, 69, 70
 religious charities 57–65, 69–76
 supporting machinery or harmony of civil society 62–63
Norway, religious entities in
 deregistering process 67–68, 69
 grants and subsidies to 66–68
 increasing secularisation and 66
 registration system 66–67
Nottingham, Lord 25

O
***Oppenheim* test** 62–64, 106
Orwell, George
 Nineteen Eighty-Four 10, 103, 116–117

P
Parachin, A 127, 129, 130, 143
partnerships with corporations 6
PASC Report 82–83, 85
paternalistic power relations
 'beneficiaries' 161
 disability service charities 161, 162
Peel, Robert 28
***Pemsel* test** 30–31, 61–62, 83, 87, 105, 106, 113, 128, 175, 229
People and Pets Animal Welfare 236
Pepys, Samuel 16
perpetual charitable trusts *See also* ***cy-près* doctrine** 8
 incentivising privilege, as 143
Picton, John 50
Picton, John and Sigafoos, Jennifer 150, 241
Piepzna-Samarsinha, Leah Lakshmi 163
Plummer, Sir Thomas MR 23
police efficiency, promoting 176
police reports
 Commission investigations following 185–186, 235
political advocacy 4, 166–167, 195–196
 animal welfare organisations, by 231, 232, 244
political agenda, charities with 193–197

political influence, state funding and 5
poor boxes 16
Poor Laws 15, 20
poverty, relief of
charitable purpose, as 30, 61, 83, 175, 176
public benefit rule 31–32
statutory inquiries into charities providing 183
precedent, doctrine of
cy-près doctrine 50–51
Private Action, Public Benefit 84–85, 99
private initiative
public responsibility and 4–5, 8, 12–13
professionalisation of sector 3–4, 7, 189–190, 201
profit *See* **commercialisation**
public benefit rule
animal welfare organisations 229–231
assessing public benefit 131–136
boundaries of charitable status 6, 63–64, 81, 87
charitable purposes, definition 164–165
commercialisation and 5, 6, 7, 10
concept of 5–6, 10, 21, 30, 81–82
constitutive accountability 167–168
controversial charities 70–72
cost to detriment of society 65
cy-près doctrine 51
detriments/harm to be considered 123, 142
disability, references to 164
discriminatory practice 10, 123–124, 125, 126, 127–128, 129–138, 141–144, 166
express determination of benefit 63–65
expressive harm 124, 138–145
generally 3, 5, 61, 80–83, 129, 142
government contracts 5
historical background of concept 21, 32, 81, 84, 86–87
indirect benefits 65
intangible and nebulous nature 64–65
legal requirement for 5, 7, 21, 32, 63–65
liberality and benevolence 21–22
material harm 124, 136–138, 142, 145
mission drift 5, 7
New Zealand 62–65, 69, 70–71
Oppenheim test 62–64, 106
presumed benefit 82
relieving distress, services directed towards 165–167
religious charities 31–32, 57, 59–60, 63–65, 69, 70–76, 86
RNLI 97
sufficient section of public 63
supporting machinery or harmony of civil society 62–63
test of 63–65
Public Benevolent Institutions (PBIs) 154, 159, 165–166
public funding 5, 191
government contracts 5, 9, 10–11, 12–13, 84–85, 98–100, 168, 174, 175, 225, 232–233
political influence, risk of 5
public policy, vague nature 128
public purpose, gifts for 22–23
public responsibility
private initiative and 4–5, 8, 12–13
public services
delusional optimism, keeping citizens in 100
emotionally driven decision-making 100
ever-increasing demands 99–100
infantilisation of society 100
privatisation 4–5, 8, 12–13
provision 5, 10–11, 12–13, 84–85, 98–100, 174
state outsourcing 5, 9, 10–11, 12–13, 84–85, 98–100, 168, 174, 225, 232–233
state provision 89, 100
VCSE government contracts 175
public trust and confidence 3–4, 7, 85, 89–92, 97–98, 99, 101, 174–175, 176
Purkis, Andrew 195

R
Raz, J 137
Redesdale, Lord 26
reformation, individualist mindset 95–96
registration
China 202, 216
establishment of UK register 83
exempt charities 173–174
incorporated charities 173
number of UK registered charities 85, 173
religious organisations 58, 67–68, 73, 74, 76
requirement for 173
revocation 67–68
regulation *See also* **charity law**
accounts, preparation and filing 193
animal welfare organisations 12
Attorney General's role 25, 26–27
Australia *See* Australian Charities and Not-for-profits Commission
charity commissioners 20, 24, 27–30

Chinese regulatory framework 201–221
conflict of interests 12, 13, 89–90, 187–188, 190, 196
Court of Chancery 16, 20, 23, 24–27, 28, 30
definition of charity 19–23, 30–31
double defaulters 180, 182–183, 185, 193, 199, 235, 236
England and Wales *See* Charity Commission for England and Wales
factors triggering investigations 184–187, 235
financial control 187–190, 193
financial mismanagement 191–192
generally 3
interim manager, appointment 190, 193, 197
limits 29–33
political battles over 193–197
principles of good regulation 179–180, 198–199
proportionality principle 180, 198–199
registration of donations 25
statutory inquiries 11, 179–199
transparency 179, 180, 198–199

religious charities
Australia 73, 74
Belgium 68, 71
belief which cannot be proven 59
benefits enjoyed by 58, 60
Canada 73–74
charitable purposes 30, 58, 61, 83, 113, 175
contemporary, role 57–76
controversial 70–72
cost to detriment of society 65
discriminatory practice 6, 10, 68, 129–130
economic benefit to society 57, 64–65, 72–76
freedom of religion 68, 71
generally 86
halo effect 111–116
justifying 17, 24, 57
legal validity 63–65, 66
New Zealand 57–65, 69–76
Norway 66–68, 69
outworkings, range of 72, 76
public benefit rule 31–32, 59–60, 63–65, 66, 69, 70–71
public opinion, impact 66–72
registration 58, 67–68, 73, 74, 76
Roman Catholic 20
secular social pressures 9, 57–61, 62, 64, 66, 68, 69, 72
statutory inquiries into 183
United States 73, 74

rescue service efficiency, promoting 176
Retreat Animal Rescue 188
Rheema Church London 192–193, 197
Richmond J 104
Richmond Psychosocial Foundation 186
Romilly, Sir Samuel 21, 25–26, 31
Royal National Lifeboat Institution (RNLI) 24, 97
Royal Society for the Prevention of Cruelty to Animals (RSPCA) 24, 231, 232, 235, 236–237, 238
Runnymede Trust 194

S

Sales LJ 126
secularisation
religious charities and 9, 57–61, 62, 64, 66, 68, 69, 72
self-determination 96, 163, 164, 171
sexual abuse
Australian National Redress Scheme 148, 168–169
disability service charities 147, 149, 152, 155–159, 162, 167, 169, 175, 178–179
trustees, allegations against 178
VCSE government contracts 175
Shelford, Leonard
A Practical Treatise ... 24, 25
Sigafoos, Jennifer 235
social benefits *See also* **public benefit rule**
presumed 79–83, 86–89, 92, 93–94
social change
role of charity 88
social cohesion
risk presented by charitable activity 94–97
social harm critique
arguments for 80, 93–95
conditionality, imposition 96
delusional optimism 100
demands for accountability 96
discrimination as detriment 123–145
emotionally driven decision-making 100
financially unsustainable model 94–95, 98–100, 191–192
infantilisation of society 100
presumed positives of charity law 79–83, 86–89, 92, 93–94
role of charity, social conception 77–89, 91–92

social cohesion and charitable activity 94–97
social subordination 96
state support, charity given 79, 80, 82, 84, 85, 89, 93, 94, 98, 138–139, 141–142, 143
vagaries of donor favour 97–98

social norms
changing 3–4, 5, 6, 70–72, 78, 123
injuries of normality 170

social subordination
deserving and undeserving poor 96

Society for the Suppression of Vice 18

Somerville, Margaret 239

state role
charitable status, granting 138–139, 141–142, 143–144
charity accountability 168
facilitative 4–5
oscillating emphasis 3
outsourcing to charitable sector 5, 9, 10–11, 12–13, 84–85, 98–100, 168, 174, 225, 232–233
public services, provision 89, 100
regulatory intervention 5
support provided to charities 79, 80, 82, 84, 85, 89, 93, 94, 98, 143
VCSE government contracts 175

statutory inquiries 11, 179–199, 241
animal welfare organisations 224, 228, 235–239, 241, 243

Stolen Generations 170

Story, Joseph 33

subscriber organizations 16–17, 18
growth 24
hierarchical patronage 24

Sunnyfield 154–155, 162, 165

Support the Heroes 190

T

Tamaki, Brian 59

Tarnopolsky JA 131

tax exempt status
China 202–205, 215
exploitation 6
generally 3, 5, 6, 31, 87–90, 97–98, 141, 143, 148
historical background 19–20, 22

testamentary gifts 18–19
decline of endowment charities 23–24
definition of charity 21–23
discriminatory 126, 127
litigation 18, 21–23, 25, 90
mortmain restrictions 18–19, 21–23, 24, 31

third sector 9, 87
public services outsourced to 5, 9, 10–11, 12–13, 84–85, 98–100, 168, 174, 225, 232–233

third way politics 99

transparency 3, 5, 7, 179, 190

trustees
accounts, preparation and filing 193
animal welfare organisations 225, 238–239
China 208
disqualification 92, 180, 188, 190, 197–198, 236, 238, 239
disqualification as company directors 191
dominant individuals 192–193, 238–239
expenses 174
financial mismanagement by 191–192
insufficient financial control by 187–190, 193
insufficient number of 188
liability 26
Official Warning issued to 188
payment 174
reports 186
schisms in trustee boards 186
trustee statements, filing 193
voluntary 174

trusts
charity law as trusts law 87
cy-près doctrine *See cy-près* doctrine
income vested in 19
legal personality 17, 188
perpetual 143; *See also cy-près* doctrine
private beneficiaries 84
public purpose 22–23

Tudor, Owen Davies 8

U

United Nations Convention on the Rights of Persons with Disabilities (CRPD) 162

United States
religious charities 73, 74

V

virtuous, charities regarded as 10, 101–103, 107, 108–116, 118–119, 165

visitors 30

vivisection
anti-vivisection campaigning 230

voluntarism 23, 100, 174
decline in 99
trustees 174

W

Weinert, Kim 165
welfare state 8, 79
Wilberforce LJ 30
Wilberforce, William 18
Williams, Rowan 95
Withers, AJ 163
Wood J 49
Woodward, EL
Oxford History of England 9, 78, 86
Wright LJ 108

Z

Zacaroli J 46

www.ingramcontent.com/pod-product-compliance
Ingram Content Group UK Ltd.
Pitfield, Milton Keynes, MK11 3LW, UK
UKHW021909150926
475560UK00003B/263

9 781509 979271